North American Discovery

DOCUMENTARY HISTORY OF THE UNITED STATES

Edited by Richard B. Morris

Chronological Volumes:

David B. Quinn THE DISCOVERY OF AMERICA HR/1505
Alden T. Vaughan: THE PURITAN TRADITION IN AMERICA
Charles Gibson: THE SPANISH TRADITION IN AMERICA HR/1351
Y. F. Zoltvany: THE FRENCH TRADITION IN AMERICA HR/1425
Milton M. Klein: THE DUTCH AND QUAKER TRADITIONS IN AMERICA
Aubrey Land: BASES OF PLANTATION SOCIETY HR/1429
Jack P. Greene: GREAT BRITAIN AND THE AMERICAN COLONIES, 1606-1763 HR/1477
Richard B. Morris: THE AMERICAN REVOLUTION, 1763-1783 HR/1504
Forrest McDonald: CONFEDERATION AND CONSTITUTION HR/1396
Noble E. Cunningham, Jr.: THE EARLY REPUBLIC, 1789-1828 HR/1394
Jack M. Sosin: THE OPENING OF THE WEST HR/1424
Gilbert C. Fite: THE WEST, 1830-1890
Robert V. Remini: THE AGE OF JACKSON
Stanley Elkins & Gerald Mullin: DOCUMENTS IN THE HISTORY OF SLAVERY
Walter Hugins: THE REFORM IMPULSE (1828-1847)
James P. Shenton: THE CIVIL WAR
La Wanda and John Cox: RECONSTRUCTION, THE NEW SOUTH, AND THE NEGRO
John A. Garraty: THE TRANSFORMATION OF AMERICAN SOCIETY, 1870-1890 HR/1395
Richard M. Abrams: THE ISSUES OF THE POPULIST AND PROGRESSIVE ERAS, 1892-1912 HR/1428
Earl Pomeroy: THE FAR WEST IN THE TWENTIETH CENTURY
Stanley Coben: WORLD WAR, REFORM, AND REACTION
William E. Leuchtenburg: THE NEW DEAL: *A Documentary History* HR/1354
Louis Morton: UNITED STATES AND WORLD WAR II
Robert E. Burke: DOMESTIC ISSUES SINCE 1945

Topical Volumes:

Alan F. Westin: THE SHAPING OF THE CONSTITUTION (2 volumes)
Herbert G. Gutman: THE LABOR MOVEMENT (2 volumes)
Robert D. Cross: THE IMMIGRANT IN AMERICAN HISTORY
Douglass C. North & Robert Paul Thomas:
THE GROWTH OF THE AMERICAN ECONOMY TO 1860 HR/1352
William Greenleaf: AMERICAN ECONOMIC DEVELOPMENT SINCE 1860 HR/1353
Hollis R. Lynch: THE AMERICAN NEGRO IN THE TWENTIETH CENTURY
I. B. Cohen: HISTORY OF SCIENCE IN AMERICA
Richard C. Wade: THE CITY IN AMERICAN HISTORY
Robert H. Ferrell: FOUNDATIONS OF AMERICAN DIPLOMACY, 1775-1872,
Volume I HR/1393
Robert H. Ferrell: AMERICA AS A WORLD POWER, Volume II HR/1512
Robert H. Ferrell: AMERICA IN A DIVIDED WORLD, Volume III
Stanley J. Reisor: HISTORY OF MEDICINE
Robert T. Handy: RELIGION IN AMERICA

North American Discovery

Circa 1000–1612

edited by

David B. Quinn

HARPER & ROW, PUBLISHERS

New York, Evanston, San Francisco, London

NORTH AMERICAN DISCOVERY

Introduction, editorial notes and compilation copyright
© 1971 by David B. Quinn.

STANDARD BOOK NUMBER: 06–139244–8

LIBRARY OF CONGRESS CATALOG NUMBER: 72–162566

CONTENTS

Preface   xiii
Introduction: From Discovery to Settlement   xv

I. THE GREENLAND ROAD TO NORTH AMERICA

1. Bjarni's Discovery of Land Beyond Greenland   3
2. Leif Eiriksson's Voyage   4
3. Thorvald Eiriksson's Voyage and Settlement in Vinland   7
4. Karlsefni's Voyage to Vinland and his Unsuccessful
   Attempt at Colonization   9

II. THE WESTERN ISLANDS AND THE ROUTE TO ASIA

5. European Contacts with Vinland after the Voyages of
   the Greenlanders   18
6. An Early Fifteenth-Century View of the Ocean Between
   Spain and Asia   23
7. Portuguese Tales of Early Discoveries in the Atlantic   25
8. Toscanelli on the Westward Route to Asia, 1474   27
9. Map Inscriptions as Guides to the Oceanic Lands and
   Islands   28
10. Portuguese Grants to Discover the Island of the Seven
    Cities, 1474–87   30

III. THE EARLIEST NORTH AMERICAN VOYAGES

11. Attempts of the Bristol Men to find the Island of Brasil,
    1480–81   34
12. The First Voyage of Christopher Columbus, 1492   36
13. John Cabot's Reception in England   38
14. John Cabot's Voyage, 1497   39
15. John Cabot's Last Voyage, 1498   45
16. The Portuguese Voyages of the Corte Real Brothers,
    1500–03   48

IV. THE DISCOVERY OF THE NORTH
AMERICAN SHORELINES
17. Sebastian Cabot's Voyage to the Northwest 56
18. The Voyage of Giovanni da Verrazzano Along the
American Shoreline, 1524 58
19. The North American Voyage of Estevão Gomes, 1524–25 71
20. John Rut's Voyage, 1527–28 74

V. THE SPANISH DEFINITION OF SOUTHEASTERN
NORTH AMERICA
21. The Expeditions of Ponce de León, 1513–21 80
22. Antonio de Alaminos Touches Florida, 1517 81
23. The Expeditions of Lucas Vásquez de Ayllón, 1521–26 83
24. The Disastrous Voyage of Pánfilo de Narváez, 1528–36 86
25. The Mission of Fray Luis de Cáncer, 1549 90
26. The Luna Colonizing Expeditions, 1559–61 91

VI. JACQUES CARTIER'S RIVER ROUTE
INTO THE INTERIOR
27. The First Voyage, 1534 97
28. The Second Voyage and the First Colony, 1534–36 102
29. The Voyage of Richard Hore, 1536 112
30. The Third and Fourth Voyages and the End of the
Colonizing Attempt, 1541–43 115

VII. SPANIARDS RECONNOITER THE INTERIOR
31. Hernando de Soto Explores the Southeast, 1540–43 123
32. Coronado Finds the Seven Cities of Cíbola and Searches
for Quivira, 1540–41 131

VIII. FRENCH FLORIDA, 1562–80
33. The Ribault Expedition, 1562 141
34. The Failure of the Laudonnière Colony, 1564–65 150
35. The Last Phase, 1568 160

IX. SPANISH FLORIDA, 1565–1612
36. The Capture of Fort Caroline and the Foundation of
St. Augustine, 1565 165

37. Annexation of the North Carolina Coast, 1566   172
38. The Jesuit Mission on the York River, 1570–71   173
39. Sir Francis Drake's Raid on St. Augustine, 1586   177
40. The Exploration of Chesapeake Bay, 1588   178
41. Florida and Its Surroundings, about 1612   182

X. The Roanoke Voyages and the First English Settlements

42. The Discovery of the Carolina Outer Banks and of Roanoke Island, 1584   187
43. The 1585 Virginia Voyage   193
44. Ralph Lane on the Scope of the Activities of the 1585–86 Colony   195
45. Thomas Harriot on Cultivation by the Carolina Algonkian Indians   197
46. The End of the Roanoke Colony, June 1586   202
47. The Planting of the New Colony, 1587   204
48. The Search for the Lost Colony, 1590   207

XI. The Northwest Passage Search

49. A Portuguese Attempt to Find the Northwest Passage in 1574   212
50. Sir Humphrey Gilbert's Summary of the Advantages of a Northwest Passage   213
51. The First Voyage by Martin Frobisher, 1576   215
52. The Third Voyage by Martin Frobisher, 1578   218
53. The Voyages of John Davis, 1585–87   221
54. The Discovery of Hudson Strait and Hudson Bay by Henry Hudson in 1610   226

XII. Newfoundland and the Approaches to the St. Lawrence

55. The Newfoundland Shore Fishery, 1578   233
56. The Basque Fishing and Whaling Fleets, 1574   235
57. Sir Humphrey Gilbert at Newfoundland, 1583   236
58. A French Voyage to the Bay of Fundy and to Maine, 1583   240

59. Reasons for English Colonization of What Is Now New
England, *circa* 1592   244
60. Englishmen Prospect the Whaling Industry of the Gulf
of St. Lawrence   247
61. English Separatists Are Released from Prison to Go to
America   249
62. An Abortive English Colony in the Magdalen Islands,
1597   251

XIII. NEW ENGLAND AND THE HUDSON RIVER, 1602–09
63. Bartholomew Gosnold Explores New England, 1602   258
64. A Summer Voyage to Cape Cod, 1603   264
65. The French Exploration and Attempted Settlement of
the Coast from Nova Scotia to Massachusetts, 1604–07 266
66. George Waymouth Surveys Monhegan, Georges Islands
and the St. Georges River, 1605   271
67. The Establishment and Abandonment of St. George's
Fort, 1607–08   276
68. Henry Hudson Ascends the Hudson, 1609   279

XIV. THE FOUNDATION OF FRENCH CANADA, 1603–11
69. The St. Lawrence Valley, 1603   286
70. Quebec Is founded, 1608   289
71. War and Exploration Around Lake Richelieu, 1609   291
72. Champlain Attempts to Plan for Expeditions Beyond
the Lachine Rapids, 1611   294

XV. THE BEGINNINGS OF VIRGINIA
73. George Percy Reports on the First Landing and the
Selection of the Site of Jamestown, 1607   300
74. Powhatan Is Made an English Subject, 1608   302
75. Captain John Smith Explores the Head of Chesapeake
Bay, 1608   305
76. Jamestown in 1610   309

Bibliography   315

MAPS

1. The Vinland Map, *circa* 1440–50 from Skelton, Marston & Painter, *The Vinland Map and the Tartar Relation.* Copyright © 1965 by Yale University Press.
2. The Castiglione Map, 1525 taken from W. P. Cumming, *The Southeast in Early Maps.* Courtesy Harvard University Library.
3. Florida and the Southeast
4. Virginia
5. The Approaches to the Northwest Passage
6. The Entrance to the St. Lawrence
7. New England and the Hudson
8. The Velasco Map, 1610

Acknowledgments

Permission to reproduce copyright materials has been received from Cambridge University Press, the Canadian Archives Department, the Champlain Society, Florida Historical Quarterly, the Hakluyt Society, Rear Admiral Samuel Eliot Morison, Oxford University Press, the University Press of Virginia, and Yale University Press. To all of these my thanks are offered.

Preface

THE PURPOSE OF this collection is to give some idea of the range and variety of European contacts with North America before the time that the first colonies of Spaniards, English and French had become deeply rooted there. It is worth remembering that human history in the Americas does not go back more than 20,000 years but that 19,000 of these were virtually self-contained. Outside influence, since the earliest movements of peoples from Asia, has been confined to the period since about the year A.D. 1000. From the first Norse voyages until 1492, such little light as we have relates to European links with North America. Thereafter, Central and South America fill the main part of the picture. But what goes on in North America is vital for the understanding of what followed once European discovery had begun to give place to settlement and the foundations of the history of the United States and Canada were laid. In selecting from a wide variety of documents an attempt has been made to show how eastern North America, and something of the West, was gradually revealed to European eyes so that it could be described in words and on maps and could be successively surveyed, exploited and settled. If this collection has a bias, it is a geographical one: it does not deal systematically with the West; it has very little on the Amerindian population and the problem of culture contact. It does attempt to keep the activities of the different European nations in North America in balance, and it stresses a number of minor episodes as well as the major ones in order to demonstrate the multiplicity of early voyages, which is often forgotten.

Though the basis for a selection of this sort is bound to be a personal one I am grateful to many more persons that I can name for advice and also for help with translations (though I have often relied on those already in print). The older collections by Ramusio, Hakluyt and Purchas are still the basis for the documentation of this subject, and the Hakluyt Society, which built on their work, is the main modern source for texts. While there is inevitably some overlap with Professor J. H. Parry's fine collection, *The European Reconnaissance*, this has been kept as small as possible. Alison Quinn did much of the preliminary work with me and has helped materially in the selection and paring down of texts. Brigid Quinn drew the outline maps. Sally Chidwick, Beryl Hart and Lesley Roberts did much of the typing. Professor Morris gave much wise advice. To all of them, and to others unnamed, thanks are offered.

Texts (when not translated) have been left in the spelling and (usually) punctuation in which I found them; but the letters u, v, i and j, as well as y^e (the) and y^t (that) have been treated in a modern manner. After the introduction of the Julian calendar in 1582, English dates remain ten days ahead of those normally in use in France and Spain: they have not been altered. Contractions have been silently expanded. Square brackets are used to complete words imperfect in the text, to indicate linking passages supplied by the compiler where it was not possible to retain the words of the document and to provide brief identifications. Parentheses are used in translations to add material necessary for the full understanding of the matter translated, but which does not appear in the original text. It is with great regret that so many fine narratives were abbreviated for reasons of space and emphasis, but it is to be hoped that readers will use the references given to read the full texts for themselves. This is a fruitful and exciting field to which a collection of this nature can provide only an elementary introduction.

College of William and Mary   David B. Quinn
University of Liverpool

Introduction
From Discovery to Settlement

I
Preliminaries to the study of the period
of discovery and exploration

North America only gradually emerged as a geographical entity to Europeans and was only slowly revealed by successive explorers. Exploration was far from complete by 1612 when this selection ends, but the whole of the east coast from the southern tip of Florida to Cape Chidley (the northern tip of Labrador) was known by the latter date, and some idea had been gained of the nature and extent of the interior and of a substantial part of the west coast as well. This volume emphasizes the East, since the evolution of the knowledge of the West will be developed in subsequent volumes in this series; but it is not possible to ignore the Coronado expedition, which, with that under Hernando de Soto, was a decisive event in the definition of the extent of the interior.

The exploration of North America in the sixteenth century cannot be understood unless some account is taken of what went before. The Norse expeditions from Greenland at the opening of the twelfth century, however tenuous the documentary material on them may be, must come into the exploration story, though we do not yet know whether there was any degree of continuity of knowledge between the twelfth and the late fifteenth century. Similarly, it is essential to see the westward voyages of the fifteenth century, with the thinking which lay behind them, as both searches for islands which could be exploited in their own right, and an attempt, or series of attempts, to determine whether or not Asia could be reached from Europe by sailing westwards. These two lines of thought and action could be pursued independently but they were not mutually exclusive. Islands might be found and exploited independently, but they might also be looked for and used as jumping off points from which Asia might be reached more easily than by the very long haul by sea which most mathematical geographers, rightly, predicted.

The more study that is devoted to the Norse voyages—and the excavations which are now at last beginning to throw valuable light on them—and also to the knowledge and theories about the Atlantic and the islands in it, and the cosmographical concepts of the layout of land and water on the globe, the better we will understand the reactions of the earlier explorers to the transatlantic lands when they were at last located. At the same time there is, almost inevitably, a temptation to read more into the early records than they will carry.

The student of early exploration has an interesting but exacting task. Because there is very little evidence available on so many points, he must use what there is as fully as he possibly can. He will find that it is necessary to speculate beyond the limits of accurate knowledge in order to gain some general picture of what may have been happening at the time. But speculation is a risky undertaking, and without noticing it persons who speculate on the implications of inadequate evidence are liable to find themselves drifting from the probable to the possible and from the unlikely to the fantastic without fully realizing what they are doing. They can frequently end up with an obsession about some particular event which has little or no relationship to reality. This is true of many writers on the Norse and other voyages, so that there is what we may call a make-believe literature on the subject as well as a scholarly one. The situation is complicated still further by the fact that scholars who are sound judges of most of the evidence they handle may become so obsessed with one particular interpretation that they bring touches of fantasy into what may otherwise be sensible and reliable articles or books.

At the same time the student, like the scholar, must learn how to speculate up to the limit of what is probable, otherwise there would be little chance of our knowledge of these early periods developing. But student and scholar alike have to learn to be realistic and critical about their speculations and to avoid the temptation to claim that their guesses are facts. If this is done, and if, when new evidence or more satisfying intellectual formulations appear, there is a genuine willingness to discard older assumptions and take a fresh view of the evidence, then the early history of discovery can be a lively and exciting subject, while remaining a scholarly one. The student of the early attempts to find land across the ocean and to pin down its reality in space has valuable material on which to cut his critical teeth. He must, on the one hand, reject easy textbook formulas which assume that all he will ever know is already known and, on the other, treat as fiction most of the attempts to prove that some unlikely people of the past (the Romans or the Carthaginians perhaps) discovered America. His real task is first to read and assess what historians say about the subject and then to study the documents in the case for himself. Only then can he make up his mind where the balance of probabilities lies.

This volume can indicate what kinds of documents are available and give a good many samples of the types of materials on which judgment may be based, but to go further the major collections of documents on individual voyages would have to be explored. We are fortunate in that reliable versions now exist in English for most of the documentary material on early North American exploration and discovery, although there are still gaps in what is accessible to students on some significant episodes. Behind collections in English, also, there frequently lie documents in Latin, French, Spanish, Portuguese or Italian, the original versions of which may be essential for the establishment of some point or other. This collection is, consequently, a starting point only for the study of its field. But the era of discovery and exploration, in North America in particular, is a rewarding one. Moreover, the bulk of the surviving material for individual expeditions is not usually too great and it is often available as a whole to an enquirer. Publishing societies, like the Hakluyt Society, have brought together many of the surviving materials into convenient groups and have made them available in English.

Much of the value of studying what the first discoverers of America found can be brought out by following as far as is possible in their footsteps. There are nowadays many opportunities to follow the routes which the explorers took along the coast, whether by water or by flying over their routes, or by duplicating in automobile and on foot their wanderings on the ground. North America can still provide, to those who re-explore the routes of the explorers, fascinating insights into the problems they encountered and the character of the terrain which had to be met. The value of the historical imagination in reconstituting the American land-scape and seascape is very great and it can even now be employed in what is largely an industrialized and urbanized society. The inte-grative value of exploration history, when pursued in one's own country in particular, is very substantial. It can help to explain the preoccupation of the early explorers with the navigability of even small rivers; it can underline their interest in timber for boat- and shipbuilding and repairing, and in so many other natural growths for their value as foodstuffs as well as their longer term economic value for dyes, textiles, medicines, grain crops. The herbaria, the botanic gardens and arboreta of many present-day cities and uni-versities can assist very greatly in bringing to life the study of these earlier voyages. Natural history museums can give a genuine insight into the animals, particularly fish and birds, which the explorers saw and hoped to exploit.

The interactions between the earliest explorers and the Amer-indian peoples they encountered was a complex one, so complex that in the extracts from documents which follow it has only been possible to present a very limited amount of material on culture contact. The subject requires independent documentary treatment to illustrate it fully. We must remember that, on the one hand, the Indians were regarded as savage enemies whose existence threat-ened the lives and purposes of the explorers; on the other, they could be thought of as the key to the understanding of the new lands, to their geographical relations on both the small and the large scale, to their edible plants and their huntable animals, to the cultivability or otherwise of particular areas. A third point of view saw them, as Hernando de Soto saw them, mainly as load-bearers, animal-like creatures who could be exploited by explorers for their physical qualities alone. A fourth approach saw them as innocent, or relatively innocent, heathens who would become acceptable in some degree to Europeans if they could be made to listen to mis-sionaries and to become Christians and accept European theologi-cal preferences in place of their own.

At every casual contact and in every collective encounter the complications of culture contact dog the steps of the explorers. Such relations offered more difficult problems for the Europeans than the comparatively simple physical barriers which the east coast imposed. We know, thanks to the early narratives, a good deal about the Indian peoples who occupied the coastal areas of eastern North America at the time of contact; but we must remember that many of those peoples disappeared very rapidly after such contact, and that many others had their society quickly and drastically modified before any considerable account was taken of it.

Archeology, so far as sites of the early contact period are concerned, has not brought forth many materials which throw graphic light on the Indians of this period on the east coast—largely because many of the articles they used were of perishable wood or other vegetable matter. Consequently, few ethnological collections in museums exist which allow us to visualize in detail what the Indians who were in touch with the explorers of the sixteenth century were like. We should not forget, however, that we have, in the drawings of John White and the engravings made after the drawings of Jacques Le Moyne, graphic illustrations of both the coastal Algonkian and Timucua Indians for the period roughly between the years 1560 and 1590. We should also realize that normal museum exhibits are of later Plains Indians and can be misleading if they are applied uncritically to the indigenous peoples of the east coast.

In any process of historical change, it is necessary to try to understand the men who participated in it and the means by which they achieved their ends. The men who found, explored and eventually settled North America were members of a limited group of European countries who shared in their own society many features of a common civilization. They shared techniques as well as outlooks, even though there were interesting and sometimes important differences in their culture and their artifacts. They employed ships, arms and means of navigation which were part of the stock in trade of western European technology of the time. The changes which took place in the outlook of men who crossed the Atlantic and in the technological means at their disposal during the sixteenth and early seventeenth centuries were ones which took place in Europe. The study of these aspects of the background of North American history belongs, primarily, to the history of Europe, though it is an essential part of the process of understanding the framework in which exploration and exploitation in North America took place.

It is important to realize that North America (and indeed all other parts of the world to which the Europeans went during the early phases of overseas expansion) was studied and valued much less for its own sake than for what it would contribute to Europe in the way of economic and possibly political resources. Explorers were often blind to aspects of North America which would now appear important to us and particularly to present-day North Americans. As Europeans they were interested mainly in adding American resources to those of Europe, so that North American history at this period must be seen as a special aspect, a new extension, of European history rather than as a detached field of its own, except insofar as the native Amerindian peoples are concerned.

Finally, study of the indigenous peoples of the Americas as a whole before and during the period of contact with Europeans can add greatly to our understanding of what the process of culture-mingling involved. It is possible now for us to be far more aware of its implications than Europeans could have been at the time. They saw America as a field open to them to use as they wished: we see it as a territory belonging to its own people which Europeans first explored, then invaded and finally appropriated for their own profit.

II
The nature and limitations of European
access to eastern North America

In many ways the explorers of eastern North America were fortunate. Once they had learned to navigate the ocean, they had ready access to the Americas. The voyage might be fairly long, it might be dangerous at certain seasons of the year, it might be hidebound by the nature of winds and currents, but it lay well within the range of human accomplishment from quite early in the sixteenth century, even though the risk of loss or damage to sailing vessels remained considerable. Expeditions to North America—except for those attempting to penetrate the Northwest Passage—were on the average much less demanding in human and technological skills and much less costly in money and in life than the really long hauls by way of the Cape to India and the Spice Islands or by the Strait of Magellan across the Pacific. North America thus rapidly came within the sailing orbit of the countries of western Europe.

That eastern North America was not exploited sooner or more thoroughly was a question of economics, and possibly also one of politics, rather than of the limits of human capacity at this time. Only slowly did demand build up for more than casual or inter-mittent contacts and for the close connections which settlement in North America represented. Nor was it exceptionally difficult for Europeans to explore the East after their ships had made the western Atlantic crossing. There were no impenetrable tropical rain forests, no animals or diseases which offered a really formidable barrier to Europeans. The climatic conditions were not much more extreme than those to be found in various parts of western Europe. The only limiting factor which was fairly serious was ice. North of Cape Breton the long season of the icebound St. Lawrence and the ice-infested coasts of northern Newfoundland and Labrador pre-vented European contacts during a considerable part of the year and made winter residence in those areas a difficult matter of adjustment. Floating ice might continue to endanger shipping in these waters throughout a considerable part of the summer.

There were, of course, a number of barriers which might hold up and delay European access to various parts of eastern North America even if they did not prevent it. The coastal swamps of South Carolina and parts of North Carolina were such physical barriers. Shoals might be a nuisance, particularly off the Carolina Outer Banks and south of Cape Cod. Islands off the coast of Maine might be too numerous for the comfort of navigators. Fogs, especially at Newfoundland, might confuse, delay and even imperil ships. Hurricanes might make traveling along the southeastern coast hazardous in late summer and fall ("Winter begins in August," said one hurricane-fearing Spaniard), but none of these were so great an impediment as to prevent European contact or exploration in eastern North America. Thick stands of virgin timber and heavy undergrowth offered greater obstacles to the penetration of the country than anything else the explorers encountered.

It is true that in the sixteenth century climate could be a factor of some significance in circumscribing European exploration and settlement. The extreme cold of the St. Lawrence Basin in winter was undoubtedly an element in the long French failure to colonize the area, first in the mid-sixteenth century and then during the early part of the seventeenth century. It was a major influence in leaving Newfoundland unsettled by Europeans until a much later date, and entirely prevented the occupation of Labrador and the establishment in this period of forward approaches to the presumed Northwest Passage, even though Hudson's men did manage to survive a winter in the bay to which his name was afterwards given. In Maine, to De Monts and Champlain at St. Croix in 1604–05 and George Popham at Sagadahoc in 1607–08, exceptionally severe winters were factors of some importance in bringing to an end settlements which, under more normal conditions, might have persisted much longer. Europeans were not always equipped adequately with clothing and sufficient warmth-creating food or even with the means of shelter to enable them to endure extremes of climate in winter which were only occasionally found in England or France even though they might be quite characteristic of Scandinavia.

In the case of settlement in the more northern regions also, scurvy was a major impediment. An almost total dependence over the winter on protein derived from salted and dried fish, flesh and beans, brought serious consequences to most French attempts at settlement in the St. Lawrence Basin and the Maritimes between 1535 and 1609. Scurvy did not prove so deadly farther south as there were usually greenstuffs or roots to be found throughout the winter. But other diseases played a considerable part in reducing the efficiency and depleting the numbers of settlers both in the case of English and French colonizing ventures. Whether malaria was indigenous to Florida and Virginia or was brought from the Caribbean and the Thames is not finally established, but it had some effects in weakening the settlers. More important were dysentery and diarrhea, whether predominantly from amoebic infection carried from the Caribbean or the result of food intolerance or deficiency. Typhoid was also significant at Jamestown.

Maize apparently caused digestive upsets in Europeans unused to it, and so possibly did other American Indian foods. It is probable that one main source of deaths in Jamestown, for example, was debilitation owing to inadequate quantities or variety of food and the consequent lack of resistance to relatively minor ills, whether these were native or European in origin. While smallpox was brought by Europeans to North America, it would appear that measles, influenza and colds were even more deadly to Amerindians in contact with Europeans, and in the longer run they were, as in Mexico in the sixteenth century, the main decimating agents resulting from European intrusions. It is not unlikely that diseases such as these took considerable toll of the settlers themselves, given the fact that they were not getting enough of the right kinds of food to maintain their normal resistance.

Heat, on the other hand, may have offered some of the disadvantages that cold did. In the North it was often too cold for unacclimatized men to work outside during a long winter season. In the South it was, at times, too hot or too humid for men brought up in western Europe to display much energy in looking after their material needs. The steamy heat of the James River Basin in summer is not unlikely, besides encouraging fever and dysentery, to have been a factor in the apparent incapacity of the Jamestown settlers to grow rapidly for themselves sufficient quantities of food and vegetables of types that they could assimilate and that would have contributed greatly to improving their health. The same is possibly true of the French in Florida between 1562 and 1565. There are, on the other hand, no indications that this was true of Spaniards in their various attempts to settle northwards from the Gulf of Mexico to Chesapeake Bay, though it could well have been a factor in the deterrence of settlement under Ayllón and Luna between 1526 and 1560. The hot summers of the Iberian peninsula and the acclimatizing of Spanish colonials in the West Indies would, together, account for a certain immunity both to climate and to disease such as developed at summer temperatures between 25° and 37° N. latitudes in eastern North America.

Economic uncertainties seem to have accounted for a great deal of the slowness of Europeans to adapt themselves to North American conditions. Spaniards were slow to surmount the problem of growing any appreciable quantity of foodstuffs or other plants in the sandy coastal lands in the vicinity of St. Augustine and San Mateo. By 1586 they had cornfields and some fruit trees growing at St. Augustine, but only by the end of our period had they entirely mastered horticultural and agricultural obstacles. The French at Charlesfort and Fort Caroline were, it might seem, unable to establish around their settlements the gardens which were features of almost all the French settlements further north. At Ste. Croix, Port Royal and Quebec, gardens for salads and summer vegetables proved an invaluable adjunct to imported or purchased food supplies, although the failure to grow adequate supplies of root crops, which could be preserved unsalted over the winter, was a factor in the winter dominance of scurvy at sites such as these. The English settlers on Roanoke Island in 1585 were convinced that they ought to be able to grow there sugar, oranges and lemons, though the failure of their experiments to make these crops flourish proved that they were not suited to the climate. In Jamestown, after 1607, repeated attempts appear to have been made to grow northern European types of wheat, oats and barley. The failure to ripen European grain, or to get more than limited crops from it in the coastal plain, seems to have taken some time to be clearly appreciated by the settlers. The Roanoke settlers had lost their cereal seeds on landing and were forced to plant Indian corn in 1586 (though this had not ripened before they were taken off the island by Drake). The Jamestown settlers took rather longer to follow the same pattern although, as has been indicated, there was some digestive resistance to any great dependence on the local cereal, Indian corn. The settlers spent a good deal of their time attempting to grow such things as oranges and lemons, French grapevines, madder and woad—all crops which could replace English imports from Spain, Portugal, the Atlantic islands and southern France.

The presence of mulberry trees in the Southeast rapidly led to experiments in cultivating silk worms, once it was found that tent caterpillars were not capable of spinning silk fibers. Expert French cultivators were eventually sent out to get this type of plantation cultivation going. Similarly, the English do not seem to have cultivated Virginia tobacco in the early days, since the local variety, *Nicotiana rustica*, does not appear to have been congenial to English smokers. The experiments that led to the establishment of a tobacco industry based on Trinidad tobacco, which was vital to provide Virginia with an adequate export, took place shortly after 1612.

There seems to be no evidence that at Ste. Croix, Port Royal, Fort St. George (Sagadahoc) or Quebec, any early attempts were made to grow the vegetable products other than corn which were planted with greater or lesser success by the local Indians. In the case of the Roanoke settlement, however, Harriot took careful note of how the Indians grew not only maize, but also beans, squash, salt bush and sunflowers as well as tobacco. He believed that the colonists might need, largely, to depend on such local vegetable products. At Jamestown, it would seem from the writings of William Strachey and John Smith, there was some realization that the settlers might need to depend largely on Indian cultivated plants which they would take over for their own gardens, though this view may have been somewhat slow in making itself felt.

There is clear evidence that a major element in the deterioration of European-Indian relations was the demand of the settlers for quantities of grain, especially during late winter and spring, which the native economy was not geared to supply. The Timucua Indians had extensive village storehouses but even they had not a surplus sufficient to keep Laudonnière and his men going in the early part of 1565. Relations rapidly deteriorated when the French attempted to impose pressure on the Indians for corn. The same story emerges in the Roanoke colony. Pressure was already mounting before March 1586; when supplies failed to arrive from England, these pressures became unbearable for the Indians. (The English were competing with the Indians in casual seashore gathering at the same time.) In June there was a showdown in which the Indian chief Pemisapan was killed. The English were taken off by Drake before it could be fully seen what effects this breach would have on longer term relations, but there is evidence that both later in 1586 and in 1587 these were still bad as a result of the antagonizing of the local Indians at Roanoke Island by the demands of the English settlers for food in the winter of 1585–86.

In the Jamestown colony some of the quarrels between Europeans and Indians resulted from variations in the terms which one side would give and the other accept for surplus grain. The English seem to have had no idea that in acquiring surplus corn from the Indians, they were causing an upset to the local economy, and that the value of stored corn to the Indians varied very greatly according to whether it was asked of them in September, in December or in May. John Smith's tirades against those who gave the Indians too good barter rates and his compliments to himself for his business-like astuteness seem to show no understanding at all of the relative seasonal plentifulness or scarcity of food in Indian hands. What we do not know is whether the Indians were quick to appreciate that the demands on them for corn were likely to recur if the whites stayed on at Jamestown and that they rapidly responded by grow-ing more food to meet their demands for a surplus.

Much of the friction between natives and settlers at the stage before the settlers appropriated substantial areas of Indian land arose from food purchase pressure. Here the Spaniards followed a different policy from the English. They made clear to the Indians at an early stage in their relationship that continued friendship was conditional entirely upon levies of corn being paid by each tribe. If it was not, punitive action was taken as soon as possible. When peaceful relations were restored by agreement, the Spaniards al-ways insisted that the primary requirement was that the Indians should supply the Europeans with appropriate amounts of corn annually. This taxation system, once established, could lead more easily to the extension of the areas cultivated by the Indians than the casual purchase of crops in the Jamestown settlement. At the same time a poor season or some political or social revulsion against the Spaniards could disrupt the system and revive the cycle of revolt, repression and re-exploitation.

The establishment of a food exchange pattern was easier in settled areas such as Florida or Virginia than it was farther north. The Spaniards complained about the mobility of the Indians and did all they could to modify the traditional social pattern by settling the Indians into stable villages. But the mobility of the coastal Algonkians and Muskhogeans was seasonal only. Movement took place along the coast during the early summer shore-gathering and fishing season, and so did migration of all or much of the population into the interior during the short winter hunting season. This left the Indians settled (apart from war raids) for the greater part of the year. Farther north the degree of mobility was greater: the Indians of the St. Lawrence Valley traveled very much further afield to their fishing and shore-gathering grounds in summer; they moved further away and stayed longer in their winter hunting season. Consequently, the ties which bound them to their summer village and cultivation patches were slighter. A profitable season away from home could extend either of their migration periods and lead them to neglect their village bases. Their war raids also took them further afield or for longer periods. North of the St. Lawrence River the Montagnais Indians seemed to early observers almost completely nomadic, although their annual movement cycle followed a fairly consistent pattern also. Indians, however, who were more mobile than settled could not be as consistently exploited for foodstuffs by the settlers as those who were fixed in their villages for a substantial part of the year. In the North, Europeans were much more dependent, necessarily, on their own food resources than they were farther south.

Although North America came in the longer run to be valued for its own sake, and although eventually there was a considerable degree of inter-European rivalry for the acquisition of territory on the east coast, many of the Europeans who played their part in the exploration of the east coast continued to regard North America as a *pis aller*, a second-best to the route to the Golden East. Consequently, in the sixteenth century as much effort was devoted to seeing how to get to the Pacific by way of North America as to finding out exactly what the coastline was like and what use it might be to European traders or settlers. From Sebastian Cabot's voyage in the first decade of the sixteenth century to the discovery of Hudson Bay by 1612, the attempt to get around North America took up the greater part of the English westward effort during more than a century. Little attempt was made to find out what could or could not be exploited along the shores of Greenland, Labrador, Baffin Island and the other islands met with, although in the longer run the extension of the cod fishery northwards to southern Labrador, the development of a whale fishery in Davis Strait, and the systematic catching of walrus and seal in waters to the north of

Newfoundland derived to some extent from the experience of Northwest Passage voyaging. It was the supposed discovery of gold-bearing ores on Frobisher Sound in 1576 which led to the first and only large-scale exploitation of native resources in this area. But it was one, as was proved in 1578, that was wholly futile, as no extractable gold or silver could in the end be obtained. Thereafter the Passage alone was the prime objective.

From Hamilton Inlet all the way south to the rivers of the Florida coast the search went on for a passage through North America. Verrazzano's mistaking of the Carolina Outer Banks for an isthmus similar to, if narrower than, that of Darien, was a myth of the map makers and a hope of explorers until almost the end of the sixteenth century, even though the greater number of those who had practical experience of the east coast were fairly quick to discard it. The penetration of the St. Lawrence River by Cartier was the most encouraging of all signs that North America might be divided into fragments through which a westward passage might be traced. Though Cartier was discouraged by the rapids beyond Montreal he was not dismayed; he handed on his hopes to his nephew Jacques Nöel, and it is possible that after 1580 Nöel not only heard about but reached Lake Ontario and believed the Indian stories of still further water links to the west. Indeed, the Indians who encouraged Cartier, Nöel and Champlain with stories about Hudson Bay and the copper of Lake Superior and even vaguer tales of a brackish sea to the west kept alive hopes of a water approach to the Pacific Ocean long after 1612. Ralph Lane in 1586 threw most of his exploring energies into attempting to find whether the Roanoke River rose near to a western sea as the Indians had seemed to indicate. He reported in the end that only a good mine or the discovery of a passage to the South Sea would really put the colony on its feet. (Cartier had consoled himself for his failure to find an open passage to the Pacific by loading his ship in 1542 with the clear quartz of Canada diamonds and other mineral specimens.)

The Virginia Company in 1606 instructed Christopher Newport to found the first settlement well up a navigable river so that it could be used as a forward base to penetrate the interior waterways and, ultimately, to gain access to the Pacific. John Smith, too, penetrated as far as possible up each river running into Chesapeake Bay in the hope of finding it continuing westward in a navigable manner, but in all cases he was disappointed. Contacts with the Iroquois from the Susquehanna River, however, gave him some expectation of finding an interior river system, although he never returned to investigate how far it might bring him. George Way-mouth found it necessary in 1605 to state that the Georges River was much wider and longer than it was in reality since he was anxious to exaggerate its value as an approach to the interior. Hudson in 1609 was excited by the width of the Hudson River as far as the modern site of Albany; he was disappointed at the rapid change in its character beyond that point. Similarly, Champlain had found that the great estuary of the Penobscot River was not an indication that the river led far inland, although he followed it as far as it was practicable to do so. The Delaware alone of the major rivers of the East lacked persistent explorers in this period.

The belief that an easy approach to the Pacific might be possible lasted well into the period after settlement was begun by the English and French. It soon became clear, however, that the best that could be hoped for (except possibly in the case of the St. Lawrence) was a watershed from which a new stream might be followed toward the Pacific Ocean. The Spaniards, indeed, established in the 1540's how intractable were East-West communications in North America, and how vast were the distances between the two oceans. Situated as they were in Mexico and in Central America, where they already had easy access to the Pacific, the possibilities of finding a passage through North America did not interest them, although they occasionally manifested some concern lest the English should indeed discover and exploit a Northwest Passage. But ignorance of these conditions amongst even the Spaniards could at times emerge, as when Gonzalo Méndez de Canzo at the opening of the seventeenth century appeared to be convinced that New Mexico, recently reentered by the Spaniards, was no great distance from Chesapeake Bay and could easily be reached from a Spanish colony placed there.

The Fall Line was of peculiar importance in the exploration of the East. It marked the limit of inland water exploration by sizable boats or vessels for all rivers except the St. Lawrence (and in some respects the Susquehanna) and consequently few large-scale expeditions inland were mounted by European explorers for a long time after 1612 to press beyond the limits of water navigation—except, of course, in the case of Canada. The only explorers before 1612 to use the Piedmont above the Fall Line for traveling were Hernando de Soto in 1540 and Pardo and Boyano in 1566, all of whom found it easier for movement than the more congested and swampy Tidewater. Penetration of the coastal plain was not difficult on the fringes of peninsular Florida, although it was complicated by great swamps a little way inland; but the coasts of Georgia South Carolina and much of North Carolina were swamp-ridden to a greater or lesser degree and offered greater barriers to exploration. Coastal occupation was thus confined to the drier and higher riverbanks and to sites along the rivers themselves. The swamp forests of South Carolina and North Carolina were peculiarly impenetrable.

Elsewhere, coniferous forests might be so thick as to offer comparable barriers. In Newfoundland in 1583, Sir Humphrey Gilbert found the woods so choked with dead and fallen timber that he could make no headway at all into the interior behind the harbor of St. John's. The only solution appeared to be to burn rides into the forest, but the fishermen were against such action and it was not taken on this occasion. Elsewhere, the Indians made a practice of burning undergrowth to render hunting more effective and to allow them to make their way more easily through heavily forested areas. The Virginia Tidewater was by no means wholly impenetrable to the Jamestown settlers as we find a number of shortish expeditions being made by land, but whether this was because the Indians kept the woods open or because their own old cultivation patches had produced sufficient cleared land is not certain. One of the attractions of the land behind the New England shoreline was that the forests were, in places, not too thick. The parklike expanses and meadows near the Georges River were remarked by Rosier in 1605, with greater or lesser exaggeration, and Waymouth's men managed to make an inland expedition from the head of the St. George River without suffering any more inconvenience than too much heat from too much armor on a hot day in early summer.

The limiting factor to coastal exploration or to inland penetration almost everywhere was the existence or otherwise of waterways, navigable at least by boats but preferably by small or even substantial ships. Though a ship could safely reach the Fall Line on, for example, the James or the Potomac, penetration farther inland involved the use of small boats and possibly even of portable skiffs or, where the Indians had them (in Maine, the Maritimes and Canada), birchbark canoes. Champlain was the first major explorer to trust himself and his men to Indian war bands, who took him to explore the interior in their own birch bark canoes.

Natural conditions and inhibitions on the initiative of European explorers thus placed major limitations on the penetration of the interior behind the east coast by both the English and the French, and the same factors operated largely to determine and circumscribe the settlements of these peoples. The Spaniards, with a long period of American experience behind them, were less inhibited, but they had also less use for North America than the English and French and so gave less attention to its exploitation in detail.

III
The resources of the East
and their capacity for exploitation

Practically every explorer who left any extended account of his visits to North America in the period of exploration and discovery mentioned at some point his interest in or search for minerals, either precious or utilitarian, and for pearls. Close attention was given to the copper ornaments found in the hands of Indians and, as communications were established with them, frequent attempts were made to obtain information from them on indigenous metals. It is curious how both English and Spaniards derived the idea that the Indians knew of two sorts of copper, one reddish (and therefore clearly simply copper) and the other yellow (and therefore possibly gold). This is what the Europeans desired to hear. On the other hand, most Indians in replying to such questions merely indicated they had or knew of sources of metal, and their words were not for individual minerals such as copper or gold since they made no distinction, so far as we can gather, between different metals. They usually emphasized also that their metal, namely, copper, came from some distance away in the interior. Little attempt was made by the Indians to indicate precise distances, and this was not easy to do in any case since the Indians spoke in terms of days' travel by canoe and such categories were scarcely intelligible to Europeans who did not know the country.

Both the French in Florida and the English at Roanoke Island obtained from the Indians descriptions of the alluvial washing out of metals. Though it is clear that the eastern Amerindians could not smelt copper, the view which has for long been maintained that they did not collect and possibly wash out particles of pure copper from the Appalachian ranges is likely to have been mistaken. Mound-building Indians in Georgia may well have obtained part of their plentiful supply of copper locally, and the same may be true of the Indians of the Connecticut Valley. The main source of copper ornaments and artifacts throughout the East was clearly Lake Superior, and the long-distance trade in natural copper from this area justified the Indians in repeated statements that their metal came from great distances even though they might know nothing precise about its place of origin. The Hurons were eventually able to convey to Champlain something of the nature of the Lake Superior copper beds.

In the Southeast the Indians had some gold and some silver ornaments, but these were in almost all cases made from metal salvaged from the wrecks of vessels of the Spanish Indies fleet. This, in turn, caused confusion to the French and perhaps, one suspects, even to the Spaniards, so that the existence of indigenous sources of gold and silver was believed in by Europeans who had contacts with the southeastern Indians. It seems that occasionally small natural nuggets of pure silver were used by Indians for decoration, though there is no clear record of any gold being so employed. In the case of Hernando de Soto, the Indians had an obvious excuse for insisting always, when asked for gold, that there was plenty further on, and this technique was used throughout the East whenever there was any pressure on the Indians from white explorers or settlers to reveal the sources of metals.

But although the Europeans were primarily interested in precious metals, common minerals were of interest to them also. Had copper been available in natural form or in an ore which could have been recognized, it would have been gladly exploited by any of them, as indeed would lead or iron or alum. The existence of large sources of iron in Newfoundland was recognized by Anthony Parkhurst as early as 1578. Sir Humphrey Gilbert gladly picked up traces of iron (though there was no great quantity in any place he is known to have searched) and he found, apparently, a lead ore which his mineral expert seems to have convinced him was rich in silver. Farther south, iron was also searched for and bog iron in some quantity was several times identified. The value of indigenous iron sources in forested territory arose not so much from the rareness or value of the ore itself but from its presence in association with timber which could be used to smelt it. This was a result of the shortage of timber for iron smelting in England. The smelting of bog ore with Virginia timber was tried with little success in the early days of the Jamestown settlement.

From the time of the earliest voyages onwards, North American timber proved potentially attractive, especially to Englishmen. England depended largely for coniferous timber products—planking, masts, tar and resin (with subsidiary naval stores like hemp and rope)—on the Baltic area. As early as 1519 the fir trees in North America were thought of as an asset which might be worth exploiting. Once voyagers were familiar with the transatlantic passage, it became clear that the transport of rough timber in bulk would scarcely be economical, since the transport costs were likely to be too high. But this was not true of more specialized timber products. Certainly, masts would be worth bringing over, and were frequently mentioned in descriptions although they are rarely known to have been carried to Europe before 1612. A number of exploring and fishing vessels, however, are likely to have been remasted with American timber. The first product of the Maine settlement of 1607–08 was the vessel *Virginia*, whose hull and masts were hewn from the Maine woods. To what extent, if at all, timber was taken from Newfoundland by the fishing fleets remains undocumented, although great quantities were used on the spot for installations needed in the shoredrying of fish.

In later expeditions the virtue of Swamp Cypress and Red Cedar (the latter identified with some qualification as the Cedar of Lebanon) were appreciated as high-grade, furnishing timbers. Red Cedar was brought back from Roanoke Island in 1585 and from the Elizabeth Islands in 1602. The objective here was cabinetmaking, so that high-quality sawn or log timber of this sort could prove valuable enough for it to be transported across the Atlantic. Such timber was exported from the Jamestown colony, although a certain amount of coarse timber was also cut and sawn there for export as barrel staves. The Jamestown settlement also saw several experiments in making tar and potash, and possibly in tapping trees for resin. These scarcely proved viable commercially and such commodities did not become a major export of Virginia. Timber in North America, indeed, was considered by the English as a great potential reserve against future shortages in England itself, but it did not prove very profitable to exploit in the short run.

Sassafras as a medicine was identified by the French apothecaries between 1562 and 1565. It was then exploited by the Spaniards, Dr. Nicolas Monardes building it up into an all-purpose cure, especially valuable for the cure of syphilis. The roots, the bark, the leaves and even the timber were all supposed to have curative qualities. Monardes's description was available in five languages by 1605; in 1602 a cargo from the Elizabeth Islands was sufficient to have depressed the price of the London market, where it had reached a level of from 10 to 20 shillings a pound, apparently for the roots. The reason for this high price was that it had had to come from Florida to Spain, from Spain to France because England and Spain were at war, and only thence to England. Sassafras was regularly brought from Virginia under the Virginia Company although it was difficult to keep its price sufficiently high for really profitable exploitation. A typical cargo from Virginia in 1611 was made up of black walnuts, sassafras and sturgeon.

Sumac was early identified too for its qualities as a black dye, and red dyes were also obtained from the Indians, derived from Pocone and other roots. The search for dyes was part of the drive to obtain new sources for the ancillaries to cloth production, alum, madder and woad being objectives of several English colonizing expeditions while potash and vegetable oils for soap were in the same category. The French and English equally sought for such things as dyes and metals, but there is not the same evidence that the French attempted to exploit timber products as the English did, apart from using them to build their elaborate *habitations* at Ste. Croix, Port Royal and eventually Quebec.

The French, on the other hand, were the real pioneers of the fur trade. It seems likely that both in Newfoundland and at Cape Breton they were acquiring some furs quite early in the sixteenth century. To the Bretons and Normans who early crossed the Atlantic were added Basques from both sides of the artificial border which divided them politically, but not economically or culturally, between France and Spain. (It should be understood that subsequently Basques could sail under either French or Spanish colors as suited their particular interests at any one time.) It seems likely that the Basques were the main pioneers in the fur trade and that the bulk of the fine furs they obtained (probably not in very great quantity) came into St. Jean-de-Luz and the other French-Basque fishing ports, although some may also have gone to Spain.

Whether, before the time of Cartier, the French knew of the Amerindian fur trade of the St. Lawrence Valley is not clear. In any case, in 1534, Cartier found Iroquois and possibly Montagnais Indians fishing at Gaspé and probably bartering furs as well as copper with the Micmac they met there. This opened the way to the French attempt to exploit a native trade already established. Cartier's voyages in 1535–36 and 1541–42, along with Roberval's in 1542–43, can be seen as the first attempts to do this systematically. But the French did not yet know enough of the Indian polity and did not learn sufficient of the techniques of living through the Canadian winter to enable the fur trade to be placed, at this time, on a firm footing. How much in value furs brought home in 1534–43 amounted to is not known. Thereafter, from 1543 to about 1580, the main French trade seems to have been carried on with the Indian traders at Tadoussac, to which both Indians and French came in summer, but very little is known of its participants or the scale of their enterprise.

During this period, the Basques were dominant in the Gulf of St. Lawrence. Their specialty had long been whale fishing in European waters and now they found the Gulf ideal for both Right Whale and Beluga (White Whale) fishing, western Newfoundland and Anticosti being their main hunting grounds where they sometimes wintered. They also obtained furs along the Gulf shores from Eskimo, Montagnais, Beothuk and Micmac, as well as from the upstream summer traders from Huronia and the middle reaches of the St. Lawrence whom Cartier had met at the mouth of the river in 1534. The Basques were active too in the Maritimes, although both Breton and Norman competition existed in this area, and a limited but steady fur trade was carried on. In the 1580's there were regular Breton fur-trading fleets going to Tadoussac, but by that time ships were again penetrating far upstream as well. By 1590 the Bretons had intruded successfully into the Basque walrus fishery at the Magdalen Islands, while before that time Norman vessels were making their way into the Bay of Fundy and one at least, in 1583, down the coast of Maine.

It would seem that a few Englishmen were also visiting the New England coast looking for furs and minerals about 1580, and it is known that the English also tried a short spell of intervention in the Gulf of St. Lawrence between 1593 and 1597. Before the end of the sixteenth century the craze for beaver hats had hit France. The incentive which this provided to develop the American fur trade led to fiercer competition amongst the French ports and it was necessary to have state intervention to regulate the trade. This led on to attempted settlements at Tadoussac, Ste. Croix, Port Royal and Quebec during 1600 to 1608. The growth of the fur trade is the key to French intervention, in a permanent way, in North America, and the character of the French occupation of the St. Lawrence River Valley was, until long after 1612, dominated by the exigencies of the trade.

The presence of fish in American littorine waters was the first major economic incentive to Europeans to cross the Atlantic in order to exploit American resources directly and not as incidental to a search for western passages to the Pacific. The English may have been exploiting Newfoundland fish before 1490, but John Cabot was the first to publicize stories of the rich fishery off Newfoundland as a result of his voyage in 1497. It is probable that the trading and exploring expeditions from Bristol between 1501 and 1505 were employed in part in fishing off Newfoundland or elsewhere on the North American coast—although we have no direct evidence that this was so. But by the time Sebastian Cabot knew enough of the character of North America to set out to bypass the continent on the way to Asia, ships from France, Spain and Portugal were all crossing the Atlantic to the Newfoundland fisheries. The growth of regular English participation in the fishery cannot be traced in detail, but between 1519 and 1522 there is evidence that this participation was already appreciable.

There is no doubt, however, that for most of the sixteenth century the French (including the French Basques) were the most active group in the Newfoundland fishery. How the English and Portuguese and those Basques who came from Spain compared in numbers with the English is not very clear. English and Portuguese participation in the fishery was probably fairly well balanced over the greater part of the time down to 1580. The French trade was soon highly organized and extensively capitalized. The continued French involvement in the fishery, combined with French and Spanish Basque fur trading and whale fishing, gave them a real predominance in northeastern North America during the greater part of the sixteenth century. In the latter part of the century, the area dominated by the French extended from southern Labrador down both the east and west coasts of Newfoundland to the south coast (the west coast being Basque-dominated and the South divided between them and the Bretons). The Cape Breton fishery (more important than its furs) was divided between Bretons and Basques, and its tentacles stretched down the coast of the Maritimes.

A number of the French vessels were "Bankers," that is, they set out early in the year and took a rapid catch of cod well offshore on the Grand Bank, wet-salting it and sailing as soon as possible for home and then, if they reached France by May or early June, revictualing and making a second voyage in the same season. Most of the French vessels, however, made a single voyage. The French had good supplies of salt and brought back the bulk of their catch wet-salted in their holds, some of it being shore-dried at home to make it keep better and to serve as a more versatile foodstuff. Part of their catch—especially that caught by Bretons and Normans who could not necessarily rely on dry late summers and warm autumns —was dried on shore in Newfoundland. This meant that the same harbors were occupied each summer by ships from the same places. The Portuguese also had plenty of salt in their own country, but they sold much of what they brought out to the English and did some shore-drying of fish themselves in Newfoundland, although they also brought home wet-salted fish to dry in Portugal. The English found salt too expensive to use in large quantities and they could not in any case rely on dry weather for drying fish when they got home, so that they dried almost all their fish on land. The English and Portuguese both centered their activities on the harbor of St. John's and on the bays to the north and south of it on the east side of the Avalon peninsula.

Shore-drying involved extensive land installations, which were renewed or repaired each season—stages where boats could unload and where the cutting tables on which the fish were dressed could be placed; flakes on which the split fish could be dried; cookrooms for rendering and storing oil; boatslips for repairing boats on shore and bringing them on land for the winter; and possibly temporary shore accommodation for the men engaged in fish-drying and their stores. A shore-drying port was thickly inhabited for a few months from late May to late August or September. A routine of rough justice by the fishing admirals appointed by the captains at each port was instituted by the third quarter of the sixteenth century. The bulk of the shore-dried fish was caught in boats working close inshore, some of which were housed on land at the end of the season. From September to May, Newfoundland was occupied only by a few Indians whose robberies of fishing gear and boats were kept down only by killing them off like animals whenever they were seen during the fishing season.

A rough estimate of the number of ships frequenting eastern Newfoundland by 1550 would be in the region of fifty to seventy-five each year; in 1580, a hundred to a hundred and fifty; and in 1600, two to three hundred. There was probably some decline in the French fishery as a whole (or it did not, at least, expand) toward the end of the century. There was a corresponding rise in the English fishery. The Portuguese were badly hit when, after the occupation of Portugal in 1580, they were treated as Spanish enemies by the English, though they held on to a small share of the fishery. The Basques suffered severely between 1580 and 1600.

The incentives to them to expand their fishery to supply, largely, the naval victualing demands of the Spanish fleet were great, but the French government, at war with Spain for much of the time, tried to prevent French Basques from aiding the enemy. Similarly, the English captured a large number of Basque vessels, some French, some Spanish-owned, but usually manned by Basques from both sides of the border. The Basques from the Spanish side were also frequently conscripted into the Spanish navy and so were unable to man their fishing vessels to the same extent. The result was that by the early seventeenth century Basque participation, and, particularly, the share of the Spanish Basques in the fishery, had been substantially reduced. Some of the Breton fishermen were involved on the side of the Catholic League in the French civil wars and this provided an excuse for the English to attack Catholic or alleged Catholic French vessels, even though England was allied with Henry IV and his partly Protestant and partly Catholic supporters.

Though English fishing at Newfoundland was sometimes embargoed for naval reasons and the men taken from the ships into the Queen's Navy, the trade was given a good deal of encouragement during the war because fish was needed for foodstuffs by the armies and the fleets. By 1604, when the Anglo-Spanish War ended, the French were still the strongest single element in the Newfoundland fishery, but the English were almost equal to them in numbers of ships and in activity. Although Sir Humphrey Gilbert had planned to exploit the Newfoundland fishery by imposing taxes on fishermen in 1583, no attempt was made in practice to collect them. The first Newfoundland colony sent out from Bristol in 1610 was not a bid to take over the fishery but an experiment to discover whether it was possible for one or two small permanent colonies (in sample Newfoundland ports) to support themselves agriculturally and also to gain some advantages over the seasonal fisherman by starting to catch fish early in the year before ships could come from Europe. By 1612 this experiment had not shown decisive results either way. The fishery was, however, to remain largely, indeed almost wholly, a seasonal one until well into the eighteenth century. The fishery at Newfoundland did not in any meaningful terms lead on to early colonization, but was an economic entity complete in itself and dependent rather on European economic and political relations than on anything that took place inside North America.

Just as timber attracted almost all the explorers as they recorded their impressions of the American shore lands, so too many of them noted the presence of fish on the mainland coasts. The French and Spaniards were interested in the whales which ranged the Florida coast and they also watched with interest the way in which the Indians used weirs and nets to take fish in the rivers and on the shores. The Indians of Roanoke Island used fish weirs extensively in the Carolina Sounds, and John White and Thomas Harriot made illustrations of them and notes on American fishes, although they remarked that the colonists in 1585–86 proved hopelessly ill-equipped to catch fish for themselves. In the Jamestown colony, sturgeon seemed to be of great economic potential and was exploited to some extent; many other fish which might become profitable were noted by John Smith and William Strachey. Gosnold praised Cape Cod Bay greatly for its fine fish and so may have been the first to publicize the riches of the inshore waters of New England, just as Waymouth stressed the value of the fishing on Georges Bank in the Gulf of Maine, and the value of Monhegan Island and Georges Islands as bases for summer fishing.

The establishment of year-round settlements, which would exploit fishing as well as furs and timber products, brought the Plymouth merchants into the Virginia Company in 1606, although the failure of the Sagadahoc colony in 1608 rather disillusioned them on the value of a permanent shore base for the fishery. From 1609 onwards it was the summer fishery in New England which attracted them, and which by 1612 was beginning to employ an appreciable number of fishing vessels although it had not led, so far, to any year-round settlement. The possibility of fishing did attract Englishmen to New England in the early seventeenth century, but the creation of a shore fishery was not a primary incentive to settlement there even if it remained a secondary one. In the case of the Roanoke and Virginia colonies the existence of fisheries open to exploitation by the colonists was a bonus on the side, but again it did not appreciably affect the plans for the creation of settlements. Fish, therefore, brought Europeans to American waters and created the only large-scale economic nexus in the sixteenth century, but fishing, because it could be carried out on a seasonal basis by ships operating from Europe, cannot be said to have had any major influence on settlement before 1612.

IV
Political motives for settlement

Many of the expeditions which worked their way along the coasts of North America were investigatory, looking for water entries, scouting out economic resources, making tentative approaches toward their exploitation. Only in the case of the fur trade did this type of reconnaissance lead directly to occupation for the purpose of exploiting a product which was derived from the North American mainland. For the most part, the economic motive which led to settlement on the part of the English in the Roanoke and Virginia colonies was the desire to make parts of North America substitute for Europe and to produce for England products of a Mediterranean, or Baltic, or even Caribbean, character which could not be effectively grown in England and which were expensive to obtain from foreign powers in Europe.

More powerful as an inducement to settlement were political factors though, of course, these often had economic bases. Spain was willing to allow her subjects, men like Ponce de León, and Ayllón, to experiment in establishing settlements for themselves and their followers in the Southeast, but did not hold out any special economic inducements to them to do so. But from early in the sixteenth century, Spain assumed the right to occupy, as and when she wished, the whole of the eastern mainland. She was prepared to concede Newfoundland to Portugal, since Portugal had considered that Gaspar Corte Real's discoveries in 1501 were to the east of the Tordesillas line of 1494. But from Newfoundland southward she reserved her own right both to colonize and to ward off attempts by others to occupy this coastline. Yet Spain was not prepared to invest government money in settlement in this area unless she was forced to do so. It was only when the French had begun to establish themselves in the Southeast that Spain became vitally interested in this area. The French at Charlesfort in 1562 and at Fort Caroline in 1564–65 were Huguenot enemies of Spain who could use their foothold in North America to seize Spanish ships on their way to Europe by way of the Florida Channel. Already by this time some colonial officials held that the Spanish government should have a foothold in Florida in order to rescue shipwrecked crews and vessels cast ashore on their way to Europe via the Gulf Stream. Thus the abandoned French fort on Port Royal Sound was destroyed in 1564 and Pedro Menéndez de Avilés was sent in 1565 with government money and forces (though he had to use his private resources as well) to create a political and strategic bulwark against French intervention in southeastern North America.

Even though Spanish Florida failed to become more than a military outpost, attempts at agricultural colonization having largely failed, the main Spanish aim was kept in mind and no European colonies were able to install themselves in a position from which they could easily molest the Spanish fleet as it passed through the relatively narrow Florida Channel before following the Gulf Stream deflection to the northeast. Florida in this period was therefore almost wholly a political instrument in Spain's policy of keeping other Europeans away from her colonies and her shipping routes.

News of the landing of the Roanoke colonists in 1585, when it reached Florida and Spain, aroused similar sentiments to those which the earlier French settlements had done, although not in so extreme a form. The Spaniards continued to believe during the following years that they could, whenever they wished to do so, wipe out any settlements the English might establish to the north of Florida. The English, it is true, hoped to use the colony at Roanoke Island as a base against the Spanish fleet. Sir Richard Grenville picked off a valuable straggler off Bermuda in 1585 on his way back from Roanoke Island. The fort there was deliberately hidden from Spanish observation on the Outer Banks; but there was no good harbor for raiders and Chesapeake Bay was later thought of as a better substitute. Spain kept in rather fitful touch with what the English were doing and was ready in 1590 to send an expedition to Chesapeake Bay and establish her own settlement there. Pedro Menéndez Marqués, who was to lead the expedition, was suddenly recalled from Florida for other duties, however, and the expedition abandoned.

By the opening years of the seventeenth century the supposed threat from English colonies in the Roanoke Island or Chesapeake Bay areas had faded into the background. In 1602 there were notions of abandoning Florida altogether, although a suggestion was again made to expand Spanish settlements to Chesapeake Bay. Nothing was done until after peace was made with England in 1604. The crushing in 1605 of a French attempt to demarcate lines of territory in modern South Carolina showed that Spain was still determined to keep her monopoly in the Southeast, but no interference with the settlement of Jamestown in 1607 took place. The capture of a ship going by way of the West Indies to Maine in 1606 had been made the occasion of an attempt by Spain, which lasted from 1606 to 1608, to get King James to repudiate the Virginia Company and to force it to withdraw from any colonizing attempts on the American coast. James, indeed, wished to make every possible concession to Spain, as he hoped for a Spanish alliance; but the Spanish pressure on him in this instance was too overt for him to yield. In fact, the Spaniards made it a matter of prestige that he should underwrite the Virginia Company, so that Spain, after Ecíja's abortive reconnaissance in 1609, put up with the nonaggressive presence of Virginia in what she continued to regard as Spanish territory. Virginia was not settled originally to act as a countercheck to Florida, but once its continued existence had become a matter of English national prestige it became such. A political motive as well as an economic one thus lay behind its continuance and helps to explain why its financial losses were condoned and royal assistance found to keep it going.

In New England, also, there were political overtones in the early years of the seventeenth century. The English had retracted their probings of the Gulf of St. Lawrence by the time the Tadoussac settlement was tried by the French in 1600, and they thereafter kept away from this area. Farther south, De Monts and Champlain in 1604 were given authority to explore and if necessary to hold for France the North American shoreline down to 40° N. This was apparently because Henry IV knew of the English voyages of 1602 and 1603 and wished to exercise a balancing effect on English expansion. Champlain and Waymouth were both on the New England coast in 1605, and if English settlement had been proceeded with in 1606, a clash with France would have been possible. But no effective English settlement was in fact made in 1606, and before the Sagadahoc fort was built in 1607 the French had decided to withdraw from the New England coast altogether, keeping a foothold on the Bay of Fundy only. New England was thus left open not only to English fishermen but to English settlers, although none remained there in 1612. We cannot yet tell whether this sequence of events was the result of design, calculation or accident.

By 1612, New England was in effect an English sphere of influence already, while the Maritimes and Canada were French preserves. Virginia was alive and growing around Jamestown although it still had many problems to face. St. Augustine and its dependencies were similarly alive but static. The coast from Port Royal Sound to Chesapeake Bay was and remained a no-man's-land. The same was true of the coast from the eastern shore of Virginia to Rhode Island. In 1609 Henry Hudson had sketched out a possible sphere of economic activity for the United Provinces in this zone which, rather unaccountably, had been neglected by English and French alike; but by 1612 the Dutch had not yet begun to enter it. Effective appropriation of the whole coastline had still some way to go.

V
Other Incentives
to the Exploration of North America

Two widely different groups of men were interested in North America and especially in its Amerindian inhabitants for their own sakes.

The Spanish conquerors of the sixteenth century regarded it as their duty to impose Christianity on the occupants of the countries they invaded. The objective of this was twofold: to destroy non-Christian practices and to make the native peoples amenable to Spanish government. This policy was followed through systematically in Spanish Florida between 1565 and 1598, as it had been in other parts of the Spanish empire; but with few lasting results, since Spanish power was too slight and too intermittently exercised in this area to have lasting effects on the life and outlook of the Timucua Indians. There was, however, in Spanish imperialism an alternative trend. A certain number of the Catholic clergy came to realize that if the objective was genuinely to convert American Indians to Christianity, the missionaries must identify themselves with the native peoples rather than with the Spanish authorities. Consequently, men like these felt they must take the risk of preaching their religion to the Indians without the protection of the state. Several attempts were made to do this in North America during the sixteenth century. The Dominican friar, Luis Cáncer, attempted to establish himself amongst the Indians of the Gulf coast of Florida in 1549 but was killed by them before he had made any headway with his mission. Similarly in 1570 the Jesuit fathers, Juan de Segura and Luis de Quirós, persuaded the repressive governor of Florida, Pedro Menéndez de Avilés, to permit them and their assistants to land unprotected on the shores of Chesapeake Bay so that they could attempt, with the aid of a Hispanized Indian only, to convert the people we know as the Powhatan Indians. They too were overwhelmed and their mission on the York River wiped out. (Menéndez, when he discovered this, took a sanguinary revenge.)

These episodes did not reflect so much on the Indians as on the reputation the Spanish authorities gave themselves amongst nearly all the native peoples with whom they came in contact. In Florida, after the 1597 Indian rising, attempts were made to turn the Timucua Indians into a slave population. But this policy of enslavement was countermanded in Spain and a less draconic policy toward them was advocated. As a result, members of the Franciscan Order succeeded gradually in establishing a number of mission stations outside the orbit of the soldiers and officials, where they created a core of genuine converts and in the end provided a useful screen of friendly and partially converted Indians around the small nucleus of Spanish authority. Whether or not the teaching of Christianity to the Amerindians was justified, the response of the Indians to genuinely altruistic missionary work indicated that it was possible for Europeans to identify themselves with the country and its native peoples if they made the emotional effort to do so. The way was thus prepared for the efforts and achievements of the Jesuit Order in Canada in the seventeenth century.

North America also offered an intellectual challenge to a number of men who were not concerned with spreading the Christian religion. Young men brought up in the schools and universities of western Europe, which were steeped in the knowledge of the classical world, had a trained curiosity about contemporary life and found in North America a stimulus to their powers of observation. In the narrative of the Florentine, Giovanni da Verrazzano, we find a fresh excitement at the new land, a desire to put down sharply the reactions its unfamiliar contours and vegetation excited in him, and, above all, a lively and sensitive curiosity about the Amerindian peoples he encountered. Even though he was sent to look for a passage to the Pacific, Verrazzano displayed a keen interest and absorption in North America for its own sake. Thomas Harriot, in the Roanoke Island colony, showed a similar spirit, although inspired more directly by science. He took his work of conducting a survey of the natural resources of the area with great seriousness and thoroughness, and became excited at every manifestation of the differences between the plants and creatures of North America and those of Europe. His specialized task was to study the coastal Algonkian peoples amongst whom the settlers had planted themselves. He learned their language and absorbed their customs and outlook, seeing them as a community which in its own cultural orbit was as competent and intelligent as that of the Europeans in theirs. Regrettably, we have only the outlines of the extended study he could have written about them. Marc Lescarbot was a third European intellectual who enjoyed North America. He accompanied Champlain in 1606 on an expedition along the New England coast and around the Maritimes, amused at as well as interested in what he saw and found so different from Europe. There is a little of the dilettante in him, but his involvement in the new environment is genuine though limited. In the plainer narratives also, those of the Cartier and Champlain voyages in particular, but in those of Rosier and of Laudonnière as well, there is frequently the same sense of absorption, the surrendering of conscious objectives in discovery to the effects of the new setting on the senses and feelings of the explorer. Through men like these, exploration becomes an activity which is of interest and value for its own sake.

North American Discovery
circa 1000–1612

I

The Greenland Road
to North America

THE FIRST European contacts with North America came by way of Greenland. Greenland may be looked at historically as a western extension of Europe or as an eastern extension of America. The Norse settlers who came from Iceland in the tenth century A.D., by settling on the western side of Greenland unwittingly gave it an American aspect. Inevitably, since they were seamen and hunters, Greenlanders were bound to extend their hunting grounds to Baffin Island and so, probably, to the American mainland. That they did so is undoubted, but the sources which record the Greenlanders' voyages to America, the Greenland Saga and the Saga of Eirik the Red, are based partly at least on oral tradition, the first perhaps written down about 1200 and the latter about 1270, though possibly with earlier written versions behind them. As traditional tales they cannot be taken literally as recorded fact, and historians have rightly been very cautious in relying on the specific data which they record. It is now accepted that they represent, in some form, events that took place. Yet nearly every writer on American discovery has had his own theory about some part of the sagas and there is no entire consensus of opinion on precisely what they represent. The careful student will treat every conclusion based on them with due skepticism, especially when it is stated dogmatically.

The standard text is Halldór Hermannson, The Vinland Sagas (1944); the best translations are in Gwyn Jones, The Norse Atlantic Saga (1964) and Magnus Magnusson and Hermann Pálsson, The Vinland Sagas (1965). Fridtjof Nansen, In Northern Mists (2 vols., 1911), is an excellent example of a skeptical and learned approach; Helge Ingstad, Land Under the Pole Star (1966), and The Western Way to Vinland (1969) are good on the Greenland background and on the geographical setting of the Vinland voyages; Jones's Norse Atlantic Saga is the best concise account so far published; in The Vikings (1968) he places the western voyages in their European setting.

The sagas have been supplemented by archeological discoveries. From 1691 to 1968 Helge Ingstad excavated eight sites at L'Anse aux Meadows, just inside the Strait of Belle Isle, at the northeast tip of Newfoundland. One six-room long house, seven smaller houses, two cooking pits and one charcoal pit were revealed. The long house had fireplaces and ember pits as in Norse sites. Some rusted nails, fragments of iron and slag, a small piece of smelted copper, a fragment of a bone needle and a spindle whorl, both of Norse types, and finally a ring-headed bronze pin have been found. Twelve carbon-14 samples gave mean datings of plus or minus A.D. 1000 (see H. Ingstad, "The Norse Discovery of Newfoundland," The Book of Newfoundland, ed. Joseph R. Smallwood, III [1967], 218–224, and The Western Way to Vinland, pp. 193–219). There is a strong disposition to accept this as one of the sites reached and occupied by explorers from Greenland.

Contact between Greenland and eastern North America was maintained between about 1000 and about 1013. The most northerly area touched by the explorers was called by them Helluland (and is believed to have comprised Baffin Island and possibly the treeless northern tip of Labrador), Markland (the forested area including most of Labrador and extending conceivably much further south), and Vinland (hotly debated as Newfoundland, or the St. Lawrence, or the Atlantic coasts of the Maritimes and New England). It is necessary to include extracts from both the Greenland Saga and Eirik the Red's Saga, but there is no agreement amongst scholars on how these differences should be reconciled. It has been pointed out that the Greenland Saga regards Vinland as almost equivalent to a single place, Leisbudir, discovered by Leif Eiriksson, while Eirik the Red's Saga distinguishes between Straumfjord and Hop, and gives considerably greater geographical detail, especially for the final expeditions of Thorfinn Karlsefni. A reasonable hypothesis in the present state of knowledge might be that "Vinland" could represent two distinct locations: one, reasonably certain, would be northern Newfoundland; the other, the existence of which is more problematical, could be considerably farther south. Until further tangible remains of Norse intrusions are found the saga stories can be taken to indicate in some way or other what occurred, with the reservation that all the more elaborate topographical reconstructions based on them are almost certainly false, if only because the indications of locations in the sagas are, by their very nature, highly generalized.

1. Bjarni's Discovery
of Land Beyond Greenland

FROM Greenland Saga, Jones, The Norse Atlantic Saga, pp. 146–148. According to the saga, Bjarni Herjolfsson followed his father from Iceland to Greenland in A.D. 986, catching sight of land to the westward of Greenland when he was driven off course.

Bjarni brought his ship to Eyrar that same summer his father had sailed away in the spring. He was taken heavily aback by the news, and had no mind to discharge his ship's cargo. His shipmates asked him what he proposed to do, and he replied that he meant to carry on as usual and enjoy winter quarters at his father's home. "I shall steer my ship for Greenland, if you are prepared to go along with me." They all said they would stand by his decision. "Our voyage will appear foolhardy," said Bjarni, "since no one of us has entered the Greenland Sea." Even so they put out the moment they were ready, and sailed for three days before losing sight of land. Then their following wind died down, and north winds and fogs overtook them, so that they had no idea which way they were going. This continued over many days, but eventually they saw the sun and could then get their bearings [or determine the quarters of the heavens]. They now hoisted sail, and sailed that day before sighting land, and debated among themselves what land this could be. To his way of thinking, said Bjarni, it could not be Greenland. They asked him whether he proposed to sail to this land or not. "My intention," he replied, "is to sail close in to the land." Which they did, and could soon see that the land was not mountainous and was covered with forest, with low hills there, so they left the land to port of them and let their sheet turn towards the land.

 After this they sailed for two days before sighting another land. They asked whether Bjarni thought this in its turn was Greenland. In his opinion, he said, this was no more Greenland than the first place—"For there are very big glaciers reported to be in Greenland." They soon drew near to this land, and could see that it was flat country and covered with woods. Then their following wind died on them. The crew talked things over and said they thought it common sense to put ashore there; but this Bjarni would not allow. They reckoned they were in need of both wood and water. "You lack for neither," said Bjarni, and got some hard words for this from his crew.

 He gave orders to hoist sail, which was done; they turned their prow from the land and sailed out to sea three days with a southwest wind, and then they saw the third land, and this land was high, mountainous, and glaciered. They asked whether Bjarni would put ashore there, but no, he said, he had no wish to. "For to me this land looks good for nothing." So without so much as lowering their sail they held on along the land, and came to see that it was an island.

Once more they turned their prow from the land and held out to sea with the same following wind. Soon the wind freshened, so Bjarni ordered them to reef, and not crowd more sail than was safe for their ship and tackle. This time they sailed for four days, and then saw the fourth land. They asked Bjarni whether he thought this was Greenland or not. "This is very like what I am told about Greenland," replied Bjarni, "and here we will make for the land." So that is what they did, and came to land under a certain cape in the evening of the day. There was a boat on the cape, and there too on the cape lived Herjolf, Bjarni's father. It was for this reason the ness got its name, and has been known ever since as Herjolfsnes.

2. Leif Eiriksson's Voyage

BJARNI COMMUNICATED his discovery of land to the west to the family of Eirik the Red after he reached Greenland. About fourteen to sixteen years later (that is, around A.D. 1000 or 1002), Leif Eiriksson is said to have traveled in Bjarni's ship to follow up the discovery. The sagas differ in their representation of the time and nature of the voyage. Extract A is from the Greenland Saga (Jones, Norse Atlantic Saga, pp. 148–153), and Extract B from Eirik the Red's Saga (ibid., pp. 172–173).

A.

There was now much talk about voyages of discovery. Leif, son of Eirik the Red of Brattahlid, went to see Bjarni Herjolfsson, bought his ship from him, and found her a crew, so that they were thirty-five all told. Leif invited Eirik his father to lead this expedition too, but Eirik begged off rather, reckoning he was now getting on in years, and was less able to stand the rigours of bad times at sea than he used to be. . . . Leif rode on to the ship and his comrades with him, thirty-five of them all told. There was a German on the expedition named Tyrkir.

They now prepared their ship and sailed out to sea once they were ready, and they lighted on that land first which Bjarni and his people had lighted on last. They sailed to land there, cast anchor and put off a boat, then went ashore, and could see no grass there. The background was all great glaciers, and right up to the glaciers from the sea as it were a single slab of rock. The land impressed them as barren and useless. "At least," said Leif, "it has not happened to us as to Bjarni over this land, that we failed to get ourselves ashore. I shall now give the land a name, and call it Helluland, Flatstone Land." After which they returned to the ship.

After that they sailed out to sea and lighted on another land. This time too they sailed to land, cast anchor, then put off a boat and went ashore. The country was flat and covered with forest, with extensive white sands wherever they went, and shelving gently to the sea. "This land," said Leif, "shall be given a name in accordance with its nature, and be called Markland, Wood Land." After which they got back down to the ship as fast as they could.

From there they now sailed out to sea with a north-east wind and were at sea two days before catching sight of land. They sailed to land, reaching an island which lay north of it, where they went ashore and looked about them in fine weather, and found that there was dew on the grass, whereupon it happened to them that they set their hands to the dew, then carried it to their mouths, and thought they had never known anything so sweet as that was. After which they returned to their ship and sailed into the sound which lay between the island and the cape projecting north from the land itself. They made headway west round the cape. There were big shallows there at low water; their ship went aground, and it was a long way to get sight of the sea from the ship. But they were so curious to get ashore they had no mind to wait for the tide to rise under their ship, but went hurrying off to land where a river flowed out of a lake. Then, as soon as the tide rose under their ship, they took their boat, rowed back to her, and brought her up into the river, and so to the lake, where they cast anchor, carried their skin sleeping-bags off board, and built themselves booths. Later they decided to winter there and built a big house.

There was no lack of salmon in river or lake, and salmon bigger than they had ever seen before. The nature of the land was so choice, it seemed to them that none of the cattle would require fodder for the winter. No frost came during the winter, and the grass was hardly withered. Day and night were of a more equal length there than in Greenland or Iceland. On the shortest day of winter the sun was visible in the middle of the afternoon as well as at breakfast time.

Once they had finished their house-building, Leif made an announcement to his comrades. "I intend to have our company divided now in two, and get the land explored. Half our band shall remain here at the hall, and the other half reconnoitre the countryside—yet go no further than they can get back home in the evening, and not get separated." So for a while that is what they did, Leif going off with them or remaining in camp by turns. Leif was big and strong, of striking appearance, shrewd, and in every respect a temperate, fair-dealing man.

One evening it turned out that a man of their company was missing. This was Tyrkir the German. Leif was greatly put out by this, for Tyrkir had lived a long while with him and his father, and had shown great affection for Leif as a child. He gave his shipmates the rough edge of his tongue, then turned out to go and look for him, taking a dozen men with him. But when they had got only a short way from the hall there was Tyrkir coming to meet them. His welcome was a joyous one. Leif could see at once that his foster-father was in fine fettle. He was a man with a bulging forehead, rolling eyes, and an insignificant little face, short and not much to look at, but handy at all sorts of crafts.

"Why are you so late, foster-father," Leif asked him, "and parted this way from your companions?"

By way of a start Tyrkir held forth a long while in German, rolling his eyes all ways, and pulling faces. They had no notion what he was talking about. Then after a while he spoke in Norse. "I went no great way further than you, yet I have a real novelty to report. I have found vines and grapes."

"Is that the truth, foster-father?" Leif asked.

"Of course it's the truth," he replied. "I was born where wine and grapes are no rarity."

They slept overnight, then in the morning Leif made this announcement to his crew. "We now have two jobs to get on with, and on alternate days must gather grapes or cut vines and fell timber, so as to provide a cargo of such things for my ship." They acted upon these orders, and report has it that their tow-boat was filled with grapes [?raisins]. A full ship's cargo was cut, and in the spring they made ready and sailed away. Leif gave the land a name in accordance with the good things they found in it, calling it Vinland, Wineland; after which they sailed out to sea and had a good wind till they sighted Greenland and the mountains under the glaciers.

B.

Leif put to sea as soon as he was ready, was storm-tossed a long time, and lighted on those lands whose existence he had not so much as dreamt of before. There were wheatfields growing wild [literally, "self-sown"] there and vines too. There were also those trees which are called maple, and they fetched away with them samples of all these things. . . .[1]

Leif landed in Eiriksfjord and went home to Brattahlid, where everybody welcomed him with open arms.

3. Thorvald Eiriksson's Voyage and Settlement in Vinland

THE FIRST attempt to colonize Vinland soon followed. The extract is from the Greenland Saga (Jones, Norse Atlantic Saga, pp. 152–153).

There was now much discussion of Leif's expedition to Vinland. His brother Thorvald considered that the land had been explored in too restricted a fashion. So Leif said to Thorvald, "If you want to, go you to Vinland, brother, in my ship; but first I want her to go for the timber which Thorir had on the reef."

That was done, and now Thorvald made preparations for this voyage along with thirty men, under the guidance of Leif his brother. Later they put their ship ready and sailed out to sea, and nothing is recorded of their voyage till they came to Vinland, to Leifsbudir, where they saw to their ship and stayed quiet over the

1. Another manuscript says that some of the trees were large enough to be used for building houses.

winter, catching fish for their food. But in the spring Thorvald ordered them to make their ship ready, and for the ship's boat and certain of the men to proceed along the west coast and explore there during the summer. It looked to them a beautiful and well-wooded land, the woods scarcely any distance from the sea, with white sands, and a great many islands and shallows. Nowhere did they come across habitation of man or beast, but on an island in the west found a wooden grain-holder. They found no other work of man, so returned and reached Leifsbudir that autumn.

Next summer Thorvald set off eastwards with the merchant-ship and further north along the land. Off a certain cape they met with heavy weather, were driven ashore, and broke the keel from under the ship. They made a long stay there, mending their ship. Said Thorvald to his shipmates: "I should like us to erect the keel on the cape here, and call it Kjalarnes, Keelness." This they did, and afterwards sailed away and east along the land, and into the mouth of the next fjord they came to, and to a headland jutting out there which was entirely covered with forest. They brought the ship to where they could moor her, thrust out a gangway to the shore, and Thorvald walked ashore with his full ship's company. "This is a lovely place," he said, "and here I should like to make my home." Then they made for the ship, and saw three mounds on the sands up inside the headland. They walked up to them and could see three skin-boats there, and three men under each. So they divided forces and laid hands on them all, except for one who got away with his canoe. The other eight they killed, and afterwards walked back to the headland, where they had a good look round and could see various mounds on up the fjord which they judged to be human habitations. Then atfer this so great a drowsiness overtook them that they could not keep awake, and all fell asleep. Then a cry carried to them, so that they were all roused up, and the words of the cry were these: "Rouse ye Thorvald, and all your company, if you would stay alive. Back to your ship with all your men, and leave this land as fast as you can!" With that there came from inside the fjord a countless fleet of skin-boats and attacked them. "We must rig up our war-roof," ordered Thorvald, "each side of the ship, and defend ourselves to the utmost, yet offer little by way of attack." Which they did. The Skraelings kept shooting at them for a while, but then fled away, each one as fast as he could.

Thorvald now inquired among his men whether anyone was wounded. Not a wound among them, they assured him. "I have got a wound under my arm," he told them. "An arrow flew in between gunwale and shield, under my arm. Here is the arrow, and it will be the death of me. I command you, make the fastest preparations you can for your return. As for me, you shall carry me to that headland where I thought I should so like to make my home. Maybe it was truth that came into my mouth, that I should dwell there awhile. For there you shall bury me, and set crosses at my head and feet, and call it Krossanes for ever more."

Now Thorvald died. They did everything he had asked of them, and afterwards set off and rejoined their comrades, and they told each other such tidings as they had to tell. They stayed there that winter and gathered grapes and vines for the ship. The following spring they prepared to leave for Greenland, and brought their ship into Eiriksfjord, and the news they had to tell Leif was great news indeed.

4. Karlsefni's Voyage to Vinland and his Unsuccessful Attempt at Colonization

THE MOST complete account of an attempted settlement is given in the narratives of Thorfinn Karlsefni's expedition. It extended over three years and was brought to an end by attacks by the Skraelings, who were Eskimo or American Indians or both. No attempt is made to identify the locations named although it is clear that, on this occasion, more than one location was visited and occupied for some time by the settlers. Precise dates have proved difficult to calculate. Gwyn Jones concludes that "all these voyages were over and done with by 1020 at the latest" (The Vikings, p. 303); others have thought that 1013 or thereabouts would mark a terminal date. Extract A is from the Greenland Saga (Jones, Norse Atlantic Saga, pp. 156–158), and Extract B from Eirik the Red's Saga (ibid., pp. 178–186).

A.

That same summer a ship arrived in Greenland from Norway. Her captain was a man named Thorfinn Karlsefni, a son of Thord Horsehead, the son of Snorri Thordarson of Hofdi. Thorfinn

Karlsefni was a very well-to-do man, and spent the winter at Brattahlid with Leif Eiriksson. It did not take him long to set his heart on Gudrid; he asked for her hand, and she left it to Leif to answer for her. So now she was betrothed to him and their wedding took place that winter.

There was the same talk and to-do over the Vinland voyages as before, and the people there, Gudrid as well as the rest, put strong pressure on Karlsefni to undertake an expedition. So his voyage was decided on, and he secured himself a ship's company of sixty men and five women. Karlsefni entered into this agreement with his shipmates, that they should receive equal shares of everything they made by profit. They took with them all sorts of livestock, for it was their intention to colonize the country if they could manage it. Karlsefni asked Leif for his house in Vinland. He would lend the house, he said, but not give it.

Next, then, they sailed their ship to sea and reached Leifsbudir all safe and sound, and carried their sleeping-bags ashore. They soon enjoyed a big and splendid catch, for a fine big whale was stranded there. They went and cut it up, and had no problem with regard to food. The livestock went on up ashore there, but it was soon found that the males grew unmanageable and played havoc all round. They had brought the one bull with them. Karlsefni had timber felled and dressed for his ship, laying the wood out on the rock to dry. They took every advantage of the resources the country had to offer, both in the way of grapes and all kinds of hunting and fishing and good things.

After that first winter came summer. It was now they made acquaintance with the Skraelings, when a big body of men appeared out of the forest there. Their cattle were close by; the bull began to bellow and bawl his head off, which so frightened the Skraelings that they ran off with their packs, which were of grey furs and sables and skins of all kinds, and headed for Karlsefni's house, hoping to get inside there, but Karlsefni had the doors guarded. Neither party could understand the other's language. Then the Skraelings unslung their bales, untied them, and proffered their wares, and above all wanted weapons in exchange. Karlsefni, though, forbade them the sale of weapons. And now he hit on this idea; he told the women to carry out milk to them, and the moment they saw the milk that was the one thing they wanted to buy, nothing else. So that was what came of the Skraelings' trading; they carried away what they bought in their bellies, while Karlsefni and his comrades kept their bales and their furs. And with that they went away.

The next thing to report is how Karlsefni had a formidable stockade built around his house and they made their preparations. At this time too his wife Gudrid gave birth to a boy whom they named Snorri. Early in the second winter the Skraelings came to visit them; they were much more numerous than last time, but had the same wares as before. "And now," Karlsefni ordered the women, "you must fetch out food similar to what made such a hit before, and not a thing besides." And once the Skraelings saw that they tossed their packs in over the palisade. . . .

One of the Skraelings was killed by a housecarle [servant] of Karlsefni's because he had tried to steal their weapons; and away they ran as fast as they could, leaving their clothes and their goods behind them. . . .

"We had best lay our heads together now," said Karlsfni, "for I fancy they will be paying us a third and hostile visit in full force. So let us follow this plan, that ten men move forward on to the ness here, letting themselves be seen, while the rest of our company go into the forest to clear a passage there for our cattle, in readiness for when their host advances from the wood. Also we must take our bull and let him march at our head."

The ground where their clash was to take place was set out after this fashion, that there was lake on one side and forest on the other, so they followed Karlsefni's plan. The Skraelings advanced to the spot Karlsefni had fixed on for battle, battle was joined, and many fell from among the Skraelings' host. There was one big, fine-looking man in the Skraeling host who Karlsefni imagined must be their chief. One of the Skraelings had picked up an axe, he stared at it for a while, then swung at a comrade of his and cut at him. He fell dead on the instant, whereupon the big man caught hold of the axe, stared at it for a while, then flung it as far out over the water as he could. After which they fled to the forest, each as best he might, and that was the end of their encounter.

Karlsefni and his troop spent the entire winter there; but in the spring Karlsefni announced that he would be staying there no longer. He wanted to go to Greenland. They made ready for their journey, and fetched away with them many valuable commodities in the shape of vines, grapes and furs. And now they sailed to sea, and reached Eiriksfjord safe with their ship, and it was there they spent the winter.

B.

This same winter long discussions took place at Brattahlid. Karlsefni and Snorri resolved to go and find Vinland, and men debated this a good deal. The upshot was that Karlsefni and Snorri fitted out their ship, meaning to go and find Vinland in the summer. Bjarni and Thorhall resolved to make the journey with their ship and the crew which had served with them. . . . They then sailed away for the Western Settlement and for Bjarneyjar, Bear Isles. From Bjarneyjar they sailed with a north wind, were at sea two days, and then found land. They rowed ashore in boats and explored the country, finding many flat stones there, so big that a pair of men could easily clap sole to sole on them. There were many arctic foxes there. They gave the land a name, calling it Helluland, Flatstone Land. Then they sailed with a north wind for two days, when land lay ahead of them, with a great forest and many wild animals. Off the land to the south-east lay an island, where they found a bear, so called it Bjarney, Bear Island. But the land where the forest was they called Markland, Wood Land.

Then when two days were past they sighted land, and sailed to the land. Where they arrived there was a cape. They beat along the coast and left the land to starboard; it was an open harbourless coast there, with long beaches and sands. They put ashore in boats, came across the keel from a ship, so called the place Kjalarnes, Keelness. Likewise they gave a name to the beaches, calling them Furdustrandir, Marvelstrands, it was such a long business sailing past them. Then the land became bay-indented, and towards these bays they headed their ships.

It happened when Leif was with king Olaf Tryggvason, and he commissioned him to preach Christianity in Greenland, that the king gave him two Scots, a man named Haki, and a woman Hekja.

The king told Leif to make use of these people if he had need of fleetness, for they were fleeter than deer. These people Leif and Eirik provided to accompany Karlsefni. So when they had sailed past Furdustrandir they put the Scots ashore, ordering them to run into the region lying south, spy out the quality of the land, and come back before three days were past. They were so attired that they were wearing the garment which they called *Bjafal:* this was so put together that there was a hood on top, it was open at the sides and sleeveless, and buttoned between the legs, where a button and loop held it together; while for the rest they were naked. They cast anchor and lay there this while, and when three days were past they came running down from the land, and one of them had grapes in his hand, and the other self-sown wheat. Karlsefni said they appeared to have found a choice, productive land. They took them on board ship and went their ways until the land was indented by a fjord. They laid the ships' course up into this fjord, off whose mouth there lay an island, and surrounding the island strong currents. This island they called Straumsey. There were so many birds there that a man could hardly set foot down between the eggs. They held on into the fjord, and called it Straumsfjord, and here they carried their goods off the ships and made their preparations. They had brought all sorts of livestock with them, and looked around at what the land had to offer. There were mountains there, and the prospect round was beautiful. They paid no heed to anything save exploring the country. There was tall [or abundant] grass there. They spent the winter there, and a hard winter it proved, with no provision made for it; they were in a bad way for food, and the hunting and fishing failed. Then they went out to the island, hoping it would yield something by way of hunting or fishing or something drifted ashore. But small store of food was there, though their stock did well there. . . . In the spring they went up into Straumsfjord and got supplies from both sources, hunting on the mainland, eggs in the breeding grounds and fishing from the sea.

Now they talked over their expedition and made plans. . . .

Karlsefni sailed south along the land with Snorri and Bjarni and the rest of their company. They journeyed a long time till they reached a river which flowed down from the land into a lake and so to the sea. There were such extensive bars off the mouth of the estuary that they were unable to get into the river except at full flood. Karlsefni and his men sailed into the estuary and called the place Hop, Landlock Bay. There they found self-sown fields of wheat where the ground was low-lying, and vines wherever it was hilly. Every brook there was full of fish. They dug trenches at the meeting point of land and high water, and when the tide went out there were halibut in the trenches. There were vast numbers of animals of every kind in the forest. They were there for a fortnight enjoying themselves and saw nothing and nobody. They had their cattle with them.

Then early one morning when they looked about them they saw nine skin-boats, on board which staves were being swung which sounded just like flails threshing—and their motion was sunwise.

"What can this mean?" asked Karlsefni.

"Perhaps it is a token of peace," replied Snorri. "So let us take a white shield and hold it out towards them."

They did so, and those others rowed towards them, showing their astonishment, then came ashore. They were small, ill-favoured men, and had ugly hair on their heads. They had big eyes and were broad in the cheeks. For a while they remained there, astonished, and afterwards rowed off south past the headland.

Karlsefni and his men built themselves dwellings up above the lake; some of their houses stood near the mainland, and some near the lake. They now spent the winter there. No snow fell, and their entire stock found its food grazing in the open. But once spring came in they chanced early one morning to see how a multitude of skin-boats came rowing from the south round the headland, so many that the bay appeared sown with coals, and even so staves were being swung on every boat. Karlsefni and his men raised their shields, and they began trading together. Above all these people wanted to buy red cloth. They also wanted to buy swords and spears, but this Karlsefni and Snorri would not allow. They had dark unblemished skins to exchange for the cloth, and were taking a span's length of cloth for a skin, and this they tied round their heads. So it continued for a while, then when the cloth began to run short they cut it up so that it was no broader than a finger-breadth, but the Skraelings gave just as much for it, or more.

The next thing was that the bull belonging to Karlsefni and his mates ran out of the forest bellowing loudly. The Skraelings were terrified by this, raced out to their boats and rowed south past the headland, and for three weeks running there was neither sight nor sound of them. But at the end of that period they saw a great multitude of Skraeling boats coming up from the south like a streaming torrent. This time all the staves were being swung anti-sunwise, and the Skraelings were all yelling aloud, so they took red shields and held them out against them. They clashed together and fought. There was a heavy shower of missiles, for the Skraelings had warslings too. Karlsefni and Snorri could see the Skraelings hoisting up on poles a big ball-shaped object, and blue-black in colour, which they sent flying inland over Karlsefni's troop, and it made a hideous noise where it came down. Great fear now struck into Karlsefni and all his following, so that there was no other thought in their heads than to run away up along the river to some steep rocks, and there put up a strong resistance. . . .

It now seemed plain to Karlsefni and his men that though the quality of the land was admirable, there would always be fear and strife dogging them there on account of those who already inhabited it. So they made ready to leave, setting their hearts on their own country, and sailed north along the coast and found five Skraelings in fur doublets asleep near the sea, who had with them wooden containers in which was animal marrow mixed with blood. They felt sure that these men would have been sent out from that country, so they killed them. Later they discovered a cape and great numbers of animals. To look at, this cape was like a cake of dung, because the animals lay there the nights through.

And now Karlsefni and his followers returned to Straumsfjord. It is some men's report that Bjarni and Freydis had remained behind there, and a hundred men with them, and proceeded no farther, while Karlsefni and Snorri had travelled south with forty men, yet spent no longer at Hop than a bare two months, and got back again that same summer. Then Karlsefni set off with one ship to look for Thorhall the Hunter,[1] while the rest of the party stayed behind. They went north past Kjalarnes, and then bore away west, with the

---

1. One of their companions who had left them earlier.

land on their port side. There was nothing but a wilderness of forest-land. And when they had been on their travels for a long time, there was a river flowing down off the land from east to west. They put into this river-mouth and lay at anchor off the southern bank. . . .

Then they moved away and back north, believing they had sighted Winfaetingaland, Uniped Land.[2] They were unwilling to imperil their company any longer. They proposed to explore all the mountains, those which were at Hop and those they discovered.

They went back and spent that third winter in Straumsfjord. There was bitter quarrelling, for the unmarried men fell foul of the married. Karlsefni's son Snorri was born there the first autumn and was three years old when they left.[3]

They got a south wind and reached Markland, where they found five Skraelings, one of them a grown man with a beard, two women and two children. Karlsefni captured the boys but the others escaped and sank down into the ground. These boys they kept with them, taught them their language, and they were baptized. They gave their mother's name as Vaetilldi, that of their father as Uvaegi. They said that kings ruled over Skraelingaland, one of whom was called Avalldamon and the other Valldidida. There were no houses there, they said; the people lodged in caves or holes. A country lay on the other side, they said, opposite their own land, where men walked about in white clothes and whooped loudly, and carried poles and went about with flags. They concluded that this must be Hvitramannaland.[4] And now they came to Greenland and spent the winter with Eirik the Red.

---

2. A one-legged creature, a uniped, had been said earlier to have killed Thorvald with an arrow.
3. "The first known person of European origin to be born on the North American continent" (Jones, The Vikings, p. 493).
4. Another manuscript called it "Ireland the Great," on which words many fantastic theories have been erected.

II
The Western Islands and the Route to Asia

BETWEEN THE early voyages of the Greenlanders in the eleventh century and the new expeditions of the later fifteenth century there is so far no proof of any continuity in the contacts between Europe and North America. Two brief statements, one in the twelfth century and one in the fourteenth, indicate that some connections still persisted between Greenland and Vinland before the Greenland colony faded away shortly after 1400.[1] The Vinland Map now indicates that there was probably some knowledge of Vinland in fifteenth-century Europe. But the principal cause of the growing interest, theoretical and practical, in the Atlantic Ocean owed nothing to the earlier Greenland voyages. This was the revival in the late fourteenth and early fifteenth century of classical views of the possible accessibility of Asia across the Atlantic Ocean, accelerated later in the fifteenth century by calculations which seemed to establish that Asia was much nearer to Europe than had formerly been thought. The growing rash of mythical islands which adorned the sea charts of the fourteenth and fifteenth centuries was partly a reflection of the searches for and discoveries of real islands. Late in the fifteenth century those who thought voyages to Asia worth attempting by a westward route came to think that islands yet to be found would make stepping-stones on the way, which would make the Asia voyage almost easy.

Economic motives—the desire to find fertile islands on which settlers could grow sugar, grapes and woad, and round which a successful fishery could be carried on—drew Spaniards and Portuguese into the Atlantic. In this way the Spaniards acquired the Canaries, the Portuguese Madeira, the Azores and the Cape Verdes. When the western Azores were occupied about 1450, the Portuguese had mastered nearly a thousand miles of westward ocean sailing. Thus expeditions were planned to find and exploit further fertile islands and this was one reason why Portuguese and English explorers attempted to push further and further to the west.

W. H. Babcock, Legendary Islands in the Atlantic (1922) and

---

1. Gwyn Jones (The Vikings, pp. 309–311) is prepared to accept that the abandoned colony survived down to the period of rediscovery (circa 1500), but the lack of reliable evidence still leaves this very problematical.

Richard Hennig, Terrae Incognitae (4 vols. in German, 2nd edn. 1951–
56) contain a full story but must be used with caution. For the Spaniards,
F. Perez Embid, Los Discubrimientos en el Atlántico . . . hasta el
Tradado de Tordesillas (1948), is useful; for the Portuguese, see S. E.
Morison, Portuguese Voyages to America in the Fifteenth Century
(1940), with D. Peres, A History of the Portuguese Discoveries (1960)
and A. Teixiera da Mota, Portuguese Navigations in the North Atlantic
in the Fifteenth and Sixteenth Centuries (1965).

5. European Contacts with Vinland
after the Voyages of the Greenlanders

The Vinland Map (Plate 1), which, if its authenticity can be held to
be wholly established, was made about 1440 or a little later, shows
a large insular land mass to the west and southwest of Greenland, extending one might think from about 47° N. latitude to about 67° N.
latitude. This is penetrated from the east by two great inlets, which thus
divide the island into three zones (which could possibly be intended for
the Helluland, Markland and Vinland of the sagas, although they are
not named as such). An inscription alongside the island makes the
statement that it was discovered by Leif and Bjarni and was called
Vinland, without any dates being indicated. Another inscription above
the island repeats this information with a little more detail, saying that
Vinland was fertile and had vines. It also adds that Bishop Eirikr later
visited Vinland and spent some time there, returning in the last year of
Pope Pascal II, namely, 1117–18.

Comparable information is contained in the Icelandic annals, though
Bishop Eirikr is said only to have gone to look for Vinland and the date
is given as 1121. Adam of Bremen, writing in northern Europe before
1076, included in his history of the archbishoprics of Hamburg and
Bremen references to both Greenland and "Winland" (thought to mean
Vinland). After the twelfth century there is a single entry only in the
Iceland annals on western lands, when in 1347 a ship from Markland,
unable to make Greenland, arrived instead at Iceland. This would sug-
gest that some commerce in timber, perhaps only intermittent, continued
between the declining Greenland colony and the lands to the west, but
it is very slight evidence on which to base any conclusions. The Greenland colony is believed by many to have died out in the early fifteenth
century. The Dane, Claudius Clavus, between 1424 and 1430 added a
map of Greenland (shown as a peninsula extending from northern
Europe around the north and to the west of Iceland) to the cartographic
information available in southern Europe. About 1440 (again with some
question of its authenticity) the Vinland Map put an insular Greenland

on the map of the western ocean as well as the new "island" of Vinland. It has not yet been established whether this view was in circulation in the fifteenth century as the map is so far known only in a single manuscript version. Two Germans, Didrick Pining and Hans Pothorst, employed by the king of Denmark in Iceland, are known to have made a voyage to Greenland some time between 1473 and 1494, though nothing is known of their discoveries. Greenland is not known to have been seen again until Gaspar Corte Real sighted Cape Farewell in 1500 and used it as a landmark in setting off for the exploration of new lands to the west in 1501.

Much of the literature on the supposed relations of the Greenlanders with Helluland, Markland and Vinland after 1013 is conjectural or fictional. Jones, The Norse Atlantic Saga, pp. 91–97, 220–222, and The Vikings, pp. 303–311, and also F. Nansen, In Northern Mists, II, 95–290, remain invaluable. Helge Ingstad's Land Under the Pole Star and The Western Way to Vinland are interesting but less self-critical. R. A. Skelton, T. E. Marston and G. D. Painter, The Vinland Map (1965), is essential reading: it aroused immense interest and much controversy. A short review of the problems it raises is given in D. B. Quinn and P. G. Foote, "The Vinland Map," Saga-Book, XVII (1966), 63–89, and more comprehensively in Wilcomb C. Washburn, ed., The Vinland Map Reconsidered (1971). The status of the map must be considered unproven, though the present writer considers that it is somewhat more likely than not to be genuine.

A. Bishop Eirikr

THE FOLLOWING statements are from the Icelandic Annals, Kunungsannáll and Gottskalksannáll, respectively:[1]

i. 1121. Bishop Eirik of Greenland set out for Vinland.

ii. 1121. Eirik the Greenlanders's bishop went to look for Vinland.

B. 1347. A ship from Markland

THE FOLLOWING entries appear in the Icelandic Annals, Skálholtsannáll and Flateyjarannáll, respectively:[2]

i. 1347. There came also a ship from Greenland, smaller than the small Icelandic boats; she came into the outer Straumfjord [near Budir, on Snaefellsnes], and had no anchor. There were seven-

1. As printed in Gustav Storm, Islandske Annaler indtil 1578 (1888), pp. 112, 320, translated in Jones, The Norse Atlantic Saga, p. 96.
2. Storm, pp. 213, 403, translated in Jones, The Norse Atlantic Saga, p. 96. Jones (The Vikings, p. 303) regards both A and B, and also D (below) as "important and trustworthy references."

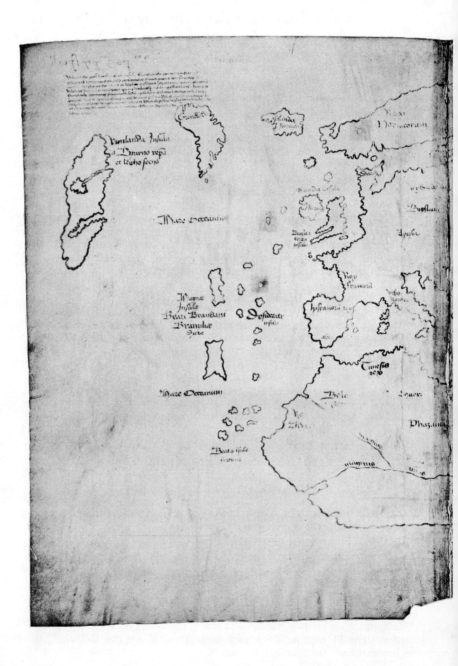

Vinlanda Insula
a Bruno reppa
er leipho socio

Mare Occeanum

Magna
Insula
Beati Brandani
Branalue
Siete

Desidata
insule

Mare Occeanum

Beate insule
fortunate

teen men on board. They made a voyage to Markland, but were afterwards storm-driven here.

ii. 1347. At this time came a ship from Greenland, which had made a voyage to Markland, and had eighteen men on board.

C. The Legends of the Vinland Map

THE LEGENDS on the Vinland Map are in Latin; their texts and translations are given in Skelton, Marston and Painter, The Vinland Map, legends 66 and 67, pp. 139–141. (The translation of the second legend has been slightly modified in accordance with the suggestions of Professor P. G. Foote in Saga-Book, XVII, 75–80.)

i. Legend 66
Island of Vinland [Insula Vinilanda], discovered by Byarni and Leiph in company.

ii. Legend 67
By God's will, after a long voyage from the island of Greenland to the south toward the most distant remaining parts of the western ocean sea, sailing southward amidst the ice, the companions Byarni and Leiph Erisson discovered a new land, extremely fertile even having vines, the which island they named Viniland. Henry [Eirikr], legate of the Apostolic See and bishop of Greenland and the neighbouring regions, arrived in this truly vast and very rich land, in the name of Almighty God, in the last year of our most blessed father Pascal [Pascal II], and later returned southeastward towards Greenland and then proceeded in most humble obedience to a higher will.

D. Adam of Bremen writes
on Iceland and Vinland, circa 1070

ADAM OF BREMEN was for a time at the court of Svein Estridsson, king of the Danes (died 1076), and there learned a good deal about the northern parts of the world which he included in his History of the Archbishops of Hamburg-Bremen, translated by Francis J. Tschan (1959). The following extracts are taken from Nansen, In Northern Mists, I, 193–195, where they are accompanied by a useful commentary.

The island of Thyle [Thule, Iceland], which is separated from the others by an infinite distance, lies far out in the middle of the Ocean and . . . is scarcely known.

Furthermore there are many other islands in the great Ocean of which Greenland is not the least. It lies farther out in the Ocean opposite the mountains of Suedia [Sweden] or the Riphean range.[1] To this island, it is said, one can sail from the shore of Nortmannia [Norway] in five or seven days, as likewise to Iceland. The people there are bluish-green from the salt water; and from this their region takes its name. They live in a similar way to the Icelanders, except that they are more cruel and trouble seafarers by predatory attacks. To them also, as is reported, Christianity has lately been wafted. . . .

Moreover he [Svien Estridsson] mentioned yet another island, which had been discovered by men in that ocean, and which is called Wineland [Vinland], because vines grow there and give the noblest wine. And that there is abundance of unsown corn we have obtained certain knowledge, not by fabulous superstition, but from trustworthy information of the Danes. Beyond this island, he said no habitable land is found in this Ocean, but all that is more distant is full of intolerable ice and immense darkness.[2]

6. An Early Fifteenth-Century View of the Ocean Between Spain and Asia

THE French cardinal, Pierre d'Ailly, wrote a famous geography in 1410 called Ymago mundi. It circulated in manuscript and was later printed. Columbus took it almost as his bible and made many notes on the margins of his copy, since it contained optimistic suggestions on the accessibility of Asia by a westward passage from Spain, based partly on the opinions (not always accurately recorded) of ancient writers. Edmond Buron's edition, with French translation and the notes of Columbus, Ymago Mundi (3 vols., 1930), gives all the known information. The passage translated is in Vol. I, pp. 206–215.

OF THE EXTENT OF THE HABITABLE EARTH

To investigate the extent of the habitation of the earth, it must be understood that habitability should be considered in two ways.

1. Which he places to the east of Sweden.
2. Perhaps the Great Sea of Darkness of some medieval writers; perhaps only the fog characteristic of the Greenland-Labrador-Newfoundland area.

In one way it must be examined in regard to climate, or how much is habitable by reason of the Sun's heat and how much is not. . . . In a second way it can be considered in respect of water, or to what extent habitability is limited by water; and of this we are now to consider. Concerning it the wise are of different opinions. In his book of the disposition of the sphere, Ptolemy holds that about a sixth part of the earth is habitable with respect to water, and all the rest is covered by water. Also in his second book of the Almagest he states that habitation is known only in a quarter of the earth, or that which we inhabit, the length of which from east to west is half that of the equatorial line, and its breadth is from the equator to the Pole and covering a fourth of a great circle. Aristotle also says, towards the end of his book of the sky and the earth, that the habitable area is greater than a quarter, which Averroes confirms. Aristotle says that the sea is small between the western extremity of Spain and the eastern part of India.[1] . . . Moreover, Seneca in the fifth book of the things of nature says that this sea is navigable in a few days if the wind be favorable.[2] And Pliny teaches in the second book of natural history that one can navigate from the

1. Buron (*Ymago Mundi*, I, 205–211) demonstrates that many of d'Ailly's references to earlier authors are misleading. For example, Ptolemy's estimate of the size of the inhabited earth was solely that it extended 180° eastwards from the Fortunate Islands, and from south to north ranged from 17° 25′ south of the equator to Thule at 63° in the north (E. L. Stevenson, *The Geography of Claudius Ptolemy* [1932], pp. 160–164); similarly Aristotle, *De coelo*, II, 14, merely says the world is circular and a sphere of no great size and that the ocean between Europe and eastern Asia might well be continuous—"Hence one should not be too sure of the incredibility of those who conceive that there is a continuity between the parts about the pillars of Hercules [Straits of Gibraltar] and the parts about India" (Aristotle, *Works*, ed. W. D. Ross, II [1930], section 297b). See also G. H. T. Kimble, *Geography in the Middle Ages* (1938), pp. 162–163.
2. Seneca, *Quaestiones naturae*, preface, bk. 5. His *Medea*, lls. 376–380, had also an encouraging reference (as translated in Nathaniel Carpenter, *Geography delineated* [1631], p. 9):

> In after years shall Ages come,
> When th'Ocean shall unloose the bands
> Of things, and shew vast ample lands;
> New Worlds by Sea-men shall be found
> Nor Thule be the utmost bound.

Arabian Gulf to the Columns of Hercules in no very great time.[3] For these and many other reasons, on which I shall have to enlarge when I speak of the Ocean, some conclude that, apparently, the sea is not so great that it can cover threequarters of the earth. We can call on the authority of Esdras in his fourth book to support this, who says that six parts of the earth are inhabited, and the seventh is covered with the waters.[4] . . . From what we have said, and from what is to be said below, it appears that the habitable earth is not round like a disc [ad modum circuli], as Aristotle says,[5] but is as the fourth part of the surface of a sphere, of which fourth the two outermost parts are to some extent cut off, namely those which are not inhabited by reason of too great heat or cold.

7. Portuguese Tales
of Early Discoveries in the Atlantic

CHRISTOPHER COLUMBUS collected many of the stories which were current in the later fifteenth century about islands in the Atlantic. His son Fernando Colón brought some of them together in a memoir of his father. The Life appeared first in Italian in 1571 (translated, as The Life of the Admiral Christopher Columbus, by Benjamin Keen [1959]). But Bartolomé de las Casas in his Historia de las Indias (in Obras, edited by Juan Perez de Tudela [5 vols., 1957–58], I, 48–49) preserved a part of a better version from which this extract is translated. The placing of islands in the ocean by such classical writers as Pliny and Seneca has just been considered, and also the belief in the existence by residents of Madeira and the Azores of further islands farther to the west.

A.

From which it followed that in the sea charts which were made in times past there were drawn certain islands in those seas and regions, especially the island which they called Antilla, and they

3. Pliny, Historia naturalis, bk. 7, 17.
4. II Esdras, III. vi. 42 (Apocrypha, King James's Version): "Upon the third day thou didst command that the waters should be gathered in the seventh part of the earth, sixe parts hath thou dried up and kept them, to the intent that of these, some being planted of God, might serve thee."
5. Aristotle, De coelo, bk. 2, 13; Meteorologia, bk. 2, 5, 10–16.

placed it a little more than two hundred leagues to the west of the Canary Islands and the Azores. This was the Portuguese estimate, and to this day they retain the opinion that it may be the Island of the Seven Cities, whose fame and the desire for which have come down to us also, and has caused many to act in a foolish manner in searching for it and to spend much money unprofitably and with great loss. . . . This island of the Seven Cities is said, according to the Portuguese, to be that peopled by them in the time when King Rodrigo lost his kingdom [in Spain]. And they say that, flying from that persecution, seven bishops and many people embarked, and with their ships arrived at this island where each set up his household and burnt the ships lest anyone should think of turning back. And it is said that in the time of the Infante Dom Henrique of Portugal a ship which had set out from Oporto ran before a storm, not stopping until it reached there. And when they landed those of the island took them to the church to see whether they were Christians and used the Roman rites, and seeing that they were, asked them to wait until their lord, who was away from there, should come. But the seamen fearing lest they should burn the ship and keep them there, and suspecting that they did not desire to become known to anyone, returned to Portugal very willingly, hoping to receive rewards from the Infante. He, they say, treated them roughly and ordered them to return, but the master and the rest did not dare to do so. For this reason, once having left this land, they never returned to it. They say also that the seamen gathered some earth or sand for their cookroom, and they found that a large part of it was gold.

B.

THE SAME, or a similar, tale is told by Antonio Galvão, The discoveries of the world, translated by Richard Hakluyt [1582], pp. 72–73; first published in 1563, translated into English 1601.

In this year also [1447], it happened that there came a Portugall ship through the streight of Gibraltar; and being taken with a great tempest, was forced to runne westwards more then willingly the men would, and at last they fell upon an island which had seven cities, and the people spake the Portugall toong, and they demanded if the Moores did yet trouble Spaine, whence they had fled for the loss which they received by the death of the king of Spaine, Don Roderigo.

The boateswaine of the ship brought home a little of the sand, and sold it unto a goldsmith of Lisbon, out of which he had a good quantitie of gold.

Don Pedro, understanding this, being then governor of the realm, caused all the things thus brought home, and made known, to be recorded in the house of justice [casa do tombo, literally, house of record].

There be some that thinke, that those Islands whereunto the Portugals were thus driven, were the Antiles, or Newe Spain, alleaging good reasons for their opinion, which here I omit, because they serve not to my purpose. But all their reasons seeme to agree, that they should be that countrey, which is called Nova Spagna.

8. Toscanelli
on the Westward Route to Asia, 1474

IN 1474 a Florentine scholar, Paolo Toscanelli, wrote to his friend, Fernão Martins, a canon of Lisbon, enclosing a chart from which King Afonso V of Portugal could see how near Asia was by westward sailing from Europe. The chart, the main features of which he described, is now lost, as is the original of the letter. Columbus heard of it and obtained in about 1481 another copy of it from Toscanelli, which he transcribed into a book that is still preserved. Accepting that Marco Polo's narrative established that Eurasia extended farther east than had been accepted, that Japan lay 1,500 miles due east of Polo's Cathay (a misleading inference) and that the circumference of the globe was in the region of 20,000 instead of some 25,000 miles (the approximate range of existing estimates), then some 2,500 miles of Atlantic sailing from the Canaries would bring a ship to Japan. Extracts are taken from S. E. Morison, Journals and Other Documents on the Life and Voyages of Christopher Columbus (1963), p. 14, with one variation in interpretation.

From the city of Lisbon westward in a straight line to the very noble and splendid city of Quinsay, 26 spaces are indicated on the chart, each of which covers 250 miles. . . . This space[1] is approximately one third of the entire globe. . . .

But from the island of Antilia, known to you, to the far-famed *Cippangu* [Japan], there are 10 spaces. That island is very rich in gold, pearls and gems; they roof the temples and royal houses with solid gold. So there is not a great space to be traversed over unknown waters.[2]

9. Map Inscriptions as Guides to the Oceanic Lands and Islands

MAP LEGENDS *in the fifteenth century contain interesting guesses about islands in the ocean and throw some light on the nature of geographical speculations at the time. Those here translated concern the possibilities of there being land to the west of Europe or to the east of Asia, and include a little on Cipangu (Japan).*

A. Vinland Map, circa 1440

LEGEND 56 *on the Vinland Map (as Skelton, Marston and Painter, The Vinland Map, pp. 64–68, 136, point out) perverts a passage in the Tartar Relation about a woman who came from a "Country [which] is situated at the very end of the world, and beyond it no land is found, but only the ocean sea," which implies some knowledge of the limit of eastern Asia but none about any new land beyond it.*

The Tartars affirm beyond doubt that a new land [nova terra] is situated in the outermost parts of the world, and beyond no land is found but only the ocean sea.

1. In the original this is "hoc spacium." Admiral Morison, because the sentence is in the middle of the description of Quinsay, takes it to refer to China and translates "It [China] has an area of approximately. . . ." This, of course, is possible, but one-third of the globe in Toscanelli's terms would be the 26 spaces of 25 miles each, 6,500 in all, which separated Quinsay in his view from the Canary Islands.
2. These calculations would put Quinsay [Hangchow] 6,500 miles from the Canaries, Japan 5,000 miles, Antilia 2,500, with 19,500 miles as the earth's circumference. The actual distance would depend on the length of the mile used.

B. The Florence Map, 1457

THE Florence Map of 1457, believed by some to have been made in Genoa, is thought by others (e.g., S. Crinò, Come scoperta l'America [1943]) to be a map of the type described by Toscanelli in his 1474 letter. Whatever its character, its legends are of interest. Legend 37 is attached to a smallish island to the east of the East Indies, opposite to which, on the mainland, is Cathay (Catayum).

Beyond these islands no other land occupied by men is known nor is it easy for pilots to pass beyond them, since the sailors are stopped by the fog.

C. The Paris Map, circa 1490

THE Paris Map of circa 1490 is a Genoese-type map which Charles de la Roncière (La carte de Cristophe Colomb [1924]) believed was drawn by Christopher Columbus or by his brother Bartholomew in 1491. It bears as inscriptions a number of quotations from Pierre d'Ailly (see p. 000) which were known to Columbus or were annotated by him. One feature is the Island of the Seven Cities, placed far to the west of Ireland, and alleged in its legend (translated below) to have been already settled by the Portuguese. Columbus, when sailing westwards in 1492, is known to have expected to find this island in latitude 28° N. or thereabouts. This—with Toscanelli's "Cippangu" being absent also—has seemed to many an adequate reason for rejecting the Columbus association of the map; but the question is by no means finally decided. The inscription is the sole pre-Columbian evidence for a Portuguese discovery of land west of the Azores. Compare document no. 7 above.

Here is the island, called the Island of the Seven Cities, now settled by the Portuguese, where, the Spanish seamen say, silver is found in the sands.

D. The Behaim Globe, 1492

THE EARLIEST surviving globe was constructed at Nuremberg in 1492 under Martin Behaim, who had traded to Africa from Portugal and had lived in the Azores. He believed that Japan (Cipangu) lay on the Tropic of Cancer some 4,500 miles westward from the Canary Islands. He places the Azores correctly; Antilia comes about halfway across the ocean between the Canaries and Japan on the Tropic of Cancer extending as far south as the equator; St. Brendan's Island is farther south in a similar position between the Cape Verde Islands and the southern tip of Japan. The inscriptions that follow are translated in E. G. Ravenstein, Martin Behaim (1908), pp. 77, 89.

INSULA DE SANT BRANDON

In the year 565 after Christ, St. Brandon in his ship came to this island where he witnessed many marvels, and seven years afterwards he returned to his country.

INSULA ANTILIA—SEPTE CITADE

In the year 734 of Christ, when the whole of Spain had been won by the heathen of Africa, the above island Antilia, called Septe citade (Seven Cities), was inhabited by an archbishop from Porto in Portugal, with six other bishops, and other Christians, men and women, who had fled thither from Spain, by ship, together with their cattle, belongings and goods. In 1414 a ship from Spain got nighest it without being endangered.

CIPANGU INSULA

[a] The island Cipangu has a King and language of its own; the inhabitants worship idols.
[b] Cipangu where grows much gold.
[c] Cipangu is the most noble and richest island in the east, full of spices and precious stones. Its compass is 1,200 miles. In this island are found gold and shrubs yielding spices.

10. Portuguese Grants
To Discover the Island of the Seven Cities,
1474–87

THE Portuguese finally located and settled the Madeiras between 1411 and about 1419 and the Azores between about 1427 and 1453. Grants to Portuguese subjects to search for and discover further islands in the Atlantic were frequently made, such as those to Diogo de Tieve (1452), Ruy Gonsalves de Camara (1473), Fernão Telles (1475) and *Fernão Dulmo and João Afonso do Estreito (1485–87). The grants, extracts from which are given below, to Telles by King Afonso V and those to Dulmo and Estreito by King John II specify the Island of the Seven Cities, which the Portuguese usually equated with Antilia. They appear in Alguns documentos da Torre do Tombo (1892), pp. 37, 58, and are translated in J. A. Williamson, The Cabot Voyages (1962), pp. 184–186. It is not thought that any voyages made under these grants were successful in finding new land. (See Morison, Portuguese Voyages to America in the Fifteenth Century.)*

A.

Dom Affonso, etc. to all who shall see this my charter I make known that I have made a grant by a charter to Fernam Tellez, governor and chief majordomo of the Princess my very beloved and esteemed daughter, of any islands to be discovered by him, and by his ships or men that he sends for this purpose, or that go to seek them for him, provided that they [the islands] be not in the seas of Guinea. According to what at greater length is contained in the said charter it does not make clear [a distinction?] between uninhabited islands and those which the said Fernam Tellez by himself or others may cause to be peopled. And it might happen that, in thus sending out to seek them, his ships or people might find the Seven Cities or some other inhabited islands which at the present time have not been navigated to or discovered or traded with by my subjects, and it might be said that the grant I have thus made must not extend to them on account of their being thus inhabited. I declare by this my [present] charter that my intentions and purpose then at the time I thus gave them was that the said charter comprises islands both inhabited and uninhabited, and that it is my pleasure that he shall have in them all the lordship and jurisdiction and power over the inhabitants and for them the same privileges and liberties, that I have by the said charter for the inhabitants of the other islands. . . . [November 10, 1475]

B.

Dom Johan, by the grace of God King of Portugal and of the Algarve on this side of the sea, and on the other in Africa Lord of Guinea [John II], we make known that Fernam Dulmo, gentleman and Captain in the island of Terceira for the Duke Manuel my very esteemed and beloved cousin, came now to us and told us how he wished to discover a large island or islands or mainland by the coast which is supposed to be the Island of the Seven Cities, and all this at his own cost and expense, and that he prayed us that we should make him a grant and royal donation of the said island or islands or mainland that he, or another by his orders, may thus discover or find; and so we grant him the right of all justice with power of death and of all other penalties of the said island. . . . [August 4, 1486][1]

1. This grant is re-cited in another grant of 1487 which also mentions a contract entered into between Dulmo and João Afonso do Estreito, of Funchal, Madeira, to co-operate in prosecuting the venture.

III

The Earliest North American Voyages

IT IS impossible to state dogmatically which expedition first rediscovered America in the fifteenth century. Though no satisfactory evidence has yet appeared which indicates that any of the Portuguese expeditions of the later fifteenth century was successful in reaching land, it is still possible that evidence can be found which could give them a pre-Columbian priority. English voyages in search of islands were being made by 1480, possibly before. Evidence from the John Day letter (first published in 1956, see below, p. 40) indicates that an English discovery of the Isle of Brasil (perhaps Newfoundland) was probably made known to Columbus before he sailed in 1492. This discovery could have been made before 1480, in 1481 (the most likely date so far indicated) or between 1481 and 1492. It is not unlikely to have been one which was regarded mainly as a landmark for a fishery off the Newfoundland coast. Columbus made his famous voyage in 1492 in an attempt to reach Asia. As is suggested below (p. 37), this could well have resulted in the discovery of North America. Instead, Columbus turned southwest to the Caribbean, and his conviction that what he had found was near the shores of Asia, as well as his continued adherence to this view, in the face of mounting evidence, until his death in 1506, held back the recognition that what he had found was a new hemisphere or pair of continents. Yet, from 1493 onwards, the Caribbean Islands were being settled by Spain and expeditions were going out to encounter mainland coasts to south and west and north. For practical purposes, whatever intellectual hesitations there might be in accepting the existence of a new continent, this was the effective discovery of America. The Cabot voyages of 1497 and 1498, followed by other voyages from Bristol, 1501–05, together with the Portuguese voyages of the Corte Real brothers, 1500–03, built up a picture of a land farther north which did not in any way appear to be Asiatic. Amerigo Vespucci became identified in the years after 1504 with the view that what had been discovered was a New World. In 1507, in the light of this belief, Martin Waldseemüller made the guess that there were, in fact, two continental-sized land masses lying between Europe and Asia. His map showed the southern one with the name America (from "Americus," as Vespucci was known); the northern one was unnamed. By 1520 Waldseemüller's theory had been accepted as fact, and the name America had been extended to North America as well. By that time fishing fleets from Portugal, Spain, France and England were all fishing for cod at Newfoundland and were laying up a store of practical knowledge on how to cross the Atlantic and how to exploit the coastal waters of North America when they did so.

11. Attempts of the Bristol Men to find the Island of Brasil, 1480–81

THE early attempts by Englishmen to search the Atlantic for new lands have hitherto been examined largely in research papers. Between 1479 and 1481 merchants and seamen at Bristol were already well informed about the Azores and Cape Verde Islands (R. A. Skelton, "English Knowledge of the Portuguese Discoveries in the 15th Century: A New Document," Congresso Internacional de História dos Descobrimentos, Actas, II [1961], 365–374). A licence granted to Thomas Croft, a customs official in Bristol, and three Bristol merchants, on June 18, 1480, allowed them to send ships to sea under special conditions, it is thought to make voyages of exploration (E. M. Carus-Wilson, The Overseas Trade of Bristol in the Later Middle Ages [1937], p. 157). In 1480 an expedition in search of the Island of Brasil, under a captain named Lloyd, left Bristol but returned unsuccessful. About July 6, 1481, the ships Trinity and George, in which Thomas Croft had an interest, left Bristol "in search of the Isle of Brasile": they had returned before September 24, and may have found land, possibly part of Newfoundland, but if so this discovery was not made public (D. B. Quinn, "Edward IV and Exploration," Mariner's Mirror, XXI [1935], 280–284; J. A. Williamson, The Cabot Voyages, pp. 19–23; D. B. Quinn, "The Argument for the English Discovery of America Between 1480–1494," Geographical Journal, CXXVII [1961], 277–285).

William Worcestre's rough notes tell us all we know about the 1480 voyage (Williamson, Cabot Voyages, pp. 187–88; William Worcestre, Itineraries, ed. John H. Harvey, [1969], p. 309), and an Exchequer inquiry into Thomas Croft's trading activities all that has been found on the 1481 venture (extract from E. M. Carus-Wilson, The Overseas Trade of Bristol, p. 164).

A. 1480

1480, on July 15, the ship[1]   and of John Jay, the younger of 80 tons burden, began a voyage from the Kyngrode,[2] the port of Bristol, to the island of Brasylle in the western part of Ireland, ploughing the seas for[3]   and Thloyde[4] is the ship's master, the most knowledgeable[5] seaman of the whole of England. And news came to Bristol on Monday, September 18, that the said ship had sailed the seas for some nine months[6] and did not find the island but had been turned back by storms at sea to the port[7]   in Ireland to rehabilitate the ship and the sailors.

B. 1481

It is found amonges othir thynges that Thomas Croft of Bristowe [Bristol] Squier on' of our Custumers in oure said port of Bristowe the vi[t] day of July the xxi[th] yere of our Reigne at Bristowe forsaid was possessid of the viii[th] parte of a Shippe or Balynger callid the Trinite and of the viii[th] parte of an other shipp or Balynger callid the George & into every of the said Shipps or Balingers the said Thomas Croft the same vi[th] day of July the forsaid xxi[th] yere of our Reigne at Bristow aforsaid shipped and putt xl busshels of salt to the value of xx s. for the rep[ar]acion' and sustentacion of the said shippys or Balingers and not by cause of marchaundise but [to] thentent to serch and fynd a certaine Ile callid the Isle of Brasile as in the said inquisicion [of September

1. The space for the name of the ship and for one or more names of part owners was never filled.
2. King Road.
3. The gap is for the period spent at sea.
4. The gap is either for the name of the captain, if she had one, or for the Christian name of the master. In the first case the master may be Thomas Lloyd; in the second, he is "[   ] Lloyd" (there was a Bristol seaman called John Lloyd).
5. Literally, *scientificus*.
6. A mistake for "weeks."
7. Space for the name of the port.

24, 1481] annexed to the forsaid commission more playnly it dothe appier.

12. The First Voyage
of Christopher Columbus, 1492

COLUMBUS, after a long campaign to get support from either the king of Portugal, John II, or the Spanish sovereigns, Ferdinand and Isabella, for a voyage westwards to Asia, finally succeeded in obtaining privileges and assistance in Spain in 1492. He left with the Santa Maria, Pinta and Niña on August 3, 1492. His plan was to work south to the Canaries and then sail westward down the latitude of 28° N. (Had he done so he would have made his landfall in North America, on the Florida coast somewhat to the south of Cape Canaveral.) He expected to find Antilia some 1,200 nautical miles to the west. He kept on course from Gomera from September 8 until September 19, when he was in longitude 41° W. At that point he believed that north and south of him there were islands (the Antilia and Satanazes of the maps) and that "he was going through between them," but sighted no land. From there he expected to reach Japan after a further voyage of not more than the same length. Light, variable winds forced him to deviate from his course and to take a somewhat more southerly track so that he was in latitude 24° 20′ N. and longitude 74° W. when the first clear indications of land were discerned on October 11. The first island sighted was Watling Island in the Bahama group, which he called San Salvador. When Columbus left it on October 14, he did not attempt to make his way northward to his original objective on the 28th parallel, but worked his way south, thus a second time turning away from North America. Asia's riches, he was certain, lay to the south. His exploration of the major Caribbean islands and his return to Europe (he reached Lisbon on March 3, 1493) make another story. On his discovery Spain and Portugal based the division of the non-Christian world between them in the Treaty of Tordesillas in 1494.

Rear Admiral S. E. Morison's three books, Admiral of the Ocean Sea (2 vols., 1942), Christopher Columbus (1 vol., 1942, without notes) and Christopher Columbus, Mariner (1956), contain the classic accounts of his voyage: the documents are most easily accessible in his Journals and Other Documents on the Life and Voyages of Christopher Columbus (1963), which contains the journal of the voyage and also the letter to the Spanish sovereigns, which was published in 1493, from which extracts are taken (pp. 182–186).

Sir, forasmuch as I know that you will take pleasure in the great triumph with which our Lord has crowned my voyage, I write this to you, from which you will learn how, in twenty days (correctly, thirty-three) I reached the Indies with the fleet which the most illustrious King and Queen, our Lord, gave to me. And there I found very many islands filled with people without number, and of all of them I have taken possession for Their Highnesses by proclamation and with the royal Standard, and nobody objected. To the first island which I found I gave the name *Sant Salvador*, in recognition of His Heavenly Mercy, who marvelously hath given all this; the Indians call it *Guanahani*. . . .

When I reached *Juana* (Cuba), I followed its coast to the westward and found it to be so long that I thought it must be the mainland (of Asia), the province of Catayo. . . . I went 107 leagues in a straight line from west to east along the coast of the island *Juana*, and . . . beyond . . . there remain to the westward two provinces where I have not been. . . . The provinces cannot have a length of less than 50 or 60 leagues. . . . The other, *Española*, in circuit is greater than all Spain, from *Colonya* (Collioure) by the coast to *Fuenterauia* (Fuentarabia) in Viscaya, since I went along one side 188 great leagues in a straight line from west to east. . . . In this *Española* . . . is the best district for the gold mines and for all trade both with this continent and with that over there belonging to the Great Khan, where there will be great trade and profit, I have taken possession of a large town to which I gave the name *La Villa de Navidad*, and in it I have built a fort and defenses . . . and I have left enough people for such a purpose, with arms and artillery and provisions for more than a year. . . .

And this is enough. And the Eternal God, Our Lord, Who gives to all those who walk in His way victory over things which appear impossible; and this is notably one. For, although men have talked or have written of these lands, all was conjecture, without getting a look at it, but amounted only to this; that those who heard for the most part listened and judged it (the Cathay of Marco Polo?) more a fable than that there was anything in it, however, small.

13. John Cabot's Reception in England

JOHN CABOT, a Genoese by birth and a Venetian by citizenship, is now thought to have come to England from Valencia in Spain some time between 1493 and 1495. He had tried to get support in Spain and Portugal for an expedition to the Indies, believing, like Columbus, that it was possible to cross the Atlantic to Asia. After Columbus returned, it appeared possible to make a shorter voyage in higher latitudes from England. He may have tried, unsuccessfully to do so in 1495 (p. 00 below). Late in 1495 or early in 1496, the Spanish representative in England, González de Puebla, reported in a letter now lost that Cabot had offered Henry VII a scheme for getting to the Indies without breaking the monopoly Spain and Portugal had claimed for themselves by the Treaty of Tordesillas in 1494: the reply of the Spanish monarchs (Extract A) instructed him to warn the English king against any such project. But on March 5, 1496, John Cabot and his sons Lewis, Sebastian and Sancio received a patent from the Crown authorizing them to occupy any new lands they found, in any direction except the South, in the name of England (Extract B). This formally launched England into competition with the Iberian powers for a share of the new American lands. The extracts below are taken from H. P. Biggar, The Precursors of Jacques Cartier (1911), pp. 710–711, 713–715. Williamson, The Cabot Voyages, pp. 45–53, 202–205, provides the best account and reprints the extracts given.

A. King Ferdinand and Queen Isabella to González de Puebla, March 28, 1496

In regard to what you say of the arrival there of one like Columbus for the purpose of inducing the King of England to enter upon another undertaking like that of the Indies, without prejudice to Spain or to Portugal, if he [Henry VII] aids him as he has us, the Indies will be well rid of the man. We are of opinion that this is a scheme of the French King's [Charles VIII's] to persuade the King of England to undertake this so that he will give up other affairs. Take care that you prevent the King of England from being deceived in this or in anything else of the kind, since wherever they can the French will endeavour to bring this about. And things of this sort are very uncertain, and of such a nature that for the present it is not seemly to conclude an agreement therein;

and it is also clear that no arrangement can be concluded in this matter in that country without harm to us or to the King of Portugal.

B. *Letters Patent to John Cabot and his sons, March 5, 1496*

Be it known and made manifest that we have given and granted as by these presents we give and grant, for us and our heirs, to our well-beloved John Cabot, citizen of Venice, and to Lewis, Sebastian and Sancio, sons of the said John, and to the heirs and deputies of them, and of any one of them, full and free authority, faculty and power to sail to all parts, regions and coasts of the eastern, western and northern sea, under our banners, flags and ensigns, with five ships or vessels of whatsoever burden and quality they may be, and with so many and with such mariners and men as they may wish to take with them in the said ships, at their own proper costs and charges, to find, discover and investigate whatsoever islands, countries, regions or provinces of heathens and infidels, in whatsoever part of the world placed, which before this time were unknown to all Christians. We have also granted to them and to any of them, and to the heirs and deputies of them and any one of them, and have given licence to set up our aforesaid banners and ensigns in any town, city, castle, island or mainland whatsoever, newly found by them. And that the before-mentioned John and his sons or their heirs and deputies may conquer, occupy and possess whatsoever such towns, castles, cities and islands by them thus discovered that they may be able to conquer, occupy and possess, as our vassals and governors lieutenants and deputies therein, acquiring for us the dominion, title and jurisdiction of the same towns, castles, cities, islands and mainlands so discovered.

14. John Cabot's Voyage, 1497

JOHN CABOT left Bristol in May 1497 in the ship Mathew, reached land across the Atlantic on June 24, explored shorelines said to lie between Cape Breton Island and Cape Bauld, the northern tip of Newfoundland (though latitude determinations could be anything up to 140 miles out in either direction), and returned to Bristol on August 6, confident that he had found the land of the Great Khan, in eastern Asia. Much of our knowledge of the voyage formerly came from the gossipy letters of Italian diplomats in London (Extracts A and B). Professor L. A. Vigneras (in "New light on the 1497 Voyage," Hispanic-American Historical Review, XXXVI [1956], 503–509) published an important letter from John Day, an English merchant, to the Grand Admiral, most probably Columbus (below, Extract C, in full), which threw new light on the voyage, as well as indicating that the land found by Cabot had been discovered much earlier by the Bristol men. John Day has now been shown to be, under another name, a Londoner named Hugh Say (A. A. Ruddock, "John Day of Bristol," Geographical Journal, CXXXII [1966], 222–233). Controversy still flourishes on the precise implications of the letter (see Quinn in Geographical Journal, CXXVII, 277–285 noted above, and "John Day and Columbus," CXXXIV [1967], 202–209). Williamson, The Cabot Voyages, pp. 54–83, 207–214, supplies the fullest account and reprints the documents, S. E. Morison, The European Discovery of America. The Northern Voyages (1971), Ch. VI, gives a new translation and an interesting critical commentary.

A. Lorenzo Pasqualigo to his Brother in Venice, August 23, 1497

That Venetian of ours who went with a small ship from Bristol to find new islands has come back and says he has discovered mainland 700 leagues away, which is the country of the Grand Khan, and that he coasted it for 300 leagues and landed and did not see any person; but he has brought here to the king certain snares which were spread to take game and a needle for making nets, and he found certain notched trees so that by this he judges that there are inhabitants. Being in doubt he returned to his ship; and he has been three months on the voyage; and this is certain. And on the way back he saw two islands, but was unwilling to land, in order not to lose time, as he was in want of provisions. The king here is much pleased at this; and he says that the tides are slack and do not run as they do here. The king has promised him for the spring ten armed ships as he desires and has given him all the prisoners to be sent away, that they may go with him, as he has requested; and has given him money that he may have a good time until then, and he is with his Venetian wife and sons at Bristol. His name is Zuam Talbot and he is called the Great Admiral and vast honour is paid to him and he goes dressed in silk, and these English run after him like mad, and indeed he can enlist as many of them as he pleases, and a number of our rogues as well. The discoverer of these things planted on the land which he has found a large cross with a banner of England and one of St. Mark, as he is a Venetian, so that our flag has been hoisted very far afield.

B. Raimondo de Raimondi de Soncino
to the Duke of Milan, December 18, 1497

Reprinted from Calendar of State Papers, Milan, I (1912), No. 552.

Perhaps amid the numerous occupations of your Excellency, it may not weary you to hear how his Majesty here has gained a part of Asia, without a stroke of the sword. There is in this Kingdom a man of the people, Messer Zoane Caboto by name, of kindly wit and a most expert mariner. Having observed that the sovereigns first of Portugal and then of Spain had occupied unknown islands, he decided to make a similar acquisition for his Majesty. After obtaining patents that the effective ownership of what he might find should be his, though reserving the rights of the Crown, he committed himself to fortune in a little ship, with eighteen persons. He started from Bristol, a port on the west of this kingdom, passed Ireland, which is still further west, and then bore towards the north, in order to sail to the east, leaving the north on his right hand after some days. After having wandered for some time he at length arrived at the mainland, where he hoisted the royal standard, and took possession for the king here; and after taking certain tokens he returned.

This Messer Zoane, as a foreigner and a poor man, would not have obtained credence, had it not been that his companions, who are practically all English and from Bristol, testified that he spoke the truth. This Messer Zoane has the description of the world in a map, and also in a solid sphere, which he has made, and shows where he has been. In going towards the east he passed far beyond the country of the Tanais. They say that the land is excellent and temperate, and they believe that Brasilwood and silk are native there. They assert that the sea there is swarming with fish, which can be taken not only with the net, but in baskets let down with a stone, so that it sinks in the water. I have heard this Messer Zoane state so much.

These same English, his companions, say that they could bring so many fish that this kingdom would have no further need of Iceland, from which place there comes a very great quantity of the fish called stockfish. But Messer Zoane has his mind set upon even greater things, because he proposes to keep along the coast from the place at which he touched, more and more towards the east, until he reaches an island which he calls Cipango, situated in the equinoctial region, where he believes that all the spices of the world have their origin, as well as the jewels. He says that on previous occasions he has been to Mecca, whither spices are borne by caravans from distant countries. When he asked those who brought them what was the place of origin of these spices, they answered that they did not know, but that other caravans came with this merchandise to their homes from distant countries, and these again said that the goods had been brought to them from other remote regions. He therefore reasons that these things come from places far away from them, and so on from one to the other, always assuming that the earth is round, it follows as a matter of course that the last of all must take them in the north towards the west.

He tells all this in such a way, and makes everything so plain, that I also feel compelled to believe him. What is much more, his Majesty, who is wise and not prodigal, also gives him some credence, because he is giving him a fairly good provision, since his return, so Messer Zoane himself tells me. Before very long they say that his Majesty will equip some ships, and in addition he will give them all the malefactors, and they will go to that country and form a colony. By means of this they hope to make London a more important mart for spices than Alexandria. The leading men in this enterprise are from Bristol, and great seamen, and now they know where to go, say that the voyage will not take more than a fortnight, if they have good fortune after leaving Ireland.

I have also spoken with a Burgundian, one of Messer Zoane's companions, who corroborates everything. He wants to go back, because the Admiral, which is the name they give to Messer Zoane, has given him an island. He has given another to his barber, a Genoese by birth, and both consider themselves counts, while my lord the Admiral esteems himself at least a prince.

I also believe that some poor Italian friars will go on this voyage, who have the promise of bishoprics. As I have made friends with the Admiral, I might have an archbishopric if I chose to go there, but I have reflected that the benefices which your Excellency reserves for me are safer, and I therefore beg that possession may be given me of those which fall vacant in my absence, and the necessary steps taken so that they may not be taken away from me by others, who have the advantage of being on the spot. Meanwhile I stay on in this country, eating ten or twelve courses at each meal, and spending three hours at table twice every day, for the love of your Excellency, to whom I humbly commend myself.

C. John Day to the Grand Admiral
[probably Christopher Columbus],
December 1497 or January 1498

Johan Day to the Most Magnificent and Most Worthy Lord the Lord Grand Admiral

Your Lordship's servant brought me your letter. I have seen its contents and I would be most desirous and most happy to serve you. I do not find the book *Inventio Fortunata*, and I thought that I [or, he] was bringing it with my things, and I am very sorry not to find it because I wanted very much to serve you. I am sending the other book of Marco Polo and a copy of the land which has been found. I do not send the map because I am not satisfied with it, for my many occupations forced me to make it in a hurry at the time of my departure; but from the said copy your lordship will learn what you wish to know, for in it are named the capes of the mainland and the islands, and thus you will see where land was first sighted, since most of the land was discovered after turning back. Thus your Lordship will know that the cape nearest to Ireland is 1800 miles west of Dursey Head which is in Ireland, and the southernmost part of the Island of the Seven Cities is west of the river of Bordeaux,[1] and your Lordship will know that he landed at only one spot of the mainland, near the place where land was first sighted, and they disembarked there with a crucifix and raised banners with the arms of the Holy Father and those of the King of

1. Dursey Head is in latitude 51° 34′ N., and the mouth of the river of Bordeaux, the Gironde, in 45°35′ N.

England, my master; and they found tall trees of the kind masts are made from, and other smaller trees, and the country is very rich in grass. In that particular spot, as I told your Lordship, they found a trail that went inland, they saw a site where a fire had been made, they saw manure of animals which they thought to be farm animals, and they saw a stick half a yard long pierced at both ends, carved and painted with brazil, and by such signs they believe the land to be inhabited. Since he was with just a few people, he did not dare advance inland beyond the shooting distance of a crossbow, and after taking in fresh water he returned to his ship. All along the coast they found many fish like those which in Iceland are dried in the open and sold in England and other countries, and these fish are called in English "stockfish"; and thus following the shore they saw two forms running on land one after the other, but they could not tell if they were human beings or animals; and it seemed to them that there were fields where they thought might also be villages, and they saw a forest whose foliage looked beautiful. They left England towards the end of May, and must have been on the way 35 days before sighting land; the wind was east-north-east and the sea was calm going and coming back, except for one day when he ran into a storm two or three days before finding land; and going so far out, his compass needle failed to point north and marked two rhumbs below. They spent about one month discovering the coast and from the above mentioned cape of the mainland which is nearest to Ireland, they returned to the coast of Europe in fifteen days. They had the wind behind them, and he reached Brittany because the sailors confused him, saying he was heading too far north. From there he came to Bristol, and he went to see the King to report to him all the above mentioned, and the King granted him an annual pension of twenty pounds sterling to sustain himself until the time comes when more will be known of this business, since with God's help it is hoped to push through plans for exploring the said land more thoroughly next year with ten or twelve vessels—because in his voyage he had only one ship of fifty tons[2] and twenty men and food for seven or eight months —and they want to carry out this new project. It is considered

2. The *Mathew*.

certain that the cape of the said land was found and discovered in the past by the men from Bristol who found "Brasil" as your Lordship knows. It was called the Island of Brasil, and it is assumed and believed to be the mainland that the men from Bristol found.[3]

Since your Lordship wants information relating to the first voyage, here is what happened: he went with one ship, his crew confused him, he was short of supplies and ran into bad weather, and he decided to turn back.

Magnificent Lord, as to other things pertaining to the case, I would like to serve your Lordship if I were not prevented in doing so by occupations of great importance relating to shipments and deeds for England which must be attended to at once and which keep me from serving you; but rest assured, Magnificent Lord, of my desire and natural intention to serve you, and when I find myself in other circumstances and more at leisure, I will take pains to do so; and when I get news from England about the matters referred to above—for I am sure that everything has to come to my knowledge—I will inform your Lordship of all that would not be prejudicial to the King my master. In payment for some services which I hope to render you, I beg your Lordship kindly to write to me about such matters, because the favour you will thus do me will greatly stimulate my memory to serve you in all the things that may come to my knowledge. May God keep prospering your Lordship's magnificent state according to your merits. Whenever your Lordship should find it convenient, please remit the book or order it to be given to Master George.

I kiss your Lordship's hands,

Johan Day

15. John Cabot's Last Voyage, 1498

MUCH EFFORT was exerted to fit out a fleet to return to the land Cabot had described, and to work down toward Marco Polo's Japan and Cathay,

3. The original text reads: "Se presume cierto averse fallado e descubierto en otros tiempos el cabo de la dicha tierra por los de Bristol que fallaron el Brasil como dello tiene noticia Vra S^a la qual se dezia la Ysla de Brasil e presumese e creese ser tierra firme la que fallaron los de Bristol."

which the English thought to lie far to the westward of the Spanish Indies. King Henry contributed £113 8s to equip a ship in London, which joined four smaller ships, laden by Bristol and London merchants, at Bristol. A rich trade was expected. The ships set out in May; in July news came that the vessels had been struck by a gale, and one, somewhat damaged, had put into an Irish port. At least one of the ships returned—the rest were never heard of, while John Cabot was presumed lost at sea. What news the returning ship brought is not known; it may have been that the new land could not be used as a route to Cathay, since King Henry made no further substantial investments in westward ventures. A sketch map of the land found in 1497 (probably that brought to Spain by John Day) was used by Juan de la Cosa to show an "English coast" on his world map begun in 1500. J. A. Williamson, The Cabot Voyages, pp. 84–115, 220, 224–225, 228–229, provides the narrative and reprints the documents.

Voyages were made from Bristol for trading purposes between 1501 and about 1506 to the new lands across the ocean, which were not then thought to be Asia. A number of Portuguese from the Azores, led to begin with by João Fernandes, took part with the Bristol men. It seems that the first syndicate may have broken up in 1502 when Fernandes disappeared, perhaps lost at sea. The second syndicate of 1502 included two Portuguese, João Gonsalves and Francisco Fernandes, and one Bristol man, Thomas Asshehurst, from that of 1501, with Hugh Elyot, a former associate of the Cabots. It is possible that Sebastian Cabot, still living in Bristol and rewarded by the king in 1505, may have been linked with the group. Voyages from 1503 to 1505 or 1506 ended in financial difficulties. Hawks, eagles, wild cats, "cats of the mountain" (bobcats) and popinjays (Carolina paroquets) were brought to England. The Newfoundland fishery is likely at this time to have been increasingly frequented by English ships.

A. A London Chronicler Reports
on Cabot's Departure in 1498

Reprinted from The Great Chronicle of London, edited by A. H. Thomas and I. D. Thornley (1939), pp. 287–288.

Thys yere also, the kyng by meanys of a venyzian which made hym sylf verray expert & kunnyng In knowlage of the cyrcuyte of the world and Ile landis of the same, as by a caart & othir demonstracions Reasonable he shewid. Cawsid the kyng to man & vytayll a Shypp at Brystow to serche for an Ile land which he said he knewe well was Rich & Replenysshid with Rych commodytees, Which shyp thus mannyd & vitaylid at the kyngis Cost dyvers marchauntis

of london aventrid In [hir] small stokkys beyng In hir as chieff
patron the said venezian, and In the Company of the said shypp
saylid also owth of Brystow iij or iiij smale shyppis frawgth wyth
sleygth & groos marchandysis as course cloth cappis lasis poyntis &
other tryfyls And so departid from Brystow In the begynnyng off
maii, Of whoom this mayris tyme¹ Retournd noo tydyngis.

B. Pedro de Ayala
to the Spanish Sovereigns, July 25, 1498

*Reprinted from H. P. Biggar, The Precursors of Jacques Cartier (1911),
pp. 27–29, with an alteration on the ninth line.*

I think Your Highnesses have already heard how the king of
England has equipped a fleet to explore certain islands or mainland
which he has been assured certain persons who set out last year
from Bristol in search of the same have discovered. I have seen the
map made by the discoverer, who is another Genoese like Columbus, who has been in Seville and at Lisbon seeking to obtain
persons to aid him in this discovery. For the last seven years the
people of Bristol have equipped two, three [and] four caravels to
go in search of the island of Brasil and the Seven Cities,
as this Genoese reckons. The king made up his mind to send
thither, because last year sure proof was brought him they had
found land. The fleet he prepared, which consisted of five vessels,
was provisioned for a year. News has come that one of these, in
which sailed another Friar Buil, has made land in Ireland in a great
storm with the ship badly damaged. The Genoese kept on his way.
Having seen the course they are steering and the length of the
voyage, I find that what they have discovered or are in search of is
possessed by Your Highnesses because it is at the cape which fell to
Your Highnesses by the convention with Portugal. It is hoped they
will be back by September. I let [?will let] Your Highnesses know
about it. The king has spoken to me several times on the subject.
He hopes the affair may turn out profitable. I believe the distance
is not 400 leagues. I told him that I believed the islands were those
found by Your Highnesses, and although I gave him the main

1. That is, up to mid-September 1498.

reason, he would not have it. Since I believe Your Highnesses will already have notice of all this and also of the chart or mappemonde which this man has made, I do not send it now, although it is here, and so far as I can see exceedingly false, in order to make believe that these are not part of the said islands.

C. *Polydore Vergil* (*in his* Anglica Historia)
Records the Presumed Death of John Cabot

Reprinted from The Anglica Historia of Polydore Vergil, edited by *Denys Hay* (1950), pp. 116–117.

There was talk at about this time that some sailors on a voyage had discovered lands lying in the British ocean, hitherto unknown.[1] This was easily believed because the Spanish sovereigns in our time had found many unknown islands. Wherefore King Henry at the request of one John Cabot, a Venetian by birth, and a most skilful mariner, ordered to be prepared one ship, complete with crew and weapons; this he handed over to the same John to go and search for those unknown islands.[2] John set out in this same year and sailed first to Ireland. Then he set sail towards the west. In the event he is believed to have found the new lands nowhere but on the very bottom of the ocean, to which he is thought to have descended together with his boat, the victim himself of that self-same ocean; since after that voyage he was never seen again anywhere.

16. The Portuguese Voyages
of the Corte Real Brothers, 1500–03

PORTUGUESE WRITERS *often claim that João Vaz Corte Real, who had settled in the Azores, discovered Newfoundland sometime in the 1470's, but this depends on a rambling chronicle written about 1590 which is*

1. This could possibly refer to the rumors of a pre-Columbian discovery by the English.
2. He assumes that the rumors refer to the period after Columbus's discovery and that Cabot's 1498 voyage was his first. Vergil was writing in 1512 or 1513.

often inaccurate, so that the claim is rejected by many historians (see Morison, Portuguese Voyages to America, pp. 33–50). King Manuel in 1500 granted his son, Gaspar Corte Real, in view of his earlier voyages (of which we know nothing), a charter to occupy the lands he might find (Extract A). It seems probable that in 1500 he did no more than discover the southern tip of Greenland, Cape Farewell. He mobilized two ships to follow up his voyage in 1501, turned westward from Greenland and encountered Labrador, which he coasted. He also examined the east coast of Newfoundland and part of the mainland farther south. He kidnapped a cargo of Indians as slaves, sent a ship home with them, and was himself lost in his flagship. For this voyage we have letters describing the people and objects brought back (Extracts B and C). This led the Portuguese to claim "the land of the King of Portugal" in the Atlantic as lying east of the imaginary line between the Spanish and Portuguese zones drawn at Tordesillas in 1494. Miguel Corte Real, another brother, went out with two ships in 1502 and did some further exploration. Again, the second ship came home; his own and himself were lost. A rescue expedition in 1503 found no trace of either brother. Out of this discovery the Portuguese fishery at Newfoundland developed. A third brother, Vasco Eannes Corte Real, was empowered to continue the family explorations in 1506 (Extract D), and it is possible that the family continued to send ships to America later in the century. The extracts are from Biggar, The Precursors of Jacques Cartier, pp. 35–36, 63–64, 66–67, 94–95. Williamson, The Cabot Voyages, pp. 118–122, and Morison, Portuguese Voyages to America in the Fifteenth Century, pp. 64–72, have short narratives.

A. King Manoel V Grants Gaspar Corte Real
Authority to Discover Unknown Territories,
May 12, 1500

To as many as shall see this grant of ours we make known, that forasmuch as Gaspar Corte Real, a nobleman of our court, has made efforts in the past, on his own account and at his own expense, with ships and men, to search out, discover and find by dint of much labour and expenditure of his wealth and at the risk of his life, some islands and a mainland, and in consequence is now desirous of continuing this search and of setting to work and doing whatever is possible in order to discover the said islands and mainland; and we taking into consideration how greatly it will redound to our service and honour, and to the increase of our kingdoms and domains, if such islands and mainlands should be discovered and found by subjects of ours, and since the said Gaspar Corte Real in virtue of his desire to carry this out, at such risk and the expenditure of so much labour, is worthy of all honour, favour and augmentation; for this cause it is our pleasure, and we are pleased of our own motion, royal and absolute power, should he discover and find any island or islands, or mainland, to grant and give him, and we do grant him by right and heredity for ever, the governorship of any islands or mainland he may thus discover or find afresh.

B. Alberto Cantino to Hercules d'Este, Duke of Ferrara, October 17, 1501

Nine months have now passed since this most serene monarch sent to the northern parts two well-equipped ships, for the sole purpose of finding out if it were possible to discover in that region any lands or islands. Now on the eleventh of the present month one of them has arrived safe and with some booty; and has brought people and news, which it appeared to me ought not to pass without your Excellency's hearing thereof; and thus I have set down here below clearly and exactly all that in my presence was told the king by the captain. First of all they relate that after setting sail as they did from the port of Lisbon, they made their way for four months continuously, always in the same direction and towards the same pole, and never in all that time did they see anything at all. Nevertheless in the fifth month, still wishing to push on, they say that they met huge masses of solid snow floating upon the sea and moving under the influence of the waves, from the summit of which by the force of the sun's rays a clear stream of sweet water was melted and once dissolved ran down in little channels made by itself, eating its way splashingly to the base. Since the ships now lacked fresh water, the boats approached and took as much as was then needed. Fearing to remain in that region by reason of this present danger, they wished to turn back, but yet, spurred by hope, decided to go forward as best they could for a few days more, and having got under way, on the second day they again discovered the sea to be frozen, and were forced to give up the undertaking. They then began to turn towards the north-west and the west, in which direction they made their way for three more months, always with favourable weather. And on the first day of the fourth month they caught sight between these two courses of a very large country which they approached with very great delight. And since throughout this region numerous large rivers flowed into the sea, by one of these they had their way about a league inland, where on landing they found abundance of most luscious and varied fruits, and trees and pines of such measureless height and girth, that they would be too big as a mast for the largest ship that sails the sea. No corn of any sort grows there, but the men of that country say they live altogether by fishing and hunting animals, in which the land abounds, such as very large deer, covered with extremely long hair, the skins of which they use for garments and also make houses and boats thereof, and again wolves, foxes, tigers and sables. They affirm that there are, what appears to me wonderful, as many falcons as there are sparrows in our country, and I have seen some of them and they are extremely pretty. They forcibly kidnapped about fifty men and women of this country, and have brought them to the king. I have seen, touched and examined these people, and beginning with their stature, declare that they are somewhat taller than average, with members corresponding and well-formed. The hair of the men is long, just as we wear ours, and they wear it in curls, and have their faces marked with great signs, and these signs are like those of the Indians. Their eyes are greenish and when they look at one, this gives an air of great boldness to their whole countenance. Their speech is unintelligible, but nevertheless is not harsh but rather human. Their manners and gestures are most gentle; they laugh considerably and manifest the greatest pleasure. So much for the men. The women have small breasts and most beautiful bodies, and rather pleasant faces. The colour of these women may be said to be more white than otherwise, but the men are considerably darker. In fine, except for the terribly harsh look of the men, they appear to me to be in all else of the same form and image as ourselves. They go quite naked except for their privy parts, which they cover with a skin of the above-mentioned deer. They have no arms or iron, but whatever they work or fashion, they cut with very hard sharp stones, with which they split in two the very hardest substances. This vessel came home thence in one month and they say the distance is 2800 miles. The other consort decided to make her way far enough along that coast to be able to learn whether it is an island or yet mainland. And thus the king awaits with great eagerness both that one and others, and when they have arrived, should they bring anything worthy of your Excellency's consideration, I shall immediately send you word of the same.

C. Pietro Pasqualigo
to the Signory of Venice,
October 18, 1501

On the ninth of the present month arrived here one of two caravels which his majesty sent out last year to discover land in the northern parts, and it has brought back seven natives, men, women and children, from the land discovered. It was towards the north and west, 1800 miles away. These men in aspect, appearance and stature resemble gypsies: they have their faces marked here and there, some with many, others with few signs, [and are] clothed in the skins of divers animals, but chiefly of otter. Their speech is utterly different from any hitherto heard in this kingdom; nor does any one understand it. They are exceedingly well-formed in their limbs, and have most gentle countenances, but most bestial habits and manners, like wild men. The crew of this caravel believes that the above-mentioned land is mainland, and that it joins another land which was discovered last year in the north by other caravels belonging to this king. It seems they could not land in that country as the sea there was frozen over with great masses of snow, like mountains. They are also of opinion that this land is connected with the Antilles, which were discovered by the sovereigns of Spain, and with the land of the Parrots recently found by this king's vessels on their way to Calicut.[1] To this belief they are moved in the first place, because after ranging the coast of said land for the space of 600 miles and more, they did not find it come to an end; next, because they say they have discovered many exceedingly large rivers which there enter the sea. The other caravel, the captain's, is expected from day to day, and from it will be learned positively the nature and condition of the above-mentioned land, because she set off to range that coast further, in order to

1. Cabral's discovery of Brazil in 1500.

discover as much of it as possible. This news has given the king here great pleasure, since it seems to him that this country will be most useful to his plans in several respects, but chiefly because being very near to his kingdom, he will be able to secure without difficulty and in a short time a very large quantity of timber for making masts and ships' yards, and plenty of men-slaves, fit for every kind of labour, inasmuch as they say that this land is very well populated and full of pines and other excellent woods. And said news has so pleased his majesty that it has made him desirous of sending ships again to said region, and of increasing his fleet for India, in order to conquer more quickly, now that he has discoveries in view; because it seems to him that God is with his majesty in his labours and brings every plan of his to fulfilment.

D. Confirmation of the Discoveries
made by His Brothers to Vasco Eannes Corte Real,
September 17, 1506

Since through the death of his said brother the said grant, according to the tenour thereof, comes and passes to him, the said Vasco Annes Corte Real, he asks us as a favour to order our letters of confirmation to be given to him in due form, and in view of his request, and considering and remembering how his brother, the said Gaspar Corte Real, was the first to discover the said lands, at his own expense, and at the expenditure of much labour and at the risk of his life; how finally he perished therein with many servants and men whom he had taken with him; and likewise how afterwards his brother Michael Corte Real, who was our major-domo, on searching for his said brother with men and ships, fitted out at his own expense, wherein he expended much of his patrimony in order to look for, find and recover his said brother, and also in order to serve us in the discovery of the said lands, at which he laboured as far as was possible, likewise died after his said brother, and lost his life therein, and with him many of his father's, his own and the said Vasco Annes's servants, whom he had with him; and we bearing this in mind and also how in all this the said Vasco Annes always assisted his said brothers with his own property, servants and men, and even to this day pays and liquidates with his money the debts, charges and obligations left behind on account of this by his said brothers; for which reasons it is right and proper that the reward and praise for the services in which his said brothers lost their lives, should be perpetuated in the said Vasco Annes Corte Real and in his descendants: We by these present letters patent assign the succession of our said grant to the said Vasco Annes Corte Real and to all his heirs and successors.[1]

---

1. This grant was confirmed to him on September 7, 1522 (Biggar, *The Precursors of Jacques Cartier,* pp. 143–145).

IV

The Discovery of
the North American Shorelines

BETWEEN THE years 1507 and 1510, and most probably between the early summer of 1508 and the early summer of 1509, Sebastian Cabot sailed northwestward from England and attempted to make his way past the land barriers in the west in the hope of reaching Asia. North America had thus been recognized as a major land mass, the illusion that it was Asia or a string of islands close to Asia having been abandoned. This knowledge may have been acquired from the earlier English voyages or from Martin Waldseemüller's map of 1507 which showed two continents, the southern one named "America" after Amerigo Vespucci, between Europe and Asia. Sebastian Cabot, as a result of his voyage, believed he had found a strait round the western continents which only floating ice prevented him from following to Asia. By 1520 at the latest, the more northern continents had also come to bear the name America, though the Spaniards continued to speak of the whole western land complex as the West Indies (India Occidentalis).

The next stage in definition was Balboa's discovery in 1513 of the South Sea, which showed that another ocean must be traversed to reach Asia. This set in motion Spanish attempts to find the Southwest Passage to the South Sea, and the return of Elcano in Magellan's ship the Victoria in 1522 demonstrated that it existed and that Asia, indeed, could be reached across the newly named Pacific Ocean, even though with great difficulty. The reaction to the circumnavigation in both France and England was that it was now clearly worth while looking for passages through or round the northern American continent. This led first to the voyage of Giovanni da Verrazzano, sponsored by Francis I of France in 1523–24, which revealed a great stretch of coastline from Florida to Nova Scotia, and produced also the concept of a North American isthmus at about 35° N. latitude. The Spaniards, the next year, (1525), sponsored a parallel voyage under Estevão Gomes, which traversed a similar section of the North American coast but returned with no indications of passages or an isthmus. The English were a little later in the field. On the one hand, Robert Thorne was speculating on the chances of an ice-free passage over the Pole to Asia, although this did not lead to any voyages being made; and, on the other, plans were made to follow

Sebastian Cabot's track to the northwest while also keeping in reserve a possible search for Verrazzano's alleged isthmus far to the south. The expedition of 1527, led by John Rut, ended with one ship lost somewhere off Labrador or beyond, and the other making a complete coasting from Newfoundland to the West Indies and home to England. By 1530 it could be said that from the tip of Florida to southeast Labrador the broad outlines of the North American shores had been delimited, although the shorelines depicted by Verrazzano and Gomes, respectively, which dominated North American cartography for so long, were elementary outlines only and, even so, differed in a number of particulars from each other. At the same time, the greater part of eastern North America could now be visualized for the first time by Europeans, and its great latitudinal extent fully appreciated.

17. Sebastian Cabot's Voyage
to the Northwest

BECAUSE IT was frequently confused in the sixteenth century with John Cabot's voyage of 1498, the expedition made by his son, Sebastian, with two ships to the coast of Labrador (possibly as far north as 60°) remained for long a debatable one. The classic accounts, placing it in 1508–09, are in G. P. Winship, Cabot Bibliography (2nd edn., 1900), and J. A. Williamson, The Voyages of the Cabots (1929) and The Cabot Voyages (1962). There are still discrepancies in what we have that need to be explained: Cabot's maps have been lost since the late sixteenth century. See D. B. Quinn, Sebastian Cabot and Bristol Exploration (1968), and Dictionary of Canadian Biography, I (1965).

A. The Earliest Account
of Sebastian Cabot's Voyage

Pietro Martire d'Anghiera (usually referred to as Peter Martyr) published his famous history of the discoveries, De Orbe Novo Decades, in installments between 1516 and 1530. To the version given in Decade III (1516, f.52), an extract from which is given below (written 1515), he added in Decade VII written in 1524 (1530), f.92ᵛ, that Cabot had made his voyage sixteen years before (i.e., in 1508). In 1536 Marcantonio Contarini reported to the Venetian Signory that Henry VII had despatched Cabot with two ships and that when he returned "He found the King dead" (i.e., it was after April 21, 1509). Peter Martyr's evidence alone would support a voyage in 1507–08 as well as 1508–09; it could also *reasonably be stretched to cover a voyage in 1509–10. Contarini's evidence sounds probable but is not so authoritative. (See Williamson, The Cabot Voyages, pp. 269–270, and Biggar, The Precursors of Jacques Cartier, pp. 182–183).*

A certain Sebastian Cabot has examined those (frozen coasts), a Venetian by birth but carried by his parents whilst yet a child into the island of Britain, they going thither as the habit is of Venetians, who in the pursuit of trade are the guests of all lands. He equipped two ships at his own cost in Britain, and with three hundred men steered first for the north, until even in the month of July he found great icebergs floating in the sea and almost continuous daylight, yet with the land free by the melting of the ice. Wherefore he was obliged, as he says, to turn and make for the west. And he extended his course furthermore to the southward owing to the curve of the coastline, so that his latitude was almost that of the Straits of Gibraltar and he penetrated so far to the west that he had the island of Cuba on his left hand almost in the same longitude with himself. He, as he traversed those coasts, which he called the Bacallaos, says that he found the same flow of the waters to the west, although mild in force, as the Spaniards find in their passage to their southern possessions. Therefore it is not only probable but necessary to conclude that between these two lands hitherto unknown lie great straits which provide a passage for the waters flowing from east to west. . . . Cabot himself called those lands the Baccallaos because in the adjacent sea he found so great a quantity of a certain kind of great fish like tunnies, called bacallaos by the inhabitants, that at times they even stayed the passage of his ships. He found also the men of those lands clothed in skins and not anywhere devoid of intelligence. He says there are great numbers of bears there, which eat fish. For the bears plunge into the midst of a shoal of those fish, and falling upon them with their claws grasping the scales draw them to shore and eat them; on which account, he says, the bears are less dangerous to men. Many say that they have seen copper ore in places in the hands of the inhabitants. I know Cabot as a familiar friend and sometimes as a guest in my house; for, having been summoned from Britain by our Catholic King after the death of the older Henry, King of Britain, he is one of our councillors, and is daily expecting shipping to be provided for him wherewith he may reveal this secret of Nature hitherto hidden.

B. A Report of
Sebastian Cabot's Map in 1577

A NUMBER of references to maps and papers of Sebastian Cabot, surviving in later sixteenth-century England, are given in Williamson, The Cabot Voyages, pp. 278–280. They include Richard Willes, The history of Travayle in the West and East Indies (1577), ff. 231–233.

Wel, graunt the West Indies not to continue continent unto the Pole, graunt there be a passage betwyxt these two landes, let the goulph lye neare[1] us than commonly in cardes[2] we fynde it set, namely, betwyxt the 61. & 64. degrees north . . . so left by our countriman, Sebastian Cabote, in his table[2], the which my good Lorde your father[3] hath at Cheynies . . . for that Cabote was not only a skilful sea man but a long travailer, & such a one as entred personally that streiete, sent by King Henry the seventh to make this aforesaid discovery, as in his owne discourse of navigation you may reade in his carde drawen with his owne hands, the mouth of the north-westerne streict lieth neare the 318 Meridian, betwixt 61. and 64. degrees in elevation, continuying the same breadth about 10. degrees west, where it openeth southerly more and more, untyll it come under the tropike of Cancer, and so runneth into Mar de Zur,[4] at the least 18 degrees more in breadth there, then it was where it fyrst began.

18. The Voyage of Giovanni da Verrazzano Along the American Shoreline, 1524

VERRAZZANO'S VOYAGE in the ship Dauphine was of particular importance as it was largely the means by which non-Iberian peoples in Europe were

1. For "nearer."
2. Both words are sixteenth-century terms for "maps."
3. The Earl of Bedford, father of Frances, Countess of Warwick, whom Willes is addressing.
4. The Pacific Ocean.

able to obtain some clear idea of the eastern seaboard of North America and also to learn something of the natural resources of the country and the characteristics of the Indian peoples along a considerable stretch from South to North. Verrazzano's letter to Francis I, written on his return to France, probably circulated in manuscript before it was printed in G. B. Ramusio's Navigationi et Viaggi, Vol. III (Venice, 1556), while the maps made from his charts by his brother Girolamo were also discreetly publicized. The first English version of the letter was made by Richard Hakluyt for his Divers voyages touching the discoverie of America in 1582. A superior text of the letter was found in the present century which contained notes by Verrazzano himself. English versions of this were printed by Edward Hagemann Hall in the American Scenic and Preservation Society's Fifteenth Report (1914), pp. 135–226, and by I. N. Phelps Stokes, The Iconography of Manhattan Island, Vol. IV (1922), pp. 15–19. In the extracts below, Hakluyt's translation is followed, with some slight modernization, but additions from the Cellare Manuscript, as it is called, are put in parentheses; divergences between the two versions are noted in the footnotes.

Verrazzano is one of the most literate and detached of the early observers of North America. Educated in the classics and informed by the Renaissance spirit of inquiry, Verrazzano gives a distinctive flavor to his observations. It is clear also that he is very anxious to link France as closely as possible to the new discoveries by giving names of members of the French royal house and other French notables to regions, bays, islands and capes. His alleged discovery of an inland sea (the Pacific, he thought), was due to his misunderstanding of the character of the sounds behind the Carolina Outer Banks.

Lawrence C. Wroth, The Voyages of Giovanni da Verrazzano, 1524–1528 (1970), is the first major study to appear in English, and contains a further version of this letter; a good edition is in C. A. Julien, Les Français en Amérique pendant la première moitié du XVIe siècle (1946), pp. 53–76.

To the most Christian King of France, Francis the first. The relation of John de Verrazzano a Florentine, of the land by him discovered in the name of his Majesty. Written in Dieppe the eighth of July, 1524. . . .

The 17 of January the year 1524 by the grace of God we departed from the dishabited rock by the isle of Madeira, appertaining to the king of Portugal, with 50 men, with victuals, weapons, and other ship munition very well provided and furnished for 8 months: and sailing Westwards with a fair easterly wind,[1] in 25

1. "East-south-east wind."

days we ran 500 leagues,[2] and the 20 of February[3] we were over-taken with as sharp and terrible a tempest (towards the sixteenth hour) as ever any sailors suffered: whereof with the divine help and mercifull assistance of Almighty God, and the goodness of our ship, accompanied with the good hap of her fortunate name, we were delivered, and with a prosperous wind followed our course West and by North. And in other 25 days we made above 400 leagues more, where we discovered a new land, never before seen of any man either ancient or modern.

At the first sight[4] it seemed somewhat low, but being within a quarter of a league of it, we perceived by the great fires that we saw by the sea coast, that it was inhabited: and saw that the land stretched to the Southwards. In seeking some convenient harbor wherein to anchor and to have knowledge of the place, we sailed fifty leagues in vain, and seeing the land to run still to the South-wards (in order not to meet with the Spaniards), we resolved to return back again towards the North, where we found ourselves troubled with the like difficulty (where we found the same place). At length being in despair to find any port, we cast anchor upon the coast, and sent our boat to shore, where we saw great store of people which came to the sea side; and seeing us approach, they fled away, and sometimes would stand still and look back, be-holding us with great admiration: but afterwards being animated and assured with signs that we made them, some of them came hard to the sea side, seeming to rejoice very much at the sight of us, and marvelling greatly at our apparel, shape and whiteness, showed us by sundry signs where we might most commodiously come aland with our boat, offering us also of their victuals to eat. . . .

Not far from these (on the shore) we found another people, whose living we think to be like unto theirs—as hereafter I will declare unto your Majesty—shewing at this present the situation and nature of the foresaid land. The shore is all covered with small

2. "Eight hundred leagues." Using leagues of 4 Roman miles (5,924 meters or 3.679 statute miles), Verrazzano made the voyage some 2,945 statute miles or 2,558 nautical miles.
3. "The 24 day of February."
4. The landfall cannot be precisely determined. It appears to have been some considerable way south of Cape Fear.

sand, and so ascendeth upwards for the space of 15 foot, rising in form of little hills about 50 paces broad. And sailing forwards, we found certain small rivers and arms of the sea, that fall down by certain creeks, washing the shore on both sides as the coast lieth. And beyond this we saw the open country rising in height above the sandy shore with many fair fields and plains, full of mighty great woods, some very thicke, and some thin, replenished with divers sorts of trees, as pleasant and delectable to behold, as is possible to imagine. And your Majesty may not think[5] that these are like the woods of Hyrcania or the wild deserts of Tartary,[6] and the northern coasts full of fruitless trees: but they are full of palm trees, bay trees, and high cypress trees, and many other sorts of trees unknown in Europe, which yield most sweet savours far from the shore. (We baptized this land "Laurel Forest"—Forêt-de-Lauriers—and a little further down on account of the beautiful cedars it was given the name "Cedar Field"—Champ-de-Cèdres. We smelled the odour a hundred leagues and farther when they burned the cedars and the winds blew from the land.) The property whereof we could not learn for the cause aforesaid, and not for any difficulty to pass through the woods, seeing they are not so thick but that a man may pass through them. Neither do we think that they, partaking of the East world round about them, are altogether void of drugs or spicery, and other riches of gold, seeing the colour of the land doth so much argue it. And the land is full of many beasts, as stags, deer and hares, and likewise of lakes and pools of fresh water, with great plenty of fowls, convenient for all kind of pleasant game.[7]

This land is in latitude 34 degrees (like Carthage and Damascus),[8] with good and wholesome air, temperate, between hot and cold; no vehement winds do blow in those regions, and those that do commonly reign in those coasts, are the Northwest and West winds in the summer season—in the beginning whereof we were there—the sky clear and fair with very little rain: and if at any time the air be cloudy and misty with the Southern wind, immediately it

5. "And do not believe Your Majesty."
6. "Scythia."
7. "Pleasure of the hunt."
8. Damascus is, in fact, 33° 30′ N. latitude and Carthage 36° 51′.

is dissolved and waxeth clear and fair again. The sea is calm, not boisterous, the waves gentle: and although all the shore be somewhat shoaled and without harbor, yet is it not dangerous to the sailors, being free from rocks and deep, so that within 4 or 5 foot of the shore, there is 20 foot deep of water without ebb or flood, the depth still increasing in such uniform proportion. There is very good riding at sea: for any ship being shaken in a tempest, can never perish there by breaking of her cables, which we have proved by experience. For in the beginning of March—as is usual in all regions—being in the sea oppressed with northern winds, and riding there, we found our anchor broken before the earth failed or moved at all.

We departed from this place, still running along the coast, which we found to trend toward the East, and we saw everywhere very great fires, by reason of the multitude of the inhabitants. While we rode on that coast, partly because it had no harbor, and for that we wanted water, we sent our boat ashore with 25 men: where by reason of great and continual waves that beat against the shore, being an open coast, without succour, none of our men could possibly go ashore without losing our boat. We saw there many people which came unto the shore, making divers signs of friendship, and showing that they were content we should come aland, and by trial we found them to be very courteous and gentle, as your Majesty shall understand by the success. . . .

(We called it Annunciata[9] from the day of arrival, where was found an isthmus a mile in width and about two hundred miles long, in which, from the ship, was seen the oriental sea between the west and north. Which is the one, without doubt, which goes about the extremity of India, China and Cathay. We navigated along the said isthmus with the continued hope of finding some strait or true promontory at which the land would end toward the north, in order to be able to penetrate to those happy shores of

9. Annunziata (Lady Day) was March 25; 200 miles in his measure would be about 176 statute miles. The coast is clearly that of the Carolina Outer Banks, extending northwards from-Cape Fear. The Sounds, seen inside the Banks, were optimistically taken to be an eastward extension of the Pacific Ocean. The Banks were subsequently called the Isthmus of Verrazzano and the Sounds the Sea of Verrazzano.

Cathay. To which isthmus was given by the discoverer [the name] Verazanio: as all the land found was named Francesca for our [King] Francis.)

Departing from hence following the shore which trended somewhat toward the North, in 50 leagues space we came to another land which showed much more fair and full of woods. . . .

We saw in this country many vines growing naturally, which growing up, took hold of the trees as they do in Lombardy[10] which if by husbandmen they were dressed in good order, without all doubt they would yield excellent wines. . . . We found also roses, violets, lilies, and many sorts of herbs, and sweet and odoriferous flowers different from ours. . . .

Having made our abode three days in this country, and riding on the coast for want of harbors, we concluded to depart from thence, trending along the shore between the North and the East, sailing only in the day-time, and riding at anchor by night. . . .

(In Arcadia, which we named Arcadia on account of the beauty of the trees, we followed a coast very green with forests but without ports, and with some charming promontaries and small rivers. We named the coast "Côte-de-Lorraine" on account of the Cardinal; the first promontory "d'Alençon," the second "Bonnivet," the largest river "Vendôme" and a small mountain which stands by the sea "Saint-Pol" on account of the Count.)[11]

In the space of 100 leagues' sailing we found a very pleasant place situated amongst certain little steep hills. From amidst the which hills there ran down into the sea an exceeding great stream of water, which within the mouth was very deep, and from the sea to the mouth of the same with the tide which we found to rise 8 foot, any great ship laden may pass up. But because we rode at anchor in a place well fenced from the wind, we would not venture ourselves without knowledge of the place: and we passed up with our boat only into the said river, and saw the country very well peopled.

10. "Cisalpine Gaul."
11. The coast is probably that between Cape Charles and Cape May. The names were given, respectively, in honor of Jean de Guise, cardinal de Guise; Charles IX, duc d'Alençon; Guillaume Gouffier, seigneur de Bonnivet, admiral of France; Charles de Bourbon, duc de Vendôme; and François II de Bourbon-Vendôme, comte de Saint-Pol.

. . . We entered up the said river into the land about half a league, where it made a most pleasant lake about 3 leagues in compass: on the which they rowed from the one side to the other to the number of 30 of their small boats, wherein were many people which passed from one shore to the other to come and see us. And behold upon the sudden—as it is wont to fall out in sailing—a contrary flaw of wind coming from the sea, we were enforced to return to our ship, leaving this land to our great discontentment, for the great commodity and pleasantness thereof, which we suppose is not without some riches, all the hills showing mineral matters in them. (We called it Angoulême from the principality which Your Majesty held when in lesser fortune, and the bay which that land makes Santa Margarita from the name of your sister who vanquishes the other matrons in modesty and talent.)[12]

We weighed anchor, and sailed toward the East, for so the coast trended, and so always for 50 leagues[13] being in sight thereof, we discovered an island in form of a triangle, distant from the mainland 10 leagues, about the bigness of the island of Rhodes: it was full of hills covered with trees, well peopled, for we saw fires all along the coast: we gave it the name of your Majesty's mother (Aloysia),[14] not staying there by reason of the weather being contrary.

And we came to another land being 15 leagues distant from the island where we found a passing good haven,[15] wherein being entered,[16] we found about 20 small boats of the people, which with divers cries and wonderings came about our ship, coming no nearer than 50 paces towards us: they stayed and beheld the artificialness of our ship, our shape and apparel: then they all made a loud shout together, declaring that they rejoiced. When we had something animated[17] them, using their gestures, they came so

12. King Francis I was comte d'Angoulême before his accession to the French throne; Marguerite was duchesse d'Alençon and later queen of Navarre.
13. "80 leagues."
14. Louise de Savoie, mother of Francis I. The island is Block Island.
15. Narragansett Bay.
16. "And before we entered it."
17. "Reassured."

near us, that we cast them certain bells and glasses, and many toys, which when they had received, they looked on them with laughing, and came without fear aboard our ship. There were amongst these people two kings of so goodly stature and shape as is possible to declare: the eldest was about 40 years of age, the second was a young man of 20 years[18] old. Their apparel was on this manner: the elder had upon his naked body a hart's skin wrought artificially with divers branches like damask: his head was bare with the hair tied up behind with divers knots: about his neck he had a large chain, garnished with divers stones of sundry colors: the young man was almost apparelled after the same manner. This is the goodliest people, and of the fairest conditions that we have found in this our voyage. They exceed us in bigness: they are of the color of brass, some of them incline more to whiteness: others are of yellow color, of comely visage, with long and black hair, which they are very careful to trim and deck up: they are black and quick eyed, and of sweet and pleasant countenance, imitating much of the old fashion. I write not to your Majesty of the other parts of their body, having all such proportion as appertaineth to any handsome man. The women are of the like conformity and beauty: very handsome and well favored, of pleasant countenance, and comely to behold: they are as well mannered and continent as any woman, and of good education.[19] They are all naked save their privy parts, which they cover with a deer's skin branched or embroidered as the men use: there are also of them which wear on their arms very rich skins of luzernes:[20] they adorn their heads with divers ornaments made of their own hair, which hang down before on both sides their breasts: others use other kind of dressing themselves like unto the women of Egypt and Syria, these are of the elder sort: and when they are married, they wear divers toys, according to the usage of the people of the East, as well men as women. Among whom we saw many plates of wrought copper, which they esteem more than gold, which for the color they make no account of, for that among all other it is counted the basest: they make most

18. "24 years."
19. "Of habits and behaviour as much according to womanly custom as pertains to human nature."
20. "Lynx."

account of azure and red. The things that they esteem most of all those which we gave them, were bells, crystal of azure color, and other toys to hang at their ears or about their neck. They did not desire cloth of silk or of gold, much less of any other sort, neither cared they for things made of steel and iron, which we often showed them in our armor which they made no wonder at, and in beholding them they only asked the art of making them: the like they did at our glasses, which when they beheld, they suddenly laughed and gave them us again. They are very liberal, for they give that which they have: we became great friends with these, and one day we entered into the haven with our ship,[21] whereas before we rode a league off at sea by reason of the contrary weather. They came in great companies of their small boats unto the ship with their faces all bepainted with divers colors, showing us that it was a sign of joy, bringing us of their victuals, they made signs unto us where we might safest ride in the haven for the safeguard of our ship keeping still our company.

And after we were come to an anchor, we bestowed 15 days in providing ourselves many necessary things, whither every day the people repaired to see our ship, bringing their wives with them, whereof they were very jealous: and they themselves entering aboard the ship and staying there a good space, caused their wives to stay in their boats, and for all the intreaty we could make, offering to give them divers things, we could never obtain that they would suffer them to come aboard our ship. And oftentimes one of the two kings coming with his queen, and many gentlemen for their pleasure to see us, they all stayed on the shore 200 paces from us, sending a small boat to give us intelligence of their coming, saying they would come to see our ship: this they did in token of safety, and as soon as they had answer from us, they came immediately, and having stayed a while to behold it, they wondered at hearing the cries and noises of the mariners. The queen and her maids stayed in a very light boat, at an island a quarter of a league off, while the king abode a long space in our ship uttering divers conceits with gestures, viewing with great admiration all the furniture of the ship, demanding the property of every thing particu-

21. "And one day, before we had entered with the ships in the port."

larly. He took likewise great pleasure in beholding our apparel,[22] and in tasting our meats, and so courteously taking his leave departed. . . .

We were oftentimes within the land 5 or 6 leagues, which we found as pleasant as is possible to declare, very apt for any kind of husbandry of corn, wine and oyle: for that there are plains 25 or 30 leagues broad, open and without any impediment, of trees of such fruitfulness, that any seed being sown therein, will bring forth most excellent fruit.[23] We entered afterwards into the woods, which we found so great and thick, that any army were it never so great might have hid itself therein, the trees whereof are oaks, cypress trees, and other sorts unknowen in Europe. We found *Pomi appii*[24] (or cherries), damson trees, and nut trees, and many other sorts of fruit differing from ours: there are beasts in great abundance, as harts, deer, luzernes, and other kinds which they take with their nets and bows which are their chief weapons: the arrows which they use are made with great cunning, and instead of iron, they head them with flint, with jasper stone and hard marble and other sharp stones which they use instead of iron to cut trees, and to make their boats of one whole piece of wood, making it hollow with great and wonderful art, wherein 10 or 12 men[25] may sit commodiously: their oars are short and broad at the end, and they use them in the sea without any danger, and by main force of arms, with as great speediness as they list themselves.

(Going further) we saw their houses made in circular or round form 10 or 12 paces in compass,[26] made with half circles of timber, separate one from another without any order of building, covered with mats of straw wrought cunningly together, which save them from the wind and rain: and if they had the order of building and perfect skill of workmanship as we have, there were no doubt but that they would also make eftsoons great and stately buildings. For all the sea coasts are full of clear and glistering stones, and ala-

22. "Imitating our manners."
23. "Open and devoid of every impediment of trees, of such fertility that any seed in them would produce the best crops."
24. "Lucullian apples."
25. "14 to 15 men."
26. "Of 14 to 15 paces compass."

baster, and therefore it is full of good havens and harbors for ships. They move the foresaid houses from one place to another according to the commodity of the place and season wherein they will make their abode, and only taking off the mats, they have other houses builded incontinent. The father and the whole family dwell together in one house in great number: in some of them we saw 25 or 30 persons. They feed as the others do aforesaid of pulse which grow in that country with better order of husbandry than in the others. They observe in their sowing the course of the moon and the rising of certain stars,[27] and divers other customs spoken of by antiquity. Moreover they live by hunting and fishing. They live long, and are seldom sick, and if they chance to fall sick at any time,[28] they heal themselves with fire without any physician, and they say that they die for very age. They are very pitifull and charitable towards their neighbors, they make great lamentations in their adversity: and in their misery, the kindred reckon up all their felicity. At their departure out of life, they use mourning mixed with singing, which continueth for a long space.[29] This is as much as we could learn of them.

This land is situated in the parallel of Rome, in 41 degrees and 2 terces:[30] but somewhat more cold by accidental causes and not of nature—as I will declare unto your highness elsewhere—describing at this present the situation of the foresaid country,[31] which lieth East and West. I say that the mouth of the haven (which on account of its advantages we called "Refugio"), lieth open to the South half a league broad, and being entered within it between the East and the North, it stretcheth twelve leagues: where it waxeth broader and broader, and maketh a gulf about 20 leagues in compass, wherein are five small islands very fruitfull and pleasant, full of high and broad trees, among which islands any great navy may

27. "The rising of the Pleiades."
28. "If they are oppressed with wounds, without crying."
29. "The relations, one with another, at the end of their life use the Sicilian lamentation, mingled with singing lasting a long time."
30. "Forty and two thirds degrees." Newport Harbor where the *Dauphine* anchored is in 41° 30′ N.
31. "Port."

ride safe without any fear of tempest or other danger. Afterwards turning towards the South in the entering into the haven on both sides there are most pleasant hills, with many rivers of most clear water falling into the sea. In the midst of this entrance there is a rock of free stone produced by nature apt to build any castle or fortress there, for the keeping of the haven (which, on account of the nature of the stone and on account of the family of a gentlewoman, we called "La Petra Viva": on whose right side at said mouth of the port is a promontory which we called "Jovium Promontarium").[32]

The fifth of May[33] being furnished with all things necessary, we departed from the said coast keeping along in the sight thereof, and we sailed 150 leagues, (within which space we found shoals which extend 50 leagues from the continent into the sea. Upon them there was scarcely 3 feet of water, which made navigation very perilous. We passed through with difficulty and named it "Armellini,"[34] finding it always after one manner: but the land somewhat higher with certain mountains (with a high promontory which we named "Pallavicino"),[35] all which bear a show of mineral matter. We sought not to land there in any place, because the weather served our turn for sailing (along the coast): but we suppose that it was like the former. The coast ran Eastward for the space of fifty leagues.

And trending afterwards to the North[36] we found another land, high, full of thick woods, the trees whereof were firs, cypresses and such like as are wont to grow in cold countries. The people differ much from the other, and seeing how much the former seemed to be courteous and gentle, so much were these full of rudeness and ill manners, and so barbarous that by no signs that ever we could make, we could have any kind of traffic with them . . . (they are

32. Jovio Head, apparently after Paolo Jovio, the scholar. It may well be Sakonnet Point.
33. "The 6th day of May."
34. From Francesco Armellino, cardinal of Pérouse. The shoals are those extending eastwards and southeastwards from Nantucket and Cape Cod.
35. From Gian Ludovico Palavicini, marquis of Corte Maggiore. The headland may be the Cape Cod Highlands or, possibly, Cape Ann.
36. "In the space of fifty leagues, holding more to the North."

in 43⅔).[37] And when we went on shore[38] they shot at us with their bows making great outcries, and afterwards fled into the woods. We found not in this land any thing notable, or of importance, saving very great woods and certain hills, they may have some mineral matter in them, because we saw many of them have beadstones of copper hanging at their ears.

We departed from thence keeping our course Northeast along the coast, which we found more pleasant champion and without woods, with high mountains within the land (growing smaller toward the shore of the sea). Continuing directly along the coast for the space of fifty leagues, we discovered 32 islands (among which we called the three larger "Les Trois Filles de Navarre"),[39] lying all near the land, being small and pleasant to the view, high and having many turnings and windings between them, making many fair harbors and channels as they do in the gulf of Venice in Sclavonia, and Dalmatia;[40] we had no knowledge or acquaintance with the people: we suppose they are of the same manners and nature as the others are.[41]

Sailing Northeast[42] for the space of 150 leagues we approached to the land that in times past was discovered by the Britons, which is in fifty degrees.[43] Having now spent all our provision and victuals, and having discovered about 700 leagues[44] and more of new countries, and being furnished with water and wood, we concluded to return into France.

37. This is the coast of the northern part of Massachusetts and the southern part of Maine. On the map of Girolamo da Verrazzano it is called "Terra onde de mala gente," Bad Men's Land.
38. "When we descended to the shore."
39. Possibly the islands Monhegan, Metinic and Matinicus, off the Maine coast.
40. "As are found in the Adriatic Gulf, in the Illyrias and Dalmatia."
41. "Like the others, devoid of morals and culture."
42. "Between east-south-east and north-north-east."
43. Cape Breton itself is in 45° 57': 50° would bring the *Dauphine* to the northern limits of Newfoundland.
44. "Six hundred leagues." The range is between about 2,207 and 2,575 statute miles.

19. The North American Voyage of Estevão Gómes, 1524–25

JUST AS Verrazzano was an Italian in the service of France, so Estevão Gómes was a Portuguese in the service of Spain, thus keeping up the tradition of employing foreign pilots for American discovery. Gómes left Coruña on September 27, 1524, and traversed the coast of eastern North America from South to North, returning to the same port on August 21, 1525. We have no narrative of the course of his ship, La Anunciada, but a map made by Diego Ribero in 1525, and sent to Rome by Baltusar de Castiglione, the papal representative in Spain, records his discoveries clearly.

There is no satisfactory account in English. L. A. Vigneras, "El Viaje de Estaban Gómez a Norte América," Revista de Indias, XVII (1957), 189–207; "The Voyage of Estaban Gomez from Florida to the Baccaloos," Terrae Incognitae, II (1970); "The Cartographer Diego Ribero," Imago Mundi, XVI (1962), pp. 76–83 (for the Castiglione Map, plate 2), modified all previous accounts of the voyage through discoveries made in the Spanish archives.

Alonso de Santa Cruz composed in about 1540 his Islario general de todas las islas del mundo (ed. Antonio Blasquez, Madrid, 1922), which contained (pp. 440 ff.) some indications, and maps, of the discoveries made by Gómes. Santa Cruz is not a very precise writer but he conveys even in translation an impression of what was found.

ISLANDS OFF THE LAND DISCOVERED BY THE PILOT ESTEVAN GÓMEZ

The pilot, Estevan Gómez . . . in the expedition made by him at the command and by licence of the emperor, our master, in search of and in order to discover Cathay or the eastern city of India, as well as that so-much-sought-for strait or passage leading to the sea commonly called the South Sea, discovered, during the ten months[1] he was absent, a large number of islands along the coast of this continent, and especially a very wide deep river which he named Rio de los Gamos[2] (Deer River), on account of the number

1. Ten months and twenty-six days. Vigneras, "El viaje de Estaban Gómez," 198.
2. The Penobscot, the Rio de Gamas, as it was more usually called, tended to be regarded as the Rio de Gomez.

of these animals found there. This river is everywhere dotted with islands, on which in summer the Indians from the mainland took up their quarters for the sake of the quantities of salmon, shad, pickerel and other kinds of fish found in these waters. Gómez sailed for some distance up this river, thinking it was the strait of which he was in search. Eventually he discovered it to be a large deep river. From this fact an idea may be formed of the size and extent of that continent.

And although he shared the general opinion about the strait or passage which, as we have already stated, separates the Bacallaos[3] from the land called Labrador,[4] yet he was convinced it was unnecessary to attempt it because of the cold in those parts which would always be an obstacle. This opinion and his excuse for not attempting that passage were accepted as so reasonable that no further attempt has been made to proceed with this matter, although of great importance to your majesty's interests and service, since through that channel a claim was laid to the trade and conquest of the Moluccas and to many more islands in those parts belonging of right to your royal crown. . . . Returning to the islands in the Rio de los Gamos and those lying off the neighboring continent, these, as I have already explained, are nearly all of them inhabited in the summer by Indians like those of Santo Domingo . . . although these men and women have finer bodies. They sharpen the bows, arrows and spears with which they fight by placing them near fire. Their land has a temperate climate and is covered with the trees common to those regions such as evergreens, oaks and olives.[5] Many wild vines are found which bear grapes, and many plants and herbs similar to those of Spain. There is much marcasite which they mistook for gold. They brought home to Spain in the galleon[6] many Indians, whom they afterwards set at liberty.[7]

3. Newfoundland and Labrador.
4. Greenland.
5. Mistaken.
6. *La Anunciada.*
7. At least fifty-eight were brought to Spain, of whom thirteen died in September 1525. Most of the remainder were baptized and given provisional liberty (Vigneras, "El Viajede Estaban Gómez," 197–201).

20. John Rut's Voyage, 1527–28

EXPEDITIONS HAD been planned in 1517 and in 1521 to follow up Sebastian Cabot's voyage of 1508–09, but it was not until 1527 that an expedition was launched to investigate the chances of a passage round North America or, alternatively, a passage or an isthmus in lower latitudes (on account of the presentation to Henry VIII about 1526 of a map showing Verrazzano's discoveries). The Mary Guildford was the king's wine ship and John Rut was her usual captain; she lost company with the Samson, which disappeared off the Labrador coast, went south to St. John's Harbour in Newfoundland and then coasted North America southwards, appearing at Mona in the West Indies on November 19, 1527. Finally, after a brush with the Spaniards at Santo Domingo, the Mary Guildford appears to have left on her homeward voyage about the end of November and was back on her run from London to Bordeaux for the wine season of 1528.

The best account of the voyage is by H. P. Biggar, "An English Expedition to America," in Mélanges offert à M. Charles Bémont (1913), pp. 459–472; see also Williamson, The Voyages of the Cabots, pp. 254–261, and Dictionary of Canadian Biography, I, 585–586.

A. Letter from John Rut to Henry VIII, August 3, 1527

This was first printed by Samuel Purchas, Hakluytus Posthumus, or Purchas his Pilgrimes, III (1625), 809 (reprinted XIV [1906], 304–305). Purchas was unable to read it accurately.

King Henrie the eight to set forth two ships for discoverie, one of which perished in the North parts of New-found Land. The Master of the other, John Rut, writ this Letter to King Henrie, in bad English and worse Writing. Over it was this superscription.

Master Grubes [Rut's] two ships departed from Plymouth the 10. day of June, and arrived in the New-found Land in a good Harbour, called Cape de Bas, the 21. day of July: and after we had left the sight of Selle [Isles of Scilly], we had never sight of any Land, till we had sight of Cape de Bas.

Pleasing your Honorable Grace to heare of your servant John Rut, with all his Company here, in good health, thanks be to God, and your Graces ship. The Mary of Gilford, with all her [   ] thanks be to God: And if it please your honorable Grace, we ranne in our course to the Northward, till we came into 53. degrees, and there we found many great Ilands of Ice and deepe water, we found no sounding, and then we durst not goe no further to the Northward for feare of more Ice, and then we cast about to the Southward, and within foure dayes after we had one hundred and sixtie fathom, and then wee came into 52. degrees and fell with the mayne Land, and within ten leagues of the mayne Land we met with a great Iland of Ice, and came hard by her, for it was standing in deepe water, and so went in with Cape de Bas,¹ a good Harbor, and many small Ilands, and a great fresh River going up farre into the mayne Land, and the Mayne Land all wildernesse and mountaines and woods, and no naturall ground but all mosse, and no inhabitation nor no people in these parts; and in the woods wee found footing of divers great beasts, but we saw none not in ten leagues. And please your Grace, the Samson and wee kept company all the way till within two dayes before wee met with all the Ilands of Ice, that was the first day of July at night, and there rose a great and a marvailous great storme, and much foule weather; I trust in Almightie Jesu to heare good newes of her. And please your Grace, we were considering and a writing of all our order, how we would wash us² and what course wee would draw and when God doe send foule weather, that with the Cape de Sper³ shee should goe, and he that came first should tarry the space of sixe weeks one for another, and watered at Cape de Bas ten dayes, ordering of your Graces ship and fishing, and so departed toward the Southward to seeke our fellow: the third day of August we entered into a good Haven, called Saint John, and there we found eleven saile of Normans, and one Brittaine, and two Portugall Barkes, and all a fishing, and so we are readie to depart toward Cape de Bas,⁴ and that is twentie five leagues, as shortly as we have fished, and so along the coast till we may meete with our fellow, and so with all

1. Cape de Bas, probably on Sandwich Bay, Labrador.
2. Corrupt: possibly "how we would wish us," in the old sense of "how we would recommend ourselves to act."
3. Cape Spear.
4. Clearly a mistake for Cape de Ras, the modern Cape Race.

diligence that lyes in me toward parts to that Ilands that we are commanded by the grace of God, as we were commanded at our departing: and thus Jesu save and keepe your honorable Grace, and all your honourable Rever.[5] in the Haven of Saint John, the third day of August, written in haste. 1527.

> By your servant John Rut, to his uttermost of
> his power.

B. Evidence on Rut's Voyage
Obtained by Spaniards in the West Indies

THE Mary Guildford was located first of all by the Spaniards at the small island of Mona and later anchored off Santo Domingo (from which she was eventually driven by a warning shot). Depositions by a number of persons are preserved in the Archivo de Indias, Seville, and are printed in Biggar, Precursors of Jacques Cartier, pp. 165–168, and Irene A. Wright, Spanish Documents Concerning English Voyages to the Carribbean, 1527–1568 (1929), and partly reprinted in Williamson, Voyages of the Cabots, pp. 108–111.

(1) FROM THE DEPOSITION OF GINES NAVARRO

The statement obtained from the English ship when at the Island of Mona on her way to Hispaniola.

That while he was loading the said caravel with cassava, last Tuesday the nineteenth of the present month of November, there arrived a vessel of 250 tons burden, and three main-tops; and taking her for a ship from Spain, he went towards her in his boat. And they came off in their pinnace manned by 25 or 30 men with as many as 25 men in the boat and the captain of the said ship[1] in command. All were armed with corselets, bows and arrows and some cross-bows and in the bow were two lombards,[2] the matches of which were still alight.

On reaching them, he inquired from what country they came. They answered they were Englishmen from the city of London, and that the vessel belonged to the king of England. He asked

5. For "Reverences"?
1. Evidently John Rut.
2. Light artillery.

them what they had come to look for in those parts. They told him the king had fitted out that vessel and another to go and discover the land of the Great Khan, but that on the way, they met with a storm, during which they lost sight of their consort and had never seen her again. They held on their course and reached the frozen sea where they met large islands of ice. Being unable to pass that way, they altered their course but ran into a sea as hot as a boiler.[3] For fear lest the water would melt the pitch of their vessel, they turned about and came to explore the Baccalaos,[4] where they found some 50 Spanish, French and Portuguese fishing vessels. They desired to land there in order to have tidings of the Indians, but on reaching the shore the Indians killed the pilot, who they said was a Piedmontese by birth.[5] Setting sail thence they made their way for some 400 leagues and more along the coast of the new land where Ayllon took his colony.[6] Thence they crossed over and came to explore the island of St. John.[7]

(II) Deposition by Cristóbal Lebron
and Alonso Zuazo,
Judge of the Audiencia of Santo Domingo,
November 26, 1527

Whereas yesterday, Monday, in the afternoon, there arrived off the mouth of this river and port a large three-masted ship belonging to the king of England; and its master with 10 or 12 seamen came ashore in a boat, and told them that the ship belonged to the king of England; and that this ship, together with another, cleared perhaps nine months ago from England,[8] to make a certain exploration towards the north, between Labrador[9] and the Baccalaos, in the belief that in that region there was a strait through which to

3. Either a traveler's tale or the result of mistranslation.
4. Cape Race, Newfoundland.
5. The first landfall is probably that made after leaving Cape Race (p. 00 above), and could have been in the Maritimes or New England. The name of the Italian pilot is not known.
6. See p. 83.
7. San Juan de Puerto Rico.
8. In fact, less than six months ago.
9. Greenland.

pass to Tartary and that they had sailed as far north as fifty and some degrees where certain persons died of cold, the pilot had died, and one of the said vessels was lost; for which reasons they came to this land to take in water and subsistence and other things which they needed.

(III) DEPOSITION OF DIEGO MARTEL

. . . these men answered witness that the King of England had sent them out with two ships to discover a certain strait which was towards Noruega,[10] whence they had cleared, and because they sailed far enough north to reach 64 degrees, since it was winter, they found all the land frozen, and it was so cold that four or five of the crew had died of it.

10. Norway (Miss Wright prints "Norembega" in Spanish Documents, p. 48, but "Noruega" is in the document).

V

The Spanish Definition
of Southeastern North America

TWO SECTIONS of the North American coast were directly in the route of the Spanish conquerors of the Caribbean as they moved outward from the central islands of Hispaniola and Cuba. The first was the Gulf coast. As ships moved along the shores of central America, from Honduras to Yucatán, and from Yucatán along the coast of Mexico, it was inevitable that they should follow the curving coastline and so define the boundaries of the Gulf of Mexico as the northern perimeter of the Caribbean. Similarly, ships going northwards and eastward from Cuba and Hispaniola were bound to be taken up by the Florida Current and carried past the Keys, early called Las Cabeças de los Martires, and within sight, in some cases, of the peninsula of Florida. Juan Ponce de León, conqueror of Puerto Rico, is traditionally the first to have seen Florida in 1513, although it is very likely to have been sighted and even mapped earlier. Francisco Hernández de Córdoba in 1517 sailed round the Gulf of Mexico, after his defeat at Champotón, and refreshed his men, not without some danger from the Indians, on the western shores of the Florida peninsula. Alonso Alvarez de Pineda, in 1519, following a similar route, gave closer attention to the shores from Mexico to western Florida. Ponce de León began the attempt to settle Florida in 1521, the first of many attempts to make the peninsula a Spanish colony; but he was driven off by the Indians, possibly near Charlotte Harbor, and died of his wounds. In the same year, Lucas Vásquez de Ayllón searched the coasts well to the north of the peninsula, and located harbors in what is now South Carolina. In 1526 he made a serious attempt to settle. He died on shore, and a move to another site still did not reveal a suitable permanent site for a settlement so that the attempt was soon abandoned. Ponce de León had coveted the western as well as the eastern side of the Florida peninsula; between 1526 and 1528, Pánfilo de Narváez attempted to occupy the whole peninsula and also the Gulf coast extending westward toward the great river, the Mississippi, which was now known, but his expedition fell to pieces before starvation and Indian attack. Only Alvar Nuñez Cabeça de Vaca and a few companions, after years of wandering, emerged in western Mexico. Hernando de Soto's great march through the Southeast gave reality to the interior, but he turned away from the pedestrian prospects of settlement and set his hopes on the chance of finding precious stones and minerals. Fray Luis de Cáncer, attempting to establish a mission in western Florida in 1549, was killed by Indians who remembered the exploitation which Soto's march from Tampa Bay involved for them. Finally, after a long gap, Tristán de Luna was officially given the task of occupying the Gulf coast from Florida to the Mississippi and also of conducting overland an expedition to settle Santa Elena on the Carolina coast. The failure of his venture, 1559-61, completes a story of failure and disaster, but it was one which gradually defined, first in outline and then in detail, the coasts and hinterland of the Southeast, and slowly replaced optimistic guesses by firm knowledge, thus preparing the way for a modest but permanent Spanish settlement in the 1560's.

21. The Expeditions
of Ponce de León, 1513–21

A. The 1513 Venture

JUAN PONCE DE LEÓN was concerned in 1508 and the following years with the conquest of the Island of Puerto Rico; in 1513, hearing legends about a land containing the Fountain of Youth, he led an expedition northwards, coasting with the east and west sides of the peninsula. Gonzalo Fernández de Oviedo, Historia General y Natural de las Indias, Bk. xvi, Chap. xi (translated) (Vol. II [1959], 102), thus describes the journey.

Juan Ponce decided to equip himself and set out with two caravels toward the north, and discovered the islands of Bimini which are to the north of the island of Fernandina [Cuba]. And then he learned of the fable of the fountain which rejuvenates or makes old men young. This was in the year 1512. This was revealed and confirmed by the Indians of these parts. And the Captain Juan Ponce and his men, losing their ships, wandered amongst these islands seeking the fountain. This brought mockery from the Indians and great disbelief amongst the Christians, at spending time searching for the fountain. He had news of and saw the mainland, and saw and gave a name to the part of it which enters the sea like a sleeve for the space of eight degrees of longitude and a good fifty of latitude, and he called it La Florida. The point or promontory of it is at twenty-five degrees from the Equator northwards extending to the Northeast. It has the same latitude as the many islands and bays which are called The Martyrs.

B. The 1521 Expedition

LATER, in 1521, after Ponce de León had obtained a grant from the Crown of the land of Florida, he set out to plant a colony and, landing on the west side of the peninsula, was wounded by the Indians. His men abandoned the landing, brought him back to Havana, and there he died (see Vicente Murga Sans, Juan Ponce de León [1959]). Oviedo, Historia General y Natural de las Indias, Bk. xvi, Chap. xii (Vol. II [1959]), 105–106, has this brief (translated) account.

This captain found that land called Florida, then, as I have said, and returned to the island of San Juan (de Puerto Rico), and went to Spain and reported all this to the Catholic King, who rewarded his services by granting him the title of adelantado of Bimini and bestowing other favors on him. In this he was greatly helped by the support of his protector, Pero Núñez de Guzmán, Grand Commander of the Order of Calatrava, who was the tutor of His Serene Highness, Prince Fernando, who is now His Majesty, King of the Romans. And afterwards Ponce de León returned to the island of San Juan and made more suitable preparations to go and settle that land which had been given to him to be his adelantamiento and governorship, and he spent a lot on the fleet; but he returned defeated and wounded by an arrow, and he came to die of this wound in the island of Cuba. He was not the only one to lose his life and time and property on that quest; for many others who followed him died on that voyage or after arrival there, some killed by sickness and others by Indians; and so the adelantado and the adelantamiento came to an end.

22. Antonio de Alaminos Touches Florida, 1517

THE Gulf of Mexico was discovered and explored by Spaniards working around the main coast of Central America from the South. The voyage of Captain Francisco Hernández de Córdoba in 1517 was important because it was a stage in the opening of the way to Mexico. The Indians who defeated his men at Champotón were the most nearly civilized the Spaniards had so far met with. Hernández continued northward from Yucatán and then eastward to gain the western shore of Florida, where the men hoped to recover from their many wounds. The extract comes from Bernal Díaz del Castillo, The True History of New Spain, translated by A. P. Maudsley (5 vols., 1908–16), I, 26–31; with an alteration on line 14.

The pilot Alaminos then took council with the other two pilots, and it was settled that from the place we then were we should cross over to Florida, for he judged from his charts and observations that it was about seventy leagues distant, and that having arrived in Florida they said that it would be an easier voyage and shorter course to reach Havana than the course by which we had come.

We did as the pilot advised, for it seems that he had accompanied Juan Ponce de León on his voyage of discovery to Florida (in 1513). . . . After four days' sail we came in sight of the land of Florida. . . .

When we reached Florida it was arranged that twenty of the soldiers, these whose wounds were best healed, should go ashore. I went with them, and also the pilot, Anton de Alaminos, and we carried with us such vessels as we still possessed, and mattocks, and our crossbows and guns. As the Captain (Córdoba) was very badly wounded and much weakened by the great thirst he had endured, he prayed us on no account to fail in bringing back fresh water as he was parching and dying of thirst, for, as I have already said, the water that we had on board was salt and not fit to drink.

We landed near a creek which opened towards the sea, and the pilot Alaminos carefully examined the coast and said that he had been at this very spot when he came on a voyage of discovery with Juan Ponce de León and that the Indians of the country had attacked them and had killed many soldiers, and that it behoved us to keep a very sharp look out. We at once posted two soldiers as sentinels while we dug deep holes in a broad beach where we thought we should find fresh water, for at that hour the tide had ebbed. It pleased God that we should come on very good water, and so overjoyed were we that what with satiating our thirst, and washing out cloths with which to bind up wounds, we must have stayed there an hour. When, at last, very well satisfied, we wished to go aboard with the water, we saw one of the soldiers whom we had placed on guard coming towards us crying out "To arms! To arms! Many Indian warriors are coming on foot and others down the creek in canoes." The soldier who came shouting and the Indians reached us nearly at the same time.

These Indians carried very long bows and good arrows and lances, and some weapons like swords, and they were clad in deer-skins and were very big men. They came straight on and let fly their arrows and at once wounded six of us, and to me they dealt a slight arrow wound. However, we fell on them with such rapidity of cut and thrust of sword and so plied the crossbows and guns that they left us to ourselves and set off to the sea and the creek to help their companions who had come in the canoes and were fighting hand to hand with the sailors, whose boat was already captured and was being towed by the canoes up the creek, four of the sailors being wounded, and the pilot Alaminos badly hurt in the throat. Then we fell upon them, with the water above our waists, and at the point of the sword, we made them abandon the boat. Twenty of the Indians lay dead on the shore or in the water, and three who were slightly wounded we took prisoners, but they died on board ship. . . .

As soon as we had got the water on board and had hauled up the boats, we set sail for Havana, and during the next day and night the weather was fair and we were near some islands called *Los Martires* among the shoals . . . and the flagship struck the ground when going between the islands . . . and we were in fear of foundering. . . . Ill and wounded as we were we managed to trim the sails and work the pump until the Lord carried us into the Port of Carenas where now stands the city of Havana . . . and when we got to land we gave thanks to God.

23. The Expeditions
of Lucas Vásquez de Ayllón, 1521–26

THE VENTURES of Lucas Vásquez de Ayllón arose, it would seem from sixteenth-century accounts, from the shortage of labor in Hispaniola and the consequent desire to find slaves, notwithstanding the laws against the enslavement of Indians. Ayllón was a legal official in the island and, with a syndicate, equipped several vessels for a voyage to the Bahamas in 1521. In the course of their expedition, perhaps influenced by reports of Ponce de León's first voyage, they explored the mainland coasts of North America well to the north of those already known. They brought back reports of fertile lands, well populated with Indians, a substantial number of whom they carried off as slaves.

Ayllón received authority in 1523 to occupy the land of Chicora these ships had found. He sailed from La Plata, Hispaniola, in July 1526 with three ships and some smaller vessels, and with men and women to found a permanent settlement. He put ashore at the Cape Fear River for a short time, but soon moved up the coast to Winyah Bay where he established the town of San Miguel de Gualdape—the first Spanish settlement intended to be permanent created on the east coast of North America (thought possibly to have been on lower Waccanaw Neck near the Waccanaw River estuary). Misfortunes dogged them: their flagship had been wrecked with many supplies, the land proved swampy, food became desperately scarce. Finally, Ayllón fell ill and died. His associates were unwilling to continue the colony without him and soon deserted it and returned to the Caribbean.

There are accounts of the Ayllón expeditions in Lowery, Spanish Settlements, I, 153–157, 160–168; Paul Quattlebaum, The Land Called Chicora (1956), pp. 7–31. Accounts by Francisco López de Gómara, Historia General de las Indias, I (1932), 89–90, of the first voyage, and by Oviedo, Historia General y Natural de las Indias, IV, 325–326, are given in translation below.

A. The 1521 Expedition

Seven inhabitants of Santo Domingo, among whom was the licentiate Lucas Vásquez de Ayllón, judge of that island, equipped two ships in Puerto de Plata in the year 1520 to go to the Lucayos [Bahamas] for Indians. . . . They went but failed to find men to barter or take by surprise so as to fetch them to their mines, their flocks or their farms (granjerías). And so they resolved to go further north to look for a country where they might find them and not return empty-handed. They reached a land named Chicora and Gualdape, which is in 32° of latitude, and is what is now called the Cape of Santa Elena and the River Jordán. However, some say it was by stress of weather, and not intentionally, that they found their way there. Be it one thing or the other, it is certain that many Indians ran to the shore to see the caravels, as a thing new and strange to them, who have very small boats. Thinking them to be some monstrous fish, and seeing the men come to land bearded and clothed, they fled as fast as they could run. The Spaniards disembarked, hurried after them and took a man and a woman. They clothed them as in Spain and released them so that they might call their people. The king, thereupon, seeing them clothed after this sort, marvelled at their costume, because his own people went about naked or with skins of wild beasts. And he sent fifty men with supplies of provisions to the ships.

Many Spaniards went with them to the king, who gave them guides to explore the land, and wherever they went they gave them things to eat and little presents of boxes (*aforros*), small pearls and silver. They, having seen the riches and the state of the country, and considered what the people were like, and having taken on water and necessary supplies, invited many of them to come to see the ships. The Indians came on board without any thought of treachery. Then the Spaniards raised anchor and set sail, and came with a good prize of Chicorans for Santo Domingo. But on the way they lost one of their two ships. The Indians in the other died shortly afterwards of sorrow and hunger, for they would not eat what the Spaniards gave them. And yet they would eat dogs, asses and other beasts which they found dead and stinking behind the fence (*tras la cerca*) and on the dungheaps.

B. The Last Voyage, 1526

For this reason [delay from a government inspection] he determined to hasten his departure from Puerto de Plata on the north side of that island [Hispaniola], setting out in the middle of July 1526 with a great ship which was the flagship, and another which was called the *Bretona*, one named the *Santa Catalina*, another known as the *Chorruca*, with a brigantine and a patache or barge. Thus there were six sail in all in which there were 500 men, most of them islanders and expert in these regions, with 80 or 90 very good horses and well provided with all the provisions and things which seemed to him to be necessary for the journey.

In the aforesaid manner he sailed directly across and disembarked in a river called the River Jordán, which is 150 leagues more or less to the east of the province of Florida on the same coast of the Main Land. The mouth of this river is situated at $33\frac{2}{3}$ degrees

[33° 40′ N.lat.] on this side of the equator towards the arctic pole. [Ayllón and his fleet were seeking a land which the Indian, Francisco de Chicora, had called Chicora; but this Indian and other interpreters deserted Ayllón and fled into the interior; and Ayllón and his men were never able to find the land of Chicora or any other of the lands named by Francisco de Chicora.]

But the ruin and destruction of this fleet began when the aforesaid flagship on entering the River Jordán was lost with all the provisions (for the people were saved); though the other ships which were smaller came in without danger.

After they had been there for some days, they became discontented with the place and were deserted by their interpreters and guides whom they had brought with them. Then they agreed to go and settle the coast in front, towards the west coast, and they went to a great river called Gualdape (40 or 45 leagues from there, more or less); and there on its bank they established their camp or base, and began to make houses, because there were none, apart from some widely separated hamlets. The land was very flat and marshy, but the river was very strong and had many good fish; its mouth was shallow if the ships did not enter at high tide. And since they had no provisions and could find none in that land, and it was very cold because that land where they stopped is situated at 33 degrees and more and was bare, many people became sick and many died. And then the licenciate [Ayllón] fell ill and God took him to himself, also; he died as a good Catholic, receiving the sacraments and repenting of his sins, his plans and his fleet. And he departed this life on the day of St. Luke, 18th, 1526. [Mutiny brought about the abandonment of the colony, and only about 150 reached the West Indies alive.]

24. The Disastrous Voyage
of Pánfilo de Narváez, 1528–36

ON DECEMBER 11, 1526, Pánfilo de Narváez, a participant in the conquest of Cuba, received a grant to conquer the territories round the Gulf of Mexico from the Rio de las Palmas to the Cape of Florida. He reached *Florida near Tampa Bay on April 14, 1528, and formally annexed the country. He decided to split his forces, assigning to the ships the task of discovering suitable ports between Tampa Bay and the Panuco River, while he, with his land forces, traced the coast from the landward side. The fleet failed to find any trace of Narváez subsequently, the last ship returning in 1529. The land party made its way to the vicinity of modern Tallahassee and then turned south toward Apalachee Bay. In distress from illness and lack of food, they killed their horses and eventually built themselves five large boats. On September 22, 1528, they embarked to sail along the Gulf coast. They passed Pensacola Bay and the estuary of the Mississippi without undue hardship, but at the end of October met strong winds which made their boats unmanageable. The boats parted company and Narváez and four of the boats were never heard of again: that commanded by Gaspar Nuñez Cabeça de Vaca alone made land on the Texas coast near Matagorda Bay on November 6. Cabeça de Vaca's party gradually lost cohesion and after incredible wanderings he, himself, with three others turned up in western Mexico in 1536. Cabeça de Vaca's Relación (Zamora, 1542) is translated in F. W. Hodge and T. H. Lewis, Spanish Explorers in the Southern United States, 1528–1543 (1907), pp. 1–126. Extracts are given from Thomas Buckingham Smith, Relation of Alvar Nuñez Cabeça de Vaca (1871), pp. 19–64, 203–204. Modern narratives are Morris Bishop, The Odyssey of Cabeza de Vaca (1933), Cleve Hallenbeck, Journey and Route of Cabeza de Vaca (1940) and John Upton Terrell, Journey Into Darkness (1962).*

The Governor set sail (from Havana) with four hundred men and eighty horses, in four ships and a brigantine. . . . We came in sight (of Florida) on Tuesday the twelfth of April, and sailed along the coast. On Holy Thursday we anchored near the shore in the mouth of a bay (probably St. Clements Point, west of Tampa Bay) at the head of which we saw some houses or habitations of Indians. . . . The next day the Governor raised ensigns for your Majesty, and took possession in your royal name. . . . The Governor ordered that the brigantine should sail along the coast of Florida and search for the harbor that Miruelo, the pilot, said he knew. . . . The . . . first of May, the Governor . . . said that he desired to penetrate the interior, and that the ships ought to go along the coast until they should come to the port which the pilots believed was very near on the way to the River Palmas. He asked us for our views. I said it appeared to me that under no circumstances ought we to leave the vessels until they were in a secure and peopled harbor. . . . The Governor followed his own judgment

and the council of others. . . . On Saturday, first of May . . .
the Governor ordered to each man going with him, two pounds of
biscuit and half a pound of bacon; and thus victualed we took up
our march into the country. The whole number of men was three
hundred. . . .

We came to a wide and deep river (the Suwannee) with a very
rapid current. As we would not venture to cross on rafts, we made a
canoe for the purpose, and spent a day in getting over. . . . When
we came in view of Apalachen, the Governor ordered that I should
take nine cavalry with fifty infantry and enter the town. . . . We
found a large quantity of maize fit for plucking, and much dry that
was housed; also many deer-skins. . . . The town consisted of
forty small houses. . . . The country where we came on shore
(Tampa Bay) to this town and region of Apalachen (perhaps
round Lake Miccosukee) is for the most part level, the ground of
sand and stiff earth. Throughout are immense trees and open
woods . . . many lakes . . . some troublesome of fording. . . .
It has fine pastures for herds. . . . In view of the poverty of the
land (to the north) . . . we determined to leave that place and go
in quest of the sea, and the town of Aute (at or near modern St.
Marks) . . . where we arrived at the end of nine days' travel from
Apalache. We found all the inhabitants gone and the houses
burned. . . . Having rested two days, the Governor begged me to
go and look for the sea. . . . I sent twenty men to explore the
coast and ascertain its direction. They returned the night after,
reporting . . . that the sea shore (Apalachee Bay) was very distant. . . . (Sickness hampered the move to the coast but boats
were eventually constructed.) We commenced to build on the
fourth (of August), with the only carpenter in the company, and
we proceeded with so great diligence that on the twentieth day of
September five boats were finished, twenty-two cubits in length,
each caulked with fibre of the palmito. . . . Before we embarked
there died more than forty men of disease and hunger. . . . By
the twenty-second of the month of September, the horses had been
consumed, one only remaining; and on that day we embarked . . .
the boats were so crowded that we could not move: so much can
necessity do, which drove us to hazard our lives in this manner,
running into a turbulent sea, not a single one who went having a
knowledge of navigation.

The haven we left bears the name of Bahía de Caballos (St. Marks Bay). . . . Coming out we went . . . to move along the coast in the direction of the river Palmas, our hunger and thirst continually increasing. . . . Sometimes we entered coves and creeks that lay far in, and found them all shallow and dangerous. Thus we journeyed along them thirty days. . . . At the end of this time . . . we saw a small island, and went to it to find water; but our labor was vain as it had none. Lying there at anchor, a heavy storm came up that detained us six days. . . . Although the storm had not ceased, we resolved to . . . adventure the peril of the sea . . . at sunset doubling a point made by the land, we found shelter with much calm (in Pensacola Bay). (They set sail after getting some supplies and fighting with the local Indians.) We discovered a point made by the land, and against a cape opposite, passed a broad river. I cast anchor near a little island forming the point, to await the arrival of the other boats. The Governor did not choose to come up and entered a bay near by in which were a great many islets. We came together there, and took fresh water from the sea, the stream (the Mississippi) entering it in a freshet. . . . Keeping my course . . . I observed two boats, and drawing near I found that the first I approached was that of the Governor. He asked me what I thought we should do. I told him we ought to join the boat which went in advance, and by no means to leave her. . . . He answered that it was no longer a time in which one should command another; but that each should do what he thought best to save his own life; that he so intended to act; and saying this, he departed with his boat. . . . (Cabeza de Vaca kept company with another boat for a time then lost her.) Near the dawn of day, it seemed to me I heard the tumbling of the sea; for as the shore was near, it roared loudly. . . . Near the shore a wave took us, that knocked the boat out of the water the distance of the throw of a crowbar, and from the violence with which she struck, nearly all the people who were in her like dead, were roused to consciousness. Finding themselves near the shore, they began to move on hands and feet, crawling to land into some ravines. There we made fire, parched some of the maize we brought and found rain water. . . . The day on which we arrived was the sixth of November. (Cabeza de Vaca then tells the long story of his adventures in the interior.) . . . After we left the vessels made sail, taking their course onward; but not finding the harbor, they returned. Five leagues below the place at which we debarked, they found the port. . . . Into this haven and along this coast, the three ships passed with the other ship that came from Cuba, and the brigantine, looking for us nearly a year, and not finding us, they went to New Spain.

25. The Mission
of Fray Luis de Cáncer, 1549

AFTER THE failure of Soto's expedition, the Spanish Crown gave up for a time the attempt to establish settlements in eastern North America. Luis Cáncer de Barbastro, however, a Dominican friar and a disciple of Bartolomé de las Casas, resolved to attempt the peaceful conversion of the Florida Indians to Christianity. Obtaining royal permission, he sailed from Vera Cruz in an unarmed ship, the Santa Maria de la Encina, with three other religious and a female interpreter. The ship brought them to Tampa Bay where the Indians, recalling Soto's severities, turned hostile, killing one of the friars and, when he endeavored to make further contact with them, Cáncer himself. This effectually ended the missionary venture, the ship returning to San Juan de Ulua on July 19. There are accounts in Woodbury Lowery, The Spanish Settlements Within the Present Limits of the United States, 1513–1574, I, 411–427, 475–477; V. F. O'Daniel, The Dominicans in Early Florida (1930). The extract (translated) comes from López de Gómera, Historia General de las Indias, I (1932), 98.

Nevertheless they sent Fray Luis Cancel Balvastro [Luis Cáncer de Barbastro] with other Dominican friars who offered to pacify that land and to convert the people and bring them to serve and obey the emperor by their words alone. The friar then set out at the king's cost in 1549. He went on shore with four friars whom he had brought with him and with certain laymen—unarmed sailors— for this was the way they had to begin preaching. There came down to the shore many of the Floridians, who, without listening, clubbed him, with another or two other companions, and ate them and so they died, martyred for preaching the faith of Christ. May He keep them in His Glory. The others took refuge on board ship, preserving themselves to hear confessions as some say. Many who favored the purpose of these friars now recognized that by such means it is difficult to bring the Indians to friendship with us or to our holy faith, although if it could be done it would be better thus.

26. The Luna Colonizing Expeditions, 1559–61

HERNANDO DE SOTO's expedition has been regarded as an undirected thrust into the interior rather than as a contribution to Spanish knowledge of the southeastern coastlands, yet study of its records suggested to the Spaniards that a short and easy route to the hinterland of the Bay of Santa Elena had been found through the Piedmont by way of the Indian territory of Coosa. This was a complete misreading of the evidence, since it was the territory of the Cusabo Indians which lay in this area. Contact with relics of the Ayllón expedition had been made by Soto when he was at Cutífachíqui in the Piedmont between the Savannah and Santee River Valleys; Coosa (in modern Alabama) had been reached only after Soto had crossed the Appalachians and turned south. Continued tales of French privateers using the coast near the Bay of Santa Elena to refit and to trade with the Indians led to the first royally organized attempt to occupy the area. It took a long time to prepare: the decision to make it was taken in December 1557; Luis de Velasco, viceroy of Mexico, selected (in October 1558) Tristán de Luna y Arellano, a veteran of Coronado's expedition, to lead it; and the expedition sailed on June 11, 1559. Besides 300 soldiers it included women, white retainers and Mexican Indian servants, amounting to 1,500 in all. Having established a base at Ochuse on Pensacola Bay, ships and supplies were disrupted by a hurricane in August. Luna was to explore and settle westward as far as the Mississippi, but he had as his first task to reconnoiter the route to Coosa and make a settlement there. Short of food, he moved inland to Manicapana on the Alabama River in February 1560. His advance party reached the territory of the Coosa Indians, on the Coosa River (now Telledega County, Alabama), settled temporarily there, and sent back some corn, but could make no contact with the Atlantic coast or discover any route to Santa Elena. Luna was immobilized until June 1560; his men forced him to return to Ochuse instead of setting off for Coosa in that month: contact was established with Coosa in August and he made another attempt to set out for there, but his men forced him to abandon the attempt. He was finally relieved by Angel de Villafañe in April 1561. Villafañe left a small garrison in Ochuse and went by sea to land at Santa Elena, but his fleet was dispersed by a hurricane in the summer of 1561, without his establishing a colony, and the project was abandoned, although Pedro Menéndez de Avilés made a successful coastal reconnaissance as far north as Chesapeake Bay from which he had returned by September 1561. This was the basis for the successful Spanish occupation of Florida in 1565. There is an account in Lowery, The Spanish Settlements, I, 351–377; the documents and introduction in Herbert I. Priestley, The Luna Papers, 1559–1561 (2 vols., 1928), give the whole story, and see also his biography, Tristán de Luna (1936).

·

A. Tristán de Luna Reports
on his Expedition, 1559–61

A BALD outline of his story was given by Luna in the petition he delivered in Spain in 1561. It is taken from Priestley, The Luna Papers, I, 4–7.

When I, Don Tristán de Luna y Arellano, widower, was in New Spain, the Viceroy, Don Luis de Velasco, having heard of a certain expedition which I had made to Cíbola (with Coronado), ordered me in the name of your Majesty to make the expedition to La Florida. I accepted, and took five hundred and fifty men and one hundred and eighty horses. I took your Majesty's officials, a maestre de campo, captains, and all the other officers necessary for such an enterprise. All these positions were filled by your viceroy, and, besides the great amount which we all spent, I believe that your Majesty must have expended over three hundred thousand pesos (on this expedition). I disembarked my people from the eleven vessels which were given me (August 14, 1559), at a point some eighty or one hundred leagues farther down, toward New Spain, than where Soto landed. I took a good Port which they call Polonza (Ochuse, Pensacola Bay). I then sent out the sargento mayor (Mateo de Sauz), my nephew (Captain Cristóbal Ramírez y Arellano), with a few of the people. They informed me that they had come upon a town [Nanipacana, on the Alabama River] in which they had found some supplies. Inasmuch as these were what I lacked, I left a captain with fifty or sixty men at the port, and with the remainder of the force set out inland, penetrating forty or fifty leagues from the port to where they were awaiting me. Thence I again sent out the sargento mayor, my nephew, some other captains, and two Dominican friars (Brothers Anunciación and Salazar).

[They were to go to Coosa, make a settlement, and from there to make contact with Santa Elena on the coast, preparing the way for moving the whole colony there.] Certain of the captains and the friars whom I mention availed themselves of such wiles with the people they took with them that although the *sargento mayor* strove to establish a settlement as he had been ordered, they would not do so, but persisted in returning. [In fact Luna sent a party in September to recall them.] Nor could I (reach them), although I attempted to do so at two different times (in June before leaving Nanipacana to return to Ochuse, and in August); neither would the *maestre de campo* (Jorge Cerón Saavedra), the officials, nor the captains go with me but persisted in leaving the country and would not remain in it. [Luna was able to hand over to Villafañe only on April 9, 1561, by which time only a few men were left in Ochuse.]

B. A Report on Coosa

FRAY DOMINGO DE LA ANUNCIACIÓN *and others wrote to Luna on August 1, 1560, telling how they found the land of Coosa which they had just reached. The extract is from Priestley,* The Luna Papers, *I, 228–232.*

We reached this settlement of Coosa in sixteen days. Here we found the chief and all his people in their houses, and they made no move to take away their food or women, as if they had talked and had dealings with us before this. We took up our lodging in a small savana one or two arquebus shots' distance from the town. Here they provide us with necessities—I mean corn, beans, and other little things for which we barter. . . . There are also roasting ears and pumpkins, which have their place, so that, blessed be our Lord, there is no lack of food, nor do we even expect to lack it. As to making a settlement, it appears to us that the country is not so well suited for it as we thought. It seems very densely forested, and inasmuch as the Indians have the good part of it occupied, if a settlement were to be made it would be imperative to take their lands from them. So for this reason and for others it is desirable that you come or send orders as to what is to be done. For even though the natives have been observed to be so disposed that they can be utilized profitably, the country is so poor and with such scant opportunities for gainful pursuits that we think it would be difficult to maintain ourselves in it. . . . We are really indebted to these Indians as far as we have seen up to the present; for if twenty or thirty or ten Indians are needed to build a camp or a house they give them, showing good will in the matter. It seems that certain (other) Indians have entered their lands, demanded them and usurped them, and in so doing have caused them injuries and vexations. . . . (These Indians) asked us, as they were our friends, had given us of whatever they had, and had placed themselves under the protection of the king, Don Felipe our lord, that we would show them favor and aid so that those other Indians should not prevent their communication, trade and intercourse thus with their own natural lord.

C. Villafañe Attempts to
Settle Santa Elena, 1561

ANGEL DE VILLAFAÑE relieved Luna at Ochuse in 1561, bringing fresh soldiers and supplies. He left a small garrison in Ochuse under Captain Diego de Biedma, took Luna's unfit men back to Cuba, and set out in June with four ships to explore the coast in the vicinity of Santa Elena and settle a garrison there. Unable to find a harbor, the ships anchored off the Punta de Santa Elena, where Villafañe went ashore and took possession. The ships then sailed north along the coast past the Rio de Canóas and the Rio Jordán, when a storm struck, scattered them and drove them back to the Caribbean. A number of soldiers were examined in Hispaniola in August, their depositions being given in Priestley, The Luna papers, II, 280–311. Extracts are from pp. 294–299 (deposition of Alonso de Montalván).

As soon as Don Tristán had gone, upon the following day Angel de Villafañe caused all the captains and soldiers to be gathered together, and he made a speech to them, saying that he had come by command of his Majesty and the viceroy in his royal name to go to the Punta de Santa Elena . . . and that he wished to designate those who were to go with him and that all whom he should designate those must take oath to him as their captain. . . . When this was done Angel de Villafañe left at the port (Ochuse) Captain (Diego de) Biedma and Antonio Velásquez with fifty men, commanding them not to desert the place. . . . With the rest of the people, who must have been one hundred and sixty in all, he set out for La Havana. . . . The *maestre de campo* remained behind in La Havana, and Angel de Villafañe set out from there in perhaps three months and a half or less, with the ship *San Juan* and a lateen caravel and two frigates. . . . They passed through the (Bahama) Channel with very good weather and went to the Punta de Santa Elena. . . . They anchored at the said point three leagues out at sea because of the shoals which are many. Being thus anchored Angel de Villafañe set out in a frigate with twenty men. He went ashore, and traveled along the shore of the sea and back inland about half a league, looking for the river of the said Punta de Santa Elena until they hit upon it, and there on the bank of the river Angel de Villafañe took possession of that land in the name of His Majesty. . . . They went on, searching by sea and land along that entire coast as far as the Río Jordán and the Río de Canóas up to 34° 30', but they did not find any port or river where ships could be anchored. While they went along performing these duties a hurricane came upon them which lasted an entire night and another day until noon, and on that night they lost the two frigates. . . . The ship *San Juan*, which was at anchor broke loose. . . . The aforesaid Angel de Villafañe, seeing how he was left alone, and realizing the loss which had come upon him, asked the pilot-major what was the nearest land which was peopled with Spaniards; and the pilot said to him that it was the island of La Española, which was four hundred leagues away. So Angel de Villafañe told him that since we were left alone he should turn his prow thither and make for the nearest port.

VI

Jacques Cartier's
River Route into the Interior

THE FIRST serious penetration of the North American continent was achieved, after all, by water, in the course of four French exploring expeditions, three of them led by Jacques Cartier and one by Jean François de La Rocque de Roberval between 1534 and 1543. Verrazzano, Gomes and Rut had all, in their search for a passage into the land mass, missed both the Cabot Strait and the Strait of Belle Isle. French fishermen found the latter and were fishing inside it before 1534—probably news of this water channel to the west, possibly picked up at the Newfoundland Banks fishing ground to which many of the French ships resorted, led Cartier to promote and lead his first expedition. He was able in 1534 to explore the Gulf of St. Lawrence fully and to ascertain the existence of a great river into the interior. In 1535 he took a party of men to settle over the winter near modern Quebec, and with them explored the St. Lawrence River as far as Montreal. The Lachine Rapids acted as a brake to further westward traveling, but he learned a great deal from the Indians of the St. Lawrence Valley about the lands and waters to the north, south and, especially, to the west of the area he explored. He also experienced the deadly cold and scurvy—dangers of the Canadian winter. On his return he could map confidently a thousand miles westward from the entrance to the Strait of Belle Isle as far as Montreal. He maintained that a water passage to the Pacific, however obstructed, was still possible, and, if it was not, a watershed could be reached from the St. Lawrence River system which would give reasonably easy westward access to the ocean. Not until 1541 was he able to muster the colony necessary for the next steps in exploration. Yet his third expedition failed to penetrate the rapids beyond Montreal and to overcome the scurvy of winter; he and his men insisted on returning to France in 1542. The support party under Roberval followed a similar pattern in 1542–43, deserted their settlement in the spring and returned to France to bring this series of ventures to an end. The French had not yet mastered the techniques of the fur trade—which would give them in time both the means to penetrate Indian country and the financial returns with which to maintain permanent posts—nor indeed did they succeed in acclimatizing themselves. The accumulation of data which these expeditions provided was very important

for all the European communities interested in exploring and exploiting North America.
The best edition of the texts of the Cartier-Roberval voyages is that edited by H. P. Biggar, The Voyages of Jacques Cartier (1924). The best narratives are in French, C. A. Julien, Les Voyages de Découverte et les Premiers Établissements (1948), and Marcel Trudel, Histoire de la Nouvelle-France. I. Les Vaines Tentatives, 1524–1603 (1963); Bernard G. Hoffman, Cabot to Cartier (1961), is also useful, as are the articles in the Dictionary of Canadian Biography, I (1965).

27. The First Voyage, 1534

THE NARRATIVE of Cartier's first voyage contained in the first account of the penetration of the interior is a lucid and detailed journal, and it is of vital importance in the revelation of the interior of North America to Europeans. From the time of its first publication in 1556 (in G. B. Ramusio's Navigationi et Viaggi, III, ff. 435–436), it was taken as a guide by other explorers for its information on natural resources, American Indians and climate. It first appeared in English in 1580 in A short and briefe narration of the two navigations . . . to Newe Fraunce (reprinted in facsimile in D. B. Quinn, Richard Hakluyt, Editor [1967]). Extracts are taken from the edition by Biggar, The Voyages of Jacques Cartier, pp. 3–79.

When Sir Charles de Mouy, Knight, Lord of La Meilleraye and Vice-Admiral of France, had received the oaths of the captains, masters and sailors of the vessels, and had made them swear to conduct themselves well and loyally in the King's service, under the command of the said Cartier, we set forth from the harbour and port of St. Malo with two ships of about sixty tons' burden each, manned in all with sixty-one men, on (Monday) April 20 in the said year 1534; and sailing on with fair weather we reached Newfoundland on (Sunday) May 10, sighting land at Cape Bonavista in latitude 48° 30'. . . .

And on (Thursday) the twenty-first of the said month of May we set forth from this (Catalina) harbour with a west wind, and sailed north, one quarter north-east of cape Bonavista as far as the isle of Birds (Funk Island). . . .

In the air and round about are an hundred times as many more as on the island itself. . . . Of these, each of our ships salted four or five casks, not counting those we were able to eat fresh. . . .

On Wednesday the twenty-seventh of the month (of May) we reached the mouth of the bay of Castles (Strait of Belle Isle), but on account of the unfavourable weather and of the large number of icebergs we met with, we deemed it advisable to enter a harbour in the neighbourhood of that entrance called Karpont, where we remained, without being able to leave, until (Tuesday) June 9, when we set forth in order with God's help, to proceed farther on. Karpont (Jacques Cartier Bay) lies in latitude 51° 30′. . . .

On Wednesday June 10 we entered Brest harbour with our ships to get wood and water and trim ship and proceed on beyond the said bay (of Castles). . . .

We came to a small, very deep passage with the land running south-west and with very high shores. It is a good harbour; and a cross was set up there, and it was named St. Servan's harbour (Lobster Bay). . . . Ten leagues farther on there is another good opening somewhat larger and where there are many salmon. We named it St. James's river (Shecatica Bay?). While here we saw a large ship from La Rochelle that in the night had run past the harbour of Brest where she intended to go and fish; and they did not know where they were. . . . If the soil were as good as the harbours, it would be a blessing; but the land should not be called the New Land, being composed of stones and horrible rugged rocks; for along the whole of the north shore (of the Gulf or south shore of Labrador), I did not see one cart-load of earth and yet I landed in many places. Except at Blanc Sablon there is nothing but moss and short, stunted shrub. In fine I am rather inclined to believe that this is the land God gave to Cain. . . .

On . . . Monday the fifteenth we set sail from Brest and set our course towards the south in order to examine the land we saw there. . . .

The . . . sixteenth of the month (of June) we ran along this coast to the south-west, one quarter south, for some thirty-five leagues from cape Double, when we came to a region of very high and rugged mountains, among which was one in appearance like a barn and on this account we named this region (western Newfoundland) the Barn mountains. . . .

(On Friday, June 26, we) came to three islands, two of which were small and as steep as a wall, so that it is impossible to climb to the top. Between these there is a narrow passage. These islands were as completely covered with birds (Bird Islands), which nest there, as a field is covered with grass. . . . Five leagues to the west of these islands was the other island which is about two leagues long and as many in breadth. . . . This island was named Brion Island. In the neighbourhood of these islands the tides are strong and run to all appearance south-east and north-west. I am rather inclined to think from what I have seen that there is a passage between Newfoundland and the Breton's land. If this were so, it would prove a great saving both in time and distance, should any success be met with on this voyage. Four leagues from the said (Brion) island to the west-south-west lies the mainland (the Magdalen islands), which has the appearance of an island surrounded by islets of sand. On it stands a fine cape which we named cape Dauphin, as it is the beginning of the good land. . . .

From Brion island to this place there is fine sandy bottom and an even depth which gradually grows less as one approaches the shore. . . .

And pursuing our course we came in sight of what had looked to us like two islands, which was mainland, that ran south-south-east and north-north-west as far as a very fine headland, named by us cape Orleans (Cape Kildare, Prince Edward Island).

We headed north-east until the next morning (Wednesday), the first day of July . . . and we had sight of cape Orleans and of another cape that lay about seven leagues north, one quarter north-east of it, which we named Indian cape (North Point). . . .

On the following day (Thursday), the second of July, we caught sight of the coast to the north of us which joined that already explored, and we saw that this (mouth of Northumberland strait) was a bay about twenty leagues deep and as many in width. We named it St. Leonore's Bay . . . the third day of July, when the wind came west; and we headed north in order to examine this coast, which was a high land lying to the north-north-east of us beyond the low shores. Between these low shores and the high lands was a large bay and opening, with a depth in some places of fifty-five fathoms and width of about fifteen leagues. On account of this depth and width and of the alteration in the coast-line, we had hopes of discovering here a strait like the one at the strait of Castles. This bay (Chaleur Bay) runs east-north-east and west-south-west. The land along the south side of it is as fine and as good land, as arable and as full of beautiful fields and meadows, as any we have ever seen; and it is as level as the surface of a pond. And that on the north side is a high mountainous shore, completely covered with many kinds of lofty trees; and among others are many cedars and spruce trees, as excellent for making masts for ships of 300 tons and more, as it is possible to find. . . .

On Thursday the eighth of the said month (of July) as the wind was favourable for getting under way with our ships, we fitted up our long-boats to go and explore this (Chaleur) bay; and we ran up it that day some twenty-five leagues. The next day (Friday, July 10), at daybreak, we had fine weather and sailed on until about ten o'clock in the morning, at which hour we caught sight of the head of the bay, whereat we were grieved and displeased. At the head of this bay, beyond the low shore, were several very high mountains. And seeing there was no passage, we proceeded to turn back. . . .

Being certain that there was no passage through this bay, we made sail and set forth from St. Martin's cove on Sunday, July 12, in order to explore and discover beyond this bay. . . . But on the . . . sixteenth . . . we deemed it prudent to go farther up some seven or eight leagues, into a good and safe harbour, which we had already explored with our long-boats. . . . During that time there arrived a large number of savages, who had come to the river (Gaspé basin) to fish for mackerel, of which there is great abundance. . . . On Magdalen's day (July 22), we rowed over in our long-boats to the spot on shore where they were, and went on land freely among them. At this they showed great joy, and the men all began to sing and to dance in two or three groups, exhibiting signs of great pleasure at our coming. . . . We saw a large quantity of mackerel which they had caught near the shore with the nets they use for fishing, which are made of hemp thread, that grows in the country where they ordinarily reside; for they only come down to the sea in the fishing-season, as I have been given to understand. . . .

On (Friday) the twenty-fourth of the said month (of July), we

had a cross made thirty feet high, which was put together in the
presence of a number of the Indians on the point at the entrance to
this harbour, under the cross-bar of which we fixed a shield with
three fleurs-de-lys in relief, and above it a wooden board engraved
in large Gothic characters, where was written LONG LIVE THE KING
OF FRANCE. We erected this cross on the point in their presence
and they watched it being put together and set up. . . .

When we had returned to our ships, the chief, dressed in an old
black bear-skin, arrived in a canoe with three of his sons and his
brother; but they did not come so close to the ships as they had
usually done. And pointing to the cross he (the chief) made us a
long harangue, making the sign of the cross with two of his fingers;
and then he pointed to the land all around about, as if he wished to
say that all this region belonged to him, and that we ought not to
have set up this cross without his permission. . . . When they had
come on board, they were assured by the captain that no harm
would befall them, while at the same time every sign of affection
was shown to them; and they were made to eat and to drink and to
be of good cheer. And then we explained to them by signs that the
cross had been set up to serve as a land-mark and guide-post on
coming into the harbour, and that we would soon come back and
would bring them iron wares and other goods; and that we wished
to take two of his (the chief's) sons away with us and afterwards
would bring them back again to that harbour. And we dressed up
his two sons (Domagaya and Taignoagny) in shirts and ribbons
and in red caps, and put a little brass chain round the neck of each,
at which they were greatly pleased; and they proceeded to hand
over their old rags to those who were going back on shore. To each
of these three, whom we sent back, we also gave a hatchet and two
knives at which they showed great pleasure. . . .

[Between July 25 and August 5, he examined the south shore of
Anticosti before moving into the eastern end of Jacques Cartier
Passage which his boats found to be open to the west.]

And on arriving on board the said vessel, we assembled all the
captains, pilots, masters and sailors to have their opinion and
advice as to what was best to be done. When they had stated one
after the other that considering the heavy east winds that were
setting in, and how the tides ran so strong that the vessels only lost

way, it was not possible then to go farther; and also that as the storms usually began at that season in Newfoundland, and we were still a long way off, and did not know the dangers that lay between these two places, it was high time to return home or else to remain here for the winter; that nevertheless and moreover should a succession of east winds catch us, we should be obliged to remain. When these opinions had been heard, we decided by a large majority to return home. And as it was on St. Peter's day that we had entered that strait, we named it St. Peter's strait. . . .

From that day (Saturday, August 1) until Wednesday (August 5) we had a strong favourable wind and coasted this north shore east-south-east and west-north-west. . . .

From the said Wednesday (August 5) until Saturday (August 8) we had a heavy south-west wind and ran east-north-east, and that day we reached the west coast of Newfoundland between the Barn mountains and cape Double. . . .

And afterwards, that is to say on (Saturday) August 15, the day and feast of the Assumption of Our Lady, we set forth together from the harbour of Blanc Sablon, after hearing mass, and made our way in fine weather as far as mid-ocean . . . we reached the harbour of St. Malo whence we had set forth, on (Saturday) September 5 in the said year (1534).

28. The Second Voyage
and the First Colony, 1535–36

THE NARRATIVE of Cartier's second voyage, recording his detailed exploration of the St. Lawrence Valley and his experiences in wintering in the interior, is of great interest as a record of exploration and an illustration of the hardships which Europeans had to undergo in their first attempts to settle in the interior of North America, with its severe continental winters, and also for the information on Amerindian society obtained by the explorers.

The narrative is the only one of the series to have been published in France at the time, the Brief recit appearing in Paris in 1545. It was published in Italian by Ramusio in 1556 and in English in 1580 (see p. 97 above), and like the story of the first voyage was very influential

with later voyagers. *The extracts given are from Biggar,* Voyages of
Jacques Cartier, *pp. 85–240.*

The second voyage undertaken by the command and wish of the
Most Christian King of France, Francis the First of that name, for
the completion of the discovery of the western lands, lying under
the same climate and parallels as the territories and kingdom of
that prince, and by his orders already begun to be explored; this
expedition carried out by Jacques Cartier, native of St. Malo on the
Island, in Brittany, pilot of the aforesaid prince, in the year
1535–1536. . . .

And on the Wednesday following, May 19, the wind came fair
and in our favour and we set sail with three vessels, namely, the
Grande Hermine of some 100 to 120 tons' burden, on board of
which sailed the Commander (Cartier), with Thomas Fromont as
mate, and Claud de Pontbriant, son of the Lord of Montreal, and
cup-bearer to His Highness the Dauphin, Charles de La Pom-
meraye, John Poulet and other gentlemen. In the second ship,
called the *Petite Hermine* of about sixty tons' burden, went as
captain under Cartier, Mace Jalobert and William Le Marie as
mate; and as captain of the third and smallest vessel named the
Émerillon of some forty tons' burden, went William Le Breton
with Jacques Maingard as mate. . . .

And after separation, we in the commander's vessel had continual headwinds until (Wednesday) July 7, when we sighted
Newfoundland and made land at the isle of Birds. . . .

On (Thursday) July 8, we set sail in fine weather from this
island, and on (Thursday) the fifteenth of that month reached the
harbour of Blanc Sablon, lying inside the bay of Castles (Strait of
Belle Isle), which was the point where we had agreed to meet. We
stayed there awaiting our consorts until (Monday) the twenty-
sixth of the month, on which day they both arrived together. . . .

On (Friday) the thirteenth of that month (August), we set out
from St. Lawrence's bay and heading towards the west, made our
way as far as a cape on the south side (West Point, Anticosti),
which lies some twenty-five leagues west, one quarter south-west of
St. Lawrence's harbour. And it was told us by the two Indians
whom we had captured on our first voyage that this cape formed

part of the land on the south which was an island, and that to the south of it lay the route from Honguedo, where we had seized them when on our first voyage to Canada; and that two days' journey from this cape and island, began the kingdom of the Saguenay, on the north shore as one made one's way towards this Canada. . . .

After passing through the strait (of St. Peter, Jacques Cartier Passage) on the previous night . . . we had sight of land towards the south, which turned out to be a coast with marvellously high mountains. . . . We coasted this south shore from that day (Sunday), until noon on Tuesday, when the wind came out of the west. We then headed north in order to make our way towards the high coast we saw in that direction. And on reaching it, we found that the shore was low and flat at the water's edge, but that beyond this low shore there were mountains. This coast runs east and west, one quarter south-west. Our Indians told us that this was the beginning of the Saguenay and of the inhabited region; and that thence came the copper they call *caignetdaze*. The distance from the south to the north shore is about thirty leagues; and there is a depth of more than 200 fathoms. The two Indians assured us that this was the way to the mouth of the great river of Hochelaga and the route towards Canada, and that the river grew narrower as one approached Canada, and also that farther up, the water became fresh, and that one could make one's way so far up the river that they had never heard of anyone reaching the head of it. . . .

On (Wednesday), September the first we set sail from this harbour (Le Bic) to make our way towards Canada. . . .

On (Monday) the sixth of that month (September), we ran with a favourable wind some fifteen leagues up this river, and came to anchor at an island near the north shore, which here makes a small bay and inlet. In this bay and about this island are great numbers of large turtles. The people of the country also fish near this island for the above-mentioned *Adhothuys*. The current here is as strong as at Bordeaux on the ebbing and flowing of the tide. This (Coudres) island is some three leagues long by two in width. The soil is rich and fertile, and the island is covered with several species of fine large trees. Amongst others we found many hazel-bushes, loaded with hazel-nuts as large as ours and better-tasting, though a little more bitter. On this account we named the island "Hazel-bush island."

On (Tuesday) the seventh of the month, being our Lady's day, after hearing mass, we set out from this (Coudres) island to proceed up stream, and came to fourteen islands which lay some seven or eight leagues beyond Coudres island. This is the point where the province and territory of Canada begins. . . . After we had cast anchor between this large island (Isle of Orleans) and the north shore, we went on land and took with us the two Indians we had seized on our former voyage. . . .

On the morrow, the lord of Canada, named Donnacona (but as chief they call him Agouhanna), came to our ships accompanied by many Indians in twelve canoes. He then sent back ten of these and came alongside our ships with only two canoes. And when he was opposite to the smallest of our three ships (*Émerillon*), this Agouhanna began to make a speech and to harangue us, moving his body and his limbs in a marvellous manner, as is their custom when showing joy and contentment. And when he came opposite to the Captain's vessel, on board of which were Taignoagny and Domagaya, the chief spoke to them and they to him, telling him what they had seen in France, and the good treatment meted out to them there. At this the chief was much pleased and begged the Captain to stretch out his arms to him that he might hug and kiss them, which is the way they welcome one in that country. . . . And the Captain likewise ordered out our long-boats to make our way up the stream with the flood tide, to find a harbour and safe spot in which to lay up the ships. And we went some ten leagues up the river, coasting this island (of Orleans) at the end of which we came to a forking of the waters, which is an exceedingly pleasant spot, where there is a small river and a harbour with a bar, on which at high tide, there is a depth of from two to three fathoms. We thought this river (St. Charles) a suitable place in which to lay up our ships in safety. We named it "Sainte Croix," as we arrived there that day (September 14). Near this spot lives a tribe of which this Donnacona is chief, and he himself resides there. The village is called Stadacona. . . .

On the following day, we set sail with our ships to bring them to the spot called Ste. Croix, where we arrived the next day (Tuesday), the fourteenth of the month. And Donnacona, Taignoagny and Domagaya came to meet us with twenty-five canoes filled with Indians who were coming from the direction whence we had set out and were making towards Stadacona, which is their home. . . . The Captain asked them if they were willing to go with him to Hochelaga, as they had promised and they replied that they were and that it was their intention to go there. . . .

On the sixteenth of that month (September), we placed our two largest vessels inside the harbour and river, where at high water there is a depth of three fathoms, and at low tide, half a fathom. But the bark was left in the roadstead to take us to Hochelaga. . . . And Taignoagny told the Captain that chief Donnacona was annoyed because he (Cartier) intended to go to Hochelaga, and was most unwilling that Taignoagny should accompany him, as he had promised to do: for the river was not worth exploring. To this the Captain made reply, that notwithstanding this he would use his efforts to reach there; for he had orders from the king his master to push on as far as possible. . . .

The following day (Sunday), September 19, we made sail and got under way with the bark (Émerillon) and the two long-boats, as already stated, in order with the tide to push on up the river. . . . And when we had come to anchor some twenty-five leagues from Canada, at a place called Achelacy, which is a narrow passage in the river where the current is swift and the navigation danger-ous, both on account of the rocks as for other causes, there came several canoes to our ships; and among the rest came a great chief of this region, who made a long harangue as he came on board, pointing out to us clearly by signs and in other ways that the river was extremely dangerous a little higher up, and warning us to be on our guard. . . .

From (Sunday), the nineteenth until (Tuesday), the twenty-eighth of the month, we continued to make our way up the river without losing a day nor an hour. During this time we saw and discovered as fine a country and as level a region as one could wish, covered, as before mentioned, with the finest trees in the world. . . .

On (Tuesday) September 28, we reached a large lake (Lake St. Pierre) where for twelve leagues the river widens out to a distance of some five or six leagues. We made our way up this lake that day without finding anywhere a depth of more than two fathoms, neither more nor less. And on reaching the head of this lake, we could see no passage nor outlet. . . .

On the morrow (September 29) our Captain, seeing it was impossible to get the bark past this spot at that season, ordered the long-boats to be fitted out and provisioned, and stores to be put into them for as long a period as possible, and as the long-boats would hold. . . .

And we sailed on in as fine weather as one could wish until (Saturday) October 2, when we arrived at Hochelaga, which is about forty-five leagues from the spot where we had left our bark. . . . And on reaching Hochelaga, there came to meet us more than a thousand persons, both men, women and children, who gave us as good a welcome as ever father gave to his son, making great signs of joy; for the men danced in one ring, the women in another and the children also apart by themselves. . . .

At daybreak the next day (October 3), the Captain, having put on his armour, had his men marshalled for the purpose of paying a visit to the village and home of these people, and to a mountain (Montreal) which lies near the town. The Captain was accompanied by the gentlemen and by twenty sailors, the remainder having been left behind to guard the long-boats. And he took three Indians of the village as guides to conduct them thither. When we had got under way, we discovered that the path was as well-trodden as it is possible to see, and that the country was the finest and most excellent one could find anywhere, being everywhere full of oaks, as beautiful as in any forest in France, underneath which the ground lay covered with acorns. . . . We marched on, and about half a league thence, found that the land began to be cultivated. It was fine land with large fields covered with the corn of the country, which resembles Brazil millet, and is about as large or larger than a pea. They live on this as we do on wheat. And in the middle of these fields is situated and stands the village of Hochelaga, near and adjacent to a mountain, the slopes of which are fertile and are cultivated, and from the top of which one can see for a long distance. We named this mountain "Mount Royal." . . .

As we drew near to their village, great numbers of the inhabitants came out to meet us and gave us a hearty welcome, according to the custom of the country. . . .

On issuing forth from the village we were conducted by several of the men and women of the place up the above-mentioned mountain, lying a quarter of a league away, which was named by us "Mount Royal." On reaching the summit we had a view of the land for more than thirty leagues round about. Towards the north there is a range of mountains (the Laurentides), running east and west and another range (the Adirondacks) to the south. Between these ranges lies the finest land it is possible to see, being arable, level and flat. And in the midst of this flat region one saw the river (St. Lawrence) extending beyond the spot where we had left our long boats. At that point there is the most violent rapid (Lachine Rapids) it is possible to see, which we were unable to pass. And as far as the eye can reach, one sees that river, large, wide and broad, which came from the south-west and flowed near three fine conical mountains, which we estimated to be some fifteen leagues away. And it was told us and made clear by signs by our three local Indian guides, that there were three more such rapids in that river, like the one where lay our long-boats; but through lack of an interpreter we could not make out what the distance was from one to the other. They then explained to us by signs that after passing the rapids, one could navigate along that river for more than three moons. And they showed us furthermore that along the mountains to the north, there is a large river (the Ottawa), which comes from the west like the said river (St. Lawrence). We thought this river (Ottawa) must be the one that flows past the kingdom and province of the Saguenay. . . . The Captain showed them some copper, which they call *caignetdaze*, and pointing towards the said region, asked by signs if it came thence? They shook their heads to say no, showing us that it came from the Saguenay, which lies in the opposite direction. Having seen and learned these things, we returned to our long-boats, accompanied by a large number of these Indians, some of whom, when they saw that our people were tired, took them upon their shoulders, as on horseback and carried them. And on our arrival at the long-boats, we at once set sail to return to the bark, for fear of any misadventure. . . .

And on Tuesday, the fifth of that month (October), we hoisted sail and set forth with our bark and the long-boats to return to the province of Canada and to Ste. Croix harbour, where our ships had been left. . . .

On Monday, October 11, we arrived at the harbour of Ste. Croix

where our ships were lying, and found that the mates and sailors
who had stayed behind, had built a fort in front of the ships,
enclosed on all sides with large wooden logs, planted upright and
joined one to the other, with artillery pointing every way, and in a
good state to defend us against the whole country-side. . . .
  After this, these people used to come day by day to our ships
bringing us plenty of eels and other fish to get our wares. We gave
them in exchange knives, awls, beads and other trinkets, which
pleased them much. . . . The latter (Cartier) was warned by the
chief of the village of Hagouchonda, who had presented him with a
little girl when he was on his way to Hochelaga, to be on his guard
against Donnacona and these two rogues, Taignoagny and Domagaya, who were *Agojuda*, that is to say traitors and rogues, and he
(Cartier) was also warned against them by some of the Indians of
Canada. . . .
  Seeing their malice, and fearing lest they should attempt some
treasonable design, and come against us with a host of Indians, the
Captain gave orders for the fort to be strengthened on every side
with large, wide, deep ditches, and with a gate and drawbridge, and
with extra logs of wood set crosswise to the former. And fifty men
were told off for the night-guard in future, in four watches, and at
each change of watch, the trumpets were to be sounded. These
things were done according to the above orders. . . .
  On our return from Hochelaga with the bark and the long-boats,
we held intercourse and came and went among the tribes nearest to
our ships in peace and friendship, except for a few quarrels now
and then with some bad boys, at which the others were very angry
and much annoyed. And we learned from Chief Donnacona, from
Taignoagny, Domagaya and the others that the above-mentioned
river, named the "river of the Saguenay," reaches to the (kingdom
of the) Saguenay, which lies more than a moon's journey from its
mouth, towards the west-north-west; but that after eight or nine
days' journey, this river is only navigable for small boats; that the
regular and direct route to the (kingdom of the) Saguenay, and the
safer one, is by the river (St. Lawrence) to a point above Hochelaga where there is a tributary, which flows down from the (kingdom of the) Saguenay and enters this river (St. Lawrence) as we
ourselves saw, from which point the journey takes one moon. And
they gave us to understand, that in that country, the natives go

clothed and dressed in woollens like ourselves; that there are many towns and tribes composed of honest folk who possess great store of gold and copper. Furthermore they told us that the whole region from the first-mentioned river up as far as Hochelaga and (the kingdom of the) Saguenay is an island, which is encircled and surrounded by rivers and by the said (St. Lawrence); and that beyond the (kingdom of the) Saguenay, this tributary flows through two or three large, very broad lakes, until one reaches a fresh-water sea, of which there is no mention of anyone having seen the bounds, as the people of the (kingdom of the) Saguenay had informed them; for they themselves, they told us, had never been there. They also informed us that at the place where we had left our bark when on our way to Hochelaga, there is a river (Richelieu) flowing from the south-west, and that along it they likewise journey in their canoes from Ste. Croix (the St. Charles) for one month to a land where ice and snow never come; but in which there are continual wars of one tribe against the other. In that country grow in great abundance oranges, almonds, walnuts, plums and other varieties of fruit. They also told us that the inhabitants of that land were dressed and clothed in furs, like themselves. On inquiring if gold and copper were to be found there, they said no. From these statements, and judging from their signs and the indications they gave us, I am of the opinion that this land lies towards Florida. . . .

From the middle of November (1535) until (Saturday) the fifteenth of April (1536), we lay frozen up in the ice, which was more than two fathoms in thickness, while on shore there were more than four feet of snow, so that it was higher than the bulwarks of our ships. . . . During this period there died (of scurvy) to the number of twenty-five of the best and most able seamen we had. . . .

During the time that sickness and death were holding sway on board our ships, Donnacona, Taignoagny and several others set off, pretending to be going to hunt stags and other animals, which in their language they call *Ajounesta* and *Asquenondo*, as the snow was deep and yet they could paddle along the river (St. Lawrence) where the ice had broken up. Domagaya and the others told us that they (Donnacona etc.) would be gone about a fortnight, which we believed, but they did not return for two months. . . .

On (Friday) April 21, Domagaya came on board our vessels with several fine-looking, powerful Indians whom we had not been in the habit of seeing, and told us that Chief Donnacona would be back on the following day and would bring with him a quantity of deer's meat and other venison. And the next day, the twenty-second of the month, Donnacona did arrive at Stadacona accompanied—why or for what purpose we did not know—by a great number of Indians. . . .

The Captain, on being informed of the large number of Indians at Stadacona, though unaware of their purpose, yet determined to outwit them, and to seize their Chief (Donnacona), Taignoagny, Domagaya and the headmen. And moreover he had quite made up his mind to take Chief Donnacona to France, that he might relate and tell to the king all he had seen in the west of the wonders of the world; for he assured us that he had been to the land of the Saguenay where there are immense quantities of gold, rubies and other rich things, and that the men there are white as in France and go clothed in woollens. . . .

On (Wednesday) May 3, which was the festival of the Holy Cross, the Captain in celebration of this solemn feast, had a beautiful cross erected some thirty-five feet high, under the cross-bar of which was attached an escutcheon, embossed with the arms of France, whereon was printed in Roman characters: LONG LIVE FRANCIS I. BY GOD'S GRACE KING OF FRANCE. And that day about noon several persons arrived from Stadacona, both men, women and children, who told us that Chief Donnacona with Taignoagny, Domagaya and the rest of their party were on their way, which pleased us, as we were in hopes of being able to capture them. They arrived about two o'clock in the afternoon . . . our Captain proceeded to call to his men to seize them. At this they rushed forth and laid hands upon the chief and the others whose capture had been decided upon. The Canadians, beholding this, began to flee and to scamper off like sheep before wolves, some across the river, others into the wood, each seeking his own safety. When the above-mentioned had been captured and the rest had all disappeared, the chief and his companions were placed in safe custody. . . .

On Saturday, May 6, we set sail from Ste. Croix harbour and came to anchor at the foot of the island of Orleans, some twelve leagues from Ste. Croix. And on Sunday we reached Coudres island, where we remained until Monday, the fifteenth of the month. . . .

On the following day (Tuesday) May 16, we set sail from Coudres island, and came to anchor at an island lying some fifteen leagues below Coudres island. . . . And there we remained until (Sunday) the twenty-first of the month, when the wind came fair; and we made such good headway each day that we passed down as far as Honguedo, between the island of Assumption (Anticosti) and this Honguedo, which passage had never been discovered. And we ran on until we came opposite cape Pratto (or Meadow), which is the entrance to Chaleur bay. And as the wind was fair and entirely in our favour, we carried sail both night and day. And on the morrow, we found we were heading straight for the middle of Brion island, which was what we wished in order to shorten our route. . . . (Thursday), June 1. And (setting sail that day) we came to a high shore (Cape Breton island) lying south-east of this (Brion) island, which appeared to us to be an island, which we coasted for some twenty-two leagues. . . . This coast (of Cape Breton island) which is high and flat, we saw to be mainland, which ran north-west. . . . .

On Sunday, the fourth of that month (of June), which was the feast of Whitsuntide, we came in sight of the coast of Newfoundland, which runs east-south-east, and is distant some twenty-two leagues from the above cape (North). . . . And on Monday, the nineteenth of that month (of June), we set forth from this harbour (Renewse) and were favoured at sea with such good weather that we reached St. Malo on (Sunday) July 16, 1536.

29. The Voyage
of Richard Hore, 1536

IN 1536 a somewhat puzzling voyage was undertaken by Richard Hore, a London merchant. Hore induced a number of young London gentlemen to embark in two ships on a voyage to America. It seems possible, since they had a Breton pilot, Alain Moyne, on board, that the object was to follow the route taken by Jacques Cartier in 1534 through the Strait of Belle Isle into the Gulf of St. Lawrence. The ships revictualed with seabirds at Funk Island on the Newfoundland coast as Cartier had done. It would appear that one ship penetrated the Strait but ran out of supplies on the southern coast of Labrador (or northern Newfoundland). The men eventually resorted to cannibalism, but were able to exchange ships by force with a French fisherman and returned home much enfeebled. The other ship, the William of London—master, Richard Elyot—on which both Hore and Alain Moyne sailed, evidently turned back quite soon and proceeded down the Newfoundland coast to catch cod at the "Isle of Spear" (Spear Island), eventually returning to England with a leaking ship and a cargo of cod. It would seem that the failure to carry through this voyage efficiently discouraged other Englishmen from following the French into the St. Lawrence.

The documents in Richard Hakluyt, The principall navigations (1589), 517–519 (extracted below), are unsatisfactory, resting on the recollections of two elderly survivors fifty years later. See also Williamson, The Voyages of the Cabots, pp. 112–115, 268–271; E. G. R. Taylor, "Master Hore's Voyage of 1536," Geographical Journal, LXXVII (1933), 469–470; and "John Rut," in Dictionary of Canadian Biography, I (1965).

One master Hore of London, a man of goodly stature and of great courage, and given to the studie of Cosmographie, in the 28. yeere of king Henry the 8. and in the yeere of our Lord 1536. encouraged divers gentlemen and others, being assisted by the kings favour and good countenance, to accompany him in a voyage of discoverie upon the Northwest partes of America: wherein his perswasions tooke such effect, that within short space many gentlemen of the innes of court, and of Chauncerie, and divers other of good worship desirous to see the strange things of the world, very willingly entered into the action with him. . . . The whole number that went in the two tall shippes aforesayd, to wit, the Trinitie and the Minion,[1] were about six score persons, whereof 30 were gentlemen, which all were mustered in warlike maner at Gravesend, and after receiving of the sacrament, they embarked themselves in the end of Aprill, 1536.

From the time of their setting out from Gravesende, they were very long at sea, to witte, above two moneths, and never touched any lande until they came to part of the West Indies about Cape

1. Actually, the William and the Trinity.

Breton, shaping their course thence Northeastwardes, untill they came to the Island of Penguin [Funk Island, Newfoundland], which is very full of rocks and stones, whereon they went and founde it full of great foules white and gray, as bigge as geese,[2] and they saw infinite numbers of their egges. They drave a great nomber of the foules into their boates upon their sailes. . . .

Master Oliver Dawbeny, which . . . was in this voyage, and in the Minion,[3] tolde Master Richard Hakluyt of the middle Temple these things following: to wit, That after their arrivall in New-found land, and having bene there certaine dayes at ancre, and not having seene any of the naturall people of the Countrey, the same Dawbeny walking one day on the hatches, spied a boat with Savages of those partes, rowing downe the bay towarde them, to gase upon the shippe and our people . . . they manned out a shipboate to meete them and take them. But they spying our ship-boate making towards them, returned with maine force & fled. . . .

And further, the said Master Dawbeny told him, that lying there they grewe into great want of victuals, and that they found small reliefe, more then that they had from the nest of an Osprey, that brought hourely to her yong great plentie of divers sorts of fishes. But such was the famine that increased amongst them from day to day, that they were forced to seeke to relieve themselves of rawe herbes and rootes that they sought on the maine: but the famine increasing, and the reliefe of herbes being to little purpose to satisfie their insatiable hunger, in the fields and deserts here and there, the fellow killed his mate . . . and cutting out pieces of his body . . . broyled the same on the coles and greedily devoured them.

By this meane the company decreased. . . . And such was the mercie of God, that . . . there arrived a French shippe in that port, well furnished with vittaile, and such was the policie of the English that they became masters of the same, and changing ships and vitayling them, they set saile to come into England.

In their journey they were so farre Northwards, that they sawe mightie Islands of yce in the sommer season, on which were haukes

2. The Great Auk.
3. Apparently the *Trinity*.

and other foules to rest themselves being wearie of flying over farre from the maine. . . . They arrived at S. Ives in Cornewall about the ende of October.

30. The Third and Fourth Voyages and the End of the Colonizing Attempt, 1541–43

CARTIER INTENDED *in 1541 to settle a permanent colony at or near the site he had occupied in 1535–36. Though he began well, winter again took heavy toll of his men, the Indians turned hostile and his men, having collected much mineral ore and supposed precious stones, insisted on returning in 1542, refusing to turn back when they met the relief expedition under Roberval at Newfoundland. Roberval stepped into Cartier's place, though we know little of his colony. Once again the men refused to stay longer than a single winter, and so the venture was abandoned in 1543. The ore and stones proved worthless. These experiences gave the French much knowledge of Canada which they were able to employ in building up a summer fur trade with the Indians, but they did not encourage them to attempt to establish further colonies there in the sixteenth century.*

Incomplete narratives, all that survive, of both expeditions appeared in English in Hakluyt. The principal navigations, III (1600), 332–336 (reprinted VIII [1904], 263–289), from which the extracts are taken.

A. Cartier, 1541–42

King Francis the first . . . resolved to send the sayd Cartier his Pilot thither againe, with John Francis de la Roche, Knight, Lord of Roberval, whome hee appointed his Lieutenant and Governour in the Countreys of Canada and Hochelaga, and the sayd Cartier Captaine generall and leader of the shippes, that they might discover more than was done before in the former voyages, and attaine (if it were possible) unto the knowledge of the Countrey of Saguenay, whereof the people brought by Cartier, as is declared, made mention unto the King, that there were great riches, and very good countreys. And the King caused a certaine summe of money to be delivered to furnish out the sayd voyage with five shippes. . . . After these things thus dispatched, the winde comming faire,

the foresayd five ships set sayle together well furnished and victualled for two yeare, the 23, of May 1540 [correctly 1541] . . .
untill at length at the ende of one moneth wee met all together at
the Haven of Carpont (Grand Kirpon), in Newfoundland . . .
wee arrived not before the Haven of Saincte Croix in Canada
(where in the former voyage we had remayned eight monethes)
untill the 23 day of August. In which place the people of the
Countrey came to our shippes, making shew of joy for our arrivall,
and namely he came thither which had the rule and government of
the Countrey of Canada, named Agona, which was appointed king
there by Donacona. . . . After which things the sayd Captaine
(Cartier) went with two of his boates up the river, beyond Canada
and the Port of Saincte Croix, to view a Haven and a small river,
which is about 4 leagues higher: which he found better and more
commoditous to ride in and lay his ships, then the former. And
therefore he returned and caused all his ships to be brought before
the sayd river, and at a lowe water he caused his Ordinance to bee
planted to place his ships in more saftie, which he meant to keepe
and stay in the Countrey which were three. . . .

The sayd River is small, not past 50 pases broad, and shippes
drawing three fathoms water may enter in at a full sea; and at a low
water there is nothing but a chanell of a foote deepe or thereabout.
On both sides of the said River there are very good and faire
grounds, full of as faire and mightie trees as any be in the world,
and divers sorts, which are above tenne fathoms higher then the
rest, and there is one kind of tree above three fathoms about,
which they in the Countrey call Hanneda, which hath the most
excellent vertue of all the trees of the world. . . . To bee short, it
is as good a Countrey to plow and manure as a man should find or
desire. We sowed seedes here of our Country, as Cabages, Naveaus,
Lettises and others, which grew and sprong up out of the ground in
eight dayes. The mouth of the river is toward the South, and it
windeth Northward like unto a snake: and at the mouth of it
toward the East there is a high and steepe cliff (Cap Rouge),
where we made a way in manner of a payre of staires, and aloft we
made a Fort (Charlesbourg Royal) to keepe the nether Fort and
the ships, and all things that might passe as well by the great as by
this small river. Moreover a man may behold a great extension of

ground apt for tillage, straite and handsome and somewhat enclining toward the South, as easie to be brought to tillage as I would desire, and very well replenished with faire Okes and other trees of great beauty, no thicker than the Forrests of France. Here wee set twenty men to worke, which in one day had laboured about an acre and a halfe of the said ground, and sowed it part with Naveaus or small Turneps, which at the ende of eight dayes, as I said before, sprang out of the earth. And upon that high cliffe wee found a faire fountaine very neere the sayd Fort: adjoyning whereunto we found good store of stones, which we esteemed to be Diamants. On the other side of the said mountaine and at the foote thereof, which is towards the great River is all along a goodly Myne of the best yron in the world, and it reacheth even hard unto our Fort, and the sand which we tread on is perfect refined Myne, ready to be put into the fornace. And on the waters side we found certaine leaves of fine gold as thicke as a mans nayle. . . .

The sayd Captaine . . . determined . . . to make a voyage with two boates furnished with men and victuals to goe as farre as Hochelaga, of purpose to view and understand the fashion of the Saults of water, which are to be passed to goe to Saguenay, that hee (Cartier) might be the readier in the spring to passe farther. . . . And wee sailed with so prosperous a wind, that we arrived the eleventh day of the moneth (of September 1541) at the first Sault of water (Ste. Marie), which is two leagues distant from the Towne of Tutonaguy (Hochelaga). And after wee were arrived there, wee determined to goe and passe as farre up as it was possible with one of the boates, and that the other should stay there till it returned: and wee double manned her to rowe up against the streame of the said Sault (the Lachine Rapids). And after wee had passed some part of the way from our other boate, wee found badde ground and great rockes and so great a current, that wee could not possibly passe any further with our Boate. And the Captaine resolved to goe by land to see the nature and fashion of the Sault. And after that we were come on shore, wee founde hard by the water side a way and beaten path going toward the sayde Saultes, by which wee tooke our way. And on the sayd way, and soone after we found an habitation of people which made us great cheere, and entertained us very friendly. And after that he (Cartier) had signified unto them, that wee were going toward the Saults, and that wee desired to goe to (the kingdom of) Saguenay, foure young men went along with us to showe us the way, and they brought us so farre that wee came to another village or habitation of good people, which dwell over against the second Sault, which came and brought us of their victuals, as Pottage and Fish, and offered us of the same. After that the Captaine had enquired of them as well by signes as wordes, how many more Saults wee had to passe to goe to Saguenay, and what distance and way it was thither, this people shewed us and gave us to understand, that wee were at the second Sault, and that there was but one more to passe, that the River was not navigable to goe to Saguenay, and that the sayd Sault was but a third part farther than we had travailed, shewing us the same with certaine little stickes, which they layed upon the ground in a certaine distance, and afterwards layde other small branches between both, representing the Saults. And by the sayde marke, if their saying be true, it can be but six leagues by land to passe the sayd Saults.

B. Roberval, 1542–43

Sir John Francis de la Roche, knight, lord of Roberval, appoynted by the king as his Lieutenant general in the Countreis of Canada, Saguenay, and Hochelaga, furnished 3. tall Ships, chiefly at the kings cost: and having in his fleete 200 persons, aswel men as women, accompanied with divers gentlemen of qualitie, as namely with Monsieur Saine-terre his lieutenant, l'Espiney his Ensigne, captaine Guinecourt, Monsieur Noire fontaine Dieu lamont, Frote, la Brosse, Francis de Mire, la Salle, and Roieze and John Alfonse of Xanctoigne an excellent pilot, set sayle from Rochel the 16 of April 1542 . . . wee could not reach Newfound lande, untill the seventh of June. The eight of this Moneth wee entred into the Rode of Saint John (St. John's Harbour), where wee founde seventeene Shippes of fishers. While wee made somewhat long abode heere, Jacques Cartier and his company returning from Canada, whither hee was sent with five sayles the yeere before, arrived in the very same Harbour. Who, after hee had done his duetie to our Generall, tolde him that hee had brought certaine Diamonts, and a

quantitie of Golde ore, which was found in the Countrey. Which
ore the Sunday next ensuing was tryed in a Furnace, and found to
be good.

Furthermore, hee enformed the Generall that hee could not
with his small company withstand the Savages, which went about
dayly to annoy him: and that this was the cause of his returne into
France. . . . At length . . . wee . . . finally arrived foure
leagues Westward of the Isle of Orleans. In this place wee found a
convenient Harbour for our shipping, where wee cast anchor, went
a shoare with our people, and chose out a convenient place to
fortifie our selves in, fitte to commaund the mayne River, and of
strong situation against all invasion of enemies. . . . The sayde
Generall at his first arrivall built a fayre Fort (France Roy on the
site of Charlesbourg Royal), neere and somewhat Westward above
Canada, which is very beautifull to beholde, and of great force,
situated upon an high mountaine, wherein there were two courtes
of buyldings, a great Towre, and another of fortie or fiftie foote
long: wherein there were divers Chambers, on Hall, a Kitchine,
houses of office, Sellers high and lowe, and neere unto it were an
Oven and Milles and a stoove to warme men in, and a Well before
the house. . . . There was also at the foote of the mountaine
another lodging, part whereof was a great Towre of two stories
high, two courtes of good buylding, where at the first all our victuals, and whatsoever was brought with us was sent to be kept; and
neere unto that Towre there is another small river. In these two
places above and beneath, all the meaner sort was lodged. . . .

[The narrative breaks off after relating that Roberval went up
river "toward the said province of Saguenay" on June 5.]

VII

Spaniards Reconnoiter
the Interior

By 1540 Spaniards had behind them a great reservoir of experience in the exploration of the interior of Central and South America which enabled them to embark on the search of the interior of North America for settled Amerindian societies and mineral wealth comparable with what they had found elsewhere. The logistics of penetration were by then well known. Where supplies could not be carried by sea along the coast then stock had to be taken on the hoof, in the form of either pigs or sheep as basic resources. When long treks were needed, human porterage was essential if Spaniards were not to be worn down by the burdens of equipment and supplies, so that slaves or bearers must be available. Horses had also been shown to be an invaluable asset in war and, where the ground was suitable, for movement. Forces of 500 men or a little more were about the optimum number which could be kept moving and yet be adequate to supply losses through war, disease and inadequate food so that an expedition should not become so small as to be unduly vulnerable. The Spaniards had, above all, learned confidence. A few hundred men, it had been shown in Mexico, Peru, New Granada and elsewhere, made up a force, if adequately commanded, capable of meeting and defeating anything that Amerindian enemies might muster.

Before Spaniards ventured into the interior in strength they had defined, as has been shown, the periphery of the coastline in the Southeast and they had done the same in the Southwest. The Pánuco River and the desert area to the north of it delimited reasonably clearly the northern boundary of Mexico on the east. There was no such border area yet evident in the West where the extension of Spanish rule and reconnaissance northwestward had not yet met a clear boundary; but the Gulf of California, recently charted, marked a reasonably well-defined zone along the coast.

The culmination of Spanish expansion in the Southwest and of a long period of probing in the Southeast was a pincer movement from east and west which, taking place almost simultaneously from both directions, revealed the great extent of land which lay between Florida and the Gulf of California. Just as the earlier definition of the Gulf and southeastern Atlantic coasts was the inevitable consequence of the occupation of the Caribbean Islands and of the valley of Mexico, so the move to the north over such a wide front on both east and west was a consequence of the occupation of Mexico from sea to sea. Pánfilo de Narváez had received a grant to conquer and occupy the lands between Mexico and Florida in 1527. His expedition disappeared into the American wilderness after leaving its base at Tampa in 1528. In 1536, four battered figures, led by one who proved to be Alvar Nuñez Cabeça de Vaca, a leading member of the Narváez expedition, entered Spanish territory in northwestern Mexico. Cabeça de Vaca's narrative of lengthy wanderings was one of the elements which lay behind the organization of the expedition under Francisco Vásquez de Coronado in 1540, though Fray Marcos de Niza had also brought back news of Indian cities to the north after a reconnaissance in 1539. Meantime in the East, Hernando de Soto, who had served successfully in Central America and Peru, took up Narváez's grant in 1539, landing with 600 men at Charlotte Harbor in Florida on May 28. Until March 1540 Soto and his men explored the northern and western parts of Florida before working their way up the Piedmont to the Savannah River. But, finding no cities or gold, Soto turned westward and crossed the Appalachian Mountains into the Tennessee River Valley. During this time Coronado had been mustering at Culiacán, from which he set out on April 22, 1540, with his advance guard, leaving the main body to follow in May. Early in July Coronado sighted the first of the Seven Cities of Cíbola, the Zuni pueblo of Hawikuk, a bitter disappointment to the Spaniards who expected something more like the Tenochtítlan Cortés had found. By this time Soto was working southeastwards by way of the river valleys toward the Gulf of Mexico where ships were to await him with supplies; but losses from Indian attacks and his own pride obliged him to ignore the ships and keep the knowledge of their return with supplies from Cuba from his men. He then struck far to the northwest, wintering from December 1540 to March 1541 in the eastern part of the state of Mississippi. Coronado, after capturing Hawikuk in July 1540, had ordered up his main forces and from his base a party discovered the Grand Canyon, while others made contact with bison herds and followed the Rio Grande to Tiguex, beyond modern Albuquerque. A captured Indian told tales of a rich land, Quivira, to the east. Coronado wintered at Tiguex (Mohi), suppressed pueblo resistance to his plundering and set out eastwards. The expedition wandered into eastern Kansas, Quivira being no more than another tribal center, and returned late in the year to New Mexico. In May 1541, Soto reached the Mississippi at Sunflower Landing and crossed after boats had been constructed. He wandered northwestwards into Arkansas and at his westernmost limit was no great distance from Coronado's most eastward terminus. Little more than ten days march from Quivira southeastward would have probably enabled Coronado to cross his path. Indeed, he made contacts with Indians who were aware of Soto's westward advance.

Eventually Soto turned southeastward and wintered at Utiangue on the Ouachita River from November 1541 to March 1542. Coronado, wintering at Alcanfor in the pueblo country, had no further objectives and set out on his return in the spring of 1542, reaching Culiacán safely in June. Soto also set out in the spring to return southeastward to the Mississippi, which he reached but, worn out, died there on May 21, 1542. Deterred by swamps from further progress down the river, the new leader, Luis de Moscoso, first took the men westward in search of a land route to Mexico but was eventually forced to return to the Mississippi. From there, by constructing boats for the river passage and the coastal voyage, Moscoso eventually brought 310 men to Pánuco on September 10, 1543. Within four years, from 1539 to 1543, the greater part of south-central North America had been traversed by European exploring missions.

Soto had revealed the mountainous backbone of the East, the Appalachians, and the complex river systems which lay to the west of the mountains, culminating in the great river, the Mississippi, hitherto known only at its mouth. Much of his wandering had been following vague tales of precious metals or searching for food supplies in Indian hands. Well before his death, Soto had lost any clear objective—pride alone kept him going. Coronado was in some ways more fortunate and also more realistic. The pueblo country of New Mexico gave him a secure, if not always friendly, base; but like Soto's, his distant wanderings became in the end a pointless search for riches in the widening and empty plains. The best he could do was to return. To Spanish officials, in Mexico and at home, both expeditions had revealed a worthless land. Reports of agricultural riches were swamped by the failures to find cities and golden kingdoms in either the East or West. In official Spanish policy the North American interior could be written off, though the memory of dramatic journeys into unknown territory remained, and provided, with missionary enterprises, incentives for the revival of exploration in the West in the 1580's. In the East the Spaniards were to concentrate thereafter almost wholly on the coastline.

Narratives of the Cabeça de Vaca, Soto and Coronado expeditions are conveniently combined in Hodge and Lewis, Spanish Explorers in the Southern United States, 1528–1543. The basic text for the Soto expedition, that of the anonymous Portuguese member of the expedition, is best edited by James Alexander Robertson, True relation of the hardships suffered by Governor Fernando de Soto and certain Portuguese gentlemen during the discovery of the Province of Florida, now newly set forth by a Gentleman of Elvas (2 vols., 1933). The basic texts on Coronado were edited by G. P. Winship, "The Coronado Expedition, 1540–1542," in Smithsonian Institution, Bureau of American Ethnology, Fourteenth Report (1896), pp. 329–637, and the best modern edition is

George P. Hammond and Agapito Rey, Narratives of the Coronado Expedition, 1540–1542 (1940).
The route of the Soto expedition will be found authoritatively traced in U.S. De Soto Expedition Commission, Final Report (1939), and briefly summarized in John R. Swanton, The Indians of the Southeastern United States, Smithsonian Institution, Bureau of American Ethnology, Bulletin 137 (1946), pp. 39–59. There is no adequate modern narrative. For Coronado, Herbert E. Bolton, Coronado, Knight of Pueblos and Plains (1949), and A. Grove Day, Coronado's Quest (1940, repr. 1964), provide reliable accounts. The documentation of the revived Spanish penetration of the Southwest after 1580 is authoritatively given in works edited by George P. Hammond and Agapito Rey, The Rediscovery of New Mexico, 1580–1594 (1966), and Don Juan de Oñate Colonizer of New Mexico, 1595–1628 (2 vols., 1955).

31. Hernando de Soto
Explores the Southeast, 1540–43

So MUCH of Soto's expedition appears inconsequent that the reader is likely to get as lost as Soto frequently was himself. The Gentleman of Elvas in his famous narrative conveys a sense of continuous movement, purposeful in the shorter run, aimless in longer perspective, which is difficult to illustrate in short extracts. The selection given here covers the arrival of the expedition, after a march along the Piedmont, at the Savannah River, the crossing of the Appalachians (of which little is made in the narrative), ending with the beginnings of Soto's progress along the Tennessee River Valley.

On Sunday, the 18th day of May, in the year 1539, the Adelantado sailed from Havana with a fleet of nine vessels, five of them ships, two caravels, two pinnaces; and he ran seven days with favorable weather. On the 25th of the month, being the festival of Espíritu Santo, the land was seen, and anchor cast a league from shore, because of the shoals. On Friday, the 30th, the army landed in Florida, two leagues from the town[1] of an Indian chief named Ucita. Two hundred and thirteen horses were set on shore, to unburden the ships, that they should draw the less water; the seamen only remained on board, who going up every day a little

1. Ucita, on the point at the mouth of Charlotte Harbor, Florida.

with the tide, the end of eight days brought them near to the town.

So soon as the people were come to land, the camp was pitched on the sea-side, nigh the bay, which goes up close to the town. Presently the captain-general, Vasco Porcallo, taking seven horsemen with him, beat up the country half a league about, and discovered six Indians, who tried to resist him with arrows, the weapons they are accustomed to use. The horsemen killed two, and the four others escaped, the country being obstructed by bushes and ponds, in which the horses bogged and fell, with their riders, of weakness from the voyage. At night the Governor, with a hundred men in the pinnaces, came upon a deserted town; for, so soon as the Christians appeared in sight of land, they were descried, and all along on the coast many smokes were seen to rise, which the Indians make to warn one another. The next day, Luis de Moscoso, master of the camp, set the men in order. The horsemen he put in three squadrons—the vanguard, battalion, and rearward; and thus they marched that day and the next, compassing great creeks which run up from the bay; and on the first of June, being Trinity Sunday, they arrived at the town of Ucita[2], where the Governor tarried.

The town was of seven or eight houses, built of timber, and covered with palm leaves. The chief's house stood near the beach, upon a very high mount made by hand for defence; at the other end of the town was a temple, on the top of which perched a wooden fowl with gilded eyes, and within were found some pearls of small value, injured by fire, such as the Indians pierce for beads, much esteeming them, and string to wear about the neck and wrists. The Governor lodged in the house of the chief, and with him Vasco Porcallo and Luis de Moscoso; in other houses, midway in the town, was lodged the chief castellan, Baltasar de Gallegos, where were set apart the provisions brought in the vessels. The rest of the dwellings, with the temple, were thrown down, and every mess of three or four soldiers made a cabin, wherein they lodged. The ground about was very fenny, and encumbered with dense thicket and high trees. The Governor ordered the woods to be felled the distance of a crossbow-shot around the place, that the

2. Hirriga, on the northeast arm of the harbor.

horses might run, and the Christians have the advantage, should the Indians make an attack at night. In the paths, and at proper points, sentinels of foot-soldiers were set in couples, who watched by turns; the horsemen, going the rounds, were ready to support them should there be an alarm. . . .

The Governor sent two men on horseback, with word to those in the rear that they should advance rapidly, for that the way was becoming toilsome and the provisions were short. He came to Cale and found the town abandoned; but he seized three spies, and tarried there until the people should arrive, they travelling hungry and on bad roads, the country being very thin of maize, low, very wet, pondy, and thickly covered with trees. . . . While the people should be coming up, the Governor ordered all the ripe grain in the fields, enough for three months, to be secured. In gathering it three Christians were slain. One of two Indians who were made prisoners stated that seven days' journey distant was a large province, abounding in maize, called Apalache. . . .

On the eleventh day of August, in the year 1539, the Governor left Cale, and arrived to sleep at a small town called Ytara, and the next day at another called Potano, and the third at Utinama, and then at another named Malapaz. . . . On the seventeenth day of August they arrived at Caliquen, where they heard of the province of Apalache, of Narváez having been there and having embarked, because no road was to be found over which to go forward, and of there being no other town, and that water was on all sides. Every mind was depressed at this information, and all counselled the Governor to go back to the port, that they might not be lost, as Narváez had been, and to leave the land of Florida; that, should they go further, they might not be able to get back, as the little maize that was yet left the Indians would secure: to which Soto replied, that he would never return until he had seen with his own eyes what was asserted, things that to him appeared incredible. . . .

We marched five days, passing through some small towns, and arrived at Napetaca on the fifteenth day of September. . . . On the twenty-third day of September the Governor left Napetaca, and went to rest at a river, where two Indians brought him a deer from the cacique of Uzachil; and the next day, having passed through a large town called Hapaluya, he slept at Uzachil. He found no person there; for the inhabitants, informed of the deaths at Napetaca, dared not remain. . . . From Uzachil the Governor went towards Apalache, and at the end of two days' travel arrived at a town called Axille. . . . On the fourth day of the week, Wednesday of St. Francis,[3] the Governor crossed over and reached Uitachuco, a town subject to Apalache, where he slept. He found it burning, the Indians having set it on fire. Thenceforward the country was well inhabited, producing much corn, the way leading by many habitations like villages. Sunday, the twenty-fifth of October,[4] he arrived at the town of Uzela,[5] and on Monday at Anhayca Apalache, where the lord of all that country and province resided. . . . There were other towns which had much maize, pumpkins, beans, and dried plums of the country, whence were brought together at Anhayca Apalache what appeared to be sufficient provision for the winter. . . .

Informed that the sea was eight leagues distant, the Governor directly sent a captain thither, with cavalry and infantry, who found a town called Ochete, eight leagues on the way; and, coming to the coast, he saw where a great tree had been felled, the trunk split up into stakes, and with the limbs made into mangers. He found also the skulls of horses. With these discoveries he returned, and what was said of Narváez was believed to be certain, that he had there made boats, in which he left the country, and was lost in them at sea. Presently . . . the Governor directed Francisco Maldonado, captain of infantry, to run the coast to the westward with fifty men, and look for an entrance; proposing to go himself in that direction by land on discoveries. . . .

On Wednesday, the third of March, in the year 1540, the Governor left Anhaica Apalache to seek Yupaha. He had ordered his men to go provided with maize for a march through sixty leagues of desert. . . . The Governor left Capachiqui, passing through a desert; and on Wednesday, the twenty-first of the month, came to Toalli. . . . The Governor left Toalli on the twenty-fourth day of March, and arrived on Thursday, in the evening, at a little stream where a small bridge was made, and the

3. October 4, but this was not a Wednesday in 1539.
4. This should be Sunday, October 5.
5. Calahuchi.

people passed to the opposite side. . . . So soon as the Governor had crossed, he found a town, a short way on, by the name of Achese, the people of which, having had no knowledge of Christians, plunged into a river; nevertheless, some men and women were taken. . . . The Governor set out on the first day of April, and advanced through the country of the chief, along up a river, the shores of which were very populous. On the fourth he went through the town of Altamaca, and on the tenth arrived at Ocute. . . . On Monday the twelfth of April, the Governor took his departure, the cacique of Ocute giving him four hundred tamemes, the Indians that carry burdens. He passed through a town, the lord of which was called Cofaqui, and came to the province of another, named Patofa. . . .

From this province of Patofa, back to the first cacique we found at peace, a distance of fifty leagues, the country is abundant, picturesque, and luxuriant, well watered, and having good river margins; thence to the harbor of Espíritu Santo, where we first arrived, the land of Florida, which may be three hundred leagues in length, a little more or less, is light, the greater part of it of pine-trees, and low, having many ponds; and in places are high and dense forests, into which the Indians that were hostile betook themselves, where they could not be found; nor could horses enter there, which, to the Christians, was the loss of the food they carried away, and made it troublesome to get guides. . . . The Governor had brought thirteen sows to Florida, which had increased to three hundred swine; and the maize having failed for three or four days, he ordered to be killed daily, for each man, half a pound of pork, on which small allowance, and some boiled herbs, the people with much difficulty lived. . . .

On Monday, the twenty-sixth of April, the Governor set out for Aymay, a town to which the Christians gave the name of Socorro. . . . Four Indians were taken, not one of whom would say anything else than that he knew of no other town. The Governor ordered one of them to be burned; and thereupon another said, that two days' journey from there was a province called Cutifachiqui . . . he set out for Cutifachiqui, capturing three Indians in the road, who stated that the mistress of that country had already information of the Christians, and was waiting for them in a town.

He sent to her by one of them, offering his friendship and announc-
ing his approach. . . . After a little time the Caçica came out of
the town, seated in a chair, which some principal men having
borne to the bank, she entered a canoe. . . .

The Caçica presented much clothing of the country, from the
shawls and skins that came in the other boats; and drawing from
over her head a large string of pearls, she threw them about his
neck, exchanging with him many gracious words of friendship and
courtesy. She directed that canoes should come to the spot, whence
the Governor and his people passed to the opposite side of the
river. So soon as he was lodged in the town, a great many turkeys
were sent to him. The country was delightful and fertile, having
good interval lands upon the streams; the forest was open, with
abundance of walnut and mulberry trees. The sea was stated to be
distant two days' travel. . . . In the barbacoas were large quantities of clothing, shawls of thread, made from the bark of trees,
and others of feathers, white, gray, vermilion, and yellow, rich and
proper for winter. There were also many well-dressed deer-skins, of
colors drawn over with designs, of which had been made shoes,
stockings, and hose. The Caçica, observing that the Christians
valued the pearls, told the Governor that, if he should order some
sepulchres that were in the town to be searched, he would find
many; and if he chose to send to those that were in the uninhabited towns, he might load all his horses with them. They examined
those in the town, and found three hundred and fifty pounds'
weight of pearls, and figures of babies and birds made of them. The
inhabitants are brown of skin, well formed and proportioned. They
are more civilized than any people seen in all the territories of
Florida, wearing clothes and shoes. . . . In the town were found a
dirk and beads that had belonged to Christians, who, the Indians
said, had many years before been in the port, distant two days'
journey. He that had been there was the Governor-licentiate
Ayllón, who came to conquer the land, and, on arriving at the port,
died, when there followed divisions and murders among the chief
personages, in quarrels as to who should command; and thence,
without knowing any thing of the country, they went back to
Spain.

To all it appeared well to make a settlement there, the point being a favorable one, to which could come all the ships from New Spain, Peru, Sancta Marta, and Tierra-Firme, going to Spain; because it is in the way thither, is a good country, and one fit in which to raise supplies; but Soto, as it was his object to find another treasure like that of Atabalípa, lord of Peru, would not be content with good lands nor pearls, even though many of them were worth their weight in gold (and if the country were divided among Christians, more precious should those be the Indians would procure than these they have, being bored with heat, which causes them to lose their hue): so he answered them who urged him to make a settlement, that in all the country together there was not support for his troops a single month; that it was necessary to return to Ochua, where Maldonado was to wait; and should a richer country not be found, they could always return to that who would, and in their absence the Indians would plant their fields and be better provided with maize. The natives were asked if they had knowledge of any great lord farther on, to which they answered, that twelve days' travel thence was a province called Chiaha, subject to a chief of Coça.

The Governor then resolved at once to go in quest of that country, and being an inflexible man, and dry of word, who, although he liked to know what the others all thought and had to say, after he once said a thing he did not like to be opposed, and as he ever acted as he thought best, all bent to his will; for though it seemed an error to leave that country, when another might have been found about it, on which all the people could have been sustained until the crops had been made and the grain gathered, there were none would say a thing to him after it became known that he had made up his mind. . . .

On the third day of May,[6] the Governor set out from Cutifachiqui; and, it being discovered that the wish of the Caçica was to leave the Christians, if she could, giving them neither guides nor tamemes, because of the outrages committed upon the inhabitants, there never failing to be men of low degree among the many, who will put the lives of themselves and others in jeopardy for some mean interest, the Governor ordered that she should be placed

6. May 13, according to Ranjel.

under guard and took her with him. . . . This brought us service in all the places that were passed, she ordering the Indians to come and take the loads from town to town. We travelled through her territories a hundred leagues, in which, according to what we saw, she was greatly obeyed, whatsoever she ordered being performed with diligence and efficacy. . . . In seven days the Governor arrived at the province of Chalaque, the country poorest off for maize of any that was seen in Florida. . . . From Ocute to Cutifachiqui are one hundred and thirty leagues, of which eighty are desert; from Cutifa to Xualla are two hundred and fifty of mountainous country; thence to Guaxule, the way is over very rough and lofty ridges.[7] . . . At the end of five days the Governor arrived at Guazulle. . . . Two leagues before he came to Chiaha, fifteen men met the Governor, bearing loads of maize, with word from the cacique that he waited for him, having twenty barbacoas full; that, moreover, himself, his lands, and his vassals, were subject to his orders. On the fifth day of July the Governor entered Chiaha. . . . The horses arrived so worn out, that they could not bear their riders from weakness. . . . The Christians were greatly exposed, so much so that if at that time the Indians had set upon them, they would have been in bad way to defend themselves.

The duration of the sojourn was thirty days, in which time, the soil being covered with verdure, the horses fattened. . . . A cacique of Acoste, who came to see the Governor, after tendering his services, and they had exchanged compliments and proffers of friendship, was asked if he had any information of a rich land; he answered yes: that towards the north there was a province called Chisca, and that a forge was there for copper, or other metal of that color, though brighter, having a much finer hue, and was to appearances much better, but was not so much used, for being softer; which was the statement that had been given in Cutifachiqui, where we had seen some chopping-knives that were said to have a mixture of gold. As the country on the way was thinly peopled, and it was said there were mountains over which the beasts could not go, the Governor would not march directly

7. The only mention of the Crossing of the Appalachians to the Tennessee River Valley.

thither, but judged that, keeping in an inhabited territory, the men and animals would be in better condition, while he would be more exactly informed of what there was, until he should turn to it through the ridges and a region which he could more easily travel.

32. Coronado Finds the Seven Cities of Cibola and Searches for Quivira, 1540–41

A.

PEDRO CASTAÑEDA wrote a "Narrative of the Expedition of Cíbola" (Hodge and Lewis, Spanish Explorers, pp. 281–387; Hammond and Rey, Narratives, pp. 191–283), which is the only full account of the Coronado expedition. The extract (taken, with a few corrections, from G. P. Winship, "The Coronado Expedition, 1540–1542," in Smithsonian Institution, Bureau of American Ethnology, Fourteenth Report [1896], 482–484) gives his reaction to the discovery of Hawikuh and its associated pueblos, the only Seven Cities of Cíbola there were.

Chapter 9, of how the army started from Culiacan and the arrival of the general at Cíbola and of the army at Señora and of other things that happened.

The general, as has been said, started to continue his journey from the valley of Culiacan somewhat lightly equipped, taking with him the friars, since none of them wished to stay behind with the army. After they had gone three days, a regular friar who could say mass, named Friar Antonio Victoria, broke his leg, and they brought him back from the camp to have it doctored. He stayed with the army after this, which was no slight consolation for all. The general and his force crossed the country without trouble, as they found everything peaceful, because the Indians knew Friar Marcos and some of the others who had been with Melchior Díaz when he went with Juan de Saldibar (Zalvidar) to investigate. After the general had crossed the inhabited region and came to Chichilticalli, where the wilderness (despoblado) begins, and saw nothing favorable, he could not help feeling somewhat down-hearted, for, although the reports were very fine about what was ahead, there was nobody who had seen it except the Indians who went with the negro, and these had already been caught in some lies. Besides all this, he was much affected by seeing that the fame of Chichilticalli was summed up in one tumbledown house without any roof, although it appeared to have been a strong place at some former time when it was inhabited, and it was very plain that it had been built by a civilized and warlike race of strangers who had come from a distance. This building was made of red earth.

From here they went on through the wilderness, and in fifteen days came to a river about 8 leagues from Cíbola, which they called Red river, (Rio Bermejo) because its waters were muddy and reddish. In this river they found barbels like those of Spain. The first Indians from that country were seen here—two of them, who ran away to give the news. During the night following the next day, about two leagues from the village, some Indians in a safe place yelled so that, although the men were ready for anything, some were so excited that they put their saddles on hind-side before; but these were the new fellows. When the veterans had mounted and ridden round the camp, the Indians fled. None of them could be caught because they knew the country.

The next day they entered the settled country in good order, and when they saw the first pueblo, which was Cíbola, such were the curses that some hurled at Friar Marcos that I pray God may protect him from them.

It is a little, unattractive pueblo, looking as if it had been crumpled all up together. There are mansions in New Spain which make a better appearance at a distance. It is a pueblo of about 200 warriors, is three and four stories high, with the houses small and having only a few rooms, and without a courtyard. One patio serves for each section. The people of the whole district had collected here, for there are seven pueblos in the province, and some of the others are even larger and stronger than Cíbola. These folks waited for the army, drawn up by divisions in front of the village. When they refused to have peace on the terms the interpreters extended to them, but appeared defiant, the (battle cry) Santiago was given, and they were at once put to flight. The Spaniards then attacked the pueblo, which was taken with not a little difficulty, since they held the narrow and crooked entrance. During the attack they knocked the general down with a large stone, and would have killed him but for Don Garcia López de Cárdenas and Hernando de Alvarado, who threw themselves above him and drew him away, receiving the blows of the stones, which were not few. But the first fury of the Spaniards could not be resisted, and in less than an hour they entered the pueblo and captured it. They discovered food there, which was the thing they were most in need of. After this the whole province was at peace.

The army which had stayed with Don Tristán de Arellano started to follow their general, all loaded with provisions, with lances on their shoulders, and all on foot, so as to have the horses loaded. With no slight labor from day to day, they reached a province which Cabeza de Vaca had named Corazones, because the people here offered him many hearts of animals. . . . From here a force went down the river to the seacoast to find the harbor and to find out about the ships. Don Rodrigo Maldonado, who was captain of those who went in search of the ships, did not find them.

B.

By October 20, 1541, Coronado had returned to the pueblo of Tiguex (Mohi), now a national monument to him, after his long and unavailing journey to Quivera. His own impression of the journey conveyed his failure, but also his continued excitement at the vast area he had traversed. The full letter (from which this text is taken) is in Winship, "The Coronado Exposition," pp. 580–583; and Hammond and Rey, Narratives, pp. 185–191.

Letter from Francisco Vásquez Coronado to His Majesty, Charles V, October 20, 1541.

Holy Catholic Cæsarian Majesty: On April 20 of this year I wrote to Your Majesty from this province of Tiguex, in reply to a letter from Your Majesty dated in Madrid, June 11 a year ago. I gave a detailed account of this expedition, which the viceroy of New Spain ordered me to undertake in Your Majesty's name to this country which was discovered by Fray Marcos de Niza, the provincial of the order of Saint Francis. I described it all, and the sort of force I have, as Your Majesty had ordered me to relate in my letters; and stated that while I was engaged in the conquest and pacification of the natives of this province, some Indians who were natives of other provinces beyond these had told me that in their country there were much larger villages and better houses than those of the natives of this country, and that they had lords who ruled them, who were served with dishes of gold, and other very magnificent things; and although, as I wrote to Your Majesty, I did not believe it before I had set eyes on it, because it was the report of Indians and given for the most part by means of signs, yet as the report appeared to me to be very valuable and that it was important that it should be investigated for Your Majesty's service, I determined to go and see it with the men I have here. I started from this province [of Tiguex] on the 23rd of last April, for the place where the Indians wanted to guide me. After nine days' march I reached some plains, so vast that I did not find their limit anywhere that I went, although I marched over them for more than 300 leagues. And I found such a quantity of cows in these, of the kind that I wrote Your Majesty about, which they have in this country, that it is impossible to number them, for while I was journeying through these plains, until I returned to where I first found them, there was not a day that I lost sight of them.

And after seventeen days' march I came to a settlement of Indians who are called Querechos, who travel around with these cows, who do not plant, and who eat the raw flesh and drink the blood of the cows they kill, and they tan the skins of the cows, with which all the people of this country dress themselves here. They have little field tents made of the hides of the cows, tanned and greased, very well made, in which they live while they travel around near the cows, moving with these. They have dogs which they load, which carry their tents and poles and belongings. These people have the best figures of any that I have seen in the Indies. They could not give me any account of the country where the guides were taking me. I traveled five days more as the guides wished to lead me, until I reached some plains, with no more landmarks than as if we had been swallowed up in the sea, where they strayed about, because there was not a stone, nor a bit of rising ground, nor a tree, nor a shrub, nor anything to go by. There is much very fine pasture land, with good grass. And while we were lost in these plains, some horsemen who went off to hunt cows fell in with some

Indians who also were out hunting, who are enemies of those that I had seen in the last settlement, and of another sort of people who are called Teyas; they have their bodies and faces all painted, are a large people like the others, of a very good build; they eat the raw flesh just like the Querechos, and live and travel round with the cows in the same way as these. I obtained from these an account of the country where the guides were taking me, which was not like what they had told me, because these made out that the houses there were not built of stones, with stories, as my guides had described it, but of straw and skins, and a small supply of corn there.

This news troubled me greatly, to find myself on these limitless plains, where I was in great need of water, and often had to drink it so poor that it was more mud than water. Here the guides confessed to me that they had not told the truth in regard to the size of the houses, because these were of straw, but that they had done so regarding the large number of inhabitants and the other things about their habits. The Teyas disagreed with this, and on account of this division between some of the Indians and the others, and also because many of the men I had with me had not eaten anything except meat for some days, because we had reached the end of the corn which we carried from this province [of Tiguex], and because they made it out more than forty days' journey from where I fell in with the Teyas to the country where the guides were taking me, although I appreciated the trouble and danger there would be in the journey owing to the lack of water and corn, it seemed to me best, in order to see if there was anything there of service to Your Majesty, to go forward with only 30 horsemen until I should be able to see the country, so as to give Your Majesty a true account of what was to be found in it. I sent all the rest of the force I had with me to this province, with Don Tristán de Arellano in command, because it would have been impossible to prevent the loss of many men, if all had gone on, owing to the lack of water and because they also had to kill bulls and cows on which to sustain themselves.

And with only the 30 horsemen whom I took for my escort, I traveled forty-two days after I left the force, living all this while solely on the flesh of the bulls and cows which we killed, at the cost of several of our horses which they killed, because, as I wrote Your Majesty, they are very brave and fierce animals; and going many days without water, and cooking the food with cow dung, because there is not any kind of wood in all these plains, away from the gullies and rivers, which are very few.

It was the Lord's pleasure that, after having journeyed across these deserts seventy-seven days, I arrived at the province they call Quivira, to which the guides were conducting me, and where they had described to me houses of stone, with many stories; and not only are they not of stone, but of straw, but the people in them are as barbarous as all those whom I have seen and passed before this; they do not have cloaks, nor cotton of which to make these, but use the skins of the cattle they kill, which they tan, because they are settled among these on a very large river. They eat the raw flesh like the Querechos and Teyas; they are enemies of one another, but are all of the same sort of people, and these at Quivira have the advantage in the houses they build and in planting corn. In this province of which the guides who brought me are natives, they received me peaceably, and although they told me when I set out for it that I could not succeed in seeing it all in two months, there are not more than 25 villages of straw houses there and in all the rest of the country that I saw and learned about, which gave their obedience to Your Majesty and placed themselves under your royal overlordship. The people here are large. I had several Indians measured, and found that they were 10 palms [80 inches] in height; the women are well proportioned and their features are more like Moorish women than Indians. The natives here gave me a piece of copper which a chief Indian wore hung around his neck; I sent it to the viceroy of New Spain, because I have not seen any other metal in these parts except this and some little copper bells which I sent him, and a bit of metal which looks like gold. I do not know where this came from, although I believe that the Indians who gave it to me obtained it from those whom I brought here in my service, because I can not find any other origin for it nor where it came from.

The diversity of languages which exists in this country and my not having anyone who understood them, because they speak their own language in each village, has hindered me, because I have been forced to send captains and men in many directions to find out whether there was anything in this country which could be of service to Your Majesty. And although I have searched with all diligence I have not found or heard of anything, unless it be these provinces, which are a very small affair. The province of Quivira is 950 leagues from Mexico. Where I reached it, it is in the fortieth degree. The country itself is the best I have ever seen for producing all the products of Spain, for besides the land itself being very fat and black and being very well watered by the rivulets and springs and rivers, I found plums like those of Spain and nuts and very good sweet grapes and mulberries. I have treated the natives of this province, and all the others whom I found wherever I went, as well as was possible, agreeably to what Your Majesty had commanded, and they have received no harm in any way from me or from those who went in my company. I remained twenty-five days in this province of Quivira, so as to see and explore the country and also to find out whether there was anything beyond which could be of service to Your Majesty, because the guides who had brought me had given me an account of other provinces beyond this. And what I am sure of is that there is not any gold nor any other metal in all that country, and the other things of which they had told me are nothing but little villages, and in many of these they do not plant anything and do not have any houses except of skins and sticks, and they wander around with the cows; so that the account they gave me was false, because they wanted to persuade me to go there with the whole force, believing that as the way was through such uninhabited deserts, and from the lack of water, they would get us where we and our horses would die of hunger. And the guides confessed this, and said they had done it by the advice and orders of the natives of these provinces.

At this, after having heard the account of what was beyond, which I have given above, I returned to these provinces to provide for the force I had sent back here and to give Your Majesty an account of what this country amounts to, because I wrote Your Majesty that I would do so when I went there. I have done all that I possibly could to serve Your Majesty and to discover a country where God Our Lord might be served and the royal patrimony of Your Majesty increased, as your loyal servant and vassal. For since I reached the province of Cíbola, to which the viceroy of New Spain sent me in the name of Your Majesty, seeing that there were none of the things there of which Friar Marcos had told, I have managed to explore this country for 200 leagues and more around Cíbola, and the best place I have found is this river of Tiguex where I am now, and the settlements here. It would not be possible to establish a settlement here, for besides being 400 leagues from the North sea and more than 200 from the South sea, with which it is impossible to have any sort of communication, the country is so cold, as I have written to Your Majesty, that apparently the winter could not possibly be spent here, because there is no wood, nor cloth with which to protect the men, except the skins which the natives wear and some small amount of cotton cloaks. I send the viceroy of New Spain an account of everything I have seen in the countries where I have been, and as Don García López de Cárdenas is going to kiss Your Majesty's hands, who has done much and has served Your Majesty very well on this expedition, and he will give Your Majesty an account of everything here, as one who has seen it himself, I give way to him. And may Our Lord protect the Holy Imperial Catholic person of Your Majesty, with increase of greater kingdoms and powers, as your loyal servants and vassals desire. From this province of Tiguex, October 20, in the year 1541. Your Majesty's humble servant and vassal, who would kiss the royal feet and hands:

FRANCISCO VÁZQUEZ DE CORONADO

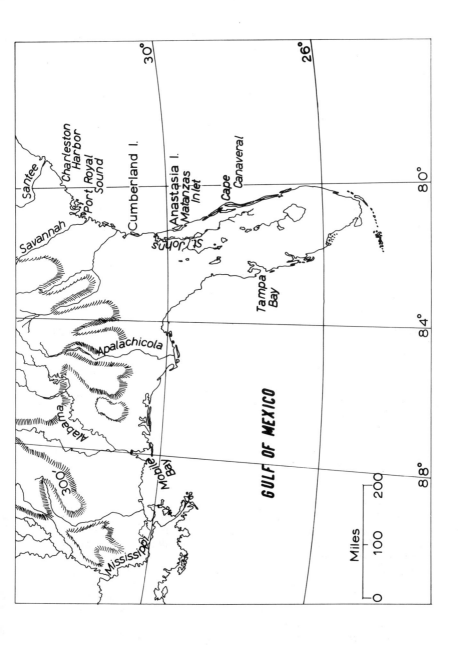

Santee
Charleston Harbor
Port Royal Sound
Savannah
Cumberland I.
Anastasia I.
Matanzas Inlet
St. Johns
Cape Canaveral

Apalachicola
Tampa Bay
Alabama

300'

Mississippi
Mobile Bay

GULF OF MEXICO

Miles
0   100   200

30°
26°
80°
84°
88°

VIII

French Florida, 1562–80

THE ATTEMPTED settlement of Florida by France provides us with a valuable counterpart to the earlier attempts to penetrate and settle the St. Lawrence Valley. Sponsored by Gaspard de Coligny, admiral of France, and Charles IX, the French expeditions were partly concerned to deny a potentially valuable area of America to the Spaniards and to work the gold and other mineral resources it was believed to contain, partly to settle militant French Protestants who might not be able to be accommodated in their own country. The latter could, in Florida, it was hoped, develop bases from which increasing pressure could be exercised on the Spanish Indies, thus diverting Spanish attention from France herself. French Florida, like Spanish Florida thereafter, was not confined to the present state of that name but comprised the eastern coastline and hinterland of what are now Florida, Georgia and South Carolina. Jean Ribault established the first French post at Charlesfort, traditionally believed to have been on Parris Island, Port Royal Sound, in 1562. A revolt by the garrison led to the killing of the commander, Albert de La Pierria, and the return of the survivors to France. A second, more ambitious venture was launched in 1564 when René Goulaine de Laudonnière established a substantial settlement at Fort Caroline on the St. Johns River. Much interesting local exploration was done and valuable information collected on the neighboring Timucua peoples. For the first time a competent artist accompanied the expedition, and the maps, drawings and engravings deriving from Jacques Le Moyne de Morgues's stay in the country are a valuable record. (They are to be published in a critical edition by the British Museum, under the editorship of Paul Hulton. The engravings first appeared in Theodor de Bry's America, part II [1591].) Laudonnière was in some difficulties with his men by the summer of 1565 and accepted a ship from the English navigator, John Hawkins, who called to see how the settlement fared. But before he set out for France he was relieved on August 28 and superseded by Jean Ribault, accompanied by a large fleet and many settlers. Before this reinforcement could be consolidated, Ribault took most of his ships and men to sea to fight a Spanish expedition under Pedro Menéndez de Avilés, sent to drive out the French and settle a strong Spanish garrison in Florida. Most of the ships were destroyed in a gale; Charlesfort was taken by a land attack; French prisoners were almost all executed, and Florida remained in the hands of the Spaniards. France did not give up all thought of resettling Florida. Dominique de Gourges in 1568 destroyed San Mateo, the fort built on the site of Fort Caroline, but this attack was not followed up. French ships operating against Spain in the Caribbean used the coast north of Santa Elena (built near the older Charlesfort) for watering and refitting their ships. In 1577 Nicolas Strozzi established a French fort somewhere close to, but to the north of, Santa Elena. Quarrels with the Indians brought about its destruction and the handing over of the survivors to the Spaniards. A supply ship, under Gilberto Gil, in 1580 ran aground and was taken by the Spaniards, the men being, as usual, executed. (See Mary Ross, "French Intrusions . . . 1577–1580," Georgia Historical Quarterly, VII [1923], 256–269; Colonial Records of Spanish Florida, 1577–1580, ed. Jeanette T. Connor, [1925], vol. I, 78–79, 318–323). The Spaniards thus succeeded for the remainder of the sixteenth century in denying any part of the Southeast to France.

Jean Ribault, The whole and true discoverye of Terra Florida (1563, facsimile edited by Jeanette T. Connor, 1927) is the primary authority for the first colony, supplemented by René de Laudonnière, L'histoire notable de la Floride (1586, facsimile, 1946), an English translation of which, A notable historie containing foure voyages . . . unto Florida (1587, facsimile, with an introduction by Thomas R. Adams, 1964) covers the years 1562–68. The best modern edition of these texts is by Susanne Lussagnet, Les Français en Amérique pendant la deuxième moitié du XVIᵉ siècle. Les Français en Floride (1958). The soundest of the older accounts is that in Lowery, The Spanish Settlements Within the Present Limits of the United States. Florida, 1562–1574 (1911); the best narratives are in French, Julien, Les voyages de Découverte et les premiers Établissements and Trudel, Histoire de la Nouvelle-France. Les Vaines Tentatives.

33. The Ribault Expedition, 1562

JEAN RIBAULT published, in an English translation, his report to Gaspard de Coligny as The whole and true discoverye of Terra Florida (1563). H. P. Biggar published a better text, "Jean Ribaut's Discoverye of Terra Florida," in English Historical Review, XXXII (1917), 253–270, which was reprinted in Jeanette T. Connor, ed., The Whole and True Discoverye of Terra Florida (1927). Extracts are given here, and can be elucidated with the aid of W. P. Cumming, "The Parreus Map (1562) of French Florida," Imago Mundi, XVII (1963), 27–40.

The 18 daye of February last past, through the favor of God, we departed with our two vesselles owt of the havon of Havor de Grace into the rode of Caux, and the next daye hoised up sailes. . . .

Thursday the last of Aprill at the breke of the daye we discovered and clearly perceaved a faire cost, streching of a gret lenght, covered with an infenite number of highe and fayre trees, we being not past 7 or 8 leages from the shore, the countrye seming unto us playn, withowt any shewe of hilles, and approching nearer within 4 or 5 leages of the land, we cast ancre at ten fadom watter, the bottom of the sea being playn with muche oose and of fast hold. On the southe side as far as a certen poynt or cape, scituate under the latitude of 29 degrees and a half, which we have named the cap Francoys,[1] we could espie nether river nor baye, wherfore we sent our boates, furnished with men of experience, to sound and knowe the coast nere the shore, who retourning agen unto us abowt one of the clocke at after none, declared that they had found, amonges other thinges, vii fadom watter at the harde bancke of the sea. Wherupon, having dilligently wayed up our ancres and hoist up saile, with wynd at will we sailed and veewed the coast all along with an inspeakeable pleasure of thoderiferous smell and bewtye of the same. And bicause there apeared unto us no sine of any porte, abowt the setting of the sonne, we cast ancre agayn, which don, we did behold to and fro the goodly order of the woodes wherwith God hathe decked everywhere the said lande. Then perceiving towardes the northe a leaping and breking of the water, as a streme falling owt of the lande unto the sea, forthewith we sett agayn up saile to duble the same while it was yet daye. And as we had so don, and passed byonde yt, there apeared unto us a faire enter[ye] of a great river,[2] which caused us to cast ancre agen and tary there nere the lande, to thende that the next mornyng we myght see what it was. And though that the wynd blewe for a tyme vehemently to the shore warde, yet the hold and auncordge is so

1. The Cape of Anastasia Island, lat. 29° 52′ N.
2. The river of May, the St. Johns River.

good there, that one cable and one ancre held us fast withowt driving or slyding.

The next daye in the morninge, being the First of Maye, we assaied to enter this porte with two rowe barges and a boate well trymed, finding littell watter at the entrye and many surges and brekinges of the water which might have astuned[3] and caused us to retourn backe to shippborde, if God had not speedely brought us in, where fynding fourthwith 5 or 6 fadom water, entered in to a goodly and great river, which as we went we found to increase still in depth and lardgnes, boylling and roring through the multytude of all sortes of fishes. Thus entered we perceved a good numbre of the Indians, inhabytantes there, coming alonge the sandes and seebanck somewhate nere unto us, withowt any taken[4] of feare or dowbte, shewing unto us the easiest landing place, and thereupon we geving them also on our parte tokens of assuraunce and frende-lynes, fourthewith one of the best of apparance amonges them, brother unto one of there kinges or governours, comaunded one of the Indians to enter into the water, and to approche our boates, to showe us the easiest landing place. We seeing this, withowt any more dowbting or difficulty, landed, and the messenger, after we had rewarded him with some loking glases and other prety thinges of smale value, ran incontenently towards his lorde, who forth-with sent me his girdell in token of assurance and Frendship, which girdell was made of red lether, aswell couried and coulored as is possible. And as I began to go towardes him, he sett fourthe and came and receved me gentlye and rejosed[5] after there mannour, all his men Following him with great silence and modestie, yea, with more then our men did. And after we had awhile with gentill usage congratulated with him, we fell to the grownd a littell waye from them, to call upon the name of God, and to beseche him to contynewe still his goodnes towardes us, and to bring to the knoweledg of our Savior Jesus Christ this pooer people. While we were thus praying, they sitting upon the grownd, which was dressed and strewed with baye bowes, behelde and herkened unto us very attentively, withowt eyther speaking or moving. And as I made a

3. Astounded.
4. Token.
5. Rejoiced.

sygne unto there king, lifting up myne arme and streching owt one
fynger, only to make them loke up to heavenward, he likewise
lifting up his arme towardes heven, put fourthe two fynge[rs]
wherby it semed that he would make us tunderstand that they
worshipped the sonne and mone for godes, as afterward we understode yt so. In this meane tyme there number increased and thither
came the kinges brother that was First with us, their mothers,
wifes, sisters and children, and being thus assembled, thaye caused
a greate nombre of baye bowes to be cutt and therwith a place to
be dressed for us, distant from theires abowt two Fadom; for yt is
there mannour to parle and bargayn sitting, and the chef of them
to be aparte from the meaner sorte, with a shewe of great obedyence to there kinges, superyours, and elders. They be all naked and
of a goodly stature, mighty, faire and aswell shapen and proportioned of bodye as any people in all the worlde, very gentill,
curtious and of a good nature. . . .

After that we had tarried in this northe side of the river the most
parte of the daye, which river we have called by the name of the
river of Maye, for that we discovered the same the First day of that
mounthe, congratulated and made alyance and entered into amytie
with them, and presented theire kinge and his brethern with
gownes of blewe clothe garnished with yellowe flowers de luce, yt
semed they were sorry for our departure, so that the most parte of
them entered into the watter up to the necke, to sett our barges on
flote, putting into us soundry kindes of Fishes, which with a
marvelus speed they ran to take them in there parkes,[6] made in the
watter with great redes, so well and cunyngly sett together, after
the fashion of a labirinthe or maze, with so manny tourns and
crokes, as yt is impossible to do yt with more cunning or industrye.

But desiering to imploye the rest of the daye on the other side of
this river, to veue and knowe those Indians we sawe there, we
traversed thither and withowt any diffycutye landed amonges
them, who receaved us verry gentelly with great humanytie, putting us of there fruites, even in our boates, as mulberies, respices[7]
and suche other frutes as thay found redely by the waye.

6. Pounds or fish weirs.
7. Raspberries.

Sone after this there came thither there kinge with his brethern and others, with bowes and arrowes in there handes, using therewithall a good and grave Fashion and bihavior, right souldier like with as warlike a bouldnes as might be. They were naked and paynted as thothers, there hear likewise long, and trussed up with a lace made of hearbes, to the top of there hedes, but they had neither there wives nor childern in there company.

After we had a good while lovengly intretayned and presented them with littell giftes of haberdasherye wares, cutting hookes and hatchettes, and clothed the king and his brethern with like robes we had geven to them on the other side, [we] enterd and veued the cuntry therabowte, which is the fairest, frutefullest and plesantest of all the worlde, habonding[8] in honney, veneson, wildfoule, forrestes, woodes of all sortes, palme trees, cipers, ceders, bayes, the hiest, greatest and fairest vynes in all the wourld with grapes accordingly, which naturally and withowt mans helpe and tryming growe to the top of okes and other trees that be of a wonderfull greatnes and height. And the sight of the faire medowes is a pleasure not able to be expressed with tonge . . . and to be shorte it is a thinge inspeakable, the comodities that be sene there and shalbe founde more and more in this incomperable lande, never as yet broken with plowc irons, bringing fourthe all thinges according to his first nature, wherof the eternall God endued yt. . . .

As we [nowe] demaunded of them for a certen towne called Sevolla,[9] wherof some have wrytten not to be farr from thence, and to be scituate within the lande and towardes the southe sea, they shewed us by signes which we understode well enough, that they might go thither with there boates by rivers in xx^{tie} dayes. Those that have wrytten of this kingdom and towne of Sevolla, and other towns and realmes therabowtes, say that ther is great aboundaunce of gould and silver, precious stouns and other great riches, and that the people hedd ther arrowes, instedd of iron, with [sharpe] poynted turqueses. Thus the night aproching, and that it was conveynient for us to retire by daye to ship bourd, we toke leve of them muche to their greif and more to oures withowt comparison,

8. Abounding.
9. Cíbola.

for that we had no meane to enter the river with our shippes. . . .

The next day in the morning we retourned to land agayne, accompaned with the captayns, gentilmen, souldiers, and others of our smale troup, carring with us a piller or colume of hard stone, our kinges armes graven therin, to plaint and sett [the same] at the entrye of the porte in some high place wher yt might be easelly sene. And being come thither bifore the Indyans were assembled, we espied on the southe side of the river a place verry fyt for that purpose upon a littell hill compassed with cipers, bayes, palmes, and other trees, and swete pleasaunt smelling shrubbes, in the mydell wherof we planted the first bounde or lymete of his majestie. Thus don, perceving our first Indians assembled and loking for us we went first unto them according to our promisse, not withowt some mislyking of those on the southe parte, wher we had sett the said lymete, who tarried for us in the same place where they mete with us the day before, seming unto us that there ys some ennemytie betwen them and the others. But when the[y] perceved our long tarr[y]ing on this side, the[y] ran to se what we had don in that place where we landed First and had sett our lymete, which they vewed a gret while withowt touching yt any waye, or abasshing, or ever speaking unto us therof at any tyme after. . . .

Being retourned to our shippes, we sailed to knowe more and more of the coast, going as nere the shore as we could. And as we had sailed so all alonge abowt six or seven leages, there apered unto us another baye where we cast ancre twart of yt, tarr[y]ing so all the night. In the morrowe, we went thither, and fynding by our sounding at the entre many bankes and beatynges, we durst not venture to entre there with our great shippes, we having named this river Some,[10] which within is a leage over and of viii, ix, x, and xi fadom deapthe, deviding yt sclf into many great rivers, that sever the cuntry into many faire and great ilandes and smale goodly medowe ground and pastures, and every where such aboundaunce of fishe as is increadeble. And on the west northewest side there is a great river that comithe from the highe country, of a great leage over, and on the other on the northest side which retourn into the

10. Satilla River, lat. 31° N.

sea. So that (my lorde) yt is a country full of havens, rivers and islandes of suche frutefullnes as cannot with tonge be expressed, and where in shorte tyme great and precyous comodyties might be founde. And besides theis, we discovered and founde also seven rivers more, as great and as good, cutting and deviding the land into faire and great ilandes, th' Indians inhabytantes therof like in manours, and the countrey in fertilitie apte and comodious throughowt to make suger and to beare and bring fourthe plentifully all that men would plant or sowe upon it. There be every where the highest, fayrerest and greatest Firr trees that can be sene, verry well smelling and whereowt might be gotton with cutting only the bark, as muche rosin, turpentyne and frankinsence as men would have; and to be shorte, there lackethe nothing. Wherfore being not able to entre and lye with our great vesselles there, where we would make no long abode, nor entre so farr into the rivers and cuntres as we would fayne have don: for yt is well inough known howe many inconvenyences have hapened unto men, not only in attempting of newe discover[ie]s, but also in all places by leving there great vesselles in the sea, farr from the lande, unfurnished of there heddes and best men. As for thother rivers, we have given them suche names as followe, and unto the Indians joining to them, the same name that the next river unto yt hathe, as ye shall see by the protacture or carte I have made thereof, as to the fourth the name of Loire, to the vth Charent, to the vith Garone, to the vijth ryviere Belle, to the viijth Riviere Grande, to the ixth Porte Royall, to the xth Belle a Veoir.[11]

Upon Whitsontide, Sondaye the xvii of Maye, after we had well perceved and considered that there was no remedye but to assaye to fynde the meanes to harborough our shippes, aswell for to amend and tryme them as to gett us fresshe water, wood and other necessaries wherof we had nede, being of opynion that there was no fayrer or fytter place for the purpose then porte Royall. [And] when we had sounded the entrey and the channell,[12] (thanked be God) we entred salfely therin with our shippes agenst the opynyon

11. Numbers 4 to 10 are, respectively (4) St. Simon Sound-Brunswick River, (5) Altamaha River, (6) Sapelo River, (7) Ogeechee River, (8) Savannah River, (9) Port Royal Sound and (10) St. Helena Sound (*Imago Mundi*, XVII, 32).
12. Port Royal Sound.

of many, fynding the same one of the greatest and fayrest havens of the worlde. Howebeyt, it must be remembred, lest that men approching nere yt within vii leages of the lande, be abasshed and afrayed, fynding on the east side, drawing towardes the south est, the ground to be flatt, for neverthelesse at a full sea ther is every where foure fadom water keping the right channell.

In this porte are many armes of the sea depe and lardg, and here and there of all sides many rivers of a meane biggnes, where without danger all the shippes in the worlde myght be harbored. We founde no Indians inhabyting there abowt the porte and river side nerer than x or xii leages upward into the cuntryes, although yt be one of the goodlyest, best and frutfullest cunteres that ever was sene, and where nothing lacketh, and also where as good and like[ly] comodities be founde as in the other places therby; for we found there a great numbre of peper trees, the peper upon them yet grene and not redy to be gatherd; also the best watter of the worlde, and so many sortes of Fishes that ye maye take them withowt nett or angle, as many as you will; also guinea foule[13] and innumerable wildfoule of all sortes. . . .

This is the river of Jordayne[14] in myne oppynion, wherof so much hathe byn spoken, which is verry faire, and the cuntrye good and of grete consequence, both for theire easye habitation and also for many other thinges which shuld be to long to wrytt. The xxii of May we planted another colme graven with the Kinges armes, on the southe side, in a comodyous pleasaunt and high place, at the entrye of a faire great river, which we have called Lybourne[15] where ther is a faire lake of Freshe water verry good, and on the same side a lyttell lower towardes the entry of the haven, is one of the fairest and best fountaynes that a made may drynke of, which falleth with voyelence down to the river from a highe place owt of a redd and sandy ground, and yet for all that frutfull and of good aire, where yt shuld seme that the Indians have had some faire habytation. . . .

13. Wild turkeys.
14. As sought for by the Spaniards.
15. The location is contested. Professor Cumming (*Imago Mundi*, XVII, 37) suggests Mackay Islands for the monument, and Skull and Mackay Auks for the River Lybourne.

Wherfore (my lorde) trusting you will not thinke yt amisse, considering the great good and comodyties that may be brought thence into France, if we leve a nombre of men there, that may fortifye and so provide themselves of thinges necessarye, for in all newe discovers yt is the chef and best thinge that may be don at the begining, to fortifye and people the country which is the true and chef possesion. I had not so sonne sett fourthe this thinge to our company, but many of them offered to tarry there, yea with suche a good will and jolly curradg, that suche a nombre did thus offre themselves as we had muche ado to staye there importunytie, and namely of our shipmasters and principall pilottes, and of suche as we could not spare. Howebeyt, we have leift there but to the numbre of xxx in all, of gentilmen, souldiers, and merryners, and that at ther own suite and prayer, and of there one fre and good willes, and by the adviz and delyberation of the gentilmen sent on the behalf of the Prynces and youres, and have leift unto them for hed and ruler (following therin your goodwill) Capten Alberte della Pirie, a souldier of long experyence and the First that from the beginning did offre to tarry; and furthere by there adviz, choise and will, installed and fortified them in an iland on the northe est side, a place of strong scytuation and comodyous, upon a river which we have called Chenonceau and the inhabytacion and fortresse Charle forte.[16]

After we had instructed and duelye admonished them of that they shuld do aswell for there mannour of proceeding as for there good and loving behavior of themselves towardes this poore and simple Indians and there conversacon with them, the xi of the mounthe of June last past, we departed from Port Riall, mynding yett to range and veue the coast untill the xl degrees of the elevation: but forasmuche as there came upon us trublesome and cloudy whither[17] and verry incomodyous for our purpose, and considering also amonges many other thinges that we had spent our cables and fur[n]iture therof . . . we concluded through the helpe of God to retourn into France to make relation unto you of the effecte of

16. Traditionally Parris Island, this too has been contested. Professor Cumming (op. cit. 37–38) considers that Charlesfort "was apparently built on Battery Creek, Port Royal Island, probably near the present site of the town of Port Royal."
17. Weather.

our navegation. Praying to God that yt may please him to kepe you
in long helthe and prossperytie and give unto you the grace to
cause this faire discoverture of this Newe France to be cuntynewed
and dylligently followed.

34. The Failure
of the Laudonnière Colony, 1564–65

RENÉ DE LAUDONNIÈRE *wrote his history of the French expeditions to
Florida between 1562 and 1568 some time after his return to France
in 1565. It gives a full and usually reliable account of the settlement
which the French made near the mouth of the St. Johns River and of
their fort, Fort Caroline, which they occupied from June 1, 1564, until
dispossessed of it by the Spaniards on September 20, 1565. The extracts are from Laudonnière's* A notable historie containing foure voyages made by certaine French captaynes unto Florida, *translated by
Richard Hakluyt, and published in 1587.*

Afterward we passed betweene Languilla and la Negada,[1] sayling
toward New Fraunce, where we arived fifteene dayes afterward, to
witte on a Thurseday the two and twenteth of June about three or
foure of the clock in the morning, and landed neere unto a little
River which is thirtie degrees distant from the Equator, and ten
leagues aboue Cape François drawing toward the South, and about
thirtie leagues above the River of May. After we had strocken sayle
and cast Anker a thwart the River, I determined to goe on shore to
discover the same. Therefore being accompanied with Monsur de
Ottigny, with Monsur de Arlac mine Ensigne, & a certaine number
of Gentlemen and souldiers I embarked my selfe about three or
foure of the clocke in the evening. And being arived at the mouth
of the River I caused the Chanell to be sounded, which was found
to be very shallow, although that farther within the same the water
was there found reasonable deepe, which separateth it selfe into
two great armes, whereof one runneth toward the South and the
other toward the North. Having thus searched the River I went on

1. Anguilla (Leeward Islands) and Anegada (Virgin Islands).

lande to speake with the Indians which wayted for us upon the shore which at our comming on land, came before us, crying with a loud voyce in their Indian language, *Antipola, Bonassou,* which is as much to say, as, brother, friend, or some such like thing. After they had made very much of us, they shewed us their Paracoussy, that is to say, their king and governour, to whom I presented certaine toyes wherewith he was wel pleased. And for mine own part I praise God continually, for the great love which I have found in these Savages, which were sory for nothing, but that the night approched, and made us retire unto our shippes. For though they endevoured by all meanes to make us tarry with them, and that they shewed by signes the desire they had to present us with some rare things, yet neverthelessse for many just and reasonable occasions I would not stay on shore all night: but excusing my selfe for al their offers, I embarked my selfe againe and returned toward my ships.

Howbeit, before my departure, I named this river, the river of Dolphines,[2] because that at mine arrivall, I sawe there a greate number of dolphines which were playing in the mouth thereof. The next day the three and twentieth of this moneth (because that toward the South I had not found any commodious place for us to inhabite, and to build a fort) I gave commaundement to weigh anker, and to hoyse our sayles to sayle towarde the river of Maye,[3] where we arrived two dayes after, and cast anker, afterwarde going overland, with some number of Gentlemen and Souldiers to knowe for a certaintie the singularities of this place, wee espyed the Paracoussy of the countrey, which came towards us (this was the very same that we saw in the voiage of Captaine John Ribault) which having espied us, cried very farre of, *Antipola, Antipola,* and being so joyful that he could not containe himselfe, he came to meet us accompanied then with two of his sonnes, as faire & mighty persons as might be found in all the world, which had nothing in their mouthes but this word, *Amy, Amy:* that is to say, friend, friend: yea and knowing those which were there in the first voyage, they went principally to them to use this speech unto

2. Matanzas Inlet, Lat. 29° 42′ N. (*Imago Mundi,* xvii, 31).
3. The St. Johns River.

them. There was in their trayne a great number of men and women, which still made very much of us, and by evident signes made us to understand how glad they were of our arival.

This good entertainment past, the Paracoussy prayed me to go to see the piller which we had erected in the voyage of John Ribault (as we have declared heretofore) as a thing which they made great account of. Having yeelded unto him and being come to the place where it was set up we found the same crowned with crownes of Bay, & at the foote therof many litle baskets ful of Myl which they call in their language *Tapaga Tapola*. Then when they came thither they kissed the same with great reverence & besought us to do the like, which we could not deny them, to the end we might draw them to be more in frendship with us. This done the Paracoussy tooke me by the hand, as if he had desire to make me understand some great secrete, and by signes shewed me very well up within the river the limits of his dominion, & said that he was called Paracussy Satorioua, which is as much as king Satourioua. His children have the selfe same title of Paracoussy: The eldest is named Athore, a man, I dare say, perfect in beautie, wisdom, and honest sobrietie, shewing by his modest gravitie that he deserveth the name which he beareth besides that he is gentle and tractable. After we had sojourned a certayne space with them, the Paracoussy prayed one of his sonnes to present unto me a wedge of silver, which hee did and that with a good will: in recompence whereof I gave him a cutting hooke & some other better present: wherewith he seemed to be very well pleased. Afterward we tooke our leave of them, because the night approached, and then returned to lodge in our ships.

Being allured with this good entertainment I fayled not the next day to embarke my selfe agayne with my Lieuetenaunt Ottigni and a number of souldiers to returne toward the Paracoussy of the River of May, which of purpose wayted for us in the same place, where the day before we conferred with him. We found him under the shadow of an Arbour accompanied with fourescore Indians at the least, and apparelled at that time after the Indian fashion, to witte, with a great Hartes skin dressed like Chamoys and painted with devises of strang and divers colours, but of so lively a portrature and representing antiquitie with rules so justly compassed,

that there is no painter so exquisite that could finde fault there-
with: the naturall disposition of this straunge people is so perfect
and well guided, that without any ayde and favour of artes, they are
able by the helpe of nature onelie to content the eye of artizans,
yea even of those which by their industrie are able to aspire unto
thinges most absolute. Then I advertised Paracoussy Satourioua,
that my desire was to discover farther up into the river, but that
this shoulde bee with such diligence that I would come againe unto
him very speedily: wherwith he was content, promising to stay for
me in the place where hee was: and for an earnest of his promise,
he offered me his goodly skinne, which I refused then, and promised to recive it of him at my returne. For my part I gave him
certaine small trifles, to the intent, to retayne him in our frendship. . . .

On the morrow about the breake of day I commaunded a
trumpet to be sounded, that being assembled we might give God
thankes for our favorable and happie arrival. There we sange a
Psalme of thanksgiving unto God, beseeching him that it would
please him of his grace to continue his accustomed goodness
toward us his poore servants, and ayde us in al our enterprises, that
all might turne to his glorie, & the advauncement of our king. The
prayers ended, every man began to take courage. Afterward having
measured out a piece of ground in forme of a triangle[4] wee en-
devored our selves of all sides, some to bring earth some to cut
Fagots, and others to rayse and make the rampyre, for there was
not a man that had not either a shovel, or cutting hook, or hatchet
aswel to make the ground plaine by cutting down the trees, as for
the building of the Fort, which we did hasten with such cheereful-
ness that within few dayes the effect of our diligence was apparent:
In which meane space the Paracoussy Satourioua our neerest
neighbour, and on whose ground we built our fort, came usually
accompanied with his two sonnes and a great number of Indians to
offer to do us al curtesie. And I likewise for my part bestowed
divers of our trifles frankly on him to thend he might know the
goodwil which we bare him, & therby make him more desirous of

4. On the south side of the St. Johns River.

our friendship, in such sort that as the dayes increased so our amity & friendship increased also: After that our fort was brought into forme, I began to build a grange to retire my munition, & things necessary for the defence of the fort: praying the Paracoussy that it would please him to commaund his subjects, to make us a covering of palme leaves, & this to thend that when that was done I might unfreight my ships, & put under coverture those thinges that were in them. Sodainely the Parracoussy commaunded in my presence all the Indians of his company to dress the next day morning so good a number of Palme leaves, that the grange was covered in lesse then two dayes: so that business was finished. For in the space of those two dayes, the Indians never ceased from working, some in fetching Palme leaves, others in enterlacing of them: in such sorte that their kings commaundement was executed as he desired.

Our Fort was built in forme of a triangle. The side toward the West, which was toward the land, was enclosed with a litle trench and raysed with turves made in forme of a Battlement of nine foote high: the other side which was toward the River was enclosed with a Pallisado of planckes of timber after the maner that Gabions are made. On the south side there was a kind of bastion within which I caused an house for the munition to be built: it was all builded with Fagots and sand, saving about two or three foote high with turves wherof the battlements were made. In the middest I caused a great court to be made of eighteene pases long and broad, in the middest wherof on the one side drawing toward the South I builded a Corpes de gard, and an house on the other side toward the North, which I caused to be raysed somwhat to high: for within a short while after the winde beat it downe: and experience taught me, that we may not build with high stages in this countrey, by reason of the winds whereunto it is subject. One of the sides that inclosed my court, which I made very fayre and large, reached unto the grange of my munitions: and on the otherside towards the River was mine own lodging, round about the which were galleries all covered. The principall doore of my lodging was in the midest of the great place, and the other was towards the River. A good distance from the Fort I built an Oven, to avoyd the daunger of fier, because the houses are of Palme leaves, which will soone bee burnt, after the fier catcheth hold of them, so that with much adoe a man shall have leasure to quench them. Loe here in breefe the description of our Fortresse, which I named Caroline in the honour of our Prince king Charles.

After we were furnished with that which was most necessary, I would not lose a minute of an houre, without employing of the same in some vertuous exercise: therefore I charged Monsieur de Ottigni my Lieuetenant, a man in truth worthy all honour for his honestie and vertue, to search up within the river what this Thimogoua might be, whereof the Paracoussy Satouriou had spoken to us so often at our comming on shore. For execution hereof the Paracoussy gave him two Indians for his guides, which taking upon them to lead him in this voyage seemed to goe unto a wedding, so desirous they were to fight with their enemies. Being embarked they hoysed sayle and having sayled about twentie leagues, the Indians which still looked on this side and that side to espie some of their enimies, discovered three Canoes. And immediately they began to crie *Thimogoua, Thimogoua*, and spake of nothing else but to hasten forward to goe to fight with them: which the Captayne seemed to be willing to doe, to content them. When they came to boorde them, one of the Indians gat holde of an Halbert, another of a Coutelas[5] in such a rage that hee would have lept into the water to have fought with them alone. Neverthelesse . . . the meaning of Ottigny was not to make warre upon them of Thimogoua, but rather to make them friendes, and to make them thencefoorth to live in peace one with another if it were possible, hoping by this meane to discover daily some new thing, & especially the certayne course of the River. For this purpose hee caused the barke to retire wherein were the two Indians his guides, & went with his toward the Canoes which were on the Rivers side. Being come unto them, he put certaine trifles into them, and then retired a goodway from them, which thing caused the Indians which were fled away to returne to their Boates, and to understand by this signe, that those of our barke were none of their enimies, but rather come onely to trafficke with them. Wherefore being thus assured of us they called to our men to come neere unto them: which they did incontinently and set foote on lande, and spake freely with them, with diverse ceremonies ouer long to recount. In the end Ottigni demaunded of them by signes if they

5. Cutlass.

had gold or silver among them. But they told him they had none as then: and that if he would send one of his men with them, they would bring him without daunger into a place where they might have some. Ottigni seeing them so willing, delivered them one of his men which seemed very resolute to undertake this voyage: this fellow stayed with them untill ten of the clock the next day morning, so that Captayne Ottigny somewhat offended with his long staye, sayled tenne great leagues farther up the river: although he knew not what way hee should goe, yet he went so farre up that he espied the boate wherein his souldier was: which reported unto him that the Indians would have carried him three great dayes journey farther, & told him that a king named Mayrra rich in gold and silver dwelt in those quarters, and that for small quantitie of marchandise inough might be had of him: yet that he would not hazard himself without his leave, and that he brought but a very litle gold. This being done our men returned toward our fort Caroline after they had left the souldier with the Indians to enforme himselfe more and more of such things as he might discover more at leasure. . . .

For if we had beene succoured in time and place, and according to the promise that was made unto us, the warre which was betweene us and Utina, had not fallen out, neither shoulde we have had occasion to offend the Indians, which with al paines in the world I entertayned in good amitie, aswell with marchandise and apparell, as with promise of greater matters, and with whome I so behaved my selfe, that although sometimes I was constrayned to take victuals in some fewe villages, yet I lost not the alliance of eight kings and Lords my neighbours, which continually succoured and ayded me with whatsoever they were able to afford. Yea this was the principall scope of all my purposes, to winne and entertaine them, knowing howe greatly their amitie might advance our enterprise, and principally while I discovered the commodities of the countrey, and sought to strengthen my selfe therein. . . .[6]

6. In 1565 Landonnière was in difficulties as no supplies arrived in the spring or early summer, so he began preparations to return. John Hawkins sold him a ship early in August, and by August 28 he was ready to set out for France.

As I was thus occupied in these conferences, the winde and the tyde served well to set sayle, which was the eight and twentieth of August, at which instant Captaine Vasseur, which commaunded in one of my shippes, and Captaine Verdier, which was chiefe in the other, now readye to goe foorth, began to discrye certayne sayles at sea, whereof they advertised me with diligence: whereupon I appointed to arme foorth a boat in good order to goe to descrye and know what they were. I sent also to the centinels, which I caused to be kept on a little knappe, to cause certayne men to clymbe up to the top of the highest trees the better to discover them. . . .

Being therefore advertised that it was Captayne Ribault, I went forth of the fort to goe to meete hym, & to doe hym all the honor I coulde by any meanes, I caused hym to bee welcommed with the artillerie, and a gentle voley of my shotte, whereunto he aunswered with his. Afterward being come on shore and receaved honorable and with joy, I brought hym to my lodging, rejoycing not a little because that in this company I knew a good number of my friendes, which I intreated in the best sort that I was able, with such victuals as I could get in the country, & small store which I had left mee, with that which I had of the English Generall. . . .

The next day the Indians came in from all partes, to know what people these were, to whome I signified that this was hee which in the yeare a thousande five hundred sixtie and two arrived in this countrie, and erected the piller whiche stoode at the entrie of the river. Some of them knew him: for in truth he was easie to be knowen by reason of the greate bearde whiche hee ware. He receaved many presents of them which were of the villages neere adjoyning, among whom there were some that he had not yet forgotten. The kinges Homoloa, Sarauahi, Alimacani, Malica, and Casti, came to visite him and welcome him with diverse giftes according to their manner. I advertised them that he was sent thither by the king of Fraunce, to remayne there in my roome, and that I was sent for. Then they demaunded and prayed him, if it might stand with his good pleasure, to cause the marchandise that he had brought with him to be delivered them, and that in fewe dayes they woulde bring him to the mountaines of Apalassy, whither they had promised to conduct mee, and that in case they performed not theyr promise, that they were content to be cut in peeces. In those mountaines, as they sayde, is founde red copper, which they call in their language *Sieroa Pira*, which is asmuch to say, as redde mettell, whereof I had a peece, which at the verie instant I shewed to Captaine Ribault, which caused his gold-finer to make an assay thereof, which reported unto him that it was perfect golde. . . .

But loe how oftentimes missfortune doth serch & pursue us, even then when we thinke to be at rest! lo see what happened after that captaine Ribault had brought up three of his small ships into the river, which was the fourth of September! Sixe great Spanish ships arrived in the rode, where foure of our greatest ships remained, which cast anker, assuring our men of good amitie. They asked how the chiefe captaines of the enterprise did, & called them all by their names and surnames. I report me to you if it could be otherwise but these men before they went out of Spaine must needs be enformed of the enterprise and of those that were to execute the same. About the breake of day they began to make toward our men: but our men which trusted them never a deale, had hoised their sayles by night, being ready to cut the stringes that tyed them. Wherefore perceiving that this making toward our men of the Spaniards was not to do them any pleasure, and knowing well that their furniture was to smal to make head against them, bicause that the most part of their men were on shore, they cut their Cables, left their ankers, and set saile. . . .

Hee [Jean Ribault] embarked himselfe the eighth of September, and tooke mine ensigne and eight and thirtie of my men away with him. I report me to those that knowe what wars meane, if when an ensigne marcheth any soldier that hath any courage in him will stay bchinde, to forsake his ensigne: Thus no man of commaundement stayed behinde with mee, for ech one followed him as chiefe, in whose name, straight after his arrival, all cryes and proclamations were made. . . . The verie day that he departed, which was the tenth of September, there rose so great a tempest accompanied with such stormes, that the Indians themselves assured me that it was the worst weather that ever was seene on that coast: where upon two or three dayes after, fearing least our shippes might be in some distresse, I sent for Monsieur Du Lys unto me, to take order to assemble the rest of our people to declare unto them what neede we had to fortifie our selves: which was done accordingly: and then I gave them to understande the necessitie and inconveniences whereinto we were like to fall, aswell by the absence of our ships, as by the neerenes of the Spaniards, at whose hands we could looke for no lesse then an open and sufficient proclamed warre, seeing they had taken lande and fortified themselves so neere unto us. . . .

Thus briefly you see the discourse of all that happened in new France since the time it pleased the kings Majestie to send his subjects thither to discover those parts. The indifferent & unpassionate readers may easily weigh the truth of my doings, & be upright judges of the endeavour which I there used. For mine owne part I will not accuse nor excuse any: it sufficeth me to have folowed the truth of the history, whereof many are able to beare witnes, which were there present. I will plainly say one thing, That the long delay that Captaine John Ribault used in his embarking, & the fifteen daies that he spent in roving along the coast of Florida before he came to our fort Caroline, were the cause of the losse that we sustained. For he discovered the coast the fourteenth of August, & spent the time in going from river to river, which had been sufficient for him to have discharged his ships in, & for me to have embarked my selfe to returne into France. I wote well that all that hee did was upon a good intent: yet in mine opinion he should have had more regard unto his charge, then to the devises of his owne braine, which sometimes be printed in his head so deepely that it was very hard to put them out: which also turned to his utter undoing: for hee was no sooner departed from us, but a tempest tooke him, which in fine wrackt him uppon the coast, where all his ships were cast away, & he with much adooe escaped drowning, to fall into their hands, which cruelly massacred him and all his company.[7]

7. The Spanish assault on Fort Caroline, September 29, is described on pp. 165 below.

35. The Last Phase, 1568

THE MASSACRE at Fort Caroline was an insult to France that Huguenot and Catholic alike resented. Dominique de Gourges took out an expedition in 1567 designed to destroy as much as he could of the Spanish settlement in Florida, and so revenge Ribault and his men. He reached Florida in April 1568 and rapidly made contact with the Indians, Satourioua assuring him that the Spaniards had made themselves his enemies and agreeing to assist in an attack on their settlements. The French fort was by now rebuilt as San Mateo and was defended downstream by two smaller forts, San Gabriel on the north bank of the St. Johns River and San Estebán on the south. Taking the two smaller forts by assault, he ambushed a reconnoitering force from San Mateo. This caused such terror in the garrison that they deserted the fort and took to the woods, where they were killed or captured by the Indians. Survivors from all three strong points were ceremonially hanged in revenge for the 1565 massacre. Gourges did not feel himself strong enough to make more than a gesture—though he might well have taken St. Augustine as well—and so sailed home. Although this represented the last overt challenge to Spain in Florida, the French continued to frequent the South Carolina rivers. In 1577 they had for a time a fort north of Santa Elena, and in 1605 the Spaniards captured a French ship in Charleston Harbor that was marking out sites for a renewed French occupation, which, however, was never attempted. The account of the 1568 attack is given in Laudonnière's History, reprinted by Hakluyt, The principal navigations, III (1600) 356–360 (IX [1904], 100–vv2).

Captaine Gourges a Gentleman borne in the Countrey neere unto Bordeaux incited with a desire of revenge, to repaire the honour of his nation, borrowed of his friends and sold part of his owne goods to set forth and furnish three ships of indifferent burthen with all things necessary, having in them an hundred and fiftie souldiers, and fourscore chosen Mariners. . . . He . . . landed 15 league from the fort, at the mouth of the River Tacacouru, which the Frenchmen called Seine. . . . [Contact was made with Satourioua who ceremonially came to visit him.] Afterward Gourges being about to speake, Satourioua prevented him, declaring at large unto him the incredible wrongs, and continuall outrages that all the Savages, their wives and children had received of the Spanyards since their comming into the Countrey and massacring of the Frenchmen, with their continuall desire if we would assist them thoroughly to revenge so shamefull a treason, aswell as their owne particular griefes, for the firme good will they always had borne unto the Frenchmen. . . .

Now he had learned that the Spanyards were foure hundred strong, devided into three forts builded and flanked, and well fortified upon the river of May, the great fort especially begunne by the French, and afterward repaired by them: upon the most dangerous and principall landing place whereof, two leagues lower and neerer towarde the Rivers mouth, they had made two smaller Forts, which were defended, the river passing betweene them, with sixe score souldiers, good store of artillery and other munition, which they had in the same. [The two smaller forts were taken with Indian assistance: Gourges then turned on San Mateo.] But the Governour hastened his unhappy destiny, causing threescore shotte to sallie foorth, which . . . advanced forward to descrye the number and valour of the French, whereof twentie . . . getting betweene the Fort and them which were now issued forth, cut off their repassage. . . . So that turning their backs as soone as they were charged and compassed by his Lieutenant, they remained all slaine upon the place. Whereat the rest that were besieged were so astonished, that they knew none other meane to save their lives, but by fleeting into the Woodes adjoyning, where neverthelesse being incountred againe by the arrowes of the Savages . . . some were constrayned to turne backe, choosing rather to dye by the hand of the French, which pursued them. . . . The Fort when it was taken, was found well provided of all necessaries: namely of five double Colverines, and foure Mynions, with divers other small pieces of all sorts, and eighteen grosse cakes of gunnpowder. . . .

The rest of the Spaniards being led away prisoners with the others, after that the Generall had shewed them the wrong which they had done without occasion to all the French Nation, were all hanged on the boughes of the same trees, whereon the French hung. . . . But instead of the writing which Pedro Melendes[1] hanged over them, importing these wordes in Spanish, I doe not this as unto Frenchmen, but as unto Lutherans, Gourges caused to

1. Pedro Menéndez de Avilés.

be imprinted with a searing iron in a table of Firrewood, I doe not this as unto Spaniardes, nor as unto Mariners, but as unto Traitors, Robbers, and Murtherers. Afterward considering he had not men inough to keepe his Forts which he had wonne, much lesse to store them . . . hee resolved to raze them. . . . This done by Gourges, that he might returne to his Shippes which were left in the River of Seyne² . . . fifteene leagues distant from thence . . . he marched by land alwayes in battell [ar]ray, finding the wayes covered with Savages, which came to honour him with presents and prayses, as the deliverer of all the countries round about adjoyning. . . . Briefly being arrived and finding his ships set in order, and everything ready to set sayle, hee counselled the kings to continue in the amities and ancient league which they had made with the king of France, which would defend them against all Nations: which they all promised, shedding teares because of his departure.

2. St. Mary's River, lat. 30° 42′ N. (*Imago Mandi*, xvii, 32).

IX

Spanish Florida, 1565–1612

AFTER SO MANY false starts, Spanish Florida got off to an effective as well as a bloody beginning. On the ruins of the French colony Pedro Menéndez de Avilés was able rapidly to build up a chain of Spanish posts and missions from Tampa Bay to Port Royal Sound and to make valuable probings into the interior. Philip II in 1565 had been willing to contribute lavishly to Menéndez's own investment. But after a year, or at most two, it became clear that the future of the colony was a dubious one. The Indians were incalculable: unwilling to pay tribute regularly, they also rapidly turned hostile to missionary activities, which threatened both their customs and their routine of living, so that the prospect of long periods of pacification by force or persuasion or both clearly lay before the Spanish authorities. Once Menédez's private resources had been depleted it became clear that the royal support for the colony, money (or supplies in lieu of payment) for 150 men of the garrison was not enough to do more than maintain a small garrison center at St. Augustine and an outpost or two at San Mateo and Santa Elena at most.

The attempt to establish civilian settlers at St. Augustine and Santa Elena failed. At neither place did agriculture flourish, while Indian robbery and attacks gradually wore down their endurance and they drifted off to the Caribbean. Menéndez became involved in various tasks for the king of Spain and was unable to give his full attention to Florida. The French raid of 1568 on San Mateo was followed by an English raid on St. Augustine in 1571; there were alarms from the French in the North from 1577 to 1580. St. Augustine was wiped out by Drake in 1586 and Santa Elena, for a time, abandoned. A major Indian rising in 1577 destroyed much of the missionary work and local diplomacy of the early years; the greater rising of 1597 devastated the colony and left a legacy of bitterness and hatred on account of its savage suppression. Only when the colony looked like being wiped out did the authorities in Spain or in the Indies send more than the regular ration of money and supplies. At the same time, the imperial objectives—the maintenance of a post on the mainland for the rescue of shipwrecked sailors and cargoes and the denial of the shore to foreign powers—were achieved, if at times by good fortune rather than contrivance. The failure of the movement to abandon the colony in 1602 testified to the confidence of the authorities that

Florida had still a small role to play in the Spanish empire. Once the English were established in Virginia, from 1607 onwards, reasons of prestige forced the Spaniards to remain where they were. Both Pedro Menéndez de Avilés and Pedro Menéndez Marqués, who dominated the first twenty years of the colony, were able soldiers and far from negligible diplomatists. The Spanish hold on North America was maintained largely through their personal efforts.

Expansion beyond Santa Elena remained an ambition before all Spanish governors. An expedition in 1566 formally annexed what are now the Carolina Outer Banks. Pedro Menéndez sponsored the Jesuit mission to Chesapeake Bay in 1570 which was so soon wiped out by the Powhatan Indians. From 1584 onward the Spaniards had the threat of the English exploration and settlement in the Carolina Outer Banks area to urge them to further efforts; the expedition of Vicente Gonzales in 1588 failed to find any English settlers on Chesapeake Bay, but produced some interesting geographical information. The extracts given below illustrate the establishment of the Florida colony on the ruins of the French experiments, something of the expansionist movement between 1566 and 1588, and an indication of the Spanish reaction to Drake's raid in 1586. A short geographical description indicates the tiny scale of Spanish activity after nearly fifty years. Nothing can be done here to illustrate the problems of day-to-day administration.

Gonzalo Solís de Merás, Pedro Menéndez de Avilés edited by Jeanette T. Connor (1923, repr. 1965), and Bartolomé Barrientos, The Life of Pedro Menéndez de Avilés in Genaro Garcia, Dos antiquos relaciones de la Florida (1902), translated by Anthony Kerrigan (1965), pp. 1–152, are the main Spanish sources for the conquest. Lowery, Spanish Settlements, II, is still the fullest narrative. The introduction and texts in Jeanette T. Connor, ed., Colonial Records of Spanish Florida, 1577–1580, and C. W. Arnade, Florida on Trial, 1593–1602 (1959) are valuable. On the expansion, see L. A. Vigneras, "A Spanish Discovery of North Carolina in 1566," North Carolina Historical Review, XLVI (1969), 398–415; Clifford M. Lewis and Albert J. Loomie, The Spanish Jesuit Mission in Virginia, 1570–1572 (1953); Irene A. Wright, ed., Further English Voyages to America, 1583–1594 (1951) (on Drake's raid); and D. B. Quinn, "Some Spanish Reactions to Elizabethan Colonial Enterprises," Transactions of the Royal Historical Society, 5th ser., I (1951), 1–23.

36. The Capture of Fort Caroline
and the Foundation of St. Augustine, 1565

SUBSTANTIAL EXTRACTS are given from Solís de Merás, Pedro Menéndez de Avilés, translated by Jeanette T. Connor, to record the first major clash between European forces in North America. Solís de Merás is strongly biased in favor of Spain (Laudonnière on the French side, though not impartial, is appreciably more detached). His account of the massacre of the French prisoners in cold blood is omitted as perhaps too strong for contemporary taste. The extracts are taken from pp. 80–107.

They sailed until August 28th, St. Augustine's Day, on which they sighted the land of Florida; all of them kneeling, saying the *Te Deum Laudamus*, they praised Our Lord, all the people repeating their prayers, entreating Our Lord to give them victory in all things.

And because they knew not in what part the Lutherans had fortified themselves, they sailed for four days along the coast, very much distressed, and in great suspense, not knowing whether the French were north or south of where the said Adelantado was going with his armada, sailing by day and anchoring at night; and one morning he saw Indians on the coast. He sent his camp master to land with 20 arquebusiers . . . the Indians awaited him, received him well and were reassured: then the camp master arrived and spoke with them, and through signs they told him that the French were about 20 leagues from there, to the north . . . they reiterated what they had said, that the French were 20 leagues from there; the Adelantado left them very happy and embarked on his ships and went sailing along the coast with his armada, and discovered 8 leagues from there a good harbor, with a good beach, to which he gave the name of St. Augustine,[1] because that was the first land he discovered in Florida, and he did so on the very day of St. Augustine. On the following day, three hours after noontime, as he was proceeding along the coast, he discovered four large galleons at anchor. As it appeared to him that that was the harbor where

1. We should probably use the Spanish form, San Agustín, for the period 1565 to 1612.

the French were,[2] that succor had come to them and that those galleons belonged to their armada, he entered into council with his captains and told them that as he held it for certain that the French armada had come and that their fort could not be taken, nor their armed harbor . . . that the Frenchmen could not reasonably expect him so soon on that coast; they would have their infantry on land and be unloading the supplies, as those vessels, being large, could not enter the harbor laden; and it seemed to him that they (the Spaniards) should go to fight with them, for if they captured them, the French would not have an armada sufficient to go out in search of him on the seas; and that they could return to the port of St. Augustine, which was twelve leagues from there, and disembark in that harbor and fortify themselves, and send the ships to Hispaniola to give tidings to the armada he was in need of; and that the infantry, horses and supplies his Majesty had ordered to be given him, should all come together in March to that port of St. Augustine, and once they had arrived there, they could go against the enemy by land and sea, capturing their harbor, because they had their fort . . . inland on the river bank . . . the said Adelantado told them that he had determined to attack the French armada, which they all approved. Then he ordered the captains to go to their ships and gave them instructions as to what they had to do, and he gave orders to the Admiral of the fleet as to what point he was to support and what position he was to take, with two vessels he indicated to him and the one whereon he was, which made three in all; the other ship, a patache, the Adelantado commanded not to leave the side of his flagship. And so, sailing along with fair weather, they were about three leagues from the French armada, which was anchored off its harbor and consisted of four large galleons, when the wind died down, and there was much thunder and lightning and a heavy shower, which lasted until 9 o'clock at night, and then the sky became very serene and clear, and the wind shifted toward land . . . he decided to anchor in front of their bows, in such manner that when the cables were let loose after the anchors had caught, the sterns of the ships of the said Adelantado would overlap the prows of the enemy's ships, and

2. The mouth of the St. Johns River.

at dawn the next morning, by loosening the cables they could board the enemy . . . and then he had the trumpets sounded hailing the enemy, and they answered him, hailing him with theirs; and presently when these salutes were ended, the said Adelantado spoke to them with much courtesy, saying: "Señores, whence comes that armada?" One only replied that it came from France. He asked them again: "What is it doing here?" They said to him: "We are bringing infantry, artillery and supplies for a fort which the King of France has in this country, and for others which he is to build." . . .

The Adelantado replied to them: "He who asks this of you is called Pedro Menéndez, this armada belongs to the King of Spain and I am the General thereof; and I come to hang and behead all the Lutherans I may find on this sea and in this land; and thus do I bring instructions from my King, which I shall fulfil at dawn when I shall board your ships; and if I should find any Catholic, I will give him good treatment."

Many together answered many shameless and insulting words against the King our Master, calling him by his name, and against the said Adelantado, saying: "Let that be for the King, Don Felipe, and this for Pedro Menéndez, and if thou beest a brave man, as they say, come and wait not until tomorrow." The Adelantado, on hearing such unseemly words to the detriment of his King, ordered the cables to be loosened to board the enemy, and as the sailors did this unwillingly, he leaped down from the bridge to hasten them. The cable was wound round the capstan; it could not be loosened so quickly; when the enemy saw this, and heard sounded the Adelantado's command, they feared him, cut the cables, unfurled the sails and fled.

The said Adelantado did the same with his ships, and pursued them in such manner that when he was in the midst of them, he followed (in the flagship) with a patache, the two (galleons) which took the direction of the north, and his Admiral pursued, with the three ships, the other two which turned to the south. . . . And thus it happened that the said Adelantado chased the two French galleons northward for about five or six leagues, until dawn, and his Admiral went as many after the other two which sailed to the south; and the said Adelantado . . . went to the harbor of St.

Augustine, where he arrived on the eve of Our Lady of September; and as soon as he reached there he landed about three hundred soldiers, and sent two captains with them, who were to reconnoitre at daybreak the next morning the lay of the land and the places which seemed to them strongest (for defense), in order that they might dig a trench quickly while it was being seen where they could build a fort, so that the next day when the said Adelantado should land, they could show him what they had observed, and decide what would be most proper to do about it.

And on the following day, the day of Our Lady of September,[3] the said Adelantado landed near noon, when he found many Indians awaiting him there, as they had had tidings of him from the other Indians with whom he had spoken four days before; he had a solemn mass said in honor of Our Lady, and when that was ended, he took possession of the country in the name of his Majesty; he received the solemn oath of the officials of his Majesty's Royal Exchequer, the camp master and the captains, that they would all serve his Majesty with entire loyalty and fidelity, and this being done, the said Adelantado had the Indians fed and dined himself. On finishing he went immediately to see the locations which appeared to the captains he had sent, suitable for the trench; and leaving the site marked out,[4] he returned to the ships . . . (and) in two days and a half he took ashore the people, the artillery, the munitions and a large part of the supplies. . . . At dawn the French armada was near there, a quarter of a league away . . . and a ship and three shallops of the enemy came on, and because of the extreme low tide and the sea's not being very calm, it was dangerous to cross the bar . . . and about two hours from the time the enemy were waiting for the tide to be high, God Our Lord performed a miracle; for the weather being fair and clear, suddenly the sea rose very high, and a strong and contrary north wind came up, which made the return to their fort and harbor difficult for the French.

Then the Adelantado said to them, having thanked them for their favorable reply:

3. Nativity of the Blessed Virgin Mary, September 8.
4. On Anastasia Island.

"Gentlemen, I feel impelled to tell you of a very good opportunity which presents itself to my soul and reason, for we must not lose it, and it behooves us to take advantage of it and not allow it to pass by, and it is that I consider—and this is common sense— that as the French armada fled from me four days ago and now comes in search of me, they must have strengthened themselves with part of the men they had as a garrison in their fort, and these must be from among the best (men) and captains: the wind is too contrary for them to return to their harbor and fort, and to all appearance it will last so for many days . . . (and) it seems to me that we must take 500 men, two thirds of them arquebusiers, the other third pikemen, and rations for 8 days in our knapsacks, without any porters, carrying our arms on our backs; and that you ten captains, each with your banner and officers, with the number of 50 men to each captain, should go (with me) to reconnoitre the country and the fort where the Lutherans are, and the way to them; for although we know not the way, with our compass I shall know how to guide you, within two leagues right or left of the right direction; and wherever we find woods, we shall open a path with the hatchets so as to pass and know how to return; for I am taking a Frenchman with me who has been more than a year in that fort;[5] he says he is acquainted with the country for two leagues around and can take us to the fort; and if we see that we are not discovered, it may be that a quarter of an hour before dawn, we can capture their fort. . . ."

The next day at daybreak they sounded reveillé with trumpets, fifes and drums; the bells chimed and all thronged to mass; and having heard it, they departed hopefully, all setting out marching in order.

The Adelantado took 20 soldiers, all Biscayans and Asturians, with their hatchets; a Biscayan captain with them who was called Martin Ochoa, and 2 Indians who had come there, brothers, who seemed to be angels that God was sending; these told them by signs that they had been in the fort of the French six days before; and he went ahead, marching as far in front as he could, marking

5. Jean François, who had been captured while on a privateering expedition to the Caribbean.

the path, blazing the trees with the hatchets . . . he approached to less than a quarter of a league from the fort, where he decided to spend that night in a very bad and swampy place; and on account of the bad night he turned back to look for the rear-guard so that they should succeed in finding the way. It was after 10 when they finished arriving. . . .

Then he said to them: "Gentlemen, are you confident that the forest is very near the fort?"

They replied that they were.

He said to them: "Then it appears to me that we ought to go and try our fortune, as has been agreed." . . . He gave the order to march, he himself going ahead, taking with him the Frenchman whom they had as guide, with his hands bound behind him by a rope, the end whereof was held by the Adelantado himself . . . and when they had arrived at a little rise in the ground, the Frenchman told him that behind there, below, was the fort; that the water from the river washed against it, and that it was about three arquebus shots from there.

The Adelantado gave the Frenchman over to Francisco de Castañeda, the captain of his guard, who never left his side; and bending forward very quickly he went to the top of the hill, discovered the river and saw some houses, but he could not see the fort, although it was near them. . . . [Menéndez and Martin Ochoa went to reconnoiter, enticed a French sentinel out and surprised him, killed two others who appeared but whose shouts brought up the other Spaniards. Whereupon] the Adelantado cried in a loud voice:

"Santiago! At them! God is helping! Victory! The French are killed! The camp master is inside the fort and has captured it!"

And then all began to run forward in disorder along the path, but the Adelantado remained motionless, always repeating this, without ceasing. The soldiers held it for certain that many had gone with the camp master and that the fort was won: they felt great joy and satisfaction, in such wise that he who could run fastest was considered the most valiant, and there were no cripples, nor maimed, nor cowards; they passed on running, and when they arrived near the fort, the postern of the principal gate was opened at the shouts raised by the people outside the fort; the camp master closed in on the postern, slew the man who opened it and stole in, and after him those who could enter the soonest: some of the Frenchmen in the houses came out in their shirts and others who were clothed, to find out what was happening: these were killed at once, and others took to flight and threw themselves down from the walls of the fort. Two flags were presently brought in: one belonged to the sergeant major, which was raised on a caballero[6] by his ensign, who was called Rodrigo Troche, of Tordesillas; the other belonged to Diego de Maya, and it was set up on another caballero by his ensign, Cristóbal de Herrera, a mountaineer: there was some quarrelling between these two ensigns as to who had been first: this could not be ascertained. The trumpeters entered at the same time as those two flags and they placed themselves on those caballeros near the flags, sounding victory; whereat all the French became terrified; and all our men came running through the gate, which was opened wide to them, and went through the quarters of the French without leaving one alive . . . except about 50 or 60, who threw themselves down from the walls of the fort and took refuge in the woods. . . .

And he made Captain Gonzalo de Villarroel, who was the sergeant major, alcalde of that fort and governor of that district; who had worked very hard and with much system and care, and who appeared to him a very good and trustworthy soldier for the office; and it was delivered to him and he took the accustomed oath, and (the Adelantado) gave the fort the name of San Mateo because the day he captured it was St. Matthew's Day.[7] He commanded that from that day forward he (the sergeant major) should hold and defend it in the name of his Majesty with 300 soldiers whom he would leave him for the guarding thereof. . . .

It took them three days to arrive in St. Augustine, for owing to the victory Our Lord had given them, they did not feel the journey, nor the hardships thereof, in the desire they had to give this good news to their comrades. . . . The people who had remained there held them for lost, because of the bad weather they had had and the news given them by those who had returned, as they knew that

6. An interior defense which was erected on a platform on the parade ground, and served to protect a part of the fort.
7. September 21.

they had no kind of food, powder nor wicks; but when the good news came, 4 priests who were there immediately set out, holding the cross aloft, and followed by all the sea and land forces, the women and children, in a procession singing the *Te Deum Lauda-mus;* they received the Adelantado with great pleasure and rejoicing, everyone laughing and weeping for joy, praising God for so great a victory; and so they escorted the Adelantado in triumph to the intrenchment and settlement of St. Augustine, where he related to them in detail the very great mercy which Our Lord had shown them through his victory.

37. Annexation of the North Carolina Coast, 1566

IN 1566 Pedro Menéndez sent Fray Pablo de San Pedro and Captain Pedro de Coronas, with Don Luis, a hispaniolized Indian taken at Chesapeake Bay in 1561, to establish a forward base for Spain on the Bay of St. Mary (Chesapeake Bay). Missing the entrance to the Bay, the ship Trinidad worked its way southward and sent a boat ashore on the Carolina Outer Banks. The latitude was estimated to be 36°30′ N. An inlet was entered but no Indians were seen. The country was then, on August 25, 1566, annexed for Spain under the name of the River of St. Bartholomew (Rio de San Bartolomé): the escrivano (recorder) of the expedition, Diego de Camargo, put the annexation on record. The ship ultimately returned to Spain without reaching Chesapeake Bay. The documents were first published in translation by Vigneras, "A Spanish Discovery of North Carolina," North Carolina Historical Review, XLVI, the extract being from 413.

And having thus entered the river, Fray Pablo de San Pedro, governor, Captain Pedro de Coronas and all the soldiers made their way to the shore in the boat. . . . And in my presence, the said captain declared that, since he had been appointed captain by the most illustrious señor Pedro Menéndez de Avilés, governor and captain general for His Majesty of the land and coast of the provinces of Florida . . . he nevertheless wished to further enhance His Majesty's service and authority, and seize and take possession of the said land and harbor, he requested that I record in the register of the expedition the said declaration of ownership and give him a transcription of the original as evidence. The said captain then walked through the land, cut branches, made a cross and planted it on the beach, and declared that he gave to the river the name San Bartolomé, because it was discovered on the day of the Blessed Apostle San Bartolomé. . . . Diego de Camargo.

38. The Jesuit Mission on the York River, 1570–1571

DON LUIS, a member of the ruling family of the Powhatan Indians, had become a Christian and was still regarded, after the failure of the 1566 venture, as an instrument who could be used by the Jesuit mission that Father Segura wished to establish beyond the Spanish sphere of influence and outside the protection of the Florida garrison. Juan Baptista de Segura, Luis de Quirós, three other Jesuits and four catechists were designated for the mission, which was to be located in the country of Don Luis's tribe on Chesapeake Bay. The ships bearing the missionaries reached the James River in September 1570 and disembarked them some distance upstream, from which the men made their way overland to the next major inlet, the York River, where they built their mission, the exact site not being known. Don Luis and his people were friendly at first but they soon turned against the mission. The Jesuits failed to prevent Don Luis from reverting to his tribal customs. The demands of the missionaries for food proved irksome and their possessions appeared desirable, so, on February 9, 1571, Don Luis led a party to the mission where all were savagely killed, with the exception of one boy catechist, Alonso de Olmos, who was spared. A supply ship failed to find the mission, but captured an Indian from whom they learned it had been destroyed. Pedro Menéndez de Avilés commanded an expedition to Chesapeake Bay in August 1572 when Alonso was rescued and a number of Indians killed in revenge. No further attempt was made to Christianize the people of this area.

A. *Father Luis de Quirós to Juan de Hinistrosa,*
from Ajacán, September 12, 1570

Lewis and Loomie, The Spanish Jesuit Mission in Virginia, pp. 89–92, extracts.

ILLUSTRIOUS LORD,

. . . After having been delayed in arriving here much more than we had expected by those adversities which you understand are usual in the discovery of new regions, and by the discomforts of the weather, as the pilot will narrate to you more at length, we arrived here and unloaded our cargo yesterday, which was the tenth day of September. We departed as you know on the fifth of August from Santa Elena. We find the land of Don Luis in quite another condition than expected, not because he was at fault in his description of it, but because Our Lord has chastised it with six years of famine and death, which has brought it about that there is much less population than usual. Since many have died and many also have moved to other regions to ease their hunger, there remain but few of the tribe, whose leaders say that they wish to die where their fathers have died, although they have no maize, and have not found wild fruit, which they are accustomed to eat. Neither roots nor anything else can be had, save for a small amount obtained with great labor from the soil, which is very parched. So the Indians have nothing else to offer to us and to those who came on the ship but good will, and certainly these Indians have shown that in a kindly manner. They seemed to think that Don Luis had risen from the dead and come down from heaven, and since all who remained are his relatives, they are greatly consoled in him. They have recovered their courage and hope that God may seek to favor them, saying that they want to be like Don Luis, begging us to remain in this land with them. . . .

Thus we have felt the good will which this tribe is showing. On the other hand, as I have said, they are so famished, that all believe they will perish of hunger and cold this winter. For only with great difficulty can they find roots by which they usually sustain themselves, and the great snows found in this land do not allow them to hunt for them. Seeing then the good will that this tribe has shown, great hope is had of its conversion and of the service of Our Lord and His Majesty and of an entrance into the mountains and to China, etc. Therefore, it has seemed best to Father to risk remaining despite such scanty stores, because on our trip we have consumed two of the four barrels of biscuit and the small amount of flour which was given us for the journey. We had to help the entire

ship with some supplies, as we were ill-provisioned for the journey.
I am convinced that there will be no lack of opportunity to exercise patience, and to succeed we must suffer much. But it has seemed good to expose ourselves to that risk and this especially so, since in your kindness you might be able to send us a generous quantity of corn to sustain us and to let all this tribe take some for sowing. As it touches the service of Our Lord and His Majesty, it would be best that you see to it that we are supplied with all speed possible. If it cannot be done in the winter, it is imperative that some provisions arrive some time during March or at the beginning of April so that we can give seeds to the tribe for planting. At this time the planting is done here, and thus many of the tribes will come here after being scattered over the region in search of food and there will be a good opportunity for the Holy Gospel. The chief has sought this very thing especially. As to information about the land that touches the route along which the pilot must be directed, he himself will give it. It is not convenient to enter by the river we did, for we did not have as good information from the Indians as was necessary about the place we should have entered. And so, today, the pilot has gone overland 2 good leagues away to see a river, which he will enter when with good fortune he comes again to help us and visit us. Through this region he can go by water up to the place where we plan to make our encampment. To reach this spot, it is two good leagues by land, and two others or more by water, so that the goods, which we have unloaded in this uninhabited place reached by the river where we now are, must be carried by the Indians on their shoulders for these 2 leagues and then embarked in canoes, which is sufficiently laborious. . . .
From this port on the 12th of September, 1570.
By order of Father Vice-Provincial.

Your chaplain
QUIRÓS

B. *Father Juan Rogel to Father Francis Borgia, General
of the Society of Jesus, from the Bay of Madre de Dios,
August 28, 1572*

Lewis and Loomie, The Jesuit Mission in Virginia, pp. 109–110, relating the account given to the punitive expedition by the boy Alonso de Olmos after his rescue.

Now I will relate to Your Paternity how Ours who were here suffered death, as this boy tells it. After they arrived there, Don Luis abandoned them, since he did not sleep in their hut more than two nights nor stay in the village where the Fathers made their settlement for more than five days. Finally he was living with his brothers a journey of a day and a half away. Father Master Baptista sent a message by a novice Brother on two occasions to the renegade. Don Luis would never come, and Ours stayed there in great distress, for they had no one by whom they could make themselves understood to the Indians. They were without means of support, and no one could buy grain from them [the Indians]. They got along as best they could, going to other villages to barter for maize with copper and tin, until the beginning of February. The boy says that each day Father Baptista caused prayers to be said for Don Luis, saying that the devil held him in great deception. As he had twice sent for him and he had not come, he decided to send Father Quirós and Brother Gabriel de Solís and Brother Juan Baptista to the village of the chief near where Don Luis was staying. Thus they could take Don Luis along with them and barter for maize on the way back. On the Sunday after the feast of the Purification, Don Luis came to the three Jesuits who were returning with other Indians. He sent an arrow through the heart of Father Quirós and then murdered the rest who had come to speak with him. Immediately Don Luis went on to the village where the Fathers were, and with great quiet and dissimulation, at the head of a large group of Indians, he killed the five who waited there. Don Luis himself was the first to draw blood with one of those hatchets which were brought along for trading with the Indians; then he finished the killing of Father Master Baptista with his axe, and his companions finished off the others. This boy says that when he saw them killing the Fathers and Brothers, he sought to go among the Indians as they inflicted the wounds so that they might kill him too. For it seemed better to him to die with Christians than live alone with Indians. A brother of Don Luis took him by the arm and did not let him go. This happened five or six days after the death of the others. This boy then told Don Luis to bury them since he had killed them, and at least in their burial, he was kind to them.

39. Sir Francis Drake's Raid
on St. Augustine, 1586

SIR FRANCIS DRAKE had left Cartagena, after ransoming it, on April 24, 1586, and appeared off St. Augustine on June 6 following. After his first bombardment of the fort, the governor, Pedro Menéndez Marqués, realized he could not withstand another and so retired, with the civilians from the town, to take shelter with the local Indians. Drake destroyed the fort and town and withdrew on June 13, intending to attack Santa Elena also but, missing the way into Port Royal Sound, was unable to find it. The English narrative by Walter Bigges (and others), A summarie and true discourse of Sir Frances Drake's West Indian voyage (1589, reprinted in Hakluyt, Principal navigations, III [1600]), is extracted in D. B. Quinn, The Roanoke Voyages, 1584–1590, I, 218–277. This letter, giving the Spanish version, is from I. A. Wright, ed., Further English Voyages to Spanish America, pp. 163–164.

Pedro Menéndez Marqués
to the president of the House of Trade,
San Agustín, June 17, 1586

Very Illustrious Sir

I am reduced to such a situation that I do not know where to begin to relate the hardship and misery which have befallen this land. Therefore this communication will not be long, as will be observed.

On the 6th instant Francis Drake arrived at this port with 42 sail, 23 being large vessels and nineteen pinnaces, frigates and shallops. At dawn on the 7th he landed 500 men and with seven large pinnaces sought me forthwith in the fort. With 80 men I had in the fort I resisted him until nearly midday. In view of my resistance he sent to the ships which lay outside the bar for reinforcements, and in nine vessels landed some 2000 men and planted four pieces of artillery among certain sand dunes near the fort, with which he began to batter it. I retired as best I could, to protect my women and children (more than 200 persons).

Having occupied the fort, the enemy took and sacked the town and burned the church with its images and crosses, and cut down the fruit trees, which were numerous and good. He burned the fort and carried off the artillery and munitions and food supplies.

We are all left with the clothes we stood in, and in the open country with a little munition which was hidden. We are without food of any sort except six hogsheads of flour which will last twenty days at half a pound per head.

I am reporting to His Majesty in full in the accompanying despatch and entreat your lordship to forward it immediately, and to favour me as far and as speedily as possible, since help for Florida must come from your lordship's hands.

Our Lord, etc.

San Agustín, June 17, 1586.

Pedro Menéndez Marqués.

40. The Exploration
of Chesapeake Bay, 1588

VINCENTE GONZALES, *a Portuguese pilot in the Spanish service, was sent by Pedro Menéndez Marqués to reconnoiter Chesapeake Bay (the Bay of Madre de Dios del Jacán to the Spaniards) in May 1588 to discover where the English colonies of which he had heard were settled. Gonzales made an exceptionally quick and efficient survey of the Bay, though he found no trace of the English there. On his way back, he put in at the Carolina Outer Banks and, by accident, stumbled on some signs of the Roanoke colony. Having pinpointed one focus of English interest he returned to St. Augustine before the end of July. Luis Geronimo de Oré, Relacion de los martires que a avido en las provincias de la Florida (1617?), evidently had a journal of the Gonzales voyage. Maynard Geiger translated it as The Martyrs of Florida, 1513–1516 (1936). The portions relating to the Gonzales voyage appear in other versions in Lewis and Loomie, The Spanish Jesuit Mission in Virginia, and in Quinn, The Roanoke Voyages, 1584–1590, II, 804–812, from which these extracts come.*

In the following year (1588), towards the end of the month of May, Captain Vicente González departed from the port and fortress of San Agustín. With Gonzalez went the sergeant-major, Juan Menéndez Marqués, and thirty soldiers and sailors in a bark of San

Lúcar which had come to Havana the year before as a packet-boat. This boat was purchased for the voyage, the purpose of the expedition being to run along the coast up to the bay of Madre de Dios del Jacán in order to obtain knowledge of and to reconnoitre the English settlement and fort. . . . Finally, they arrived at the bay of Madre de Dios del Jacán in the month of June in the year 1588.

The mouth of this bay is about three leagues wide, without shoals or reefs and is more than eight fathoms deep at its entrance. It runs N.W.–S.E. and forms a large circular gulf. Between the entrance and the place where one reaches the mainland it extends westward and north-westward for about three leagues. On the mainland, and in an east-west direction with the mouth, is a good harbor which has at its entrance a depth of three fathoms. . . .

Thereupon they departed from the said harbour, coasting along the mainland shore towards the north where they discovered another haven which seemed to be a good one and of great depth. On shore there was abundance of large stones while the cape of land to the north formed a high headland. These three harbours can be seen at one glance from the mouth of the bay, the last, however, only faintly.[1]

As they continued to sail northwards the land from the east jutted into the bay. It narrowed so much that at one point, from the western shore towards the eastern side, it was only two leagues wide. After that they discovered coves and inlets, as well as rivers, along the western shore. Then they came upon a large fresh-water river, which, where it entered the bay, was more than six fathoms deep. To the north of it there was very high land, with ravines, but without trees, cleared and like a green field and pleasant to behold. On the southern shore of this river the beach is very calm and it is covered with tiny pebbles. Farther up on the south bank of the same river appeared a delightful valley, wooded, with pleasant land, apparently fertile and suitable for stock-breeding and husbandry. This river was located in latitude 38 degrees. They named it San Pedro. . . .[2]

1. The Elizabeth River (or Nansemond River), the James and the York are probably intended.
2. This may be the Potomac.

Advancing further, they discovered many other harbours and rivers carrying much water which entered the bay from the western shore until they came to latitude 35°,[3] where they saw mountain ridges, very high, running S.W.–N.E. Still more rivers were found and soon, in the middle of the bay, a small island. Along the western shore the depth began to diminish so much that they could go no further, so they turned eastwards. Opposite the island the land was high, broken and well-wooded, while nearby on the eastern side there were shoals of greater or lesser depth. Sailing closer to the mainland on the east they found a channel of great depth. Still further north they found that the hills began to close in the view.

In different places they found mouths of rivers and coves, while, where this bay ends in a semi-circle, it is about as wide as Cadiz harbour. More than two or three leagues before they reached the head of the bay they found the water was fresh. That evening they were on the point of entering a river, west-north-west between some high hills and crags.[4] At high tide the mouth was more than three fathoms deep, but because night was falling they anchored about a quarter of a league inside. At dawn there was low tide, and it was almost a miracle that the bark avoided the great rocks by which the river was enclosed from one side to the other. At great risk, and with shouts of "Boat here!" and "Be on your guard there!" she sailed out as far as the mouth of the river which was clear. There they saw a small shad floating on the water, dead and of no use. In a rivulet which came down between the rocks some small trout were seen. This was the eve of the feast of St. John the Baptist and out of devotion they called the river San Juan de las Peñas.

They went up on the ridge at a level place and saw on the other side another river and with it ranges of hills and rolling land. Below, in the fold of this range there was a fair valley with trees and with fertile and pleasing land. From latitude 38° up to the end of the bay there is to be found a great quantity of chestnuts and large walnuts, as well as wild vines with swollen grapes. And the same day they left the river and went some distance from the coast and the shore towards the east for a good while. There they dis-

3. Probably 39° is intended.
4. This would appear to be the Susquehanna River at the head of the Bay.

covered a very agreeable inlet, with thick woods where many deer appeared. They entered it towards the north, and sailed as far as its extremity. There they landed on a pleasant beach, below some small gullies. At that end of the little bay there was a quiet and pleasant valley, with trees but without any craggy places. In it they found many deer. They killed one of these and made a feast of it on the day of the grace-giving St. John the Baptist.[5]

Captain Vicente González and the pilot Ginés Pinzón took the latitude which they found to be a little over 40°. They had taken it also at the first harbour after they had entered the bay on the mainland and there they found it to be 37° 37'. On that same day, the feast of St. John, they left the end of the bay and sailed southwards along the western shore. . . .

When they left the bay it was evening.[6] All that night they worked their way south with the aid of a strong west wind. The same was true of the whole of the next day until sunset. The wind then freshening so much they were forced to dismast the ship and to bring her to the shore by means of oars. They entered on a bar of very little depth, and inside found a large cove, the southern part of which at low tide was almost dry. The view towards the north gave on to a great part of the bay and revealed a large arm in the northwest curve which was heavily wooded. And along the shore towards the north there was another opening which appeared to be better than that by which they had entered, this part of the coast for about a league, between one bar and another, being low and free of sand. And on the inside of the little bay they had entered there were signs of a slipway for small vessels, and on land a number of wells made with English casks, and other debris indicating that a considerable number of people had been here.[7]

The next day they again departed, finding the latitude to be

5. June 24.
6. It was by then June 29.
7. This was at the inlet in the Carolina Outer Banks known to the English as Port Ferdinando (near modern Oregon Inlet). The debris was that left by three English colonizing parties, 1585–87, the most recent under John White. This enabled the Spaniards to pinpoint the location of the Roanoke Island settlement. Whether it was still inhabited in 1588 we do not know.

35½° . . . they returned to San Agustín in the month of July in the same year 1588.

41. Florida
and Its Surroundings, about 1612

In the first quarter of the seventeenth century Antonio Vásquez de Espinosa wrote "The Compendium and Description of the West Indies" (translated and published by Charles Upson Clark, in Smithsonian Miscellaneous Collections, CVIII [1942]) in which he included notes on each province of the Spanish empire compiled in 1612. The Florida material comprises pp. 106–115, the extracts here being taken from pp. 106–109. It provides a brief indication of what the Spaniards had achieved: no major settlement but some mastery of the horticultural possibilities of the area.

Of the city of St. Augustine, Florida, and its district.

Florida is a point of land projecting 100 leagues into the sea; it is on a line N. from Cuba; it is about 25 or 30 leagues across from E. to W., and forms part of the mainland with New Spain. . . . This city of St. Augustine lies near the sea at the water's edge; it contains over 300 Spanish residents, who are all married soldiers living there as as a garrison. The city is well built of stone, with an excellent parish church and a Franciscan convent with some 30 friars, who are almost all evangelizing the Indians in their villages. There is a hospital to care for the indigent sick, a shrine of Santa Barbara, and a fort with some 25 excellent bronze cannon. His Majesty appoints a Governor, who is Captain General, and two Royal Officials.

The city lies full 30° N.; its climate is like that of Spain, with winter and summer; the country is fertile, level, and wooded, with some swamps. Spanish fruit trees bear with great abundance, as do cereals, garden truck, and vegetables; they grow excellent quinces, pomegranates, pears, and other kinds of fruit, and marvelous melons.

There are many districts converted to the Faith; the Indians are very good Christians and devout. One league from the city lies the village of San Sebastián, and there are other villages, like Aîs, Moloa, Matacumbe, and others, and the Province of Surruqué to the S., as one comes from Havana, and many other settlements and provinces.

The Province of Gualé is 40 leagues N. of St. Augustine; farther on is the Province of Santa Elena, and in that direction, at 120 leagues from St. Augustine, the Sierra de Tama, all rock crystal, where fine diamonds have been found; beyond which some 40 leagues to the N., lies Virginia, or Xacal [= Jacán], an English settlement.

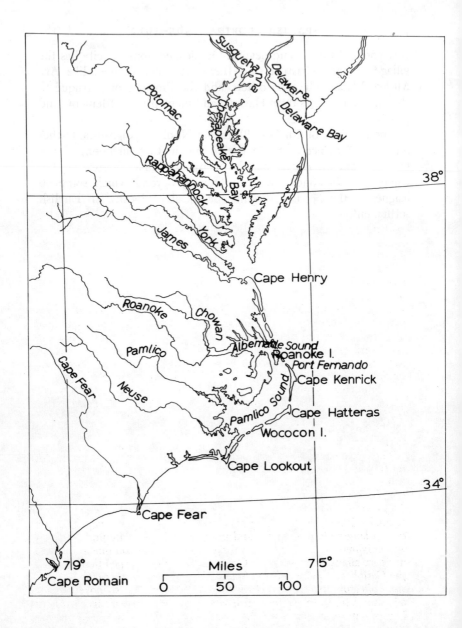

Susquehanna
Potomac
Chesapeake Bay
Delaware
Delaware Bay
38°
Rappahannock
York
James
Cape Henry
Roanoke
Chowan
Albemarle Sound
Roanoke I.
Pamlico
Port Fernando
Cape Kenrick
Cape Fear
Neuse
Pamlico Sound
Cape Hatteras
Wococon I.
Cape Lookout
34°
Cape Fear
79°
75°
Miles
0   50   100
Cape Romain

X

The Roanoke Voyages
and the First English Settlements

Not until the 1580's was any serious attention paid in England to the problems which settlement overseas presented. Sir Humphrey Gilbert had been bitten with the desire to become a landowner while he was soldiering in Ireland, and after his return he focused his attention on America for this purpose. His patent, which in 1578 allowed him to acquire and colonize unoccupied areas across the seas, did not specify America as the scene of his labors, but he intended to occupy land along its shores so as to create a great landed seignory for himself. His reconnaissance expedition in 1578 came to nothing, but between 1581 and 1583 he sold millions of acres of land in North America, which he had never seen, to anyone who would give him money for it and agree to hold it under his lordship. His first expedition to reach American waters in 1583 was diverted to Newfoundland and he was forced to turn back and was lost at sea on his return. The main focus of his activities was intended to be around Verrazzano's "Refugio," which he believed he could find and settle.

His half brother, Walter Raleigh, took up his plans in 1584 and during the next six years Raleigh, Sir Richard Grenville and Ralph Lane were the leading figures amongst those who attempted to create an American settlement.

The reconnaissance which Amadas and Barlowe carried out for Raleigh in 1584 was directed to the North American coast outside the zone of current Spanish settlement in Florida, although well inside the limits which the Spaniards had already explored and hoped to settle. The Carolina Outer Banks were sufficiently attractive and the site of Roanoke Island so promising that their report was favorable enough to win large-scale support for and investment in the enterprise. Raleigh was knighted as a symbol of royal favor, but he was too much involved in court affairs to go himself. Grenville led out an expedition through the Caribbean, spying out the Spaniards' strengths and weaknesses, and also collecting materials to stock the settlement. The Roanoke Indians allocated land to the settlers on Roanoke Island, where a small fort and houses outside it were built. Lane was left in August with 108 men to stay until the spring of 1586. His function was to experiment with agriculture, to carry out an extensive survey of the natural resources of the area, to determine how relations with the Indians could be developed, to explore in search of precious metals and to attempt to discover a harbor better than that on the Outer Banks which had already proven unsatisfactory. Under Lane, Thomas Harriot and John White carried out a survey, illustrated by many drawings; Lane attempted to track down an alleged gold mine on the Roanoke River but was unable to proceed very far into the interior; he located Chesapeake Bay as a probable deep-water harbor to which the colony could be moved. But he also fell out with the Indians and killed the Roanoke chief Wingina (Pemisapan). His men went hungry when supplies were late, so that when Sir Francis Drake put in after destroying St. Augustine, Lane proved willing to abandon the colony and return to England, bringing important news, good and bad from the English point of view, on conditions in Virginia —the name given to the area it was proposed to occupy.

Lane's return to England coincided with Grenville's arrival at Roanoke Island with reinforcements, but he left only a small holding party on the island which was soon driven off by the Indians. Raleigh and Grenville were somewhat discouraged, but John White had developed a passion for Virginia and with Raleigh's encouragement and the help of London merchants went out with settlers, including women and children, intending to pick up Grenville's men at Roanoke Island and go on to Chesapeake Bay to create there a continuing English community. White was on bad terms with the commander of the squadron, the Portuguese seaman Simon Fernandes, who took the settlers from England in April 1587 to land them in Virginia in July. Fernandes insisted they should remain at Roanoke Island as he did not wish to delay by bringing them to Chesapeake Bay. White, at the request of the planters (who included his daughter and son-in-law and their newly born daughter Virginia Dale), went home with the ships to organize rapid supplies for the colony.

Early in 1588 Raleigh and Grenville made a last attempt to create a substantial settlement. When the ships were ready to sail, the queen ordered them to join the fleet awaiting the threatened Spanish invasion. White was allowed in April to sail with supplies and a few reinforcements to Virginia, but pirates robbed him near the Azores and he was forced to turn back. After the Armada campaign there was still an embargo on sailings in 1589, so it was 1590 before White sailed back to Roanoke Island. He then found the colony deserted, with indications that at least some of the settlers had gone to friendly Indians at Croatoan, farther south along the Outer Banks. The settlers had intended to go eventually "fifty miles within the main," probably to the southern shore of Chesapeake Bay. It seems likely that some arrived there and survived until those who remained were all killed by Powhatan in 1605 or 1606. White could not get the sailors to stay for a lengthy search and gave up the attempt to find the settlers. Nor did Raleigh continue the attempt: so long as it was not established that the settlers were dead, his rights to Virginia remained good in law. He thus held his Virginia venture in reserve until he saw first what Guiana might bring and until, with the ending of the Spanish war, fresh settlers could venture to North America.

On the background see D. B. Quinn, The Voyages and Colonising Enterprises of Sir Humphrey Gilbert (2 vols., 1940), Raleigh and the British Empire (3rd ed., N.Y., 1962); A. L. Rowse, The Expansion of Elizabethan England (1955) and The Elizabethans and America (1959). On the Roanoke voyages and colonies see Quinn, The Roanoke Voyages, 1584–1590, and P. H. Hulton and D. B. Quinn, The American Drawings of John White (2 vols., 1964).

42. The Discovery of the Carolina Outer Banks and of Roanoke Island, 1584

THE REPORT which Amadas and Barlowe made of their visit to North America has an idyllic character. Clearly, the writers of this report to Walter Raleigh enjoyed what they saw and conveyed their feelings in their narrative. Simon Fernandes, a Portuguese pilot and former pirate had guided them skillfully to their destination where he had, apparently, been previously on a Spanish expedition in the 1560's. There are several indications that the narrative was appreciably altered from its original form before being circulated (in manuscript it is thought) as propaganda for the 1585 voyage. Some unpleasant incident involving a brush with Indians, possibly at Chesapeake Bay before or after the visit to Roanoke Island, was eliminated (see Quinn, Roanoke Voyages, I, 5; "Simão Fernandes, A Portuguese Pilot in the English Service," Congresso Internacional de História dos Discobrimentos, Actas, III [1961], 449–465). Details about neighboring Indians tribes could also not have been understood at the time. Some Englishmen had first to learn part of the native language, and their Indian guests, Manteo and Wanchese, who accompanied them to England, had to acquire some English before such information could be assembled. Consequently, the report is a composite document, possibly considerably rewritten by Raleigh or one of his associates some time after the return of the expedition. The document does not mention the strategic motive behind the choice of a site (the need for a base to attack Spanish shipping on its way from the Indies) or the desire to mount an exploration of the interior to find gold or a watershed with a route to the Pacific. The fertility of the land and the friendly nature of the Indians are what are stressed. The extracts come from Hakluyt, The Principall Navigations (facsimile, ed. Quinn and Skelton), II, 728–733; and Quinn, Roanoke Voyages, I, 92–115.

The 27. day of Aprill, in the yeere of our redemption, 1584. we departed the west of England, with two barkes, well furnished with men and victuals. . . .

The second of July, we found shole water, which smelt so sweetely, and was so strong a smell, as if we had bene in the midst of some delicate garden, abounding with all kinde of odoriferous flowers, by which we were assured, that the land could not be farre distant: and keeping good watch, and bearing but slacke saile, the fourth of the same moneth, we arrived upon the coast, which we supposed to be a continent, and firme lande, and wee sailed along the same, a hundred and twentie English miles, before we could finde any entrance, or river, issuing into the Sea. The first that appeared unto us, we entred, though not without some difficultie, and cast anker about three harquebushot within the havens mouth, on the left hande of the same: and after thankes given to God for our safe arrivall thither, we manned our boates, and went to viewe the lande next adjoyning, and to "take possession of the same, in the right of the Queenes most excellent Majestie, as rightfull Queene, and Princesse of the same, and after delivered the same over to your use, according to her Majesties grant, and letters patents, under her Highnes great Seale." Which being performed, according to the ceremonies used in such enterprises, wee viewed the lande about us, being whereas we first landed, very sandie, and lowe towards the water side, but so full of grapes, as the very beating, and surge of the Sea overflowed them, of which we founde such plentie, as well there, as in all places else, both on the sande, and on the greene soile on the hils, as in the plaines, as well on every little shrubbe, as also climing towardes the toppes of the high Cedars, that I thinke in all the world the like aboundance is not to be founde: and my selfe having seene those partes of Europe that most abound, finde such difference, as were incredible to be written. . . .

The next day[1] there came unto us divers boates, and in one of them the Kings brother, accompanied with fortie or fiftie men, very handsome, and goodly people, and in their behavior as mannerly, and civill, as any of Europe. His name was Granganimeo, and the King is called Wingina, the countrey Wingandacoa, (and nowe by her Majestie, Virginia,) the manner of his comming was in this sorte: hee left his boates altogether, as the first man did a little from the shippes by the shoare, and came along to the place over against the shippes, followed with fortie men. When hee came to the place, his servants spread a long matte uppon the grounde, on which he sate downe, and at the other ende of the matte, foure others of his companie did the like: the rest of his men stoode round about him, somewhat a farre off: when wee came to the shoare to him with our weapons, he never mooved from his place, nor any of the other foure, nor never mistrusted any harme to be offered from us, but sitting still, he beckoned us to come, and sitte by him, which wee perfourmed: and beeing sette, hee makes all signes of joy, and welcome, striking on his head, and his breast, and afterwardes on ours, to shewe we were all one, smiling, and making shewe the best hee could, of all love, and familiaritie. After hee had made a long speech unto us, wee presented him with divers things, which hee receaved very joyfully, and thankefully. . . .

After wee had presented this his brother, with such things as we thought he liked, we likewise gave somewhat to the other that sate with him on the matte: but presently he arose, and tooke all from them, and put it into his owne basket, making signes and tokens, that all things ought to be delivered unto him, and the rest were but his servants, and followers. A daye or two after this, we fell to trading with them, exchanging some thinges that we had for Chammoys, Buffe, and Deere skinnes: when we shewed him all our packet of merchandize, of all things that he saw, a bright tinne dishe most pleased him, which he presently tooke up, & clapt it before his breast, & after made a hole in the brimme thereof, & hung it about his necke, making signes, that it would defende him against his enemies arrowes: for those people maintaine a deadlie and terrible warre, with the people and King adjoyning. We ex-

1. Apparently July 16.

changed our tinne dishe for twentie skinnes, woorth twentie
Crownes, or twentie Nobles: and a copper kettle for fiftie skinnes
woorth fiftie Crownes. They offered us very good exchange for our
hatchets, and axes, and for knives, and would have given any thing
for swords: but we would not depart with any. After two or three
daies, the Kings brother came aboord the shippes, and dranke wine,
and ate of our meate, and of our bread, and liked exceedingly
thereof: and after a few daies overpassed, he brought his wife with
him to the shippes, his daughter, and two or three little children:
his wife was very well favored, of meane stature, and very bash-
ful. . . .

The Kings brother had great liking of our armour, a sworde, and
divers other things, which we had: and offered to laye a great boxe
of pearle in gage for them: but wee refused it for this time, because
we would not make them knowe, that wee esteemed thereof, untill
we had understoode in what places of the Countrey the pearle
grewe: which nowe your Worshippe doth very well understand.

He was very just of his promise: for many times wee delivered
him merchandize uppon his worde, but ever he came within the
daye, and performed his promise. Hee sent us every daye a brase or
two of fatte Buckes, Conies, Hares, Fishe, the best of the worlde.
Hee sent us divers kindes of fruites, Melons, Walnuts, Cucumbers,
Gourdes, Pease, and divers rootes, and fruites very excellent good,
and of their Countrey corne, which is very white, faire, and well
tasted, and groweth three times in five monethes: In Maye they
sowe, in July they reape: in June they sowe, in August they reape:
in July they sowe, in September they reape: onely they cast the
corne into the ground, breaking a little of the soft turfe with a
woodden mattocke, or pickeaxe: our selves prooved the soile, and
put some of our Pease into the ground, and in tenne daies they
were of foureteene inches high: they have also Beanes very faire, of
divers colours, and wonderfull plentie: some growing naturally, and
some in their gardens, and so have they both wheat and oates.

The soile is the most plentifull, sweete, fruitfull, and wholsome
of all the world: there are above foureteene severall sweete smelling timber trees, and the most part of their underwoods are Bayes,
and such like: they have those Okes that we have, but farre greater
and better. After they had bene divers times aboord our shippes,
my selfe, with seven more, went twentie mile into the River, that

runneth toward the Citie of Skicoake, which River they call Occam: and the evening following, we came to an Island, which they call Roanoak, distant from the harbour by which we entred, seven leagues: and at the North ende thereof, was a village of nine houses, built of Cedar, and fortified round about with sharpe trees, to keepe out their enemies, and the entrance into it made it like a turne pike very artificially. . . .

We were entertained with all love, and kindnes, and with as much bountie, after their manner, as they could possibly devise. Wee found the people most gentle, loving, and faithfull, void of all guile, and treason, and such as lived after the manner of the golden age. The earth bringeth foorth all things in aboundance, as in the first creation, without toile or labour. The people onely care to defend themselves from the cold, in their short winter, and to feede themselves with such meate as the soile affoordeth: their meate is very well sodden, and they make broth very sweete, and savorie: their vessels are earthen pots, very large, white, and sweete: their dishes are woodden platters of sweete timber: within the place where they feede, was their lodging, and within that their Idoll, which they worship, of which they speake uncredible things. . . .

Beyonde this Islande, there is the maine lande, and over against this Islande falleth into this spatious water, the great river called Occam, by the Inhabitants, on which standeth a Towne called Pemeoke, and six daies journey further upon the same is situated their greatest citie, called Schycoake, which this people affirme to be very great: but the Savages were never at it, onely they speake of it, by the report of their Fathers, and other men, whome they have heard affirme it, to be aboue one daies journey about.

Into this river falleth another great river, called Cipo, in which there is found great store of the Muscels, in which there are pearles: likewise there descendeth into this Occam, another river, called Nomopana, on the one side whereof standeth a great Towne, called Chowanoake, and the Lord of that Towne and Countrey, is called Pooneno: this Pooneno is not subject to the King of Wingandacoa, but is a free Lorde. Beyonde this Countrey, is there another King, whome they call Menatoan, and these three Kinges are in league with eache other. Towards the Sunne set, foure daies journey, is situate a Towne called Sequotan, which is the Westermost Towne of Wingandacoa. . . .

Adjoyning unto this Towne aforesaide called Sequotan, beginneth a Countrey called Ponouike, belonging to another King, whome they call Piemacum, and this King is in league with the next King, adjoyning towards the setting of the Sunne, and the Countrey Neiosioke, situate uppon the side of a goodly River, called Neus: these Kings have mortall warre with Wingina, King of Wingandacoa, but for two yeeres past, there was a peace made betweene the King Piemacum, and the Lorde of Sequotan, as these men which we haue brought with us into England, haue made us understande. . . .

When we first had sight of this Countrey, some thought the first lande we sawe, to be the continent: but after wee entred into the Haven, wee sawe before us another mightie long Sea: for there lieth along the coast a tracte of Islands, two hundreth miles in length, adjoyning to the Ocean sea, and betweene the Islands, two or three entrances: when you are entred betweene them (these Islands being very narrowe, for the most part, as in most places sixe miles broad, in some places lesse, in fewe more,) then there appeareth another great Sea, containing in bredth in some places, fortie, and in some fiftie, in some twentie miles over, before you come unto the continent: and in this inclosed Sea, there are about a hundreth Islands of divers bignesses, whereof one is sixteene miles long, at which we were, finding it to be a most pleasant, and fertile ground, replenished with goodly Cedars, and divers other sweete woods, full of Currans, of flaxe, and many other notable commodities, which we at that time had no leasure to view. . . .

Thus Sir, we have acquainted you with the particulars of our discoverie, made this present voyage, as farre foorth, as the shortnes of the time we there continued, would affoord us to take viewe of: and so contenting our selves with this service at this time, which we hope hereafter to inlarge, as occasion and assistance shall be given, we resolved to leave the Countrey, and to apply our selves to returne for England, which we did accordingly, and arrived safely in the West of England, about the middest of September.

Master Philip Amadas, ⎫
Master Arthur Barlowe, ⎬ Captaines.

43. The 1585 Virginia Voyage

THE ANONYMOUS journal of a member of the ship's company on the Tiger, flagship of the expedition, gives an outline story of the approach to the Carolina Outer Banks and the location of a settlement on Roanoke Island. The West Indies section is fuller and this part reads as if it had been considerably trimmed for publication. It was first printed in Hakluyt, The principall navigations (1589), 773–776, and is reprinted in Quinn, Roanoke Voyages, I, 178–193 (extracts on 188–193).

The 20. [June] we fell with the mayne of Florida.

The 23. wee were in great danger of a Wracke on a breache called the Cape of Feare.

The 24. we came to anker in a harbor where we caught in one tyde so much fishe as woulde have yelded us xx. pounds in London: this was our first landing in Florida.

The 26. we came to anker at Wocokon.

The 29. wee waighed anker to bring the Tyger into the harbour, where through the unskilfulnesse of the Master whose name was Fernando, the Admirall strooke on grounde, and sunke.

July.

The 3. we sent word of our ariving at Wococon, to Wingino at Roanocke.

The 6. Master John Arundell was sent to the mayne, and Manteio with him: and Captayne Aubry and Captaine Boniten the same day were sent to Croatoan, where they found two of our men left there, with 30. other by Captaine Reymond, some 20. daies before.

The 8. Captaine Aubry, and Captaine Boniten returned with two of our men found by them to us at Wocokon.

The 11. day the Generall accompanied in his Tilt boate with Master John Arundell, Master Stukelye, and divers other Gentelmen, Master Lane, Master Candish, Master Harriot, and 20. others in the new pinnesse, Captaine Amadas, Captaine Clarke, with tenne others in a ship boate, Francis Brooke, and John White in another ship boate, passed over the water from Ococon to the mayne land victualled for eight dayes, in which voyage we first discovered the townes of Pomioke, Aquascogoc and Secota, and also the great lake called by the Savages Paquype, with divers other places, and so returned with that discovery to our Fleete.

The 12. we came to the Towne of Pomeioke.

The 13. we passed by water to Aquascococke.

The 15. we came to Secotan and were well intertayned there of the Savages.

The 16. we returned thence, and one of our boates with the Admirall was sent to Aquascococke to demaund a silver cup which one of the Savages had stolen from us, and not receiving it according to his promise, we burnt, and spoyled their corne, and Towne, all the people beeing fledde.

The 18. we returned from the discovery of Secotan, and the same day came aboord our fleete ryding at Wocokon.

The 21. our fleete ankering at Wokocon, we wayed anker for Hatoraske.

The 27. our fleete ankered at Hatoraske, and there we rested.

The 29. Grangino, brother to King Wingino, came aboord the Admirall, and Manteo with him.

August.

The 2. The Admirall was sent to Weapemeoke.

The 5. Master John Arundell was sent for England.

The 25. our Generall wayed anker, and set saile for England.

About the 31. he tooke a Spanish ship of 300. tunne richly loaden, boording her with a boate made with boards of chests, which fell a sunder, and sunke at the shippes side, assoone as ever hee and his men were out of it.

September.

The 10. of September, by foule weather the Generall then shipped in the prise lost sight of the Tyger.

October.

The sixt the Tyger fell with the landes ende, and the same day came to an anker at Falmouth.

The 18. the Generall came with the prise to Plymmouth, and was courteously received by diverse of his worshipfull friends.

44. Ralph Lane on the Scope
of the Activities of the 1585–86 Colony

WHEN THE Roanoke colonists returned to England in July 1586, Ralph
Lane submitted reports to Sir Walter Raleigh and other organizers of
the expedition. Those parts of the reports which were published by
Hakluyt in The principall navigations (1589), 737–747, comprise a general account of the topographical achievements of the colonists (extracted
below), a narrative of an abortive attempt to reach an alleged gold-
producing area by way of the Roanoke River, and an account of the
breakdown of friendly relations with the Roanoke Indians and of the
removal of the colonists by Drake.

First therefore touching the particularities of the Countrey, you
shal understand our discovery of the same hath bene extended
from the Iland of Roanoak, (the same having bene the place of our
settlement or inhabitation) into the South, into the North, into
the Northwest, and into the West.

The uttermost place to the Southward of any discoverie was
Secotan, being by estimation foure score miles distant from
Roanoak. The passage from thence was thorowe a broad sound
within the mayne, the same being without kenning of land, and yet
full of flats and shoales: we had but one boate with foure oares to
passe through the same, which boat could not carry above fifteene
men with their furniture, baggage, and victuall for seven dayes at
the most: and as for our Pinnesse, besides that she drewe too deepe
water for that shalow sound, she would not stirre for an oare: for
these and other reasons (winter also being at hand) we thought
good wholly to leave the discovery of those partes untill our
stronger supplie.

To the Northwarde our furthest discoverie was to the Chesepians, distant from Roanoak about 130. miles, the passage to it was
very shalow and most dangerous, by reason of the breadth of the
sound, and the little succour that upon any flawe was there to be
had.

But the Territorie and soyle of the Chesepians (being distant
fifteene miles from the shoare) was for pleasantnes of seate, for

temperature of Climate, for fertilitie of soyle, and for the commoditie of the Sea, besides multitude of beares (being an excellent good victual, with great woods of Sassafras, and Wall nut trees) is not to be excelled by any other whatsoever.

There be sundry Kings, whom they call Weroances, and Countries of great fertilitie adjoyning to the same, as the Mandoages, Tripanicks, and Opossians, which all came to visit the Colonie of the English, which I had for a time appointed to be resident there.

To the Northwest the farthest place of our discoverie was to Choanoke distant from Roanoak about 130. miles. Our passage thither lyeth through a broad sound, but all fresh water, and the chanell of a great depth, navigable for good shipping, but out of the chanell full of shoales.

The Townes about the waters side situated by the way, are these following: Pysshokonnok, The womans Towne, Chipanum, Weopomiok; Muscamunge, and Mattaquen: all these being under the jurisdiction of the king of Weopomiok, called Okisco: from Muscamunge we enter into the River, and jurisdiction of Choanoke: There the River beginneth to straighten untill it come to Choanoke, and then groweth to be as narrowe as the Thames betweene Westminster, and Lambeth.

Betweene Muscamunge and Choanoke upon the left hand as we passe thither, is a goodly high land, and there is a Towne which we called the blinde Towne, but the Savages called it Ooanoke, and hath a very goodly corne field belonging unto it: it is subject to Choanoke.

Choanoke it selfe is the greatest Province and Seigniorie lying upon that River, and the very Towne it selfe is able to put 700. fighting men into the fielde, besides the forces of the Province it selfe.

The King of the sayd Province is called Menatonon, a man impotent in his lims, but otherwise for a Savage, a very grave and wise man, and of very singular good discourse in matters concerning the state, not onely of his owne Countrey, and the disposition of his owne men, but also of his neighbours round about him as wel farre as neere, and of the commodities that eche Countrey yeeldeth. When I had him prisoner with me, for two dayes that we were together, he gave mee more understanding and light of the

Countrey then I had received by all the searches and salvages that
before I or any of my companie had had conference with: it was in
March last past 1586. Amongst other things he tolde me, that
going three dayes journey in a canoa up his River of Choanoke, and
then descending to the land, you are within foure dayes journey to
passe over land Northeast to a certaine Kings countrey, whose
Province lyeth upon the Sea, but his place of greatest strength is an
Iland situate as he described unto me in a Bay, the water round
about the Iland very deepe.

45. Thomas Harriot on Cultivation by the Carolina Algonkian Indians

THE LITTLE BOOK, *Thomas Hariot, A briefe and true report of the new
found land of Virginia (1588), was a prospectus for the Roanoke Island-
Chesapeake Bay area as one which, in spite of reverses, should continue
to attract English settlers. But it also contains summaries of the results
of the extensive natural history and ethnographical survey that Thomas
Harriot (as the name is now spelled) and John White had carried
out between August 1, 1585, and June 1586. De Bry's America, part i,
(1590), besides carrying a reprint of his book (and translations into
Latin, French and German), contained some of Harriot's notes to engravings of Indians made by White. The latter, with the original drawings reproduced in Hulton and Quinn, The American Drawings of John
White, are other parts of the Harriot-White survey to survive. Harriot's
special responsibility was to study Indians: he learned something of the
language and reported faithfully on their way of life. The extracts from
Harriot that follow on the plants they cultivated give some idea of his
careful observation and reporting.*

The second part of suche commodities as Virginia is knowne to
yeelde for victuall and sustenance of mans life, usually fed upon by
the naturall inhabitants: as also by us, during the time of our
aboade. And first of such as are sowed and husbanded.

Pagatowr, a kinde of graine so called by the inhabitants; the
same in the West Indies is called Mayze: English men call it
Guinny wheate or Turkie wheate, according to the names of the
countreys from whence the like hath beene brought. The graine is

about the bignesse of our ordinary English peaze and not much different in forme and shape: but of divers colours: some white, some red, some yellow, and some blew. All of them yeelde a very white and sweet flowre: being used according to his kinde it maketh a very good bread. Wee made of the same in the countrey some mault, whereof was bruwed as good Ale as was to bee desired. So likewise by the helpe of hops thereof may bee made as good Beere. It is a graine of marveillous great increase; of a thousand, fifteene hundred and some two thousand fold. There are three sortes, of which two are ripe in eleven and twelve weekes at the most: sometimes in ten, after the time they are set, and are then of height in stalke about sixe or seven foote. The other sort is ripe in foureteene, and is about ten foote high, of the stalkes some beare foure heads, some three, some one, and some two: every head conteining five, sixe, or seven hundred graines within a few more or lesse. Of these graines besides bread, the inhabitants make victuall, eyther by parching them, or seething them whole untill they be broken; or boyling the floure with water into a pappe.

Okindgíer, called by us Beanes, because in greatnesse & partly in shape they are like to the Beanes in England; saving that they are flatter, of more divers colours, and some pide. The leafe also of the stemme is much different. In taste they are altogether as good as our English peaze.

Wickonzówr, called by us Peaze, in respect of the beanes, for distinction sake, because they are much lesse; although in forme they little differ: but in goodnesse of taste much, & are far better then our English peaze. Both the beanes and peaze are ripe in tenne weekes after they are set. They make them victuall either by boyling them all to pieces into a broth, or boiling them whole untill they bee soft and beginne to breake as is used in England, eyther by themselves, or mixtly together: Sometimes they mingle of the wheate with them. Sometime also beeing whole sodden, they bruse or pound them in a morter, & thereof make loaves, or lumps of dowishe bread, which they use to eat for varietie.

Macócqwer, according to their severall formes, called by us Pompions, Mellions, and Gourdes, because they are of the like formes as those kinds in England. In Virginia such of severall formes are of one taste and very good, and do also spring from one seed. There are of two sorts; one is ripe in the space of a moneth, and the other in two moneths.

There is an hearbe which in Dutch is called Melden. Some of those that I describe it unto take it to be a kinde of Orage; it groweth about foure or five foote high: of the seede thereof they make a thicke broth, and pottage of a very good taste: of the stalke by burning into ashes they make a kinde of salt earth, wherewithall many use sometimes to season their broths; other salte they knowe not. Wee our selves used the leaves also for pot-hearbes.

There is also another great hearbe, in forme of a Marigolde, about sixe foot in height, the head with the floure is a spanne in breadth. Some take it to be Planta Solis: of the seeds heereof they make both a kinde of bread and broth.

All the aforesayd commodities for victuall are set or sowed, sometimes in groundes apart and severally by themselves, but for the most part together in one ground mixtly: the manner thereof, with the dressing and preparing of the ground, because I will note unto you the fertilitie of the soile; I thinke good briefly to describe.

The ground they never fatten with mucke, dounge, or any other thing, neither plow nor digge it as we in England, but onely prepare it in sort as followeth. A few daies before they sowe or set, the men with wooden instruments, made almost in forme of mattockes or hoes with long handles; the women with short peckers or parers, because they use them sitting, of a foote long and about five inches in breadth: doe onely breake the upper part of the ground to rayse up the weedes, grasse, & olde stubbes of corne stalks with their rootes. The which after a day or twoes drying in the Sunne, being scrapte up into many small heapes, to save them labour for carrying them away; they burne into ashes. (And whereas some may thinke that they use the ashes for to better the ground, I say that then they would either disperse the ashes abroade, which wee observed they do not, except the heapes bee too great: or else would take speciall care to set their corne where the ashes lie, which also wee finde they are carelesse of.) And this is all the husbanding of their ground that they use.

Then their setting or sowing is after this maner. First for their corne, beginning in one corner of the plot, with a pecker they make a hole, wherein they put foure graines, with that care they touch not one another (about an inch asunder) and cover them with the moulde againe: and so through out the whole plot, making such holes and using them after such manner: but with this regard, that they bee made in rankes, every ranke differing from other halfe a fadome or a yarde, and the holes also in every ranke, as much. By this meanes there is a yard spare ground betwene every hole: where according to discretion here and there, they set as many Beanes and Peaze; in divers places also among them seedes of Macócqwer, Melden and Planta solis.

The ground being thus set according to the rate by us experimented, an English Acre conteining fourtie pearches in length, and foure in breadth, doeth there yeeld in croppe or ofcome of corne, beanes and peaze, at the least two hundred London bushelles, besides the Macócqwer, Melden, and Planta solis: When as in England fourtie bushelles of our wheate yeelded out of such an acre is thought to be much.

I thought also good to note this unto you, that you which shall inhabite and plant there, maie know how specially that countrey corne is there to be preferred before ours: Besides the manifold waies in applying it to victuall, the increase is so much that small labour and paines is needful in respect that must be used for ours. For this I can assure you that according to the rate we have made proofe of, one man may prepare and husband so much grounde (having once borne corne before) with lesse then foure and twentie houres labour, as shall yeeld him victuall in a large proportion for a twelvemoneth, if hee have nothing else, but that which the same ground will yeelde, and of that kinde onelie which I have before spoken of: the saide ground being also but of five and twentie yards square. And if neede require, but that there is ground enough, there might be raised out of one and the selfsame ground two harvestes or ofcomes; for they sowe or set and may at anie time when they thinke good from the middest of March untill the end of June: so that they also set when they have eaten of their first croppe. In some places of the countrey notwithstanding they have two harvests, as we have heard, out of one and the same ground.

For English corne neverthelesse whether to use or not to use it, you that inhabite maie doe as you shall have farther cause to thinke best. Of the grouth you need not to doubt; for barlie, oates and peaze, we have seene proof of, not beeing purposely sowen but fallen casually in the sorst sort of ground, and yet to be as faire as any we have ever seene here in England. But of wheat, because it was musty and had taken salt water we could make no triall: and of rye we had none. This much have I disgressed and I hope not unnecessarily: nowe will I returne againe to my course and intreate of that which yet remaineth apperteining to this Chapter.

There is an herbe which is sowed apart by it selfe & is called by the inhabitants uppówoc: In the West Indies it hath divers names, according to the severall places & countreys where it groweth and is used: The Spaniardes generally call it Tobacco. The leaves thereof being dried and brought into pouder, they use to take the fume or smoke thereof by sucking it thorough pipes made of claie, into their stomacke and heade; from whence it purgeth superfluous fleame & other grosse humors, openeth all the pores & passages of the body: by which meanes the use thereof, not only preserveth the body from obstructions; but also if any be, so that they have not been of too long continuance, in short time breaketh them: whereby their bodies are notably preserved in health, & know not many greevous diseases where withall wee in England are often-times afflicted.

This Uppówoc is of so precious estimation amongest them, that they thinke their gods are marvelously delighted therwith: Wher-upon sometime they make hallowed fires & cast some of the pouder therein for a sacrifice: being in a storme upon the waters, to pacifie their gods, they cast some up into the aire and into the water: so a weare for fish being newly set up, they cast some therein and into the aire: also after an escape of danger, they cast some into the aire likewise: but all done with strange gestures, stamping, sometime dauncing, clapping of hands, holding up of hands, & staring up into the heavens, uttering therewithal and chattering strange words and noises.

We our selves during the time we were there used to suck it after their maner, as also since our returne, & have found manie rare and wonderfull experiments of the vertues thereof; of which the rela-tion woulde require a volume by it selfe: the use of it by so manie of late men & women of great calling as else and some learned Phisitions also, is sufficient witnes.

And these are all the commodities for sustenance of life that I know and can remember they use to husband: all else that followe, are founde growing naturally or wilde.

46. The End of the Roanoke Colony, June 1586

AFTER *Sir Francis Drake had attacked and damaged Santo Domingo and Cartagena (and taken ransoms from them), he went on to attack the Spanish colony in Florida. Having destroyed St. Augustine (see pp. 177 above), he took all the portable equipment he could find from the town, and any aid in food that he could and a number of the Negroes and Central American Indians he had rescued from the Spaniards with Lane. Lane had been involved in fighting with the Indians and had not had any supplies from England. Drake offered him shipping so that he could explore Chesapeake Bay, but a storm scattered Drake's fleet. The colonists then decided to come home.*

The story of the Drake voyage was told by Walter Bigges [and others], A summarie and true discourse of Sir Frances Drakes West Indian voyage (1589), partly reprinted in Quinn, The Roanoke voyages, I, 294-303, from which extracts are taken.

Here it was resolved in full assemblie of Captaines, to undertake the enterprise of S. Helena, and from thence to seeke out the inhabitation of our English countrey men in Virginia, distant from thence some six degrees Northward.

When we came thwart of S. Helena,[1] the shols appearing daungerous, and we having no Pilot to undertake the entrie, it was thought meetest to go hence alongst. For the Admirall had bene the same night in foure fadome and halfe three leagues from the shore: and yet we understood, that by the helpe of a knowen Pilot, there may and doth go in ships of greater burthen and draught then anie we had in our Fleete.

We passed thus alongest the coast hard abord the shore, which is shallow for a league or two from the shore, and the same is lowe and broken land for the most part.

1. Santa Elena, on Port Royal Sound.

The ninth of June upon sight of one speciall great fire (which are verie ordinarie all alongst this coast, even from the Cape Florida hither) the Generall sent his Skiffe to the shore, where they found some of our English countrey men (that had bene sent thither the yeare before by Sir Walter Raleigh) & brought one aboord, by whose direction we proceeded along to the place, which they make their Port. But some of our ships being of great draught unable to enter, we ankered all without the harbour in a wild road at sea, about two miles from shore.

From whence the General wrote letters to Maister Rafe Lane, being Governour of those English in Virginia, and then at his fort about six leagues from the rode in an Island, which they call Roanoac, wherein specially he shewed how readie he was to supply his necessities and wants, which he understood of, by those he had first talked withall.

The morrowe after Maister Lane him selfe and some of his companie comming unto him, with the consent of his Captaines, he gave them the choise of two offers, that is to say: Either he would leave a ship, a Pinnace, and certaine boates with sufficient Maisters and mariners, together furnished with a moneths victuall to stay and make farther discoverie of the country and coastes, and so much victuall likewise that might be sufficient for the bringing of them all (being an hundred and three persons) into England if they thought good after such time, with anie other thing they would desire, & that he might be able to spare.

Or else if they thought they had made sufficient discoverie alreadie, and did desire to returne into England, he would give them passage. But they as it seemed, being desirous to stay, accepted verie thankefully, and with great gladnesse that which was offred first. Whereupon the ship being appointed and receaved into charge, by some of their owne companie sent into her by Maister Lane, before they had received from the rest of the Fleete, the provision appointed them, there arose a great storme (which they sayde was extraordinarie and verie straunge) that lasted three dayes together, and put all our Fleete in great daunger, to be driven from their ankoring upon the coast. For we brake manie Cables, and lost manie Ankers. And some of our Fleete which had lost all (of which number was the ship appointed for Maister Lane and his companie) were driven to put to sea in great danger, in avoiding the coast, and could never see us againe untill we met in England. Manie also of our small Pinnaces and boates were lost in this storme.

Notwithstanding after all this, the Generall offered them (with consent of his Captaines) another ship with some provision, although not such a one for their turnes, as might have bene spared them before, this being unable to be brought into their harbour. Or else if they would, to give them passage into England, although he knewe we should performe it with greater difficultie then he might have done before.

But Maister Lane with those of the chiefest of his companie which he had then with him, considering what should be best for them to doe, made request unto the Generall under their handes, that they might have passage for England: the which being graunted, and the rest sent for out of the countrey and shipped, we departed from that coast the eighteenth of June.

And so God be thanked, both they and we in good safetie arrived at Portesmouth the eight and twentieth of July 1586. to the great glorie of God, and to no small honour to our Prince, our countrey, and our selves.

47. The Planting
of the New Colony, 1587

JOHN WHITE's journal records his progress by way of the West Indies to Roanoke Island in 1587. Though he was not destined to leave many more than a hundred men, women and children in America, the attempt to form a communal colony is significant. It shows that White believed that even a small community, carefully managed, could establish itself in Indian territory and co-exist peacefully with the native society. When Simon Fernandes refused to carry the settlers on from Roanoke Island to the Chesapeake, White was not discouraged since he knew the Roanoke Island area better, and evidently believed in its potentialities. He understood too that the sense of isolation which affected the settlers required that someone of importance should return to England to make sure supplies would reach them in good time in 1588. But his departure

was a gamble, and one that did not come off. The history of the settlement after his departure is one of the intriguing question marks of early
American history. The journal appeared in Hakluyt, The principall
navigations (1589), 764–790, and is reprinted in Quinn, Roanoke
Voyages, II, 515–538.

About the 16. of July, we fell with the maine of Virginia. . . .

The two and twentieth of Julie, we arrived safe at Hatoraske,
where our shippe and pinnesse ankered: the Governour went
aboord the pinnesse, accompanied with fortie of his best men, intending to passe up to Roanoake foorthwith, hoping there to finde
those fifteene Englishmen, which Sir Richard Greenvill had left
there the yeere before, with whome he meant to have conference,
concerning the state of the Countrey, and Savages, meaning after
he had so done, to returne againe to the fleete, and passe along the
coast, to the Baye of Chesepiok, where we intended to make our
seate and forte, according to the charge given us among other directions in writing, under the hande of Sir Walter Ralegh: but
assoone as we were put with our pinnesse from the shippe, a
Gentleman by the meanes of Fernando, who was appointed to
returne for England, called to the sailers in the pinnesse, charging
them not to bring any of the planters backe againe, but leave them
in the Island, except the Governour, and two or three such as he
approoved, saying that the Summer was farre spent, wherefore hee
would land all the planters in no other place. Unto this were all the
sailers, both in the pinnesse, and shippe, perswaded by the Master,
wherefore it booted not the Governour to contend with them, but
passed to Roanoake, and the same night, at Sunne set, went aland
on the Island, in the place where our fifteene men were left, but we
found none of them, nor any signe, that they had bene there,
saving onely we found the bones of one of those fifteene, which the
Savages had slaine long before.

The 23. of July, the Governour, with divers of his companie,
walked to the North ende of the Island, where Master Ralfe Lane
had his forte, with sundry necessarie and decent dwelling houses,
made by his men about it the yeere before, where wee hoped to
finde some signes, or certaine knowledge of our fifteene men.
When we came thither, wee found the forte rased downe, but all
the houses standing unhurt, saving the neather roomes of them,

and also of the forte, were overgrowen with Melons of divers sortes, and Deere within them, feeding on those Mellons: so we returned to our companie, without hope of ever seeing any of the fifteene men living.

The same day order was given, that every man should be imploied for the repairing of those houses, which we found standing, and also to make other newe Cottages, for such as shoulde neede.

The 25. our Flie boate, and the rest of our planters, arrived, all safe at Hatoraske, to the great joye, and comfort of the whole companie. . . .

On the thirtieth of Julie, Master Stafford, and twentie of our men, passed by water to the Island of Croatoan, with Manteo, who had his mother, and many of his kinred, dwelling in that Island, of whome we hoped to understande some newes of our fifteene men, but especially to learne the disposition of the people of the Countrey towards us, and to renew our olde friendshippe with them. . . .

The 13. of August, our Savage Manteo, by the commandement of Sir Walter Ralegh, was christened in Roanoak, and called Lord thereof, and of Dasamongueponke, in reward of his faithfull service.

The 18. Elenora, daughter to the Governour, and wife to Ananias Dare, one of the Assistants, was delivered of a daughter in Roanoak, and the same was christened there the Sunday following, and because this childe was the first Christian borne in Virginia, she was named Virginia. By this time our shippes had unlanded the goods and victuals of the planters, and began to take in wood, and fresh water, and to new calke and trimme them for England: the planters also prepared their letters, and tokens, to send backe into England.

The next day, the 22. of August, the whole companie, both of the Assistants, and planters, came to the Governour, and with one voice requested him to returne himselfe into England, for the better and sooner obtaining of supplies, and other necessaries for them: but he refused it, and alleaged many sufficient causes, why he would not. . . .

The Governour beeing at the last, through their extreame intreating, constrayned to returne into England, having then but halfe a daies respit to prepare him selfe for the same, departed from Roanoake, the seven and twentieth of August in the morning. . . .

The 5. [November] the Governour landed in England at Marta-sew, neere Saint Michaels mount in Cornewall.

48. The Search
for the Lost Colony, 1590

JOHN WHITE's long-delayed return to Roanoke Island and his narrative (extracted below form Hakluyt, principal navigations, III (1600), 288–295), of the unavailing search for the settlers sharply brings to light the appearance of the deserted northwest corner of Roanoke Island in August 1590. White was at the mercy of the sailors, who were unwilling to give him the time he needed for an adequate search. In the end he left for England, leaving the mystery of the fate of the colonists unsolved. What is known or can be surmised of their fate is given in Quinn, Raleigh and the British Empire, pp. 101–109.

The 15 of August towards Evening we came to an anker at Hatorask, in 36 degr. and one third, in five fadom water, three leagues from the shore. At our first comming to anker on this shore we saw a great smoke rise in the Ile Roanoak neere the place where I left our Colony in the yeere 1587, which smoake put us in good hope that some of the Colony were there expecting my returne out of England.

The 16 and next morning our 2 boates went a shore, & Captaine Cooke, & Captain Spicer, & their company with me, with intent to passe to the place at Roanoak where our countreymen were left. At our putting from the ship we commanded our Master gunner to make readie 2 Minions and a Falkon well loden, and to shoot them off with reasonable space betweene every shot, to the ende that their reportes might bee heard to the place where wee hoped to finde some of our people. This was accordingly performed, & our twoe boats put off unto the shore, in the Admirals boat we sounded all the way and found from our shippe untill we came within a mile of the shore nine, eight, and seven fadome: but before we were halfe way betweene our ships and the shore we saw another great smoke to the Southwest of Kindrikers mountes: we therefore thought good to goe to that second smoke first: but it was much further from the harbour where we landed, then we supposed it to be, so that we were very sore tired before wee came to the smoke. But that which grieved us more was that when we came to the smoke, we found no man nor signe that any had bene there lately, nor yet any fresh water in all this way to drinke. Being thus wearied with this journey we returned to the harbour where we left our boates, who in our absence had brought their caske a shore for fresh water, so we deferred our going to Roanoak untill the next morning, and caused some of those saylers to digge in those sandie hilles for fresh water whereof we found very sufficient. That night wee returned aboord with our boates and our whole company in safety.

The next morning being the 17 of August, our boates and company were prepared againe to goe up to Roanoak. . . . Our boates and all things fitted againe, we put off from Hatorask, being the number of 19 persons in both boates: but before we could get to the place, where our planters were left, it was so exceeding darke, that we overshot the place a quarter of a mile: there we espied towards the North end of the Iland the light of a great fire thorow the woods, to the which we presently rowed: when wee came right over against it, we let fall our Grapnel neere the shore, & sounded with a trumpet a Call, & afterwardes many familiar English tunes of Songs, and called to them friendly; But we had no answere, we therefore landed at day-breake, and comming to the fire, we found the grasse & sundry rotten trees burning about the place. From hence we went thorow the woods to that part of the Iland directly over against Dasamongwepeuk, & from thence we returned by the water side, round about the Northpoint of the Iland, untill we came to the place where I left our Colony in the yeere 1586. In all this way we saw in the sand the print of the Salvages feet of 2 or 3 sorts troaden that night, and as we entred up the sandy banke upon a tree, in the very browe thereof were curiously carved these faire Romane letters C R O: which letters presently we knew to signifie the place, where I should find the planters seated, according to a secret token agreed upon betweene them & me at my last departure from them, which was, that in any wayes they should not faile to write or carve on the trees or posts of the dores the name of the place where they should be seated; for at my comming away they were prepared to remove from Roanoak 50 miles into the maine.

. . . Therefore at my departure from them in Anno 1587 I willed them that if they should happen to be distressed in any of these places, that then they should carve the letters or name, a Crosse ✠ in this forme, but we found no suche signe of distresse. And having well considered of this, we passed toward the place where they were left in sundry houses, but we found the houses taken downe, and the place very strongly enclosed with a high palisado of great trees, with cortynes and Flankers very Fort-like, and one of the chiefe trees or postes at the right side of the entrance had the barke taken off, and 5. foote from the grounde in fayre Capitall letters was graven CROATOAN without any crosse or sign of distresse; this done we entred into the palisado, where we found many barres of Iron, two pigges of Lead, foure yron fowlers, Iron sacker-shotte, and such like heavie things, throwen here and there, almost overgrowen with grasse and weedes. . . .

Presently Captaine Cooke and I went to the place, which was in the ende of an olde trench, made two yeeres past by Captaine Amadas: wheere wee found five Chests, that had been carefully hidden of the Planters, and of the same chests three were my owne, and about the place many of my things spoyled and broken, and my bookes torne from the covers, the frames of some of my pictures and Mappes rotten and spoyled with rayne, and my armour almost eaten through with rust; this could bee no other but the deede of the Savages our enemies at Dasamongwepeuk, who had watched the departure of our men to Croatoan; and assone as they were departed, digged up every place where they suspected any thing to be buried: but although it much grieved me to see such spoyle of my goods, yet on the other side I greatly joyed that I had safely found a certaine token of their safe being at Croatoan, which is the place where Manteo was borne, and the Savages of the Iland our friends.

When we had seene in this place so much as we could, we returned to our Boates, and departed from the shoare towards our Shippes, with as much speede as we could. . . .

On Saturday the 24. [October] we came in safetie, God be thanked, to an anker at Plymouth.

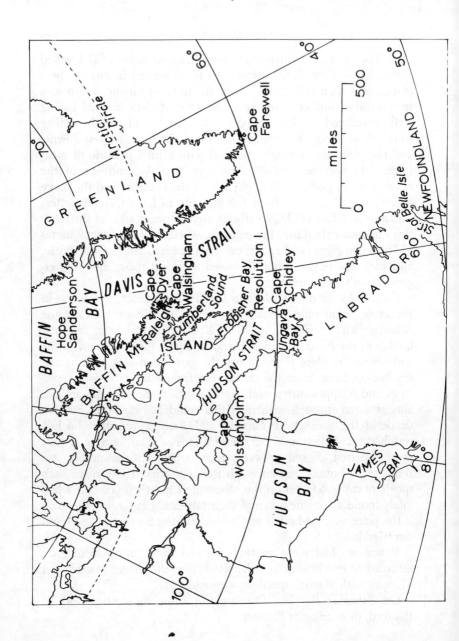

GREENLAND

Arctic Circle

70°

60°

BAFFIN BAY

DAVIS STRAIT

Hope Sanderson

Cape Raleigh

Mt Dyer

Cape Walsingham

Cumberland Sound

BAFFIN ISLAND

Frobisher Bay

Resolution I.

HUDSON STRAIT

Cape Wolstenholm

Ungava Bay

Cape Chidley

LABRADOR

HUDSON BAY

JAMES BAY

Cape Farewell

Strait Belle Isle

NEWFOUNDLAND

miles

0   500

40°

50°

60°

70°

80°

100°

XI
The Northwest Passage Search

THE DISCOVERY that North America was continental in scale and barred a direct sea approach to Asia produced a long series of attempts to find a way round America by the North. The Northwest Passage ventures had their own logic and vocabulary and were to an appreciable degree detached from the explorations and attempted settlements which make up the main part of the uncovering of North America to Europe in the sixteenth and early seventeenth centuries. They are regarded in the history of exploration as the long-drawn-out prelude to the Arctic explorations of the nineteenth and twentieth centuries. Yet if it had not been for the incentive provided by the presumed Passage, the greater part of the shores of Greenland, Labrador, Baffin Island and some of the other northern islands, the Ungava Peninsula and Hudson Bay would certainly not have been charted by 1612, nor the peculiar problems of voyaging in such northern waters investigated and experienced. The temporary attractions of gold at Baffin Island in 1577–78 and the later, more enduring whale fishery off Greenland would not, in themselves, have been effective. In the early sixteenth century Sebastian Cabot was in a real sense the inventor of the Northwest Passage concept. His own voyage was the first to have as its main objective the circumventing of North America and, though he did not get his Spanish employers (1512–48) to follow up his objectives in the North, he continued to encourage Englishmen to do so. When he returned to England in old age he revived interest in the concept, and it was not until the last minute that the exploring syndicate which he inspired decided to send its ships in 1553 in search of a Northeast and not a Northwest Passage. Other Englishmen, Robert Thorne (1527) and Roger Barlow (1540–41), advocated an approach to Asia directly over the North Pole. Anthony Jenkinson and Humphrey Gilbert debated the respective merits of a Northeast and a Northwest Passage to Asia in the 1560's. Gilbert's tract, A discourse of a discoverie for a new passage to Cataia, written in 1566 but not published until 1576, identified him with the Northwest Passage concept. This was taken up by Michael Lok, who identified himself with the Company of Cathay which sponsored the expeditions of Martin Frobisher, 1576–78. These expeditions revealed part of the west coast of Greenland, parts of Labrador and, especially, the southern part of

Baffin Island, as well as a westward trending channel, "the mistaken straits," into which Frobisher blundered on his third voyage, but which he did not follow. But the main concentration of the second and third voyages lay on the extraction of mineral-bearing rock from the shores and islets of Frobisher Sound. When these were found to be worthless, much of the drive to find Cathay by the Northwest evaporated. The ventures left behind a small core of devotees of the Northwest Passage concept which made it possible to continue them. John Davis's three voyages, 1585–87, defined the western coast of Greenland as far as 73° N. latitude, while he also clarified the land boundaries on the west of the strait later named after him, though he did not find the Passage. It was through his searches that a whale fishery was eventually made possible. He also fully explored Hamilton Inlet on the Labrador coast. George Waymouth, acting for the East India Company which wished to hedge its bets on the passage to India, entered Hudson Strait in 1602 but could not induce his men to go further. It was left to Henry Hudson to press through the Straits in 1610 to discover Hudson Bay and to winter at the head of James Bay, before being cast off by his crew the following summer because he attempted to urge them to still further feats of endurance. The discovery of Hudson Bay raised great hopes that a passage had been found. A Northwest Passage Company was founded to exploit it, but although Thomas Button (1612–13) managed to define the limits of Hudson Bay in the West and North he was not able to find any route from it to the Pacific. The search continued intermittently thereafter.

Modern accounts of the search may be found in V. Stefansson, Northwest to Fortune (1958), L. H. Neatby, In Quest of the North-West Passage (1958), and E. S. Dodge, Northwest by Sea (1961), the last being exceptionally clear.

49. A Portuguese Attempt
to Find the Northwest Passage in 1574

RICHARD HAKLUYT had just sent to the printer the first English collection of voyage narratives on North America, Divers voyages touching the discoverie of America, early in 1582, when he had word that a Portuguese voyage toward the Northwest had taken place some eight years before. He hastily added a note of this to his book. Anus Cortereal is clearly Eannes Corte Real, and is likely to have been the son or other descendant of the Vasco Eannes Corte Real to whom a grant was made by the king of Portugal in 1506, confirmed to him in 1522. This voyage does not appear to be documented in Portuguese sources. It seems not unlikely that like Frobisher in 1578 and Waymouth in 1602, Corte Real rounded Cape Chidley and entered the eastern end of Hudson Strait. Though this is in 60°, not 58° N. latitude, an error of 2° was not exceptional at this time. For the text see Divers Voyages, edited by J. Winter Jones (1851), p. 7; D. B. Quinn, Richard Hakluyt, Editor (with a facsimile of Divers Voyages, [2 vols. 1967]), p. [4].

A verie late and great probabilitie of a passage, by the Northwest part of America in 58. degrees of Northerly latitude.

An excellent learned man of portingale, of singuler gravety, authorite and experience tolde mee very lately, that one Anus Cortereal,[1] captayne of the yle of Tercera about the yeere 1574. which is not above eight yeres past, sent a Shippe to discover the Northwest passage of America, & that the same shippe arriving on the coast of the saide America in fiftie eyghte degrees of latitude, founde a great entrance exceeding deepe and broade, without all impediment of ice, into whiche they passed above twentie leagues, and found it alwaies to trende towards the South, the lande lying lowe and plaine on eyther side: And that they perswaded them selves verely, that there was a way open into the south sea. But their victailes fayling them, and being but one shippe, they returned backe agayne with joy. This place seemeth to lie in equal degrees of latitude, with the first entrance of the sounde of Denmark betweene Norway and the head land, called in latin Cimbrorum promontorium, and therefore like to bee open and navigable a great part of the yeere. . . .

50. Sir Humphrey Gilbert's Summary of the Advantages to England of a Northwest Passage

HUMPHREY GILBERT was a young soldier when he began in 1565 to consider whether there might be a career for him in discovering a Northwest Passage. For several years he endeavored to obtain backing for his proposed expedition, during the course of which he drafted in 1566 a pamphlet summarizing his geographical arguments. He was diverted from his plans by military service in Ireland, and did not revive his argument until 1574 or 1575, when he became associated with Michael Lok and

1. Probably a descendant of Vasco Eannes Corte Real of the 1506 grant.

others who were planning a fresh Northwest Passage venture. Through a mutual friend, George Gascoigne, the pamphlet was published as A discourse of a discoverie for a new passage to Cataia (1576). Gilbert took on trust recent maps and globes showing the distribution of land and water in the northern seas, but his argument is a careful one. His Discourse is discussed and reprinted in Quinn, The Voyages and Colonising Enterprises of Sir Humphrey Gilbert, pp. 6–11, 29–31, 129–164, the passage covered by the extract occurring on pp. 158–160. He is summarizing the argument which he had in 1566 with Anthony Jenkinson on whether a Northeast Passage or a Northwest Passage was the more likely to be found, and, if both were available, which it would be more advantageous for England to exploit.

How that the passage by the Northwest, is more commodious for our traffick, then the other by the East : if there were any such.

Cap. 9.

1   First, by the Northeaste (if your windes doe not give you a marvellous speedie, and luckie passage) you are in daunger (being so nere the Pole) to be benighted, almost the one halfe of the yeare, and what miserie and daunger that were, to live so long comfortlesse, voyde of light, (if the colde killes you not) eche man of reason or understanding may judge.

2   Also Mangia, Quingit, and the Molluccae, are neerer unto us by the Northwest, then by the Northeast, more than 2/5 parts which is almost by the halfe.

3   Also wee may have by the West, a yerely returne, it being at al times Navigable, wheras you have but six moneths, in the whole yere, to goe by the Northeast : the passage beinge at such elevation, as it is formerly expressed, for it cannot be any neerer the South.

4   Furthermore, it cannot be finished without divers wintrings by the way, having no havens in any temperate Climate, to harbour in ther. For it is as much as we can well sayle, from hence to S. Nicholas, in the trade of Muscovia, and return in the Navigable season of yeare, and from S. Nicholas to Cerimissi Tartarii, which standeth at 80 degrees of the Septentrional latitude, it is at the least 400 Leagues, which amounteth scarce to the thirde part of the way, to the ende of your voyage by the Northeast.

5   And yet after you have doubled this Cape, if then there might be found a navigable sea, to cary you Southeast, according to your desire, yet can you not winter conveniently, until you come to 60

degrees, and to take up one degree running Southeast, you must sayle 24 leagues 3/4 which amounteth to 495 leagues.

6 Furthermore, you may by the Northwest, saile thither with al Easterly winds, and returne with any westerly windes, whereas you must have by the Northeast sundrie windes, and those proper, accordinge to the lying of the coastes and capes, you shalbe inforced to double, which windes are not alwayes to be had, when they are looked for : wherby your journey should be greatly prolonged, and hardly endured so nere the Pole. As we are taught by Sir Hugh Wiloughbie, who was frosen to death far nerer the South.

7 Moreover, it is very doubtfull, whether we should long injoy that trade by the Northeast, if there were any such passage that way, the commodities therof once knowen to the Muscovite, what privelege soever he hath graunted, seeing policie with the Maze of excessive gaine to the enriching (so greatly) of himselfe and all his dominions, would persuade him to resume the same, having so great opportunitie, to utter the commodities of those countreys by the Narve [Narva].

But by the Northwest, wee may safely trade without daunger, or annoyance, of any prince living, Christian, or heathen, it being out of al their trades.

8 Also the Queenes Majesties dominions, are nerer the Northwest passage, then any other great princes that might passe that way, and both in their going and returne, they must of necessitie succour themselves and their shippes, upon some parte of the same, if any tempestious weather shoulde happen.

Further, no Princes Navie of the world, is able to encounter the Queenes Majesties Navie, as it is at this present : and yet it should be greatly increased, by the traffike ensuing upon this discoverie, for it is the long voyages, that increase and maintaine great shipping.

51. The First Voyage
by Martin Frobisher, 1576

MARTIN FROBISHER *in the* Gabriel *made a remarkably direct voyage to the Northwest, passing the southern tip of Greenland and making land* at approximately 61° N. latitude. This, he thought, was the northern limit of Labrador (Cape Chidley), but it was, instead, the northern point of Resolution Island (61° 25' N.), lying across Hudson Strait and the route to the West. He called it Queen Elizabeth's Foreland and continued to the north of the island, whereas had he kept to the south he would have entered Hudson Strait. He continued northwestward between coasts which he thought to be those of America and Asia, up Frobisher Bay, turning back before he reached its termination and naming it Frobisher's Straits. He returned to England convinced that he had found the Northwest Passage.

George Best, A true discourse of the late voyages of discoverie . . . under Martin Frobisher generall (1578), from which this extract comes (pp. 46–48), provides the fullest contemporary account of the three voyages. Best was reprinted in Hakluyt, The principal navigations, III (1600); in Richard Collinson, ed., The Three Voyages of Martin Frobisher (1867); and in Vilhjalmar Stefansson, ed., The Three Voyages of Martin Frobisher (2 vols., 1938).

He [Martin Frobisher] prepared two small Barkes, of twentie, and fyve and twentie tunne a peece, wherein hee intended to accomplish hys pretended voyage. Wherefore, beeyng furnished wyth the foresayde two Barkes, and one small Pinnesse of tenne tunne burthen, havyng therein victuals, and other necessaries for twelve Monethes provision, he departed uppon the sayde voyage from Blackewall the fiftenth of June Anno Domini. 1576.

One of the Barkes wherein hee wente, was named the Gabriell, and the other the Michaell, and sayling Northweast from Englande, uppon the firste of July, at length hee hadde sighte of a highe and ragged lande, whiche hee judged Freeselande,[1] (whereof some Authoures have made mention,) but durst not approche the same, by reason of the greate store of Ise that lay alongst the coast, and the greate mistes, that troubled them not a little.

Not farre from thence hee lost companye of his small Pinnesse, whyche by meanes of the greate storme, he supposed to bee swallowed uppe of the Sea, wherein he lost onely foure men.

Also the other Barke named the Michaell, mistrusting the matter, conveyed themselves privilie away from him, and returned home, wyth greate reporte that he was cast awaye.

The worthie Captayne, notwithstanding these discomfortes, al-

1. Correctly, Greenland.

though hys Mast was sprong, and hys toppe Mast blowen over-
boorde with extreame foule weather, continued hys course
towardes the Northweast, knowing that the Sea at length must
needes have an endying, and that some lande shoulde have a
beginning that way: and determined therefore at the least, to bryng
true proofe what lande and Sea the same myghte bee, so farre to
the North-weastwardes, beyonde anye man that hathe heeretofore
discovered. And the twentith of July, hee hadde sighte of a high
lande, whyche hee called Queene Elizabethes Forlande, after hyr
Majesties name. And sayling more Northerlie alongst that coast, he
descried another forlande, with a greate gutte, bay, or passage,
deviding as it were two mayne lands or continents asunder. There
he met with store of exceeding great yse al this coast along, &
coveting still to continue his course to the Northwardes, was
alwayes by contrarie winde deteyned overthwarte these straytes,
and could not get beyond. Within few days after, he perceyved the
Ise to be well consumed, and gone, eyther there engulfed in by
some swifte currants or indraftes, caried more to the Southwardes
of the same straytes, or else conveyed some other way: wherefore
he determined to make profe of this place, to see how farre that
gutte had continuance, and whether he mighte carrie himselfe
thorough the same, into some open Sea on the backe syde, whereof
hee conceyved no small hope, and so entred the same the one and
twentith of July, and passed above fyftie leagues therein, as hee
reported, having upon eyther hande a greate mayne or continent.
And that land uppon hys right hande, as hee sayled Westward, he
judged to bee the continente of Asia, and there to bee devided
from the firme of America, whiche lyeth uppon the lefte hande
over against the same.

This place he named after his name Frobishers Streytes, lyke as
Magellanus at the Southweast ende of the worlde, havyng discovered the passage to the South Sea (where America is devided from
the continente of that lande, whiche lyeth under the South Pole)
and called the same straites Magellanes streightes.

52. The Third Voyage
by Martin Frobisher, 1578

ON THE strength of supposed gold content in rock brought from Frobisher Bay in 1576, the 1577 expedition turned into a mining venture
only. The ore had not been discredited when Frobisher took out eleven
more ships in 1578. The planned mining camp had to be given up when
prefabricated buildings were partly lost on the way; when the ships came
home with their ore, they found it was worthless.

In July, on reaching Resolution Island, Frobisher found his way into
Frobisher Bay blocked with ice, so, edging his way forward with the Aid,
found himself in an open channel which he followed westward some 180
miles, and which was clearly Hudson Strait. He turned back from these
"mistaken straits" in order to dispose of his miners and their stores (discovering that Resolution Island was an island and offered entrance to
Frobisher Bay round its western shore), believing that he had at last
found the genuine entrance to the Northwest Passage. The discrediting
of the ore led to his giving up the Passage venture.

The extracts are from Best, A true discourse . . ., pp. 18–23 (third
pagination).

The tenth of July, the weather still continuing thicke and darke,
some of the Shippes in the fogge lost sighte of the Admirall and
the rest of the Fleete. And wandering too and fro, with doubtfull
opinion whether it were best to seeke backe againe to seaward
through great store of Ise, or to follow on a doubtfull course in a
Sea, bay, or straytes they knew not, or alongst a coast, whereof by
reason of the darke mistes they coulde not discerne the daungers, if
by chance any Rocke or broken ground should lye of the place, as
commonly in these partes it doth. . . .

The rest of the Fleete following the course of the Generall
whyche ledde them the way, passed up above .60. Leagues within
the sayd doubtfull and supposed straytes, havying alwayes a fayre
continente uppon their starreboorde syde, and a continuance still
of an open Sea before them.

The Generall albeit with the fyrste perchance he found out the
error, and that this was not the old straytes,[1] yet he persuaded the

1. Best adds the marginal note "Mistaken Straytes."

Fleete alwayes that they were in theyr righte course, and knowne straytes. Howbeit I suppose he rather dissembled hys opinion therein, than otherwyse, meaning by that policie (being hymself ledde with an honorable desire of further discoverie) to enduce the fleete to follow him to see a further proofe of that place. And as some of the company reported, he hath since confessed, that if it had not bin for the charge and care he had of the Fleete, and fraughted Shippes, he both would and could have gone through to the South Sea, called *Mare del Sur*, and dissolved the long doubt of the passage which we seeke to find to the ritch Countrey of Cataya.

1 Of which mistaken straytes, considering the circumstance, we have greate cause to confirme oure opinion, to like and hope well of the passage in this place. For the foresaide bay or Sea, the further we sayled therein, the wyder we found it, with great likelyhoode of endlesse continuance. And where in other places we were muche troubled wyth Ise, as in the entrance of this same, so after we had sayled 50. or 60. leagues therein, we had no lette of Ise, or other thing at all, as in other places we found.

2 Also this place seemeth to have a marvellous greate indraft, and draweth unto it most of the drift yse, and other things, which do fleete in the Sea, eyther to the North, or Eastwardes of the same, as by good experience we have founde.

3 For heere also we mette with boordes, latthes, and divers other things driving in the Sea, which was of the wracke of the shippe called the Barke *Dennys*, which perished amongst the Ise, as beforesaid, being lost at the first attempt of the entrance over-thwart the Queens foreland, in the mouth of Frobishers straytes, whiche coulde by no meanes have bin so brought thither, neyther by winde nor tide, being lost so many leagues off, if by force of the sayde Currant the same had not bin violently brought. For if the same hadde bin brought thither by the tyde of fludde, looke how farre in the said fludde had caried it, the ebbe woulde have recaryed it as farre backe agayne, and by the winde it could not so come to passe, bycause it was then sometime calme, and most times con-trary.

4 And some Marriners doe affyrme, that they have diligently observed, that there runneth in this place nine houres floud to .3. houres eb, which may thus come to passe by force of the saide

currant: for whereas the Sea in most places of the world, doth more or lesse ordinarily ebbe and flow once every twelve houres, with sixe houres ebbe, and sixe houres floud, so also would it doe there, were it not for the violence of this hastning currant, which forceth the floud to make appearance to beginne before his ordinary time one houre and a halfe, until the force of the ebbe be so greate, that it will no longer be resisted (according to the saying: *Naturam expellas furca licet usque recurrit*, Although nature and naturall courses be forced and resisted never so muche, yet at laste it will have their own sway againe).

5 Moreover, it is not possible, that so gret course of flouds and currant, so highe swelling tides with continuaunce of so deepe waters, can be digested here without unburdening themselves into some open Sea beyonde this place, which argueth the more likelihood of the passage to be hereaboutes. Also we suppose these great indrafts do growe, and are made by the reverberation and reflection of that same Currant, whiche at oure comming by Ireland, mette and crossed us, of whiche in the firste parte of this discourse I spake, whyche comming from the bay of Mexico,[2] passing by, and washing the Southweast parts of Ireland, running over to the Northest parts of the world, as Norway, Islande, &c. where not finding any passage to an open Sea, but rather is there encreased by a new accesse, and another Currant meeting with it from the Scythian Sea, passing the bay of Saint Nicholas Westwarde, doeth once againe rebound backe, by the coasts of Groenland, and from thence uppon Frobishers straites being to the Southwestwardes of the same. . . .

Oure menne that sayled furthest in the same mistaken straites, (having the maine lande uppon their starboorde side) affyrme, that they mette with the outlet or passage of water whiche commeth thorowe Frobyshers straites, and concurreth as al one into this passage.

Some of oure companye also affyrme, that they hadde sight of a continent upon their larbordside,[3] being .60. leagues within the supposed straites: howbeit excepte certaine Ilandes in the first

2. The Gulf Stream.
3. Port or left side.

entraunce hereof, we could make no part perfect thereof. All the foresaid tract of land seemeth to be more fruitful and better stored of Grasse, Deere, Wilde foule, as Partridges, Larkes, Seamews, Guls, Wilmots, Falcons and tassell Gentils, Ravens, Beares, Hares, Foxes, and other things, than any other parte we have yet discovered, & is more populous. And here Luke Ward, a Gentleman of the company, traded merchandise, & did exchange knives, bells, looking glasses, &c. with those countrey people, who brought him foule, fishe, beares skinnes, and suche like, as their countrey yeeldeth for the same. Here also they saw of those greater boates of the Country, with twentie persons in apeece.

Nowe, after the Generall hadde bestowed these manye dayes here (not without many daungers) he returned backe againe.

53. The Voyages
of John Davis, 1585–87

ONCE FROBISHER's *gold was shown to be dross, only faith in the Passage could keep the search for it alive. Dr. John Dee had such a faith, so had Sir Humphrey's brother, Adrian Gilbert; but it was a London merchant, William Sanderson, and some Exeter traders who put John Davis, a fine navigator, to sea in three expeditions, 1585, 1586 and 1587. The first expedition followed Frobisher's track, but a little to the north, reaching Baffin Island at Exeter Sound and exploring down to and into Cumberland Sound with no success in finding a passage. The second voyage continued farther north along the west coast of Greenland before crossing to Baffin Island at Cape Dyer, over the narrowest stretch of Davis Strait. From there Davis worked down the coast of Baffin Island, missed Hudson Strait and explored closely the shores of Labrador, including Hamilton Inlet, before turning homeward. The third voyage was the most daring, penetrating north along the Greenland coast through Davis Strait into Baffin Bay, and at 72° 12′ Davis named a projection of Swarton Huk Peninsula after his backer as "Sanderson his Hope." Though the sea was still open, headwinds made it impossible for the Ellen to make progress. Turning westwards, Davis encountered the "Middle Pack," the ice barrier in the middle of Baffin Bay, through which he could not pass. Eventually, he was forced south and was able to pick up Baffin Island and make his way home from there, once more covering the Labrador coast. Davis did nothing to reveal Hudson Strait,* but he showed that exploration far to the north was still possible and might disclose a passage. He also demonstrated that a small ship could penetrate far into Arctic latitudes.

Narratives of all three voyages were printed in Hakluyt, The principall navigations (1589). They were summarized by Davis himself in 1595 in The worldes hydrographical discription, from which extracts (sig. B1v.– B5v.) are given. See also Albert H. Markham, ed., The Voyages and Works of John Davis the Navigator (1878), and Clements R. Markham, A Life of John Davis (1891).

Now their onely resteth the North partes of America upon which coast my selfe have had most experience of any in our age, for thrise I was that wayes imployed for the discovery of this notable passage, by the honerable care and some charge of Syr Fauncis Walsingham knight principal secretory to her majestie, with whom divers noble men and worshipfull merchantes of London joyned in purse and willingnesse for the furtherance of that attempt, but when his honour died the voyage was frindles, and mens mindes alienated from adventuring therein. In my first voyage not experienced of the nature of those clymattes, and having no direction either by Chart Globe or other certayne relation in what altitude that passage was to bee searched I shaped a Northerly course and so sought the same towards the South, and in that my Northerly course I fell upon the shore which in ancient time was called Groynland five hundred leagues distant from the durseys[1] West Nor West Northerly, the land being very high and full of mightie mountaines all covered with snow no viewe of wood grasse or earth to be seene, and the shore two leages of into the sea so full of yce as that no shipping cold by any meanes come neere the same. The lothsome vewe of the shore, and Irksome noyse of the yce was such as that it bred strange conceipts among us, so that we supposed the place to be wast & voyd of any sencible or vegitable creatures, whereupon I called the same desolation, so coasting this shore towardes the South in the latitude of sixtie degrees, I found it to trend towards the west, I still followed the leading thereof in the same height, and after fiftie or sixtie leages, it fayled and lay directly North, which I still followed and in thirtie leages

1. Dursey Island on the coast of Co. Kerry, Ireland.

sayling upon the West side of this coast by me named desolation,[2] we were past all the yce and found many greene and pleasant Ills bordering upon the shore, but the mountains of the maine were still covered with great quantities of snowe, I brought my shippe among those Ylls and there mored to refresh our selves in our wearie travell, in the latitude of sixtie foure degrees or there about. The people of the Countrey having espyed our shipps came down unto us in their Canoes, holding up their right hand to the Sunne and crying Yliaout, would strike their brestes, we doing the like the people came aborde our shippes, men of good stature, unbearded, small eyed and of tractable conditions, by whome as signes would permit, we understood that towardes the North and West there was a great sea, and using the people with kindnesse in geving them nayles and knifes which of all things they most desired, we departed, and finding the sea free from yce supposing our selves to be past all daunger we shaped our course West Nor West thinking thereby to passe for China, but in the latitude of sixtie sixe degrees wee fell with another shore, and there found another passage of 20. leages broade directly West into the same, which we supposed to bee our hoped strayght, we entered into the same thirty or fortie leages finding it neither to wyden nor straighten, then considering that the yeere was spent for this was in the fyne of August, not knowing the length of the straight and dangers thereof, we tooke it our best course to retourne with notice of our good successe for this small time of search. And so returning in a sharpe fret of Westerley windes the 29. of September we arived at Dartmouth. And acquainting master Secretory with the rest of the honorable and worshipfull adventurers of all our proceedinges I was appointed againe the seconde yeere to search the bottome of this straight, because by all likelihood it was the place and passage by us laboured for.

In this second attempt, the merchants of Exeter, and other places of the West became adventurers in the action, so that being sufficiently furnished for six monethes, and having direction to search these straightes, untill we found the same to fall into another sea upon the West side of this part of America, we should

2. Desolation is western Greenland.

agayne returne for then it was not to be doubted, but shiping with trade might safely bee conveied to China and the parts of Asia. We departed from Dartmouth, & arriving unto the South part of the coast of desolation costed the same upon his West shore to the latitude of 66. degres, and there ancored among the ylls bordering upon the same, where wee refreshed our selves, the people of this place came likewise unto us, by whome I understood through their signes that towards the North the Sea was large. At this place the chiefe shipe wherupon I trusted, called the Mermayd of Dartmouth, found many occasions of discontment, and being unwilling to proceede, shee there forsook me. Then considering how I had given my fayth and most constant promise to my worshipfull good friend master William Sanderson, who of all men was the greatest adventurer in that action, and tooke such care for the perfourmance thereof that hee hath to my knowledge at one time disbursed as much money as any five others whatsoever out of his owne purse, when some of the companie have bin slacke in giving in their adventure. And also knowing that I should lose the favour of master Secretory, if I should shrinke from his direction, in one small barke of thirty tonnes, whereof Master Sanderson was owner, alone without farther comfort or company I proceeded on my voyage, and ariving unto this straights followed the same eightie leages untill I came among many ylandes, where the water did eb and flowe six fadome upright, and where there had bene great trade of people to make trayne. But by such thinges as there we found wee knew that they were not Christians of Europe that had used that trade, in fine by searching with our boate, wee found small hope to passe any farther that way, and therefore retourning againe recovered the sea and coasted the shore towardes the South, and in so doing (for it was to late to search towardes the North) wee founde another great inlett neere fortie leagues broade where the water entred in with violent swiftnes, this we also thought might be a passage, for no doubt but the North partes of America are all ylands, by ought that I could perceive therein, but because I was alone in a small barke of thirtie tonnes, and the yeere spent, I entred not into the same for it was now the seventh of September, but coasting the shore towardes the South we saw an incredible number of birdes, having divers fishermen aborde our barke they all concluded that there was a great scull of fish, wee beeing unprovided of fishing furniture, with a long spike nayle made a hoke, and fastening the same to one of our sounding lynes, before the bayte was changed wee tooke more then fortie great cods, the fishe swimming so abondantly thicke about our barke as is incredible to be reported, of which with a small portion of salte that we had, wee preserved some thirtie couple, or thereaboutes, and so returned for England. And having reported to master Secretory the whole successe of this attempt, hee commanded me to present unto the most honourable Lorde high thresurer of England some part of that fish, which when his Lordship saw and hearde at large the relation of this second attempt, I received favourable countenance from his honour, advising me to prosecute the action, of which his Lordship conceived a very good opinion. The next yeere although divers of the adventurers fel from the action, as all the Westerne merchantes and most of those in London yet some of the adventurers both honorable and worshipfull continued their willing favour and charge, so that by this meanes the next yere 2. shippes were appointed for the fishing and one pynace for the discovery.

Departing from Dartmouth, through Gods mercifull favour I arived at the place of fishing and there according to my direction I left the 2. shipps to follow that business, taking their faithful promise not to depart untill my returne unto them, which shoulde bee in the fine of August, and so in the barke I proceeded for the discovery but after my departure in sixteene dayes the shippes had finished their voyage, and so presently departed for England, without regard of their promise, my selfe not distrusting any such hard measure proceede in the discoverie and followed my course in the free and open sea between North and Norwest to the latitude of sixtie seven degrees and there I might see America, West from me, and Desolation East, then when I saw the land of both sides, I began to distrust that it would proove but a gulfe, notwithstanding desirous to know the full certaintye I proceeded, and in sixtie degrees the passage enlarged so that I could not see the westerne shore, thus I continued to the latitude of seventie five degrees, in a great sea, free from yce coasting the westerne shore of Desolation, the people came continually rowing out unto me in their Canoas twenty, forty, and one hundred at a time, and would give me fishe dried, Samon, Salmon peale, cod, Caplin, Lumpe, stone base, and such like, besides divers kindes of birdes, as Partrig, Fesant, Gulls, sea birdes, and other kindes of fleshe, I still laboured by signes to knowe from them what they knew of any sea towards the North, they still made signes of a great sea as we understood them, then I departed from that coast thinking to discover the North parts of America, and after I had sayled towardes the west neere fortie leages I fel upon a great bancke of yce, the wind being North and blewe much, I was constrained to coast the same towardes the South, not seeing any shore West from me, neither was there any yce towards the North, but a great sea, free, large very salt and blue and of an unsearcheable depth. So coasting towardes the South I came to the place where I left the shippes to fishe, but found them not. Then being forsaken and left in this distresse referring my self to the mercifull providence of God, shaped my course for England and unhoped for of any God alone releving me I arived at Dartmouth, by this last discoverie it seemed most manifest that the passage was free and without impediment towards the North, but by reason of the spanish fleete and unfortunate time of master Secretoryes death, the voyage was omitted and never sithens attempted. The cause why I use this particular relation of all my procedinges for this discovery, is to stay this objection, why hath not Davis discovered this passage being thrise that wayes imploied? how far I proceeded and in what fourme this discovery lyeth, doth appeare upon the Globe which master Sanderson to his verye great charge hath published whose labouring indevour for the good of his Countrie, deserveth great favor and commendations.

54. The Discovery
of Hudson Strait and Hudson Bay
by Henry Hudson in 1610

HENRY HUDSON's voyage of 1610 was the culmination of a new wave of Northwest Passage discovery beginning in 1602 with the voyage of George Waymouth, the incentive being to find a new short route to the East which could be used by the East India Company—founded in 1600.

Waymouth reached but did not penetrate Hudson Strait. John Knight took another ship out in 1606, but damaged his ship on the Labrador coast before making any discoveries. Henry Hudson made his first northern voyage in 1607 up the east coast of Greenland to 73° N., but was unable to penetrate farther. His 1608 expedition was an ineffective attempt to find a Northeast Passage. Transferring to the Dutch service, he switched his voyage from Northeast to West, discovering the Hudson River. He finally got support in England in 1610 for a Northwest Passage voyage. His summary journal (printed below: it first appeared in Samuel Purchas, Hakluytus posthumus, or Purchas his pilgrimes, III [1625], 596–597) records his entry into and passage through Hudson Strait—a notable achievement. He then took his ship into Hudson Bay itself, wintered in James Bay, and in 1611, when he attempted to renew his search to the West, mutineers turned him and six others adrift to their deaths, while the Discovery made for home. Ultimately this discovery enabled the Hudson's Bay Company to trade with northern Canada.

The narratives are reprinted in Purchas, Hakluytus Posthumus, or Purchas His Pilgrimes, XIII (1906), 374–412, and in George M. Asher, ed., Henry Hudson the Navigator, 1607–1613 (1860).

An Abstract of the Journall of Master Henry Hudson, for the Discoverie of the North-west Passage, begunne the seventeenth of Aprill, 1610, ended with his end, being treacherously exposed by some of the Companie.

The seventeenth of Aprill, 1610. we brake ground, and went downe from Saint Katharines Poole, and fell downe to Blacke-wall: and so plyed downe with the ships to Lee, which was the two and twentieth day.

The two and twentieth, I caused Master Coleburne to bee put into a Pinke, bound for London, with my Letter to the Adventurers, importing the reason wherefore I so put him out of the ship, and so plyed forth.

The second of May, the wind Southerly, at Eeven we were thwart of Flamborough Head.

The fift, we were at the Iles of Orkney, and here I set the North end of the Needle, and the North of the Flie all one.

The sixt, wee were in the latitude of 59. degrees 22. minutes, and there perceived that the North end of Scotland, Orkney, and Shotland are not so Northerly, as is commonly set downe. The eight day, wee saw Farre Ilands, in the latitude of 62. degrees 24. minutes. The eleventh day, we fell with the Easter part of Island, and then plying along the Souther part of the Land, we came to Westmony, being the fifteenth day, and still plyed about the mayne Iland, untill the last of May with contrary winds, and we got some Fowles of divers sorts.

The first day of June, we put to Sea out of an Harbour, in the Westermost part of Island, and so plyed to the Westward in the latitude of 66. degrees 34. minutes, and the second day plyed and found our selves in 65. degrees 57. minutes, with little wind Easterly.

The third day, wee found our selves in 65. degrees 30. minutes, with winde at North-east, a little before this we sayled neere some Ice.

The fourth day, we saw Groneland over the Ice perfectly, and this night the Sunne went downe due North, and rose North North-east. So plying the fift day, we were in 65. degrees, still encombred with much Ice, which hung upon the Coast of Groneland.

The ninth day, wee were off Frobishers Streights with the winde Northerly, and plyed unto the South-westwards untill the fifteenth day.

The fifteenth day, we were in sight of the land, in latitude 59. degrees 27. minutes, which was called by Captayne John Davis, Desolation, and found the errour of the former laying downe of that Land: and then running to the North-westward untill the twentieth day, wee found the ship in 60. degrees 42. minutes, and saw much Ice, and many Riplings or Over-fals, and a strong streame setting from East South-east, to West North-west.

The one and twentie, two and twentie, and three and twentie dayes, with the winde variable, we plyed to the North-westward in sight of much Ice, into the height of 62. degrees 29. minutes.

The foure and twentie, and five and twentie dayes, sayling to the West-ward about midnight, wee saw Land North, which was suddenly lost againe.[1] So wee ranne still to the West-ward in 62. degrees 17. minutes.

---

1. Side note: "East entrance into the Streightes."

The fift of July, wee plyed up upon the Souther side, troubled with much Ice in seeking the shoare untill the fift day of July, and we observed that day in 59. degrees 16. minutes. Then we plyed off the shoare againe, untill the eight day, and then found the height of the Pole in 60. degrees no minutes. Here we saw the Land from the North-west by West, halfe Northerly unto the South-west by West, covered with snow, a Champaigne Land, and called it, Desire provoketh.

We still plyed up to the Westward, as the Land and Ice would suffer untill the eleventh day: when fearing a storme, we anchored by three Rockie Ilands in uncertayne depth, betweene two and nine fathomes; and found it an Harbour unsufficient by reason of sunken Rockes, one of which was next morning two fathomes above water. Wee called them the Iles of Gods Mercies. The water floweth here better then foure fathomes. The Floud commeth from the North, flowing eight the change day. The latitude in this place is 62. degrees 9. minutes. Then plying to the South-westward the sixteenth day, wee were in the latitude of 58. degrees 50. minutes, but found our selves imbayed with Land, and had much Ice: and we plyed to the North-westward untill the nineteenth day, and then wee found by observation the height of the Pole in 61. degrees 24. minutes, and saw the Land, which I named, Hold with Hope. Hence I plyed to the North-westward still, untill the one and twentieth day, with the wind variable. Heere I found the Sea more growne, then any wee had since wee left England.

The three and twentieth day, by observation the height of the Pole was 61. degrees 33. minutes. The five and twentieth day, we saw the Land; and named it Magna Britannia. The sixe and twentieth day, wee observed and found the latitude in 62. degrees 44. minutes. The eight and twentieth day, we were in the height of 63. degrees 10. minutes, and plyed Southerly of the West. The one and thirtieth day, plying to the Westward, at noone wee found our selves in 62. degrees 24. minutes.

The first of August, we had sight of the Northerne shoare, from the North by East to the West by South off us: the North part twelve leagues, and the Wester part twentie leagues from us: and we had no ground there at one hundred and eightie fathomes. And I thinke I saw Land on the Sunne side, but could not make it perfectly, bearing East North-east. Here I found the latitude 62. degrees 50. minutes.

The second day, we had sight of a faire Head-land, on the Norther shoare six leagues off, which I called Salisburies Fore-land: we ranne from them West South-west, fourteene leagues: In the mid-way of which wee were suddenly come into a great and whurling Sea, whether caused by meeting of two streames, or an Over-fall, I know not. Thence sayling West and by South seven leagues farther, we were in the mouth of a Streight² and sounded, and had no ground at one hundred fathomes: the Streight being there not above two leagues broad, in the passage in this Wester part: which from the Easter part of Fretum Davis, is distant two hundred and fiftie leagues there abouts.

The third day, we put through the narrow passage, after our men had beene on Land, which had well observed there, That the Floud did come from the North, flowing by the shoare five fathomes. The head of this entrance on the South side I named Cape Worsenholme; and the head on the North-wester shoare, I called Cape Digs. After wee had sailed with an Easterly winde, West and by South ten leagues, the Land fell away to the South-ward, and the other Iles and Land left us to the Westward. Then I observed and found the ship at noone in 61. degrees 20. minutes, and a Sea to the Westward.

2. Side note: "A Streight which led us into the deepe Bay of Gods great Mercies," namely, Hudson Strait leading into Hudson Bay.

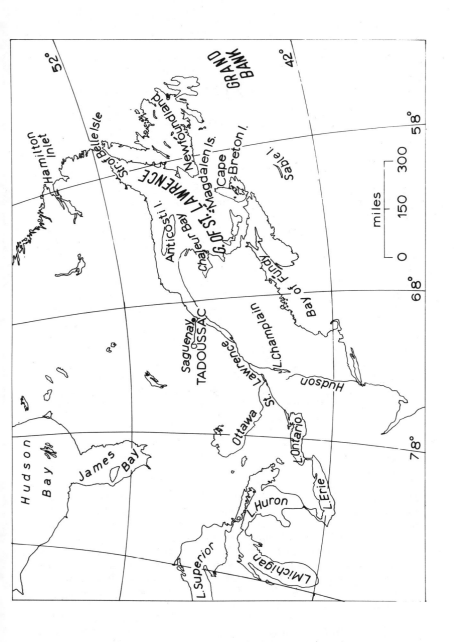

XII

Newfoundland and the Approaches
to the St. Lawrence

NEWFOUNDLAND WAS THE center of the only important industry carried on by Europeans in North America. The shore fishery brought French, French and Spanish Basques, Portuguese and English vessels to harbors and fish-drying shores for from three to four months in the year. The Banks fishery attracted other vessels—mainly French—which sometimes called at one or other Newfoundland harbor either at the beginning or end of their fishing season. Most of the Newfoundland shores were allotted by the late sixteenth century, on what were already traditional lines, amongst the nationals of one of the European powers, except for the Basques who scorned the artificial line of the Franco-Spanish boundary and worked together. The harbor of St. John's was also an exception. There, all nationalities put in for the exchange of supplies, making of repairs and social exchanges, though the shore fishery around the harbor was in English hands.

Newfoundland, because the way to it was so well known and because its ports were suitable for calls en route, was also a taking off point for voyages further west, southwest or northwest. Basque whaling, fishing and fur trading extended over the Gulf of St. Lawrence, up the St. Lawrence River and down the shores of Cape Breton and Nova Scotia. Bretons and Normans penetrated, at least from 1581, up to Tadoussac on the St. Lawrence River; from 1591, Bretons were competing with Basques at the Magdalen Islands' walrus fishery; they were active on the shores of Cape Breton, in the Bay of Fundy, along the Nova Scotia coast, sometimes penetrating down the mainland shore to Maine. The English were strong in southeast Newfoundland, which Sir Humphrey Gilbert hoped to use in 1583 as a jumping off ground for modern New England. During the 1580's the English were busy collecting data on French fishing and fur trading: between 1593 and 1597 they tried to take a share of the trade in the Gulf of St. Lawrence, settle a colony on the Magdalen Islands and fish along the Cape Breton and Nova Scotia coasts. From 1597 onward, France began to organize her interests in the area. The Marquis de la Roche sent convicted criminals with their keepers to settle Sable Island and took seal-skin cargoes home for some years; after they had killed off their keepers the surviving criminals were rescued, brought home and pardoned. A French syndicate set up a winter trading station at Tadoussac in 1600–1601, but the survivors were brought home after a bad winter. The expedition of 1603 by Samuel de Champlain, sent to make recommendations about the organization of the fur trade on the St. Lawrence, marked the virtual appropriation of the St. Lawrence Gulf and River by France. Thereafter England would have to fight France for Canada, though division of spheres of influence in Newfoundland where there were no settled colonies remained possible. The English were driven to concern themselves with areas to the south, notably New England.

H. A. Innis, The Cod Fisheries (1940) and Gillian T. Cell, The English in Newfoundland, 1580–1660 (1970), M. de la Morandière, Histoire de la Pêche de Morue française, I (1961), with the introduction to Quinn, The Voyages and Colonising Enterprises of Sir Humphrey Gilbert, I, provide material on the fishery. D. B. Quinn, "The English and the St. Lawrence, 1580–1602," in Merchants and Scholars, ed. John Parker (1965), pp. 119–143, and M. Trudel, Histoire de la Nouvelle France, I, D. B. Quinn, "The Voyage of Étienne Bellenger to the Maritimes in 1583: A New Document," Canadian Historical Review, XLIII (1962), 328–343, D. B. Quinn and N. C. Cheshire, The New Found Wand of Stephen Parmenius (1971), with articles in D.C.B., I, document the French and English in the Maritimes and Gulf of St. Lawrence.

55. The Newfoundland Shore Fishery, 1578

ANTHONY PARKHURST, who wrote the long letter to the elder Richard Hakluyt from which extracts are given, operated and commanded fishing vessels working each year from Bristol to Newfoundland, 1575–78. He was one of the few men engaged in the fishery who explored ashore in Newfoundland and who thought of the shore fishery there as only the first step in the exploitation of the St. Lawrence Gulf and River. Hakluyt was collecting material on American prospects and valued this letter as giving a good picture of what went on at the fishery. The extracts are taken from Hakluyt, The principal navigations, III (1600), 132–134.

Now to answer some part of your letter touching the sundry navies that come to New found land, or Terra nova, for fish: you shall understand that some fish not neere the other by 200. leagues, and therefore the certaintie is not knowen; & some yeeres come many more then other some, as I see the like among us: who since my first travell being but 4. yeeres, are increased from 30. sayle to 50. which commeth to passe chiefly by the imagination of the Westerne men, who thinke their neighbors have had greater gaines then in very deed they have, for that they see me to take such paines yerely to go in proper person, they also suppose that I find some secret commoditie by reason that I do search the harbors, creekes and havens, and also the land much more then ever any Englishman hath done. Surely I am glad that it so increaseth, whereof soever it springeth. But to let this passe, you shall understand that I am informed that there are above 100. saile of Spaniards that come to take Cod (who make all wet, and do drie it when they come home) besides 20. or 30. more that come from Biskaie, to kil Whale for traine. These be better appointed for shipping and furniture of munition, then any nation, saving the Englishmen, who commonly are lordes of the harbors where they fish, and do use all strangers helpe in fishing if need require, according to an old custome of the countrey, which thing they do willingly, so that you take nothing from them more then a boat or twaine of salt, in respect of your protection of them against rovers or other violent intruders, who do often put them from good harbour, &c. As touching their tunnage, I thinke it may be well neere five or sixe thousand: but of Portingals there are not lightly above 50. saile, and they make all wet in like sorte, whose tunnage may amount to three thousand tunnes, and upwarde. Of the French nation and Brittons, are about one hundred and fiftie sailes, the moste of their shipping is very small, not past fortie tunne, among which some are great and reasonably well appointed, better then the Portingals, and not so well as the Spaniards, and the burden of them may be some 7000. tunne. Their shipping is from all parts of France and Britaine [Brittany], and the Spaniards from most parts of Spaine, the Portingals from Aviero and Viana, and from 2. or 3. portes more. The trade that our nation hath to Island [Iceland], maketh that the English are not there in such numbers as other nations. . . .

Nowe to shew you my fansie what places I suppose meetest to inhabite in those parts discovered of late by our nation: There is neere about the mouth of the grand baie, an excellent harbour called of the Frenchmen Chasteau, and one Island in the very entrie of the streight called Bell Isle, which places if they be peopled and well fortified (as there are stone and things meete for it throughout all New found land) we shall bee lordes of the whole fishing in small time, if it doe so please the Queenes majestie, and from thence send wood and cole with all necessaries to Laborador lately discovered: but I am of opinion, and doe most stedfastly beleeve that we shall finde as rich Mines in more temperate places and Climates, and more profitable for fishing then any yet we have used, where wee shall have not farre from thence plentie of salt made by fire undoubtedly, and very likely by the heate of the Sunne, by reason I finde salt kerned on the rockes in nine and fortie and better: these places may bee found for salte in three and fortie. I know more touching these two commodities last remembred, then any man of our nation doth; for that I have some knowledge in such matters, and have most desired the finding of them by painefull travell, and most diligent inquirie. Now to be short, for I have bene overlong by master [Michael] Butlers means, who cried on mee to write at large, and of as many things as I call to minde woorthy of remembraunce: wherefore this one thing more. I could wish the Island in the mouth of the river of Canada [Anticosti], should bee inhabited, and the river searched, for that there are many things which may rise thereof, as I will shew you hereafter. I could find in my heart to make proofe whether it be true or no that I have red and heard of Frenchmen and Portingals to bee in that river, and about Cape Britton.

56. The Basque Fishing and Whaling Fleets, 1574

A NOTE by Cristóbal de Barros, 1574, indicating the times of departure and return from and to the Basque country, from M. Fernández de Navarrete, "Colección de los viajes y descobrimientos que hicieron . . . los Españoles", in Obras, II (1964), 117, translated.

The ships which go to the cod fishing at Newfoundland set out from that coast at the end of March and the beginning of April and return to it in the middle of September and in October. Those which go to the whale fishery set out from this coast about the middle of June and return to it in December and at the beginning of January.

57. Sir Humphrey Gilbert at Newfoundland, 1583

AFTER GETTING *many promises of support for his venture to colonize what are now the southern shores of New England, Sir Humphrey Gilbert set out in June 1583 to make a reconnaissance of the territory. He sailed by way of Newfoundland and attempted on his way to assert some measure of English control over the shore fishery at St. John's. Edward Hayes commanded the ship Golden Hind in the expedition, and gave the account from which extracts are taken. The whole proceeding was futile as Gilbert had no means of enforcing any authority on the fishery. It does, however, give some impression of the situation there. Gilbert proceeded in the direction of the mainland but, losing a ship at Sable Island, was forced to return and was lost at sea. The extracts are from Hakluyt, The principall navigations (1589), pp. 685–688.*

On Gilbert and Hayes, see Quinn, The Voyages and Colonising Enterprises of Sir Humphrey Gilbert, "Edward Hayes, Liverpool Colonial Pioneer", Transactions of the Historic Society of Lancashire and Cheshire, CXI (1959), 26–43; Quinn and Cheshire, The New Found Land of Stephen Parmenius (1971); and Dictionary of Canadian Biography, I.

Upon Tuesday the 11 of June, we forsooke the coast of England. So againe Tuesday the 30 of July (seven weekes after) we got sight of land, being immediatly embayed in the Grand bay, or some other great bay: the certeinty whereof we could not judge, so great hase and fogge did hang upon the coast, as neither we might discerne the land well, nor take the Sunnes height. But by our best computation we were then in the 51. degrees of latitude.

Forsaking this bay and uncomfortable coast (nothing appearing unto us but hideous rockes and mountaines, bare of trees, and voide of any greene herbe) we followed the coast to the South, with weather faire and cleare. . . .

We held on our course Southward, until we came against the harbor called S. Johns, about 5 leagues from the former Cape of

S. Francis: where before the entrance into the harbor, we found also the frigate or Squirril lying at ancre. Whome the English marchants (that were & alwayes be Admirals by turnes interchangeably over the fleetes of fishermen within the same harbor) would not permit to enter into the harbor. Glad of so happy meeting both of the Swallow and Frigate in one day (being Saturday the 3. of August) we made readie our fights, & prepared to enter the harbor, any resistance to the contrarie notwithstanding, there being within of all nations, to the number of 36. sailes. But first the Generall dispatched a boate to give them knowledge of his comming for no ill intent, having Commission from her Majestie for his voiage he had in hand. And immediatly we followed with a slacke gale, and in the very entrance (which is but narrow, not above 2. buts length) the Admirall fell upon a rocke on the larboord side by great oversight, in that the weather was faire, the rocke muche above water fast by the shore, where neither went any sea gate. But we found such readinesse in the English Marchants to helpe us in that danger, that without delaye there were brought a number of boates, which towed off the ship, and cleared her of danger.

Having taken place convenient in the road, we let fall ancres, the Captaines & Masters repairing aboord our Admirall: whither also came immediatly the Masters and owners of the fishing fleete of Englishmen, to understand the Generals intent & cause of our arrivall there. They were all satisfied when the General had shewed his commission, & purpose to take possession of those lands to the behalfe of the crowne of England, and the advauncement of Christian religion in those paganish regions, requiring but their lawfull ayd for repairing of his fleete, & supply of some necessaries, so farre as conveniently might be afoarded him, both out of that and other harbors adjoyning. In lieu whereof, he made offer to gratifie them, with any favour & priviledge, which upon their better advise they should demaund, the like being not to bee obteined hereafter for greater price. So craving expedition of his demaund, minding to proceede further south without long detention in those parts, he dismissed them, after promise given of their best indevour to satisfie speedily his so reasonable request. The marchants with their Masters departed, they caused forthwith to be discharged all the great Ordinance of their fleete in token of our welcome.

It was further determined that every ship of our fleete should deliver unto the marchants and Masters of that harbour a note of all their wants: which done, the ships aswell English as strangers, were taxed at an easie rate to make supply. And besides, Commissioners were appointed, part of our owne companie and part of theirs, to goe into other harbours adjoyning, (for our English marchants commaund all there) to leavie our provision: whereunto the Portingals (above other nations) did most willingly and liberally contribute. Insomuch as we were presented (above our allowance) with wines, marmalads, most fine ruske or bisket, sweet oyles and sundry delicacies. Also we wanted not of fresh salmons, trouts, lobsters and other fresh fish brought dayly unto us. Moreover, as the maner is in their fishing, every weeke to choose their Admirall a new, or rather they succeed in orderly course, and have weekely their Admirals feast solemnized: even so the General, Captaines and masters of our fleete were continually invited and feasted. To growe short, in our abundance at home, the intertainment had bene delightful, but after our wants and tedious passage through the Ocean, it seemed more acceptable and of greater contentation, by how much the same was unexpected in that desolate corner of the worlde: where at other times of the yeere, wilde beasts and birds have onely the fruition of all those Countries,[1] which now seemed a place very populous and much frequented.

The next morning being Sunday & the 4. of August, the Generall & his company were brought on land by English marchants, who shewed unto us their accustomed walkes unto a place they call the Garden. But nothing appeared more then Nature it selfe without art: who confusedly hath brought foorth roses abundantly, wilde, but odoriferous, and to sense very comfortable. Also the like plentie of raspis berries, which doe grow in every place.

Munday following, the General had his tent set up, who being accompanied with his own followers, summoned the marchants and masters, both English and strangers to be present at his taking possession of those Countries. Before whom openly was read & interpreted unto the strangers, his Commission: by vertue whereof

---

1. Side note: "Savages in the South part of Newfound land."

he tooke possession in the same harbour of S. Johns, and 200. leagues every way, invested the Queenes Majestie with the title and dignitie thereof, had delivered unto him (after the custome of England) a rod & a turffe of the same soile, entring possession also for him, his heires and assignes for ever: And signified unto al men, that from that time forward, they should take the same lande as a territorie appertaining to the Queene of England, and himselfe authorised under her Majestie to possesse and enjoy it. And to ordeine lawes for the governement thereof, agreeable (so neere as conveniently might be) unto the lawes of England: under which all people comming thither hereafter, either to inhabite, or by way of traffique, should be subjected and governed. And especially at the same time for a beginning, he posed and delivered three lawes to be in force immediatly. That is to say: the first for Religion, which in publique exercise should be according to the Church of England. The 2. for maintenance of her Majesties right and possession of those territories, against which if any thing were attempted prejudiciall, the partie or parties offending should be adjudged and executed as in case of high treason, according to the lawes of England. The 3. if any person should utter words sounding to the dishonour of her Majestie, he should loose his eares, and have his ship and goods confiscate.

These contents published, obedience was promised by generall voyce & consent of the multitude aswell of Englishmen as strangers, praying for continuance of this possession and governement begun. After this, the assembly was dismissed. And afterward were erected not farre from that place the Armes of England ingraven in lead, & infixed upon a pillar of wood. Yet further & actually to establish this possession taken in the right of her Majestie, & to the behoofe of Sir Humfrey Gilbert knight, his heires and assignes for ever: the Generall granted in fee farme divers parcells of land lying by the water side, both in this harbor of S. Johns, and els where, which was to the owners a great commoditie being thereby assured (by their proper inheritance) of grounds convenient to dresse and to drie their fish, whereof many times before they did faile, being prevented by them that came first into the harbor. For which grounds they did covenant to pay a certaine rent and service unto sir Humfrey Gilbert, his heires or assignes for ever, and yeerely to mainteine possession of the same, by themselves or their assignes.

58. A French Voyage
to the Bay of Fundy and to Maine,
1583

WHILE GILBERT was preparing to go to Newfoundland, a Rouen merchant and seaman, Étienne Bellenger, was carrying through a parallel venture in his ship the Chardon. His object was to exploit the fur trade of the shores to the south of those usually visited by French vessels, namely, the southern part of Nova Scotia and what lay beyond it, and also to reconnoiter and occupy a site for a trading post which could be used at the same time for a Catholic mission to the Indians. His exploration of the Bay of Fundy appears to have been a thorough one, and he was much attracted by the head of the Bay, yet he did not choose it as a site for his advance post but went on to investigate the Maine coast. His contacts with the Indians so far had been friendly and profitable, but after he had turned back to the Nova Scotia coast, where he seems to have thought his post could best be set up, his men were attacked, he lost his pinnace and some men and had to return.

Richard Hakluyt the younger had gone in 1583, on attachment to the English embassy at Paris, to collect information on North America on behalf of the Secretary of State, Sir Francis Walsingham. He made contact with Étienne Bellenger and jotted down a brief account of the voyage of 1583 from what he heard from him. The notes were found among the papers of Sir Julius Caesar, judge of the High Court of Admirality (British Museum, Additional Manuscript 14027, ff. 289–290), and were first published in 1962.

See Quinn, "The Voyage of Étienne Bellenger to the Maritimes in 1583: A New Document," Canadian Historical Review, XLIII, 328–343 (from which extracts are taken); T. N. Marsh, "An Unpublished Hakluyt Manuscript?", New England Quarterly, XXV (1962), 247–252; and Dictionary of Canadian Biography, I.

Master Stephen Bellanger nowe dwelling in Roan in the streete of the Augustines nexte howsse to the signe of the golden tyle in frenche thuille [Tuile] d'or; departed from Newhaven the 19th of Januarii 1583 in a barck of Fiftie Tons and a little Pinnesse loose within board accompanied with Master Cottes [Michel Costé] an excellent Pilott of Newhaven [Le Havre] and thirtie men and boyes at the charge of the Cardinal of Burbon, [Charles de Bourbon-Vendôme, cardinal of Bourbon], and within lesse then a Moneth arrived at Cape Bryton a litle to the sowthwest of Newefownde Land.

From thence he toke his course following the Coast along to the southwest for the space of Two hundreth Leagues the draught and particular discription whereof he shewed me.

He discovered all the Bayes, Harbors, Creekes, Rivers, Sandes, Rockes, Islandes, Flattes, with the depthes of Water along as he went which were in some places 15.30.40.44.50.60. fathoms which he had dilligentlie noted downe in writing within. 50. or threescore Leagues to the west and by south of Cape Briton he had drawne the Iland of St. John which lieth east and west the space of Fiftie leagues, and lieth in forme of a Triangle.[1]

In a great Bay of that Iland [Bay of Fundy] which at one place of the enteraunce is so narrowe that a Colverin shott can reache from one side to the other,[2] and after you are passed that streight is xxv leagues upp and 20 leagues broad he planted the Cardinall of Burbons Armes in a mightie highe tree[3] and gave names to many places.

To the west of that Iland about 20. leagues he fownde a great River[4] into which he ran upp with his smale Pynnasse seaven Leagues and thincketh it is navigable three or fowrescore leagues.

He wente on shoare in Tenn or twelve places which he fownde verie pleasant. And the coast lieth in 42 43 44 degrees of Latitude more or lesse, and is as warme as Bayon, Bordeux, Rochell, and Nates varieng a litle as it lieth more to the North or the south.

He thincketh verilie that verie good salte may be made there in great quantitie in divers places along the Coast seeing there wanteth no heate of the sonne nor lowe of flattes like those of Rochell fytt for the purpose.

He fownde the Countrey full of good trees to build Shipps withall

1. Bellenger gained the impression that southern Nova Scotia was insular and triangular and was the Island of St. John of earlier maps.
2. The passage from St. Mary's Bay to the Bay of Fundy, probably by way of the narrow Digby Gut.
3. Probably between Cap d'Or and Ram Head.
4. Apparently the Penobscot River.

and namely great plentie of oakes, Cypresses, Pynes, hasels etc and divers good herbes as sorrell etc.

In many places he had traffique with the people which are of verie good disposition and stature of Bodie.

They weare their hayre hanging downe long before and behynde as lowe as their Navells which they cutt short only overthwart their browes. They go all naked saving their privities which they cover with an Apron of some Beastes skynn, and tye it unto them with a long buff gerdle that comes three times about them beeing made fast behynde and at boath the endes it is cutt into litle thynn thonges, which thonges they tye rownde about them with slender quils of birdes fethers[5] whereof some are as red as if they had byn dyed in cuchanille.

Their girdells have also before a litle Codd or Pursse of Buff wherein they putt divers thinges but especiallie their tinder to keepe fire in, which is of a dry roote and somewhat like a hard sponge and will quicklie take fyer and is hardlie put out. Their weapons whereof he brought hoame store to the Cardinall are Bowes of two yardes long and arrowes of one yarde hedded with indented bones three or fower ynches long, and are tyed into a nocke at the ende with a thong of Lether.

In divers places they are gentle and tractable, But those about Cape Briton and threescore or fowerscore leagues Westward are more cruell and subtill of norture then the rest. And you are not to trust them but to stond upon your gard.[6] For among them he lost two of his men and his smale Pinesse which happned through their owne follye in trusting the salvadges to farr.

He had traffique with them in divers places and for trifles, as knyves, belles, glasses, and suche like smale marchaundize which cost hym but Fortie livers which amount but to fower Poundes Englishe he had by waie of traffique comodities that he sould in Roan at his retourne. for Fower hundreth and Fortie Crownes.

Theis were some of the Comodities which he brought hoame from thence, & showed them me at his howsse.

5. Porcupine quills, dyed red.
6. Apparently the Micmac Indians of southern Nova Scotia are meant.

1 Buff hides reddie dressed upon both sides bigger then an Oxe,[7]
2 Deere skynes dressed well on the inner side, with the hayre on the outside,
3 Seale skynns exceding great dressed on the ynnerside,
4 Marterns enclyning unto Sables,[8]
5 Bevers skynes verie fayre as many as made 600 bever hattes,
6 Otters skynnes verie faire and large,
7 A kynde of liquide muske or sivet taken out of the Bevers stones,[9]
8 The fleshe of Deere dried in the sunne in peeces a foot Long,
9 Divers excellent Cullors, as scarlet, vermillion, redd, tawny, yellowe, gray and watchett,[10]
10 Fethers the quils wherof are redd as vermillion,
11 Luserns, which the frenche call Loupcerviers [Lynx], Whereof twentie he gave to the Cardinall of Burbon for a present, and divers others to certaine of his friendes which I sawe, and was enformed that they were worth some 6.8.10.12.15 crownes a skynne,
12 A kynde of mynerall matter which as some that have seene thinck houldes sylver and tynn, whereof he gave me a peece.

Divers other comodities he fownde the secrites whereof he was loath to disclose unto me.

He affirmeth by his owne experience that fishe of that Coast on the which he hath byn thrise, is bigger and better then that of New found Land; and that the havens are exceding good.

He was out upon his voiadge but Foure Moneths and a half.

He hathe drawen a fayre Carde [chart] of all his discoverie which he presented latelie to the Cardinall of Burbon.

His first draught he shewed me at his howsse and all the comodities above mentioned and gave me parte of each of them for his kynnesmanns sake one Andrewe Mayer the Compasse maker of Roan, which made me acquaynted with hym.

He hath also made brief relation of his voiadge in the presences of divers Englishe man of Credit whome I brought into his Companie

7. Elk rather than bison.
8. Either the Fisher or the Canadian Sable.
9. Castoreum.
10. Watchet is blue.

that they might here the same And namely of one Master Harvie of Lymehouse the owner of the Barck called the Thomas & John of London, Master Malym master of the barck called the Christian of one Moyser an englishe merchaunt of Roan and one Howe a sayler & other honest men.

And this present yere 1584 he setteth fourth agayne for further Traffique in the same voiadge with a barck and a smale Pinesse which are in preparing ayenst the first of Marche at homefleur [Honfleur] upon the Coast of Normandy. . . .

59. Reasons for English Colonization of What Is Now New England, *circa* 1592

EDWARD HAYES returned from Sir Humphrey Gilbert's expedition in 1583 an enthusiast for English control of Newfoundland. But he could get no support for successive plans to occupy the island and control the fishery. After 1590, apparently in collaboration with Christopher Carleill, who had planned to follow Gilbert in 1584 but had been diverted to military service in Ireland, Hayes worked out an alternative plan for English settlement in the latitude of 40°–43° N. or thereabouts, namely, in what is now New England, although he was also interested in the St. Lawrence. This plan (written about 1592) remains, unpublished, in Cambridge University Library, Manuscript Dd. 3.85, from which an extract is given. The plan had no practical result. A shortened version of the document was published in John Brereton, A briefe and true relation of the discoverie of the north part of Virginia (1602).

See Quinn, "Edward Hayes," Transactions of the Historic Society of Lancashire and Cheshire, XCI, 37–39, and Dictionary of Canadian Biography, I.

Of the Scituation & temperature of those places we choose fyrst to inhabit. And of the dyversitie of comodities to be raysed there.

Chap. 3

Those Contries which amongst others we chiefly respect doe lye under temperat Clymes, betwen 40. & 50. degres of latitude, in the veary same Scituation & parallels of Italy, france and the most fertile & best inhabited Contries of Europe, Well agreing with the Constitution of our boddies, Which ought to be a specyall regard, in making choyse of new habitations. . . .

Then forasmuche as the places intended of our habitations in America shalbe on the same parallels of Italy & france in 40. & 44. (or thearabowts:) It canot be that those clymes which in Europe are over hoatt for our boddies, shoold be over could in America, as some have surmised the same to be.

The Course from England thyther is not long, which may be accomplished comonly in 30 dayes or under. Is alltogither through the occean, apt for most wynds that can blowe, the trade alewayes open & free from restraynt by forren prynces, which is a benifyt wanting in all our other trades, and hath ben no small anoyance unto our Marchaunts.

The Coasts along those contries are fayer, and in all respects Comodiouse for traffyck, havyng goodly Bayes, Roads and harbors for shypps, with places apt to be fortefyed & made defensible agaynst any force that can be brought thyther.

Comodities are & wylbe . videlicet

Fysh of exceeding largeries and aboundance / more vendible for England & France then the Newland fysh for the most part. Besyds that we may fysh upon those southern coasts at all tymes of the yeare, which we canot doe upon the Newfoundland & coulder regions.

Salt is found in some places so good (by relation of a frenche man) as that of Bourage [Brouage] in france, otherwayes it may be made by Arte thear to fournish all the fyshyng ether by heat of the Sonn, or by fyer whear wood is so plentifull.

Whales & Seales in aboundance, Whereof we may make oyles to serve all England. . . .

The Soyle is exceding good consisting both of woodlands, champions & pleasaunt Meadowes. But overstrong untill by manurance it be fyned. In the mean tyme it will beare aboundantly, Hemp, flax, Rape seeds, and whatsoever else that requyre suche strength of soyle as thys must have, which never was used from beginning of the world hytherto so farr as is known.

Vynes grow there withowt industry. Bearing nevertheles good grapes. In lyke sort grow peas, Roses, Respasses [raspberries], Hemp. . . .

Myneralls in many places appeare veary evydently. A ryche Moyne of Copper hath ben discovered by certayn frenche men of late. The place is made known unto us by description, and of the Mettall hath ben brought some proofe into England. Not far from the same place is gyven us also great heap of Sylver, Allam is sayd to be there also. Quarries of stone most fayer and of Sondry Coullors for curiouse buyldings. . . .

There grow myghty trees of Fyrr, pyne & cedar, abell to Mast the greatest shypps of the world. And to make Tarr, pytche, Rosen, Soap Ashes, Tymberrs and excellent Board. There grow also Oakes, Ashes and other trees servyng to all uses. . . .

Skynns & furrs wylbe ryche Comodities. As proofe hath been made by certayn frenche men, Who have in secreat manner frequented those coasts. And by trucking with the Salvages, for theyr pettie wares they have retourned of the foarsayd comodities into france wheare they have gayned 14. upon one. . . .

Ryvers, veary many descending from the Mowntayns. But how farr they extend into the land is unknown. They are all stoared aboundantly with fysh veary delicat. Amongst many other Ryvers yet unknown: Two are of most faire, One abowt 40 degrees called (thowgh falsly) Norombega [Penobscot or Narragansett Bay?] whose aboundant streame causeth the Sea whear it dischargeth to be in a maner fresh. Thother is of us comonly called St. Laurence, but of the Inhabitaunts (whose name is beareth) Canada which by sondry frenche men hath ben searched and found navygable many leagues. But for Boates or vessells of good burden it is not found portable more than a thousand english myles into the land. It leadeth further (as hath ben gathered by intelligence from those inhabitaunts) unto a great Lake[1] (which is fresh at the issue of the Ryver, but beyond is bytter or salt, and non could gyve knowledge how farr the same extendeth). At the Mowth of thys ryver is scytuated the same Land which we call Newfoundland, being an Iland or Consisting of many Ilands or broken lands. Betwen New-

1. Probably the earliest report of Lake Ontario.

foundland and Cape Brytton in 46. or thearebowts is one entrance into the sayd ryver. And at the grand Bay in 52 de[gres] is an other by the north syde of Newfoundland, whear the Byskayes have a great whale fyshing. The ryver, from grand Baye, enclyneth to Sowth west by lyttell & lyttel, and is discovered unto 45 degres of latitude, alongst the North-syde whearof lye veary goodly Contries of Canada, Saguenay, Hochelaga and others. The lyke or no dowt better, lye on the South Syde, and ar both sydes well peopled; the fyelds replenished with corne or Maiz, pasture & vynes, besyds aboundance of fruits and other delyghts, which are brought forth more by the bowntie of Nature, then by help of Arte.

So as by consideration of the premisses, we shalbe abell by the industry and skyll of our people when they are planted, to rayse these comodities both of ye Sea & land. Nam[ely] Fysh & Salt, Oyles of whales & seales, pearles, Grapes, raysins, wynes, Corne, flax, Hemp, lynen cloath, sayll cloath, cabulls, Roapes, & Tarr, pytche, Rose[n], Turpentine, Soape ashes, Soap, Rape Seeds & oyles, Masts, tymbers & Boards of ceda[r] and pynes, Hydes, Skynns & furrs, Dyes, Coulors for paynting, Mettalls & Other Myneralls, Besyds other manifold Comodities which are there to be found, Servyng both to mayntayn trade, and to sustayn armies of men wyth varietie of Beasts, fysh & fowle to content every tast.

60. Englishmen Prospect the Whaling Industry of the Gulf of St. Lawrence

ENGLISHMEN HAD learned in 1591 that Breton and Basque fishermen were profitably taking walrus at the Magdalen Islands in the Gulf of St. Lawrence. An expedition went out under George Drake in 1593 but arrived too late to do more than steal some walrus pelts from the Bretons. By 1594 a Basque pilot, Stevan de Bocall, who knew the Gulf, had been hired, and under his direction the Grace of Bristol, commanded by Sylvester Wyet, went to prospect the Basque whale fishery in the Gulf. Bocall brought Wyet to the west coast of Newfoundland where some whalebone was collected from the wreck of a Basque ship, and later took

him to search the shores of Anticosti for stranded whales, without
success. These were the first known English visits to these locations.
Bocall was dissatisfied at English unwillingness to launch a whale fishery
and returned to St. Jean-de-Luz. The extracts are taken from Hakluyt,
The principal navigations, III, 194–195.

See Quinn, "England and the St. Lawrence," Merchants and Scholars,
ed. Park, pp. 128–129, and Dictionary of Canadian Biography, I.

The voyage of the Grace of Bristol of Master Rice Jones,
a Barke of thirty five Tunnes, up into the Bay of Saint
Laurence to the Northwest of Newefoundland, as farre as
the Isle of Assumption or Natiscotec, for the barbes or
fynnes of Whales and traine Oyle, made by Silvester
Wyet, Shipmaster of Bristoll.

Wee departed with the aforesaid Barke manned with twelve
men for the place aforesaid from Bristoll the 4 of Aprill 1594. and
fell with Cape d'Espere on the coast of Newefoundland the nine-
teneth of May in the height of 47. We went thence for Cape Raz
[Cape Race], being distant from thence 18 or 19 leagues, the very
same day. . . . From the Cape de Angullie into the Bay of
S. George we ran Northeast and by East some 18 or 19 leagues.

In this bay of Saint George, we found the wrackes of 2 great
Biskaine ships, which had bene cast away three yeeres before:
where we had some seven or eight hundred Whale finnes, and
some yron bolts and chaines of their mayne shrouds & fore
shroudes: al their traine was beaten out with the weather but the
caske remained still. Some part of the commodities were spoiled by
tumbling downe of the clifts of the hils, which covered part of the
caske, and the greater part of those Whale finnes, which we understood to be there by foure Spaniards which escaped, & were
brought to S. John de Luz. Here we found the houses of the
Savages, made of firre trees bound together in the top and set
round like a Dove-house, and covered with the barkes of firre trees,
wee found also some part of their victuals, which were Deeres flesh
roasted upon wooden spits at the fire, & a dish made of a ryne of a
tree, sowed together with the sinowes of the Deere, wherein was
oile of the Deere. There were also foules called Cormorants, which
they had pluckt and made ready to have dressed, and there we

found a wooden spoone of their making. And we discerned the tracks of the feete of some fortie or fiftie men, women and children.

When we had dispatched our businesse in this bay of S. George and stayed there ten dayes, wee departed for the Northren point of the said bay, which is nine or ten leagues broade. Then being enformed, that the Whales which are deadly wounded in the grand Bay, and yet escape the fisher for a time, are woont usually to shoot themselves on shore on the Isle of Assumption, or Natiscotec, which lieth in the very mouth of the great river that runneth up to Canada, we shaped our course over to that long Isle of Natiscotec, and wee found the distance of the way to the Estermost ende thereof to be about forty foure leagues: and it standeth in the latitude of 49. Here we arrived about the middest of June at the East end. . . . From the Easter end we went to the Norther side of the Island, which we perceived to be but narrow in respect of the length thereof. And after wee had searched two dayes and a night for the Whales which were wounded which we hoped to have found there, and missed of our purpose, we returned backe to the Southwarde. . . .

Having passed Cape Raz, we passed Northwarde fourteene leagues and arrived in Farrillon, and finding there two and twentie sayles of Englishmen, wee made up our fishing voyage to the full in that harborough the twentieth foure of August to our good content: and departing thence we arrived first in Combe and staied there a seven night, and afterward in Hungrod in the river of Bristoll by the grace of God the 24 of September. 1594.

61. English Separatists
Are Released from Prison
to Go to America

ON March 25, 1597, as recorded in Acts of the Privy Council, 1597 (1897), p. 5–6, the English Privy Council instructed the London Customs officers to allow certain Brownists to leave the country with their *possessions in order to settle a colony in the Island of Ramea (the Magdalen Islands) in the Gulf of St. Lawrence.*

Wheras Abraham Van Harwick and Stephen Van Harwick merchaunt strangers and Charles Leigh merchaunt of London have undertaken to adventure a voyage of fishinge and dyscovery into the Bay of Canyda, and to plant them selves in an Island called Ramea or there aboutes whence they hope and Intend to bringe divers very necessarie comodyties of speciall use for this Realme and to establish a Trade of Fishinge there, And this present yere they have prepared to make ready two shippes to be sent thether, called the Hopewell, and the Chauncewell, the one being appointed to wynter there and thother to Retorne hether; For as moche as they have made humble suite unto her majestie to Transport out of this Realme divers Artificers, and other persons that are noted to be Sectaryes whose names are contained in a Scedule hereunto anexed whereof fower shalbe at this present sent thether in those shippes that goe this present voyage; Yow shall therefore understand that her majestie ys pleased they shall carry with them the foresaid persons this present voyage So as note be taken of theire Names by yow, and good Bondes to her Majestes use of the said merchauntes or of anie one of them that they shall not repaire againe hether unto this her majestes Realme unles they shalbe contented to reforme themselves, & to Lyve in obedyence to her Lawes established for matters of Religion, And that they nor any of them shall serve her Majestes forreine Enemyes. And before theire departure they are to tender also there othe to beare trewe faith & obedyence to her Majestie as becommeth dutyfull Subjectes;

These are, therefore, to Requier yow to cause such Bondes to be taken of the said Merchauntes, or of any one of them, and thereuppon to permytt those fower persons to be Imbarqued in the foresaid shippes. And bicause they do meane to take with them soch howshold stuff and other Implementes as may serve them for there necessary use, yow shall see what those Thinges are which they shall carry with them, and to permytt them to take those thinges with them that may be fytt for theire necessary use there, They havinge Intencion to Reside and Inhabit those partes. So

Requyring yow to take order herein accordingly, & to certyfy us the same, wee &c.

62. An Abortive English Colony in the Magdalen Islands, 1597

THE COINCIDENCE of a project to exploit the walrus and cod fishery and the desire of an English dissident group to settle a colony, led to an attempt to colonize the Magdalen Islands in 1597. A congregation of separatist Brownists, who had been imprisoned since 1592, was given the chance to leave England and settle in America. Captain Charles Leigh was commissioned by the fishing syndicate to make a reconnaissance of the islands, taking with him four members of the congregation—their pastor, Francis Johnson, his brother George, Daniel Studley and John Clarke—who were to stay over with a party of fishermen until 1598. Captain Leigh's ship, the Hopewell, duly reached the Magdalens but was driven away by the Bretons, Basques and Micmac Indians, as Charles Leigh recorded in the narratives from which extracts are given below. The other ship, the Chancewell, went aground on Cape Breton Island on the way out. Fortunately, Leigh found her men by chance on his way back from the Magdalens. The expedition went sadly homewards, cheered only by a Breton prize which they seized at Newfoundland. The would-be pilgrims brought their congregation to the Netherlands instead of to America. Richard Hakluyt, printing Leigh's narrative in The principal navigations, III, 195–201, omitted all reference to the would-be settlers.

See Quinn "The English and the St. Lawrence," in Merchants and Scholars, ed. Parker, pp. 131–138; D. B. Quinn, "The First Pilgrims," William and Mary Quarterly, 3rd series, XXIII (1966), 359–390; and Dictionary of Canadian Biography, I.

The voyage of Master Charles Leigh, and divers others to Cape Briton and the Isle of Ramea.

The Hopewell of London of the burthen of 120 tunnes, whereof was Master William Crafton, and the Chancewel of London of the burthen of 70 tunnes, whereof was Master Steven Bennet, bound

unto the river of Canada, set to sea at the sole and proper charge of
Charles Leigh and Abraham Van Herwick of London merchants
(the saide Charles Leigh himself, and Steven Van Herwick brother
to the sayd Abraham, going themselves in the said ships as chiefe
commanders of the voyage) departed from Graves-end on Fryday
morning the 8 of April 1597. . . . And with prosperous windes the
18 of May we were upon the banke of Newfoundland. . . . The
first of June we set saile from Rogneuse, and the second we put
roome to a bay under the Northside of Cape Raz being inforced in
by an extreme storme. The 4 we set saile, and this day we saw a
great Island of yce. The 5 at night we lost the Chancewell in a fog
at the mouth of the bay of Placentia. The 11 at Sunne setting we
had sight of Cape Briton. And the 12 by reason of contrary windes
we cast anker under the Northeast ende of the Isle of Menego to
the North of Cape Briton in 16 fathome reasonable ground. . . .
The 14 we came to the 2 Islands of Birds, some 23 leagues from
Menego: where there were such abundance of Birds, as is almost
incredible to report. . . . The 18 we came to the Isle of Ramea,
where we appointed to meet with our consort. And approching
neere unto the harborough of Halabolina we cast anker in 3
fadomes water and sent our great boate into the harborough, with
the masters mate and some dozen more of the company: who
when they came in, found 4 ships. Namely 2 of Saint Malo in
Britaigne, and two of Sibiburo adjoyning to Saint John de luz being
the French Kings subjects, whom they supposed to have bene of
Spaine, and so affirmed unto us. Whereupon wee went presently
into harborough, finding but eleven foote and an half of water
upon the barre and a mightie great current in, when wee had cast
anker we sent presently to speak with the masters of all the ships:
but those onely of Saint Malo came aboord, whom wee entertained
very friendly, and demaunded of whence the other two shippes
were. They sayde as they thought of Saint John de Luz or Sibiburo.
Then we presently sent our boate for the Masters of both sayd
shippes, to request them to come aboord, and to bring with them
their Charters parties and other evidences, to the ende we might
knowe of whence they were. At which message one of the sayd
Masters came aboord, with the Pilote and Masters mate of the
other shippe: whom we had examined, they sayd that they were of

Sibiburo, and the French Kings subjectes. We requested them for our better securitie in the harborough peaceably to deliver up their power and munition: promising them that if we found them to be the French Kings subjectes it should be kept in safetie for them without diminishing. But they woulde not consent thereunto: whereunto we replyed, that unlesse they would consent thereunto we would hold them to be our enemies. They not consenting, we sent the boate well manned to fetch their powder and munition from aboorde their ship: but straightly commanded our men not to touch any thing else in the ship upon their further perill: which they promised to performe. When they came aboorde the saide ships which were mored together, they were resisted by force of armes, but quickly they got the victorie: which done, they fell presently to pillaging of the Baskes, contrary to their promise: whereupon we sent another to forbidde them; but when he came to them, none was more ready of pillage then he. Whereupon I went my selfe, and tooke away from our men whatsoever they had pillaged, and gave it againe to the owners: onely I sent aboord our owne ship their powder and munition to be kept in safetie until we knew farther what they were. When I had done, I gave the Baskes possession of their shippe againe and tolde them they should not loose the valewe of one peny if they were the French Kings subjects. Then I caryed away all our men, and also tooke with me two or three of the chiefest of them, and when I came aboord went to examining of them, and by circumstances found one of the ships to belong to France: whereupon I tolde the master of the said ship, that I was throughly satisfied that he was of France and so dismissed him in peace. Of the other ship we had great presumption that she was of Spaine, but had no certaine proofe thereof, wherefore wee dismissed them likewise in peace. After I had thus dismissed them, our ships company fell into a mutiny, and more then half of them resolved to cary one of those ships away. But they were prevented of their evill purpose by ayde which the saide ships received from their countreymen in the other harborough: For the next morning, which was the twentieth of June, very earely there were gathered together out of all the ships in both harboroughs, at the least 200 Frenchmen and Britons, who had planted upon the shore three pieces of Ordinance against us, and had prepared them selves in al readinesse to fight with us, which so soone as we had discried them gave the onset upon us with at least an hundred small shot out of the woods. There were also in a readines to assault us about three hundred Savages. But after we had skirmished a while with them, we procured a parley by one of the men of Saint Malo, whose ship rowed hard by us. . . . Then we desired them to cut the bent of the cable upon the anker on shore (for we durst not send our boat lest they should have kept from us both our boat and men) which they promised to do for us, as also to send our men; but when they were on shore, they would do neither. We therefore seeing their falshood in every thing, durst no longer tary for feare of farther treachery; wherefore we concluded to cut our cable in the hawse; which we did, & so departed the harborow about 9 of the clock, leaving two of our men with our cable & anker, and 20 fadoms of a new hawser behind us. And as we were going away, they made great shewes of friendship, and dranke unto us from the shore; but more for feare then love, and requested us to come on shore for our men, whom then they delivered. . . . The next morning being the 22, we put to sea, and about 12 of the clocke the same day, the wind being at Northeast and foule weather, the master sayd he could not ply up to Grande Coste, because of the leeshore, & the wind against us, and therefore asked what we should do. I asked then how farre we had to the river of cape Briton: he sayd a little way. Then sayd I, if it be not farre, we were best to go thither to trade with the Savages while the wind is contrary, and to take in water & balist, which we wanted. . . .

The 14 of June we sent our boat on shore in great bay upon the Isle of Cape Briton for water. . . .

The 27 about tenne of the clocke in the morning we met with eight men of the Chancewell our consort in a shallope; who told us that their ship was cast away upon the maine of Cape Briton, within a great bay eighteene leagues within the Cape, and upon a rocke within a mile of the shore, upon the 23 of this moneth about one of the clocke in the afternoone.

[The Chancewell had been pillaged by French Basque fishermen and her crew were in great straits. George Johnson regarded the arrival of the Hopewell to rescue them as proof of the providence of God. Captain Leigh attempted to force the fishermen to disgorge the goods taken from the *Chancewell*, but with limited success only. He then took the *Hopewell* to the south coast of Newfoundland where, after a number of attempts to seize Basque and Breton ships, a Breton vessel was taken prize. Leigh and the four separatists (who thereupon began a fierce theological argument) transferred to her and eventually disembarked on the Isle of Wight on September 5. The separatists went secretly to London, assembled their associates, who had been temporarily released from jail, and made off with them to create an exile congregation at Amsterdam. In the end their church seems to have influenced the Pilgrims of 1620 in the choice of America as a place of refuge.]

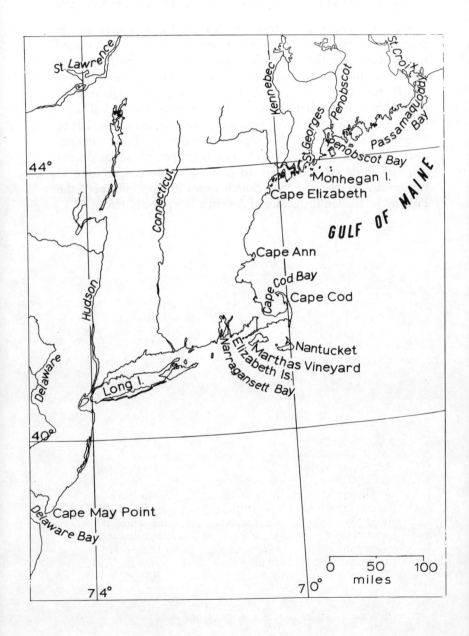

St. Lawrence

44°

Kennebec

St. Georges

Penobscot

St. Croix

Passamaquoddy Bay

Penobscot Bay

Monhegan I.

Cape Elizabeth

Connecticut

GULF OF MAINE

Cape Ann

Cape Cod Bay

Cape Cod

Hudson

Nantucket

Elizabeth Is.

Marthas Vineyard

Delaware

Narragansett Bay

Long I.

40°

Delaware

Cape May Point

Delaware Bay

0   50   100
miles

7 4°

7 0°

XIII

New England and the Hudson River, 1602–09

As THE French took over the approaches to the St. Lawrence after 1597, so English venturers, interested in competing with them in the fur trade and anxious to prospect for colonies, turned their attention to New England. Bartholomew Gosnold, attempting in 1602 to find Verrazzano's "Refugio," nearly came within sight of Narragansett Bay when he found the Elizabeth Islands and selected one of them on which to plant his trading post. But his men thought the Indians too numerous and themselves too few, so they returned to England. Martin Pring took a Bristol ship to Cape Cod in 1603 and traded peacefully with the Indians, probably in the vicinity of modern Provincetown (or conceivably Plymouth Harbor). These voyages inspired a colonizing movement. Its main support was a group of Catholics, led by Sir Thomas Arundell, and certain fishing interests at Plymouth. In order to prospect for both settlement and fishery, Captain George Waymouth brought the Archangel to Monhegan Island, explored the St. George River and brought home exaggerated reports of the suitability of the Maine coast for settlement as well as for fishing. The Catholic project fell through but the Plymouth men got a share in the large-scale Virginia Company chartered in April 1606, the "Northern" syndicate in the Company being authorized to settle between 40° and 45° N. latitude.

Meantime there had been overlapping French activity. Samuel de Champlain was based over the winter of 1604–05 at St. Croix on the Passamaquoddy River and between 1605–1607 at Port Royal in Nova Scotia, and explored extensively as far as the sounds south of Cape Cod (narrowly missing Waymouth in 1605). His authority gave him the right to occupy down to 40° N. latitude, but the proceeds of the fur trade proved too scanty and the French removed the whole enterprise in 1607, restarting it in Quebec in 1608. A reconnaissance for the new Virginia Company by Thomas Hanham and Martin Pring evidently produced a more realistic picture of the Maine coast, and the Richard under Henry Challons was sent to establish a colony at Pemaquid in 1606. Captured by the Spaniards in the West Indies, a fresh start had to be made in 1607, when the Gift of God and the Mary and John brought out the first colony under George Popham and Raleigh Gilbert to establish themselves at Fort St. George (Sagadahoc) on the Kennebec River. But the winter proved too cold and the fur trade too exiguous, so that when supplies arrived in 1608, the colony abandoned the fort. The Plymouth Virginia interests thereafter preferred to carry on only a summer fishery at the offshore islands of New England.

The Dutch had not hitherto concerned themselves with the North American mainland. But their great era of expansion was by now under way. Henry Hudson, an Englishman in their service, had been sent out in 1609 to look for a northern passage but, instead, brought the Halve Maen (Half Moon) westwards to prospect the coast northwards from the English settlement at Jamestown. By accident and perseverance he found the entrance to the Hudson River, unexplored so far as is known since 1524, and entered it, making his way as far as modern Albany, and discovering that the Indians of the Hudson Valley had many furs and were willing to trade. This was the basis for later Dutch penetration.

Between them, English, French and Dutch had clarified the outlines of the whole coast from the Hudson to Maine in the years 1602–09 and had found out a good deal about harbors, climate, agricultural possibilities, fur trade and fisheries. There was a gap in time before this knowledge was fully exploited, but it laid solid foundations for later settlement.

Warner F. Gookin and Philip L. Barbour, Bartholomew Gosnold (1963), Henry S. Burrage, The Beginnings of Colonial Maine (1914), and Richard A. Preston, Gorges of Plymouth Fort (1953), all throw light on the process of exploration and attempted settlement. Charles K. Bolton, The Real Founders of New England (1929) and Henry F. Howe, Prologue to New England (1943) provide slighter introductions. Charles H. Levermore, Forerunners and Competitors of the Pilgrims and Puritans (2 vols., 1922), is the most nearly complete collection of documents. D. B. Quinn, "Martin Pring at Provincetown in 1603?", New England Quarterly, XL (1967), 79–91, suggests a novel interpretation of the Pring expedition.

63. Bartholomew Gosnold
Explores New England, 1602

GOSNOLD'S VOYAGE from Savage Rock to the Elizabeth Islands in the Concord during May and June 1602 revealed a substantial part of the New England coast and named Cape Cod. John Brereton's A briefe and true relation of the discoverie of the north part of Virginia (1602) contained a narrative, a part of which is given below. Another, by Gabriel Archer, was printed in Samuel Purchas, Hakluytus Posthumus, or Purchas his pilgrimes, *IV* (1625), *1647–1651. Neither is easy to interpret. Savage Rock is possibly Cape Elizabeth rather than the usually accepted Cape Neddick. Gosnold explored Cape Cod Bay. Landing near modern Barnstable, he saw from a hill what looked like a channel going south-westwards into a mainland*—Vineyard Sound, the entrance, he hoped, to Verrazzano's "Refugio" (Narragansett Bay). He rounded Cape Cod to explore it and entered Nantucket Sound south of Monomoy Point. Circling round Nantucket Sound he returned to explore Cape Poge (then an island, which he named Marthas Vineyard) then on round the coast of the main island (to which the name Marthas Vineyard was transferred) which revealed his "passage" as a channel between Marthas Vineyard and the broken chain of Elizabeth Islands.*

At its western end he selected what he called Elizabeth's Isle (modern Cuttyhunk and Nashaweena then joined) as a site for his trading post. He explored the mainland as far west as Sakonnet Point, just missing the Narragansett Bay entrance, and some way northwestwards up Buzzards Bay until he saw it was not a channel. His return, when his men refused to stay at the newly built post, provided much new data on a coast with an early summer climate similar to but somewhat warmer than that of England.

A. John Brereton

May it please your Lordship therefore to understand, that upon the six and twentieth of March 1602, being Friday, we went from Falmouth, being in all, two & thirtie persons, in a small barke of Dartmouth, called The Concord, holding a course for the North part of Virginia: and although by chance the winde favoured us not at first as we wished, but inforced us so farre to the Southward, as we fell with S. Marie, one of the islands of the Açores (which was not much out of our way) but holding our course directly from thence, we made our journey shorter (than hitherto accustomed) by the better part of a thousand leagues, yet were wee longer in our passage than we expected; which happened, for that our barke being weake, we were loth to presse her with much saile; also our sailers being few, and they none of the best we bare (except in faire weather) but low saile; besides, our going upon an unknowen coast, made us not over-bolde to stand in with the shore, but in open weather; which caused us to be certeine daies in sounding, before we discovered the coast, the weather being by chance, some-what foggie. But on Friday the fourteenth of May, early in the morning, wee made the land, being full of faire trees, the land somewhat low, certeine hummocks or hilles lying into the land, the shore full of white sand, but very stony or rocky. And standing faire alongst by the shore, about twelve of the clocke the same day, we came to an anker, where eight Indians, in a Baske-shallop with mast and saile, an iron grapple, and a kettle of Copper, came boldly aboord us, one of them apparelled with a wastcoat and breeches of blacke serdge, made after our sea-fashion, hose and shoes on his feet; all the rest (saving one that had a paire of breeches of blue cloth) were naked. These people are of tall stature, broad and grim visage, of a blacke swart complexion, their eie-browes painted white; their weapons are bowes and arrowes. It seemed by some words and signes they made, that some Basks or of S. John de Luz,[1] have fished or traded in this place, being in the latitude of 43 degrees. But riding heere, in no very good harbour, and withall doubting the weather, about three of the clocke the same day in the afternoone we weighed, & standing Southerly off into sea the rest of that day and the night following, with a fresh gale of winde, in the morning we found our selves embaied with a mightie headland; but comming to an anker about nine of the clocke the same day, within a league of the shore, we hoised out the one halfe of our shallop, and captaine Bartholmew Gosnold, my selfe, and three others, went ashore, being a white sandie and very bolde shore; and marching all that afternoone with our muskets on our necks, on the highest hilles which we saw (the weather very hot) at length we perceived this headland to be parcell of the maine, and sundrie Islands lying almost round about it. . . . From this place, we sailed round about this headland, almost all the points of the compasse, the shore very bolde. . . . At length we were come amongst many faire Islands, which we had partly discerned at our first landing; all lying within a league or two one of another, and the outermost not above six or seven leagues from the maine.

B. Gabriel Archer

The sixteenth, we trended the Coast Southerly, which was all champaine and full of grasse, but the Ilands somewhat wooddie.

1. The meaning is "some [Spanish] Basques or [some French Basques] of Jean-de-Luz."

Twelve leagues from Cape Cod, we descried a point, with some breach a good distance off, and keeping our loffe to double it, wee came on the sudden into shoale water, yet well quitted our selves thereof. This breach wee called Tuckers Terror, upon his expressed feare. The Point we named Point Care, having passed it wee bore up againe with the Land, and in the night came with it anchoring in eight fadome, the ground good. The seventeenth, appeared many breaches round about us, so as wee continued that day without remoove.

The eighteenth, being faire we sent forth the Boat to sound over a Breach, that in our course lay of another Point, by us called Gilberts Point; who returned us foure, five sixe and seven fadome over. Also a Discovery of divers Ilands which after prooved to bee Hils and Hummocks, distinct within the Land. This day there came unto the ships side divers Canoas; the Indians apparelled as aforesaid, with Tobacco and Pipes steeled with Copper, Skins, artificiall strings and other trifles to barter, one had hanging about his necke a plate of rich Copper in length a foot, in breadth halfe a foot for a brest-plate, the Eares of all the rest had Pendants of Copper. Also one of them had his face over painted, and his head stucke with feathers in manner of a Turkey Cocks traine: These are more timerous then those of the Savage Rocke, yet very theevish.

The nineteenth, we passed over the breach of Gilberts Point in foure or five fadome, and anchored a league or somewhat more beyond it; betweene the last two Points are two leagues, the interim, along shoale water, the latitude here is 41. degrees two third parts. . . .

The one and twentieth, we went coasting from Gilberts Point to the supposed Iles, in tenne, nine, eight, seven and sixe fadome close aboord the shoare, and that depth lyeth a league off. A litle from the supposed Iles appeared unto us an opening, with which we stood judging it to bee the end of that which Captaine Gosnoll descrieth from Cape Cod, and as hee thought to extend some thirtie or more miles in length, and finding there but three fadomes a league off, we omitted to make further discoverie of the same, calling it Shole-hope.

From this opening the Mayne lyeth South-west, which coasting along we saw a disinhabited Iland which so afterwards appeared unto us: we bore with it, and named it Marthaes Vineyard,[1] from Shole-hope it is eight leagues in circuit, the Iland is five miles, and hath 41. degrees and one quarter of latitude . . . heere we rode in eight fathome neere the shoare, where we tooke great store of God, as before at Cape Cod, but much better. . . .

The three and twentieth wee weyed, and towards night came to Anchor at the Northwest part of this Iland, where the next morning offered unto us fast running thirteene Savages apparelled as aforesaid, and armed with Bowes and Arrowes without any feare. . . .

The foure and twentieth, we set saile and doubled the Cape of another Iland next unto it, which wee called Dover Cliffe,[2] and then came into a faire Sound, where wee roade all night, the next morning wee sent off our Boate to discover another Cape, that lay betweene us and the Mayne, from which were a ledge of Rockes a mile into the Sea, but all above water, and without danger, we went about them, and came to Anchor in eight fadome, a quarter of a mile from the shoare in one of the stateliest Sounds that ever I was in. This called wee Gosnolls Hope; the North banke whereof is the Mayne, which stretcheth East and West. This Iland Captaine Gosnoll called Elizabeths Ile,[3] where we determined our abode: the distance betweene every of these Ilands is, viz. from Marthaes Vineyard to Dover Cliffe, halfe a league over the Sound, thence to Elizabeths Ile one league distant. From Elizabeths Ile unto the Mayne is foure leagues. . . .

The eight and twentieth we entred counsell about our abode and plantation, which was concluded to be in the West part of Elizabeths Iland. The North-east thereof running from out our ken. The South and North standeth in an equall Parallel. This Iland in the Westerside admitteth some Increekes, or sandie Coves, so girded, as the water in some places of each side meeteth, to which the Indians from the Mayne doe oftentimes resort for fishing of Crabs. There is eight fadome very neere the shore, and the latitude here is 41. degrees 10. minutes. . . . Touching the fertilitie of the soyle by

1. Probably Cape Poge, Chappaquiddick, then a separate island: the name was transferred to the larger island (which still bears it) as the ship moved along the channel.
2. Gay Head, Marthas Vineyard.
3. Cuttyhunk and Nashaweena, then joined, in the Elizabeth Islands.

our owne experience made, we found it to be excellent for sowing some English pulse it sprowted out in one fortnight almost halfe a foot. In this Iland is a stage or Pond of fresh water, in circuit two miles, on the one side not distant from the Sea thirtie yards, in the Centre whereof is a Rockie Islet, contayning neere an Acre of ground full of wood, on which wee beganne our Fort and place of abode, disposing it selfe so fit for the same. . . .

The one and thirtieth, Captaine Gosnoll desirous to see the Maine, because of the distance, hee set sayle over; where comming to anchor, went ashoare with certaine of his companie. . . . In the mouth of one of these Inlets or Rivers lieth that little Ile before mentioned, called Happes Hill, from which unto the Westermost end of the Maine, appearing where the other Inlet is, I account some five leagues, and the Coast betweene bendeth like a Bow, and lyeth East and by North. Beyond these two Inlets we might perceive the Mayne to beare up Southwest, and more Southerly.[4] . . .

The first of June, we employed our selves in getting Sassafrage, and the building of our Fort. The second, third and fourth, we wrought hard to make readie our house for the provision to bee had ashore to sustaine us till our ships returne. . . .

The eighth wee divided the victuals, viz. the ships store for England, and that of the Planters, which by Captaine Gilberts allowance could be but sixe weekes for sixe monehts, whereby there fell out a controversie, the rather, for that some seemed secretly to understand of a purpose Captaine Gilbert had not to returne with supplie of the issue, those goods should make by him to be carried home. . . .

The thirteenth, beganne some of our companie that before vowed to stay, to make revolt: whereupon the planters diminishing, all was given over. The fourteenth, fifteenth, and sixteenth wee spent in getting Sasafrage and fire-wood of Cedar, leaving House and little Fort by ten men in nineteene dayes sufficient made to harbour twenty persons at least with their necessary provision. . . .

The eighteenth, we set sayle and bore for England. . . . The three and twentieth of July we came to anchor before Exmouth.

4. Gosnold realized that Buzzards Bay was not a channel into the mainland.

64. A Summer Voyage
to Cape Cod, 1603

PRING'S VOYAGE *is not important in itself, but it demonstrated how easy it was, with fortunate weather, to sail from Bristol to Cape Cod and back between April and October, having camped for a few months on a temporarily constructed trading station at Cape Cod. The summer was kind. Sassafras for medicinal purposes, furs and skins, some Indian dyes, probably paid their way. The narrative is in Purchas, Hakluytus Posthumus, or Purchas his pilgrimes, IV (1625), 1654–1656, from which this extract is taken.*

A Voyage set out from the Citie of Bristoll at the charge of the chiefest Merchants and Inhabitants of the said Citie with a small Ship and a Barke for the discoverie of the North part of Virginia, in the yeere 1603, under the command of me Martin Pringe. . . .

We set saile from Milford Haven (where the winds had stayed us a fortnight, in which space we heard of Queene Elizabeths death) the tenth of Aprill 1603. In our course we passed by the Iles of the Acores, had first sight of the Pike, and afterward of the Iland of Cuervo and Flores, and after we had runne some five hundred leagues, we fell with a multitude of small Ilands on the North Coast of Virginia, in the latitude of 43. degrees, the [   ] of June, which Ilands wee found very pleasant to behold, adorned with goodly grasse and sundry sorts of Trees, as Cedars, Spruce, Pines, and Firre-trees. Heere wee found an excellent fishing for Cods, which are better then those of New-found-land, and withall we saw good and Rockie ground fit to drie them upon: also we see no reason to the contrary, but that Salt may bee made in these parts, a matter of no small importance. We sayled to the Southwest end of these Ilands, and there rode with our ships under one of the greatest. One of them we named Foxe Iland,[1] because we found those kind of beasts thereon. . . . At length comming to the Mayne in the latitude of 43. degrees and an halfe, we ranged

1. Probably the group of islands, Foxe Islands, in Penobscot Bay.

the same to the South-west. In which course we found foure Inlets, the most Easterly whereof was barred at the mouth, but having passed over the barre, wee ranne up into it five miles, and for a certaine space found very good depth, and comming out againe, as we sailed South-westward, wee lighted upon two other Inlets, which upon our search we found to pierce not farre into the Land, the fourth and most Westerly was the best, which we rowed up ten or twelve miles.

In all these places we found no people, but signes of fires where they had beene. Howbeit we beheld very goodly Groves and Woods replenished with tall Okes, Beeches, Pine-trees, Firre-trees, Hasels, Wich-hasels and Maples. We saw here also sundry sorts of Beasts, as Stags, Deere, Beares, Wolves, Foxes, Lusernes,[2] and Dogges with sharpe noses. But meeting with no Sassafras, we left these places with all the foresaid Ilands, shaping our course for Savage Rocke,[3] discovered the yeere before by Captaine Gosnold, where going upon the Mayne we found people, with whom we had no long conversation, because here also we could find no Sassafras. Departing hence we bare into that great Gulf[4] which Captaine Gosnold over-shot the yeere before, coasting and finding people on the North side thereof. Not yet satisfied in our expectation, we left them and sailed over, and came to an Anchor on the South side in the latitude of 41. degrees and odde minutes: where we went on Land in a certaine Bay, which we called Whitson Bay[5] by the name of the Worshipfull Master John Whitson then Maior of the Citie of Bristoll, and one of the chiefe Adventurers, and finding a pleasant Hill thereunto adjoyning, wee called it Mount Aldworth, for Master Robert Aldworths sake a chiefe furtherer of the Voyage, aswell with his Purse as with his travell. Here we had sufficient quantitie of Sassafras.

At our going on shore, upon view of the people and sight of the place, wee thought it convenient to make a small baricado to keepe diligent watch and ward in, for the advertizement and succour of our men, while they should worke in the Woods. During our abode

2. Lynx.
3. Cape Elizabeth or Cape Neddick.
4. Cape Cod Bay.
5. Traditionally Plymouth Harbor, it may well be Providence Harbor.

on shore, the people of the Countrey came to our men sometimes ten, twentie, fortie or threescore, and at one time one hundred and twentie at once. We used them kindly and gave them divers sorts of our meanest Merchandize. They did eat Pease and Beanes with our men. Their owne victuals were most of fish. . . .

By the end of July we had laded our small Barke called the Discoverer, with as much Sassafras as we thought sufficient, and sent her home into England before, to give some speedie content-ment to the Adventurers: who arrived safely in Kingrode[6] above a fortnight before us. . . .

About the eighth or ninth of August, wee left this excellent Haven at the entrance whereof we found twentie fathomes water, and rode at our ease in seven fathomes being Land-locked, the Haven winding in compasse like the shell of a Snaile, and it is in latitude of one and forty degrees and five and twentie min-utes. . . .

In our returne we brought our selves into the latitude of eight and thirtie degrees about the Açores for certaine causes, and within five weekes space came from our Port of Virginia, into the Sound-ings of England, but there being long encountred with Easterly winds, we came at length into Kingrode, the second of October 1603.

65. The French Exploration
and Attempted Settlement of the
Coast from Nova Scotia to Massachusetts,
1604–07

MARC LESCARBOT was with Poutraincourt and Champlain in their Port Royal settlement only for the year 1606–07, and took part in one expedi-tion down the New England coast; but he had many opportunities for collecting information on what had been done earlier, in 1604–06. His Histoire de la Nouvelle France (1609) and other writings on America are in Works, ed. W. L. Grant (3 vols., 1907–14). Part of the Histoire was translated by Pierre Erondelle, with the title Nova Francia (1609),

6. Part of the port of Bristol.

*p. 17–94, from which the extracts below are taken. A convenient edition
is edited by H. P. Biggar (1928). Champlain's Works, also edited by
H. P. Biggar (7 vols., 1922–36) have more detail (and more authority)
than Lescarbot. His lightness of touch makes his version attractive,
especially in the contemporary translation.*

Leaving Saint Johns river, they came following the coast 20.
leagues from that place, to a great river (which is properlie sea)
where they fortified themselves in a little island [Ste. Croix] seated
in the middest of this river, which the said Champlain had beene
to discover and view. And seeing it strong by nature, and of easie
defence and keeping, besides that the season began to slide away,
and therefore it was behovefull to provide of lodging, without
running any farther, they resolved to make their abode there. . . .

During the foresaid Navigation, Monsieur de Monts his people
did worke about the Fort; which hee seated at the end of the Iland,
opposite to the place where he had lodged his Canon. Which was
wisely considered, to the end to command the river up & down. But
there was an inconvenience, the said Fort did lie towards the
North, and without any shelter, but of the trees that were on the
Ile shore, which all about hee commanded to be kept, and not cut
downe. And out of the same Fort was the Switzers lodging, great
and large, and other small lodgings, representing (as it were) a
Suburbe. Some had housed themselves on the firme land, neere the
brook. But within the fort was Monsieur de Monts his lodging,
made with very faire & artificiall Carpentrie worke, with the Banner
of France upon the same. At another part was the store-house,
wherein consisted the safety & life of everyone, likewise made with
faire Carpentrie worke, and covered with reedes. Right over against
the said store-house were the lodgings and houses of these gentlemen, Monsieur D'orville, Monsieur Champlein, Monsieur Champdoré, and other men of reckoning. Opposite to Monsieur de Monts
his said lodging, there was a gallerie covered for to exercise themselves, either in play, or for the workmen in time of raine. And
betweene the said fort and the platform, where lay the Canon, all
was full of gardens, whereunto everie one exercised himself willingly. All Autumne quarter was passed on these works, and it was
well for them to have lodged themselves, and to manure the ground
of the Iland, before winter. . . .

The most urgent things being done, and hoarie snowie father

being come, that is to say, Winter, then they were forced to keepe within doores, and to live every one at his owne home: during which time, our men had three speciall discommodities in this Iland, videlicet, want of wood, (for that which was in the said Ile, was spent in buildings) lack of fresh water, and the continuall watch, made by night, fearing some surprise from the Savages, that had lodged themselves at the foot of the said Iland, or some other enemie. . . .

There died, of this sickness [scurvy] 36, and 36 or 40, more that were stricken with it, recovered themselves by the help of the Spring, as soon as the comfortable season appeared. . . .

The rough season being passed, Monsieur de Monts wearied with his badde dwelling at Saint Croix, determined to seeke out another Port in a warmer countrie, and more to the South: And to that end made a Pinnace to be armed and furnished with victuals, to follow the coast, and discovering new countries, to seeke out some happier Port in a more temperate air. And because that in seeking, one cannot set forward so much as when in full sailes one goeth in open sea, and that finding out baies and gulfes, lying between two lands, one must put in, because that there there one may assoone find that which is sought for, as else where, he made in this voyage but about six score leagues, as we will tell you now. From Saint Croix to 60. leagues forward, the coast lieth East and West: at the end of which 60. leagues, is the river called by the savages Kinibeki [Kennebec]. From which place to Malebarre [Nauset Harbor] it lieth North and South, and there is yet from one to the other 60. leagues, in right line, not following the baies. So far stretcheth Monsieur de Monts his voyage, wherein he had for Pilot in his vessel Monsieur de Champdoré. In all this coast so farre as Kinibeki there is many places where shippes may be harbored amongst the Ilands, but the people there is not so frequent as is beyond that. . . . And there can be no great river on that coast, because there are not lands sufficient to produce them, by reason of the great river of Canada, which runneth like this coast, and is not four-score leagues distant from that place in crossing the lands. . . .

The people that be from Saint Johns River to Kinibeki (wherein are comprised the rivers of Saint Croix and Norombega) are called

Etechemins: And from Kinibeki as far as Malebarre, and farther, they are called Armouchiquois. They be traitours and theefes, and one had neede to take heed of them. . . . Monsieur de Monts was very desirous that the new habitation had beene about 40. degrees, that is to say, 4 degrees farther than Saint Croix: but having viewed the coast as farre as Malebarre, and with much paine, not finding what he desired, it was deliberated to goe and make their dwelling in Port Royal, untill meanes were had to make an ampler discovery. So everyone began to packe up his things: That which was built with infinite labour was pulled downe, except the Store-house, which was too great and painefull to be transported. . . .

The winter being come, the Savages of the country did assemble themselves, from far to Port Royal, for to truck with the Frenchmen, for such things they had, some bringing Beavers skinnes, and Otters (which are those whereof most account may be made in that place) and also Ellans [Elk] or Stagges, whereof good buffe may be made: Others bringing flesh newly killed, wherewith they made good Tabagies or feasts, living merily as long as they had wherewithall. They never wanted any bread, but wine did not continue with them till the season was ended. For, when we came thither the yeare following, they had been above three Moneths without any wine, and were very glad of our comming, for that made them to take agayne the taste of it. . . .

For the habitation of Port Royal was not judged good. And notwithstanding it is on the North and North-west sides, well sheltered with mountaines, distant some one league, some halfe a league, from the Port and the river l'Equille [Annapolis River]. So we see how that enterprises take not effect according to the desires of men, and are accompanied with many perils. So that one must not woonder if the time be long in establishing of Colonies, specially in lands so remote, whose nature and temperature of aire is not knowen, and where one must fell and cut downe forrests, and be constrained to take heed, not from the people that we call Savages, but from them that therme themselves Christians, and yet have but the name of it, cursed and abhominable people, woorse then wolves, enemies to God and humane nature. . . .

But in the meane while we must consider that they, which in these voyages have transported themselves in these parts, have an advantage over those that would plant in Florida, which is in having that refuge beforesaid, of French ships that frequent the New found lands for fishing, not being forced to build great shippes, nor to abide extreme famines, as they have done in Florida. . . .

If they have suffered famines, there was great fault in them, for not having tilled the ground, which they found plaine and champion: Which before all other thing is to be done, of them that will lodge themselves so far from ordinarie succour. But the Frenchmen, and almost all nations at this day (I mean of those that be not borne and brought up to the manuring of the ground) have this badde nature, that they think to derogate much from their dignitie in addicting themselves to the tillage of the ground. . . .

Let us returne to Monsieur de Poutrincourt, whom we have left in the Isle Saint Croix. Having made there a review, and cherished the Savages that were there, he went in the space of foure daies to Pemtegoet [the Penobscot], which is that place so famous under the name of Norombega. There needeth not so long a time in comming thither, but he taried on the way to mend his barke: for to that end he had brought with him a Smith and a Carpenter, and quantity of boards. He crossed the Iles, which be at the mouth of the river, and came to Kinibeki, where his barke was in danger, by reason of the great streames that the nature of the place procureth there. This was the cause why he made there no stay, but passed further to the Baie of Marchin, which is the name of a Captaine of the Savages, who at the arrivall of the said Monsieur De Poutrincourt began to crie out aloud: Hé Hé: whereunto the like answer was made unto him. He replied, asking in his language, What are ye? They answered him, Friends: And thereupon Monsieur De Poutrincourt approching, treated amity with him, and presented him with knives, hatchets and Matachiaz, that is to say scarves, karkenets, and bracelets made of beades, or quils made of white and blue glasse; whereof he was very glad, as also for the confederacy that the said Monsieur De Poutrincourt made with him. . . . That done, they set sailes towards Choüakoet, where the river of Captain Olmechin is. . . .

From this island they went to the river of Olmechin, a Port of Chauakoet, where Marchin and the said Olmechin brought to

Monsieur De Poutrincourt a prisoner of the Souriquois (and therefore their enemy) which they gave unto him freely. . . . From
thence Monsieur De Poutrincourt following on his course, found a
certain Port very delightfull, which had not beene seene by Monsieur de Monts. . . .

Now during the time that the said Monsieur De Poutrincourt
was there, being in doubt whether Monsieur De Monts would
come to make an habitation on that coast, as he wished it, he made
there a piece of ground to be tilled, for to sow corne and to plant
vines, which they did with the help of our Apothecary Master
Louis Hebert, a man, who, besides his experience in his art, taketh
great delight in the tilling of the ground. And the said Monsieur
De Poutrincourt may be here compared to good father Noah, who
after he had made the tillage most necessarie for the sowing of
corn, he began to plant the vine, whose effects he felt afterwards.

66. George Waymouth Surveys Monhegan,
Georges Islands and the Georges River,
1605

JAMES ROSIER, who wrote the narrative of Waymouth's voyage, remains
something of a mystery since he has not been authoritatively identified.
His narrative, A true relation of the most prosperous voyage made this
present yeere 1605 by Captaine George Waymouth, in the discovery of
the land of Virginia (1605), from which extracts are taken below, gives
an attractive picture of the Maine coast in summer. The advantages of
Monhegan and the Georges Islands for shore fishing bases are well brought
out. The beauties of Georges River, though considerable, are inflated,
and the length of the main channel, between present-day Port Clyde and
Thomaston, is greatly exaggerated. A possible place for settlement, it is
built up into a superlatively good location, though this was not endorsed
by later writers and no early settlements were made there. Rosier writes
well and observes with intelligence. His tract had some influence on the
creation of the Plymouth syndicate inside the Virginia Company of 1606.

Upon Tuesday the 5 day of March, about ten a clocke afore
noone, we set saile from Ratcliffe . . . on Saturday the 16 day

about foure a clocke after noon we put into Dartmouth Haven. . . . There we shipped some of our men, and supplied necessaries for our Ship and Voyage.

Upon Easter day, being the last of March, the winde comming at North-North-East, about five a clocke after noone we wayed anker, and put to sea. . . .

Friday, the 17 of May, about sixe a clocke at night we descried the land, which bare from us North-North-East. . . . It appeared a meane high land, as we after found it, being but an Iland of six miles in compasse, but I hope the most fortunate ever yet discovered.[1] About twelve a clocke that day, we came to an anker on the North side of this Iland, about a league from the shore. . . .

From hence we might discerne the maine land from the West-South-West to the East-North-East, and a great way (as it then seemed, and as we after found it) up into the maine we might discerne very high mountaines,[2] though the maine seemed but low land. . . .

The next day, being Whit-Sunday; because we rode too much open to the sea and windes, we wayed anker about twelve a clocke, and came along to the other Ilands more adjoyning to the maine, and in the rode directly with the mountaines, about three leagues from the first Iland where we had ankered.

When we came neere unto them (sounding all along in a good depth) our Captaine manned his ship-boat and sent her before with Thomas Cam one of his Mates, whom he knew to be of good experience, to sound & search betweene the Ilands for a place safe for our shippe to ride in . . . which it pleased God to send us, farre beyond our expectation, in a most safe birth defended from all windes. . . .

We all with great joy praised God for his unspeakable goodnesse, who had from so apparent danger delivered us, & directed us upon this day into so secure an Harbour : in remembrance wherof we named it Pentecost-harbor,[3] we arriving there that day out of our last Harbor in England, from whence we set saile upon Easterday.

1. Monhegan Island.
2. The Camden Hills, reaching only some 800 feet.
3. Georges Harbor, between Davis and Benner Islands in the Georges group.

Whitsun-munday, the 20 day of May, very early in the morning, our Captaine caused the pieces of the pinnesse to be carried a shore, where while some were busied about her, others digged welles to receive the fresh water, which we found issuing downe out of the land in many places. . . .

Wednesday, the 29 day, our shallop being now finished, and our Captaine and men furnished to depart with hir from the ship: we set up a crosse on the shore side upon the rockes.[4]

Thursday, the 30 of May, about ten a clock afore noon, our Captaine with 13 men more, in the name of God, and with all our praiers for their prosperous discoverie, and safe returne, departed in the shallop. . . .

From 10 a clocke this day we descried our Shallop returning toward us, which so soone as we espied, we certainly conjectured our Captaine had found some unexpected harbour, further up towards the maine to bring the ship into, or some river. . . .

Our Captaine had in this small time discovered up a great river,[5] trending alongst into the maine about forty miles. . . .

We manned the light horseman[6] with 7 or 8 men, one standing before carried our box of Marchandise, as we were woont when I went to traffique with them, and a platter of pease, which meat they loved: but before we were landed, one of them (being too suspitiously fearefull of his owne good) withdrew himselfe into the wood. The other two met us on the shore side, to receive the pease with whom we went up the Cliffe to their fire and sate downe with them, and whiles we were discussing how to catch the third man who was gone, I opened the box, and shewed them trifles to exchange, thinking thereby to have banisht feare from the other, and drawen him to returne: but when we could not, we used little delay, but suddenly laid hands upon them. And it was as much as five or sixe of us could doe to get them into the light-horseman. For they were strong and so naked as our best hold was by their long haire on their heads: and we would have beene very loath to have done them any hurt, which of necessity we had beene constrained to have done if we had attempted them in a multitude, which we

4. Davis Island was named Santa Cruz.
5: The Georges River.
6. A type of boat.

must and would, rather than have wanted them, being a matter of great importance for the full accomplement of our voyage.

Thus we shipped five Salvages,[7] two Canoas, with all their bowes and arrowes. . . .

Tuesday, the 11 of June, we passed up into the river[8] with our ship, about six and twenty miles.[9] Of which I had rather not write, then by my relation to detract from the worthinesse thereof. For the River, besides that it is subject by shipping to bring in all traffiques of Marchandise, a benefit alwaies accounted the richest treasury to any land: for which cause our Thames hath that due denomination, and France by her navigable Rivers receiveth hir greatest wealth; yet this place of itselfe from God and nature affordeth as much diversitie of good commodities, as any reasonable man can wish, for present habitation and planting. . . .

The River itselfe as it runneth up into the main very nigh forty miles toward the great mountaines, beareth in bredth a mile, sometime three quarters, and halfe a mile is the narrowest, where you shall never have under 4 and 5 fathoms water hard by the shore, but 6, 7, 8, 9, and 10 fathoms all along, and on both sides every halfe mile very gallant Coves. . . .

As we passed with a gentle winde up with our ship in this River, any man may conceive with what admiration we all consented in joy. . . .

I will not prefer it before our river of Thames, because it is Englands richest treasure; but we all did wish those excellent Harbours, good deeps in a continuall convenient breadth, and small tide gates, to be aswell therein for our countries good, as we found them here (beyond our hopes) in certaine, for those to whom it shall please God to grant this land for habitation. . . .

Wednesday, the twelfth of June, our Captaine manned his light-horseman with 17 men, and ranne up from the ship riding in the river up to the codde thereof, where we landed, leaving six to keepe the light-horseman till our returne. Ten of us with our shot, and some armed, with a boy to carry powder and match, marched up

7. The five Indians were to play an important part in subsequent voyages.
8. The Georges River.
9. All distances are greatly exaggerated. Above modern Thomaston the wide Georges River becomes a narrow stream.

into the countrey towards the mountaines,[10] which we descried at our first falling with the land. Unto some of them the river brought us so neere, as we judged our selves when we landed to have beene within a league of them : but we marched up about foure miles in the maine, and passed over three hilles : and because the weather was parching hot, and our men in their armour not able to travel farre and returne that night to our ship, we resolved not to passe any further, being all very weary of so tedious and laboursome a travell.

In this march we passed over very good ground, pleasant and fertile, fit for pasture, for the space of some three miles, having but little wood, and that Oke like stands left in our pastures in England, good and great, fit timber for any use. . . .

Thursday, the 13 of June, by two a clocke in the morning (because our Captaine would take the helpe and advantage of the tide) in the light-horseman with our Company well provided and furnished with armour and shot both to deffend and offend; we went from our ship up to that part of the river which trended Westward into the maine, to search that: and we carried with us a Crosse, to erect at that point, which (because it was not daylight) we left on the shore untill our returne backe; when we set it up[11] in maner as the former. . . .

Our Captaine better knowing what was fit then we, and better what they in labour were able to endure, being verie loath to make any desperate hazard, where so little necessitie required, thought it best to make returne, because whither we had discovered was sufficient to conceive that the River ran very far into the land. . . .

Sunday, the 16 of June, the winde being faire, and because we had set out of England upon a Sunday, made the Ilands upon a Sunday, and as we doubt not (by Gods appointment) happily fell into our harbour upon a Sunday; so now . . . we waied Anker and quit the Land upon a Sunday. . . .

After, we kept our course directly for England & with ordinary winds . . . upon Thursday the 18 of July about foure a clocke after noone, we came into Dartmouth. . . .

10. The Camden Hills.
11. At the head of the broad stretch of river, where Thomaston stands.

67. The Establishment
and Abandonment of St. George's Fort,
1607–08

As a result of the explorations of Hanham and Pring in 1606, the Plymouth syndicate seems to have discarded the idea of settlement on the Georges River. Instead, Captains Popham and Gilbert in 1607 were apparently given the choice of the Pemaquid peninsula or the banks of the Kennebec River. They chose the latter and picked a reasonable site for their fort. They settled down to demonstrate the value of Maine timber by constructing a stout pinnace, the Virginia, but ice came down the river early and the Gift of God had to be sent home in winter weather to save her from being damaged. Cold was severe and trade with the Indians fair, but perhaps not good enough, so the colony departed for England in 1608 leaving the Kennebec untenanted. James Davis (whom we presume to be the narrator) made a journal, extracts being given below. A copy of part of it is in the Lambeth Palace Library, London, and a summary of the concluding section is in William Strachey, The Histoire of Travell into Virginia Britania, edited by Louis B. Wright and Virginia Freund (1953), pp. 172–173. The two parts were edited by Henry O. Thayer, The Sagadahoc Colony (1892), (from which the extracts come), and in Henry S. Burrage, ed., Early English and French Voyages, 1534–1608 (1906).

Satterdaye beinge the 15th of Auguste the storme ended and the wind Cam faier for us to go for Sagadehock.[1] So we wayed our anckors and Sett Saill and stood to the estward and cam to the Illand of Sutquin[2] which was 2 Leags from those Illands we rod att anker beffor, and hear we anckored under the Illand of Sutqin in the estersyd of ytt for that the wynd was of the shore that wee could no gett into the ryver of Sagadehock and hear Captain pophams ships bott cam abord of us and gave us xx freshe Cods that they had taken beinge Sent out a fyshinge.

Sondaye beinge the 16th of Auguste Captain popham Sent his Shallop unto us for to healp us in. So we wayed our anckors and beinge Calme we towed in our ship and Cam into the Ryver of

1. The Kennebec River.
2. Seguin Island.

Sagadehocke and anckored by the gyfts Syd about xi of the Cloke the Same daye.

Mundaye beinge the 17th Auguste Captain popham in his shallop with 30 others and Captain Gilbert in his shipes bott accompaned with 18 other persons departed early in the morninge from thear ships and sailled up the Ryver of Sagadehock for to vew the Ryver and allso to See whear they myght fynd the most Convenyent place for thear plantation my Selffe beinge with Captain Gilbert. So we Sailled up into this ryver near 14 Leags and found ytt to be a most gallant ryver very brod and of a good depth. we never had Lesse Watter then 3 fetham when we had Least and abundance of greatt fyshe in ytt Leaping above the Watter on eatch Syd of us as we Sailled. So the nyght aprochinge after a whill we had refreshed our Selves uppon the shore about 9 of the Cloke we sett backward to retorn and Cam abourd our shipes the next day followinge about 2 of the Clok in the afternoon. We fynd this ryver to be very pleasant with many goodly Illands in ytt and to be both Large and deepe Watter havinge many branches in ytt. that which we tooke bendeth ytt Selffe towards the northest.

Tuesdaye beinge the 18th after our retorn we all went to the shore and thear mad Choies of a place for our plantation which ys at the very mouth or entry of the Ryver of Sagadehocke on the West Syd of the Ryver beinge almoste an Illand of a good bygness.[3] whylst we wear uppon the shore thear Cam in three Canoos by us but they wold not Com near us but rowed up the Ryver and so past away.

Wensday beinge the 19th Auguste we all went to the shore whear we mad Choise for our plantation and thear we had a Sermon delyvred unto us by our precher and after the Sermon our pattent was red with the orders and Lawes thearin prescrybed and then we retorned abord our ships again.

Thursdaye beinge the 20th of Auguste all our Companyes Landed and thear began to fortefye. our presedent Captain popham Sett the fryst spytt of ground unto ytt and after hem all the rest followed and Labored hard in the trenches about ytt.

Frydaye the 21th of Auguste all hands Labored hard about the

3. The traditional site is some little way upstream, opposite Fort Popham.

fort Som in the trentch Som for fagetts and our ship Carpenters about the buildinge of a small penis or shallop. . . .

You maie please to understand how, whilst this busines was thus followed here, soone after their first arrivall, that had dispatch't away Captain Robert Davies, in the Mary and John, to advertise of their safe arrival and forwardness of their plantacion within this river of Sachadehoc, with letters to the Lord Chief Justice,[4] ymportuninge a supply for the most necessary wants to the subsisting of a colony, to be sent unto them betymes the next yeare.

After Captain Davies departure they fully finished the fort, trencht and fortefied yt with twelve pieces of ordinaunce, and built fifty howses, besides a church and a storehowse; and the carpenters framed a pretty Pynnace of about some thirty tonne, which they called the Virginia; the chief ship wright beinge one Digby of London.

Many discoveries likewise had been made both to the mayne and unto the neghbour rivers, and the frontier nations fully discovered by the diligence of Captain Gilbert, had not the wynter proved soe extreame unseasonable and frosty; for yt being in the yeare 1607, when the extraordinary frost was felt in most parts of Europe, yt was here likewise as vehement, by which noe boat could stir upon any busines. Howbeyt, as tyme and occasyon gave leave, there was nothing omitted which could add unto the benefitt or knowledg of the planters, for which when Captain Davies arrived there in the yeare following (sett out from Topsam, the port towne of Exciter, with a shipp laden full of vitualls, armes, instruments and tooles, etc.,) albeyt he found Master George Popham, the president, and some other dead, yet he found all things in good forwardness, and many kinds of furrs obteyned from the Indians by way of trade; good store of sarsaparilla[5] gathered, and the new pynnace all finished. But by reason that Captain Gilbert received letters that his brother[6] was newly dead, and a faire portion of land fallen unto his share, which required his repaier home, and noe mynes discovered, nor hope thereof, being the mayne intended benefit expected to uphold the charge of this plantacion, and the feare that

4. Sir John Popham.
5. Presumably sassafras roots.
6. Sir John Gilbert, son of Sir Humphrey Gilbert.

all other wynters would prove like the first, the company by no means would stay any longer in the country, especyally Captain Gilbert being to leave them, and Master Popham, as aforesaid, dead; wherefore they all ymbarqued in this new arrived shipp, and in the new pynnace, the Virginia, and sett saile for England. And this was the end of that northerne colony uppon the river Sachadehoc.

68. Henry Hudson
Ascends the Hudson, 1609

A. Robert Juet

ROBERT JUET's careful but tiring journal records the details of Hudson's long voyage. Extracts are given dealing with the ascent of the Hudson River only. The journal was published by Samuel Purchas, Hakluytus Posthumus, or Purchas his pilgrimes, III, 581–595 (from which extracts are taken), and a useful version is edited by Robert M. Lunny, Juet's Journal (1959). Another is in J. F. Jameson, Narratives of New Netherlands, 1609–1664 (1909), pp. 11–28.

The third, the morning mystie untill ten of the clocke, then it cleered, and the wind came to the South South-east, so wee weighed and stood to the Northward. The Land is very pleasant and high, and bold to fall withall. At three of the clocke in the after-noone, wee came to three great Rivers. So we stood along to the Northermost, thinking to have gone into it, but we found it to have a very shoald barre before it, for we had but ten foot water. . . . The height is 40. degrees 30. minutes.

The fourth, in the morning as soone as the day was light, wee saw that it was good riding farther up. So we sent our Boate to sound, and found that it was a very good Harbour [Sandy Hook Harbor]; and foure and five fathoms, two Cables length from the shoare. Then we weighed and went in with our ship. This day the people of the Countrey came aboord of us, seeming very glad of our comming, and brought greene Tabacco, and gave us of it for Knives and Beads.

The fifth, in the morning as soone as the day was light, the wind ceased and the Flood came. So we heaved off our ship againe into five fathoms water, and sent our Boate to sound the Bay,[1] and we found that there was three fathoms hard by the Souther shoare. Our men went on Land there, and saw great store of Men, Women and Children, who gave them Tabacco at their comming on Land. So they went up into the Woods, and saw great store of very goodly Oakes, and some Currants. . . .

The eight, was very faire weather, wee rode still very quietly. The people came aboord us, and brought Tabacco and Indian Wheate, to exchange for Knives and Beades, and offered us no violence. . . .

The eleventh, was faire and very hot weather. At one of the clocke in the after-noone, wee weighed and went into the River, the wind at South South-west, little winde. Our soundings were seven, sixe, five, sixe, seven, eight, nine, ten, twelve, thirteene, and fourteene fathomes. Then it shoalded againe, and came to five fathomes. Then wee Anchored, and saw that it was a very good Harbour for all windes, and rode all night. The people of the Countrey came aboord of us, making shew of love, and gave us Tabacco and Indian Wheat, and departed for that night; but we durst not trust them.

The twelfth, very faire and hot. In the after-noone at two of the clocke wee weighed, the winde being variable, betweene the North and the North-west. So we turned into the River [the Hudson River] two leagues and Anchored. . . .

The thirteenth faire weather, the wind Northerly. At seven of the clocke in the morning, as the floud came we weighed, and turned foure miles into the River. . . . In the after-noone we weighed, and turned in with the floud, two leagues and a halfe further, and anchored all night, and had five fathoms soft Ozie ground, and had an high point of Land, which shewed out to us, bearing North by East five leagues off us.

The fourteenth, in the morning being very faire weather, the wind South-east, we sayled up the River twelve leagues, and had five fathoms, and five fathoms and a quarter lesse; and came to a Streight betweene two Points [Stony Point and Verplanck's

1. Side note: "The great-Bay in 40. degrees and 30. minutes."

Point], and had eight, nine and ten fathoms; and it trended North-east by North, one league: and wee had twelve, thirteene and fourteene fathomes. The River is a mile broad: there is very high Land on both sides. Then wee went up North-west, a league and an halfe deepe water. Then North-east by North five miles; then North-west by North two leagues, and anchored. The Land grew very high and Mountainous. The River is full of fish.

The fifteenth, in the morning was misty untill the Sunne arose: then it cleered. So wee weighed with the wind at South, and ran up into the River twentie leagues, passing by high Mountaines [the upper Highlands]. . . .

The seventeenth, faire Sun-shining weather, and very hot. In the morning as soone as the Sun was up, we set sayle, and ran up sixe leagues higher, and found shoalds in the middle of the channell, and small Ilands, but seven fathoms water on both sides.

The nineteenth, was faire and hot weather: at the floud being neere eleven of the clocke, wee weighed, and ran higher up two leagues above the Shoalds, and had no lesse water than five fathoms: wee anchored, and rode in eight fathomes. The people of the Countrie came flocking aboord, and brought us Grapes, and Pompions, which wee bought for trifles. And many brought us Bevers skinnes, and Otters skinnes, which wee bought for Beades, Knives, and Hatchets. So we rode there all night.[2]

The twentieth, in the morning was faire weather. Our Masters Mate with foure men more went up with our Boat to sound the River, and found two leagues above us but two fathomes water, and the channell very narrow; and above that place seven or eight fathomes. Toward night they returned: and we rode still all night. The one and twentieth was faire weather and the wind all Southerly: we determined yet once more to goe farther up into the River, to trie what depth and breadth it did beare; but much people resorted aboord, so wee went not this day. . . .

The two and twentieth, was faire weather: in the morning our Masters Mate and foure more of the companie went up with our Boat to sound the River higher up. . . . This night at ten of the clocke our Boat returned in a showre of rain from sounding of the

2. The highest point reached, near the site of Albany.

River, and found it to bee at an end for shipping to goe in. For they had beene up eight or nine leagues, and found but seven foot water, and unconstant soundings.

The five and twentieth was faire weather, and the wind at South a stiffe gale. We rode still, and went on Land to walke on the West side of the River, and found good ground for Corne, and other Garden herbs, with great store of goodly Oakes, and Wal-nut trees, and Chest-nut trees, Ewe [yew] trees, and trees of sweet wood in great abundance, and great store of Slate for houses, and other good stones. . . .

The nine and twentieth was drie close weather: the wind at South, and South and by West, we weighed early in the morning, and turned downe three leagues by a lowe water, and anchored at the lower end of the long Reach; for it is sixe leagues long. . . . At three of the clocke in the after-noone wee weighed, as soone as the ebbe came, and turned downe to the edge of the Mountaines, or the Northermost of the Mountaines, and anchored: because the high Land hath many Points, and a narrow channell, and hath many eddie winds. So we rode quietly all night in seven fathoms water.

The thirtieth was faire weather, and the wind at South-east a stiffe gale betweene the Mountaynes. We rode still the afternoone. The people of the Countrey came aboord us, and brought some small skinnes with them, which we bought for Knives and Trifles. This a very pleasant place to build a Towne on. . . .

The first of October, faire weather, the wind variable betweene the Weste and the North. In the morning we weighed at seven of the clocke with the ebbe, and got downe below the Mountaynes, which was seven leagues. . . .

The second, faire weather. At breake of day wee weighed, the wind being at North-west, and got downe seven leagues; then the floud was come strong, so we anchored. . . . within a while after, wee got downe two leagues beyond that place, and anchored in a Bay, cleere from all danger of them on the other side of the River, where we saw a very good piece of ground: and hard by it there was a Cliffe, that looked of the colour of a white greene, as though it were either Copper, or Silver Myne: and I thinke it to be one of them, by the Trees that grow upon it. For they be all burned, and the other places are greene as grasse, it is on that side of the River that is called Manna-hata [Manhattan]. . . .

The fourth, was faire weather, and the wind at North Northwest, wee weighed and came out of the River, into which we had runne so farre. . . .

We continued our course toward England, without seeing any Land by the way, all the rest of this moneth of October: And on the seventh day of November, stilo novo, being Saturday: by the Grace of God, we safely arrived in the Range of Dartmouth in Devonshire, in the yeere 1609.

B. Johan de Laet

J. DE LAET's *Nieuwe Wereldt* (1625) *summed up the nature and results of the penetration of the Hudson River. The Dutch text is translated in Henry C. Murphy,* Henry Hudson in Holland, *edited by Wouter Nijhoff (1909), pp. 147–148.*

They at length reached a lofty promontory or headland, behind which was situated a bay, which they entered and run up into a road-stead near a low sandy point, in lat. 40° 18′. There they were visited by two savages clothed in elk-skins, who showed them every sign of friendship. On the land they found an abundance of blue plums and magnificent oaks, of a height and thickness that one seldom beholds; together with poplars, linden trees, and various other kinds of wood useful in ship-building. Sailing hence in a northeasterly direction, they ascended a river to nearly 43° north latitude, where it became so narrow and of so little depth, that they found it necessary to return.

From all that they could learn, there had never been any ship or Christians in that quarter before, and they were the first to discover the river and ascend it so far. Henry Hudson returned to Amsterdam with this report; and in the following year, 1610, some merchants again sent a ship thither, that is to say, to the second river discovered, which was called Manhattes, from the savage nation that dwelt at its mouth. And subsequently their High Mightinesses the States General granted to these merchants the exclusive privilege of navigating this river and trading there; whereupon, in the year 1615, a redoubt or fort was erected on the river, and occupied by a small garrison.

XIV
The Foundation of French Canada, 1603–11

FROM 1577, onwards, New France had a royal viceroy; but he operated only within France. He intervened at various times before 1603 to licence syndicates of merchants to send expeditions or to enjoy temporary local monopolies in the fur trade. After 1603 the king normally entrusted nominal authority to some similar titular figure, while annual monopolies were usually granted to syndicates of Norman and Breton merchants for the fur trade of Canada. For one of these syndicates Samuel de Champlain conducted a survey of the St. Lawrence in 1603. His report, published as Les sauvages (1603), gives a vivid picture of the geography and Indian activity of the St. Lawrence Valley. The Iroquoian-speaking Indians of the Quebec area of Cartier's day had been replaced by Algonquian-speaking Montagnais, while the Iroquoian-speakers of Montreal had vanished, perhaps being re-absorbed into the main stock on Georgian Bay.

Like Cartier, Champlain was active in picking up information about river routes to the south and north of the St. Lawrence, hearing, for example, something of the Richelieu River and where it led. Once more like Cartier, he was checked by the Lachine Rapids and had to pick up what he could on the Great Lakes from Indian informants. He promised friendship and alliance to the Montagnais and to the Algonquins of the Ottawa River, but after what he heard of the hard winter in the North and of the better prospects of finding mines near the coasts south of the St. Lawrence, he advised that the river should continue to be used for seasonal, summer fur trading only and that the main exploring and trading effort should be directed further south. From 1604 to 1607 he was therefore the executive agent of France in the attempt to exploit the Bay of Fundy and to explore New England. The lack of adequate profit from these ventures led his backers to change their plans. In 1608 he was directed to establish a permanent post on the St. Lawrence, which he did at Quebec during the summer of 1608. The "Habitation" was a combination residence, barracks, fortress, magazine and trading post. It did not protect Champlain from plots or his men from the winter disease, scurvy. Only a handful survived the first winter.

Reinforced in 1609, Champlain made contact with Iroquoian-speaking Hurons coming down river for a summer's fishing and trading, and learned that they and the Algonquins were allied with the Montagnais against the main Iroquois concentration south of the river. Champlain joined the anti-Iroquois forces and took part in a raid down into the Lake Champlain area, hearing that from it contact could be made with Florida to the south. The same season, Henry Hudson was to ascend with a Dutch expedition to within eighty miles of his southernmost limit, another example of the rapidity with which the lands behind the Atlantic shorelines were being divided into European spheres of influence. In 1610 Champlain made closer contact with the Hurons and took part in a successful attack on an Iroquois fort at the mouth of the Richelieu River, before returning to France for a time.

By 1611 the French were beginning to learn to live with and through the Canadian winter. Champlain returned, and set out to meet the Hurons and Algonquins coming downsteam. He closely examined Montreal as a possible site for settlement, was brought by land to the head of the Lachine Rapids and was taught how to shoot them. He learned something of the interior lakes—great seas as they seemed to the Indians. Some of them knew of lands to the south of the Iroquois, Florida, Champlain thought—probably a contact through the Susquehanna tribe with Virginia. He did much trading and exchanged young men to become interpreters with Hurons and Algonquins, promising later to visit the trading Indians in their own countries. On his return to the Habitation he found flourishing gardens and, apparently, a garrison contented enough for him to spend a further period in France.

On his return in 1613 he was in a stronger position: a permanent monopoly had been established under royal patronage, and Champlain was to be its agent, empowered to colonize and missionize as well as trade. Professor Trudel has called the whole first phase of French settlement "Le Comptoir," the countinghouse, or trading factory, which Quebec was in 1608 and continued to be. But it was a trading post with a unique and spreading orbit of influence, much of it centering on the personality of Champlain, and sustained by the continued growing demand from France for beaver and other furs.

Samuel de Champlain's Works have been edited by H. P. Biggar in seven volumes (1922–36); the older edition by Edmund F. Slafter, The Voyages of Samuel de Champlain (3 vols., 1878–82), still being useful. The Voyages of Samuel de Champlain, edited by W. L. Grant (1909), is a valuable selection in English; so is, in French, Voyages de Samuel Champlain, edited by Hubert Deschamps (1951). Marcel Trudel, Histoire de la Nouvelle France. Le Comptoir, 1604–1627, is a thorough study; Morris Bishop, Champlain: The Life of Fortitude (1948) is the most useful life of Champlain.

69. The St. Lawrence Valley, 1603

CHAMPLAIN'S EXPEDITION in 1603 was his first reconnaissance into the St. Lawrence Valley. The extracts, translated, are from Samuel de Champlain, Les Sauvages (1603), and are represented in Champlain, Voyages, ed. O. E. F. Slafter, I, (1880), 213–277, and in Champlain, Works, ed. H. P. Biggar, I (1922), 91–165. They are selected to show what a great amount of geographical information he could collect through his Algonquian-speaking interpreters.

We set out from Honfleur, on the 15th of March 1603. . . . On the 2nd of May at eleven o'clock in the morning we reached the Bank in latitude 44° 20'. . . . On the 15th we sighted the islands of St. Pierre. On the 17th we fell in with an ice-floe near Cape May, six leagues in length, which caused us to lower sail for the whole night, so as to avoid the danger to which we were exposed. On the next day, we set sail, and sighted Cape Ray, the islands of St. Paul and Cape St. Lawrence, which is on the mainland to the south. . . .

On the 20th we sighted an island, some twenty-five or thirty leagues long, called Anticosty, which marks the entrance to the river of Canada. The next day we sighted Gaspé, a very high land, and began to enter the said river. . . .

On the 24th of the month, we came to anchor before Tadoussac, and on the 26th entered this harbor, which is like a cove at the mouth of the Saguenay river. . . . The harbor of Tadoussac is small and could not hold above ten or twelve ships; but there is water enough on the east, sheltered from the river Saguenay and along a little hill, which is almost cut off by the sea. . . .

We went to visit the savages at St. Matthew's Point, distant a league from Tadoussac. Having landed we went to the lodge of their grand Sagamore, named Anadabijou, whom we found with some eighty or a hundred of his companions, celebrating a tabagie —that is a feast. . . . They were having this celebration on account of a victory they had obtained over the Iroquois, of whom they had killed about a hundred, whose scalps they cut off, and had with them for the ceremony. Three nations engaged in the war, the Etechemins, Algonquins, and Montagnais. These, to the number of a thousand, went to war against the Iroquois, whom they encountered at the mouth of the River of the Iroquois, and of whom they killed a hundred. . . . They were in number about a thousand persons, men, women and children. . . .

On Wednesday the eighteenth of June, we set out from Tadoussac, to go to the Rapid (the Lachine Rapids beyond Montreal). . . . We came to anchor at Quebec, a narrow part of the said river of Canada, which is here some three hundred paces broad. At this passage on the north side is a very high elevation, which slopes down on two sides: elsewhere the country is level and beautiful, and there is good land covered with trees, like oaks, cypresses, birches, firs and aspens, also wild fruit trees, and vines; in my opinion, if this soil were cultivated it would be as good as our own. Along the shore of the said Quebec are diamonds in the slate rocks which are better than those of Alençon. . . .

On Monday, the 23d of this month, we set out from Quebec, where the river begins to widen. . . . The farther we went, the finer was the country. . . .

The last day of June we set out from here, and went to the mouth of the River of the Iroquois (the Richelieu), where the savages who were about to make war against these (Iroquois) were encamped and fortified. . . . We went up the River of the Iroquois some five or six leagues, but, on account of the current, could pass no farther with our long-boat. . . . This river runs approximately south-west. . . .

The savages say that some fifteen leagues from where we had been, there is a rapid coming down from a much higher level, around which they carry their canoes about a quarter of a league, where they enter a lake (Lake Champlain) at the entrance to which are three islands, and in the lake they meet with others. This lake may be some forty or fifty leagues long, and some twenty-five leagues in breadth, and into it fall as many as ten rivers, which are navigable a considerable distance for canoes. Then, when they come to the end of this lake, there is another rapid, and they enter another lake (Lake George), the same size as the former, at the extremity of which the Iroquois are encamped. They say, also, that there is a river (Hudson River), which leads down to the coast of Florida, a distance of perhaps some hundred or hundred and forty leagues from the last mentioned lake. . . .

There are here two large islands (Montreal and Perrot); one on the northern side, some fifteen leagues long and almost as many broad, begins some twelve leagues down the River of Canada, towards the River of the Iroquois, and ends beyond the rapid. The island on the south side is some four leagues long, and half a league wide. There is, besides, another island (St. Paul's) near that on the north, which may be half a league long and a quarter broad; and still another small island between that on the north, and the other near the south side, where we passed the entrance to the rapid. This being passed, there is a kind of lake, in which lie all these islands, which is some five leagues long and almost as wide, and where are many small, rocky islands. Near the rapid there is a mountain (Montreal), visible from very far into the interior, also a little river flowing from this mountain into the lake. On the south, one sees, three or four mountains, which seem to be about fifteen or sixteen leagues off in the interior (Boucherville and others). There are also two rivers; one (St. Lambert), leads to the first lake of the River of the Iroquois, along which the Algonquins sometimes make war upon them; the other near the rapid, and extending a little way inland.

As we began to approach the rapid (Lachine) with our little skiff and the canoe, I assure you I never before saw a torrent of water descend with such force as this does. . . . We went by land through the woods a league away to see the end of the rapid, and there we saw no more rocks or falls, but the water runs so swiftly that it could not be more so, and this current continues three or four leagues. . . . We questioned two or three Algonquins . . . about the extent and source of the River of Canada.

They said, according to the sketch they gave of it, that two or three leagues past the rapid which we had seen, a river (Ottawa) on the north side leads towards their territory. Continuing up the said great river, they pass . . . from first to last some twenty or twenty-five leagues. Then they enter a lake (Ontario) which is some hundred and fifty leagues in length. . . . Then arriving at the end of this lake, they come to another fall (Niagara) where they carry their canoes. Beyond this they enter another very large lake (Erie), as big perhaps as the first. The latter they have been to but very little and have heard tell that at the end of it is a sea (Lake Huron), of which they have not seen the end, nor heard that any one has; but where they have been, the water is not salt. They have not advanced any farther. The course of the waters is from the west towards the east; and they do not know whether, beyond the lakes they have seen, there is another watercourse flowing towards the west. . . .

I asked them whether they had knowledge of any mines. They told us that there is a nation called the good Iroquois (Hurons), who come to barter for the articles of merchandise which the French vessels furnish the Algonquins, who say that there is, toward the north a mine of pure copper, some bracelets made from which, obtained from the good Iroquois, they showed us. They said that if we wished to go thither, they would guide there those who should be appointed for that purpose. This is all I have been able to ascertain . . . so that, according to their account, the distance from the rapid where we had been to the salt sea (Lake Huron), which is possibly the South Sea, is some four hundred leagues (actually 700 miles). It is not to be doubted, then, from their account, that this is none other than the South Sea, the sun setting where they say. On Friday, the tenth of this month [correctly July 12] we were back at Tadoussac, where our vessel lay.

70. Quebec Is Founded, 1608

WHEN IT had been decided to move the center of French activity in North America to the St. Lawrence, Champlain, who had built establishments at Ste. Croix in 1604 and at Port Royal in 1605, knew exactly what he wished to create at Quebec. The extracts, translated, are from Champlain, Voyages (1613), and are represented in Champlain, Voyages, ed. E. F. Slafter, II (1878), 163–197, and in Champlain, Works, ed. H. P. Biggar, II (1925), 9–58. They give his account of the building of the Habitation, the third permanent European settlement (after St. Augustine and Jamestown) in North America. He also has a valuable record of the weather.

I left port (Honfleur) on the 13th (of April 1608), and arrived at the Grand Bank on the 15th of May, in latitude 45° 15'. On the 26th, in latitude 46° 45', we sighted Cape St. Mary on the island of Newfoundland. . . .

On the 3d of June we arrived . . . in the roadstead at Tadoussac, a league from the harbor which is a sort of cove at the mouth of the river Saguenay, where the tide is quite remarkable for its rapidity, and where sometimes there come violent winds bringing intense cold. . . . I set out from Tadoussac the last day of the month to go to Quebec. . . .

From the Island of Orleans to Quebec the distance is one league. I arrived there on the 3d of July. I then searched for a place suitable for our settlement, but I could not find one more convenient or better situated than the point of Quebec, so called by the savages, which was covered with nut-trees. I at once employed some of our workmen in cutting them down that we might construct our *habitation* there, some in sawing planks, some in making the cellar and digging ditches. Others I sent to Tadoussac with the pinnace to fetch our effects. The first thing we made was the storehouse for keeping our supplies under cover, which was promptly accomplished by the diligence of everyone and my own attention to the matter. . . .

Pont-Gravé set out from Quebec on the 18th September to return to France. . . . I continued the work on our quarters, which contained three buildings of two stories. Each one was three fathoms long and two and a half wide. The storehouse was six fathoms long and three wide, with a fine cellar six feet deep. All the way round our buildings, I had a gallery made, on the outside at the second story, which proved very convenient. There were also ditches, fifteen feet wide and six deep. Outside the ditches I made several spurs (salients?) which enclosed a part of the buildings, where we placed our cannon. In front of the *habitation* there is an open space four fathoms wide and six or seven long, looking out upon the river's bank. Surrounding the *habitation* are very good gardens, and an open place on the north side some hundred or hundred and twenty yards long and fifty or sixty wide. . . .

While the carpenters, sawyers, and other workmen were employed at our quarters, I set all the others to work clearing the land around our *habitation*, in order to make gardens in which to plant grains and seeds, that we might see how they would flourish as the soil seemed to be very good. . . .

On the 1st October I had some wheat sown and on the 15th some rye. On the 3d there was a white frost in some places and on the 15th the leaves of the trees began to fall. On the 24th I had some native vines planted, which flourished very well. But after I left the settlement to go back to France, they were all spoiled, for lack of attention, which distressed me very much on my return.

On the 18th of November there was a great fall of snow, which lay on the ground only two days, during which time there was a violent gale of wind. . . .

On the 5th of February it snowed heavily and there was a high wind for two days. . . . The snow and ice last for three months, from the month of January to the 8th of April, by which time it is nearly all melted. And, moreover, it is seldom that any is seen at the end of this month at our settlement. It is remarkable that two or three fathoms of snow and ice on the river is melted in less than twelve days. From Tadoussac to Gaspé, Cape Breton, Newfoundland, and the Grand Bay (Gulf of St. Lawrence), ice and snow continue in most places until the end of May, at which time the whole entrance to the great river is blocked with ice, although at Quebec there is none at all. This shows a strange difference for a hundred and twenty leagues (of distance) in longitude; for the entrance to the river is in 49° 50° and 51° degrees of latitude and our settlement in 46° 40'.

71. War and Exploration Around Lake Richelieu, 1609

CHAMPLAIN'S ALLIANCE with the Montagnais, Algonquins and Hurons *involved the French in their wars with the Iroquois. In the first campaign on the Richelieu River and Lake Champlain in 1609, Champlain demon-*

strated the value of European weapons (a lesson the Iroquois were not slow to learn), but the alliance also gave him the chance to penetrate into areas where he could not otherwise have gone. The extracts, translated, are from Champlain, Voyages, and are represented in Champlain, Voyages, ed. Slafter, II, 206–223, and in Champlain, Works, ed. Biggar, II, 64–107.

Setting out from the mouth of this river (the Richelieu), which is some four or five hundred paces wide and very beautiful, and proceeding southward, we arrived at a place in latitude 45°, and twenty-two or twenty-three leagues from Trois Rivières. . . . All this region is very level, covered with forests, vines and nut-trees. No Christians have been in this place before us; and we had considerable difficulty in ascending the river by rowing. . . .

I set out accordingly from the rapid of the Iroquois River on the 2nd of July. All the savages set to carrying their canoes, arms and baggage some half a league overland, to avoid the violence and force of the rapid, which was speedily accomplished. . . .

We set out on the following day, continuing our course up the river as far as the entrance to the lake (Lake Champlain). . . . These regions although pleasant are not inhabited by any savages, on account of their wars; for they withdraw as far as possible from the rivers into the interior, in order not to be suddenly surprised.

Next day we entered the lake which is some 80 to 100 leagues long, where I saw four fine islands about ten, twelve and fifteen leagues in length, which, were formerly inhabited by savages like the River of the Iroquois; but they have been abandoned, since the Indians have been at war with one another. . . . Continuing our course along this lake on the western side and observing the country, I noticed some very high mountains (the Green Mountains) on the eastern side on the tops of which there was snow. I enquired of the savages whether these localities were inhabited. They said they were occupied by the Iroquois, and that there were beautiful valleys and fields rich in corn in these places, such as I have eaten in this country, together with other products in abundance. They said also that the lake went close to the mountains, some twenty-five leagues from us, as I judged. I saw towards the south others (the Adirondacks), no less high than the first, but without any snow. The savages told me that it was there that we were to find their enemies, that these mountains were thickly settled, and that it was necessary (first) to pass a rapid (Ticonderoga) which I afterwards saw, whence we should enter another lake (Lake George), some nine or ten leagues long. After reaching the end of it, they said, we should have to go some two leagues by land to cross a river (Hudson River) flowing into the sea on the coast of Norumbega, near to that of Florida. . . .

Now as we began to approach within two or three days' journey of the abode of their enemy, we advanced only at night, resting during the day. . . . Then we withdrew into the interior of the forest and spent the rest of the day there. . . .

When it was evening we embarked in our canoes to continue our course, and as we paddled along very quietly and without making any noise, we met the Iroquois about ten o'clock at night on the 29th of the month at the extremity of a cape (Crown Point) which extends into the lake on the western bank. They had come to fight. We both began to utter loud cries and each got his arms in readiness. We withdrew out into the lake, and the Iroquois went on shore where they drew up all their canoes close to one another. Then they began to fell trees with the poor (iron) axes which they sometimes acquire in war, or with others of stone. Then they barricaded themselves very well. . . . After singing, dancing, and bandying words with one another for some time, when day came, my companions and myself were still under cover, lest the enemy should see us. We got our fire-arms ready in the best manner possible, being however separated, each in one of the canoes of the Montagnais Indians. After arming ourselves with light weapons, we each took an arquebus and went on shore. I saw the enemy go out of their barricade, to the number nearly of two hundred strong, in appearance stout and rugged. They came slowly to meet us with a dignity and assurance which I admired; and having three chiefs at their head. Our men also advanced in the same order, telling me that those who had the three large plumes were the chiefs, and that there were only these three, and that they could be distinguished by these plumes, which were much larger than those of their companions; and that I should do what I could do to kill them. . . .

As soon as we landed, they began to run for some two hundred yards towards their enemies, who stood firmly, not having yet noticed my (white) companions who went into the woods with some savages. Our men began to call to me with loud cries; and, in order to make way for me, they divided into two groups, and put me at their head, where I marched some twenty paces in advance until I was within some thirty paces of the enemy, who as soon as they caught sight of me halted and gazed at me as I did also at them. When I saw them making a move to draw their bows at us, I rested my arquebus against my cheek and aimed directly at one of the three chiefs. With this same shot two fell to the ground, and one of their men was so wounded that he died thereof some time after. I had loaded my arquebus with four bullets. When our people saw this shot so favorable for them, they began to raise such loud cries that one could not have heard it thunder. Meanwhile the arrows flew thick on both sides. The Iroquois were greatly astonished that two men had been so quickly killed, although they were provided with armor made of cotton thread woven together with wood (armez d'armes tissues de fil de cotton, de bois[1]), which was proof against their arrows. This caused great alarm among them. As I was loading my arquebus again, one of my companions fired a shot from the woods, which astonished them anew so much that, seeing their chiefs dead, they lost courage and took to flight, abandoning the field and their fort, and fleeing into the woods, whither I pursued them, killing still more of them. Our savages also killed several of them and took ten or twelve prisoners. The remainder escaped with the wounded. . . . After having feasted, danced, and sung, we set off three hours later on our return with the prisoners. The spot where this attack took place is in latitude 43° and some minutes, and the lake was named Lake Champlain.

72. Champlain Attempts to Plan for Expeditions Beyond the Lachine Rapids, 1611

1611 was a difficult year for Champlain. The Indians failed to come down the St. Lawrence with their furs at the usual time. In addition,

1. S. de Champlain, Voyages (1613), p. 231.

*Champlain's men had no longer a monopoly of the fur trade and many
competing French vessels had appeared. In order to tap the trade when it
should develop he moved up the river to Montreal where he was followed by other traders. Eventually, on June 13, a party of 200 Huron
Indians appeared, including a number with whom Champlain had previously had contact. They were confused by the competitive trading
which developed for the very few furs they had brought, so they turned
for explanations and friendship to Champlain. He, making the best of
his opportunities, engaged them in conversation about the interior and
suggested he should visit them during a subsequent season; this they
accepted gladly. A program of future contacts was drawn up. The
extracts, translated, are from Champlain, Voyages, and are represented in
Champlain, Voyages, ed. E. F. Slafter, III (1882), 1–24, and in Champlain, Works, ed. Biggar, II, 157–196. They show Champlain stressing
the advantages he enjoyed from his friendship with the Indians and in-
directly advocating a return to a monopoly in which he would be the
chief executive (something like this was done in 1612). But his own
record for objectivity indicates that he was not overstressing the prestige
he had acquired and the doors which this had opened to him for exploration and trade.*

We set out from Honfleur on the first day of March. . . . On
(May 2) we sighted the islands of St. Pierre, finding no ice. Continuing on our course on the next day, the third of the month, we
sighted Cape Ray, also without finding ice. On the fourth we
sighted the island of St. Paul and Cape St. Lawrence, being some
eight leagues north of the latter. The next day we sighted Gaspé.
On the seventh we were held up by a north west wind, which drove
us out of our course nearly thirty five leagues. When it dropped it
was fine and in our favour as far as Tadoussac which we reached on
the 13th day of May. Here we discharged a cannon to notify the
savages, in order to get news from our settlement at Quebec. The
country was still almost entirely covered with snow. . . .

On the 17th of the month (May) I set out from Tadoussac for
the Great Rapid (Lachine) to meet the Algonquin savages and
other tribes who had promised the year before to be there with the
young man (Étienne Brulé) whom I had given them, that I might
learn from him what he had seen during the winter. . . .

On the thirteenth day of . . . (June) two hundred Charioquois
(Huron) savages, together with the chiefs Ochateguin, Iroquet and
Tregouaroti, brother of our savage (Savignon) brought back my

servant. We were very pleased to see them. I went to meet them in a canoe with our savage. As they were approaching slowly and in order, our men got ready to salute them with a discharge of arquebuses, muskets, and small pieces. When they were near at hand, they all began to shout together, and one of the chiefs gave orders that they should make their harangue, in which they praised us greatly, commending us as worthy of trust, inasmuch as I had kept the promise to meet them at this rapid. . . .

When the next day came, I showed them a place for their cabins and there the old and leading men held a long consultation together. After their long consultation they sent for me alone with my servant, who had learned their language very well. They told him they desired to form a close alliance with me. . . . They told me that more than four hundred savages of their country who had intended to come had been kept away by certain representations of an Iroquois prisoner who had belonged to me and who had escaped to his own country. He had reported, they said, that I had given him his liberty and some merchandise, and that I intended to go to the rapid with six hundred Iroquois to await the Algonquins and kill them all, adding that the fear aroused by this intelligence had alone prevented them from coming.

I replied that the prisoner had escaped without my leave; that our savage (Savignon) knew very well how he ran away, and that there was no thought of my abandoning their friendship, as they had heard, since I had engaged in war along with them, and sent my servant (Brulé) to their country to foster their friendship. Moreover, my keeping my promise to them so faithfully was still a further confirmation. They replied that, so far as they were concerned, they had never believed such things; that they were well aware that all this talk was far from the truth, and that if they had believed the contrary they would not have come, but that the others were afraid, never having seen a Frenchmen except for my servant. . . .

I talked a great deal with them about the source of the great river (St. Lawrence) and their country, and they gave me detailed information about their rivers, falls, lakes, and lands, as also of the tribes living there, and what is found in those parts. Four of them assured me that they had seen a sea at a great distance from their country, but that it was difficult to go there not only on account of enemies, but of the intervening wilderness. They told me also that the winter before some savages had come from the direction of Florida, beyond the country of the Iroquois, who lived near our ocean (the Atlantic), and were in alliance with these latter savages. In a word, they made me a very exact statement, indicating by drawings all the places where they had been, and taking pleasure in talking to me about them. And for my part, I did not tire of listening to them, as they confirmed some things in regard to which I had been hitherto in doubt. . . .

The next day after bartering what little they had, they made a barricade about their camp partly on the side of the wood and partly on that of our pataches, and this they did for their security to avoid surprise by their enemies. . . . After a great deal of conversation they had me called also about midnight. Entering their cabins, I found them all seated in council . . . they had sent for me to assure me anew of their friendship, which would never be broken . . . and being aware that I had determined to visit their country, they said they would show it to me at the risk of their lives, giving me the assistance of a large number of men who could go anywhere; and that in future we should expect the same treatment from them as they had received from us.

Straight away they brought fifty beaver-skins and four strings of beads (wampum) which they value as we do gold chains, saying that I should share these with my brother, referring to Pont-Gravé, we being present together; and that these presents were sent by other chiefs, who had never seen me; that they desired to continue friends to me. . . . I proposed to them that, inasmuch as they were desirous to have me visit their country, I should petition His Majesty (Louis XIII) to assist us to the extent of forty or fifty men, equipped with what was necessary for the journey, and that I should embark with them on condition that they (themselves) would furnish us with the necessary provisions for the journey . . . that, moreover, if I found the country favorable and fertile, we would make many settlements there whereby we should have communication with one another, by which means we live happily in the future with each other in the fear of God, whom we would make known unto them. They were well pleased with this proposition, and begged me to see to it, saying that they on their part would do all that was possible to bring it about, and that, in regard to provisions, we should be as well supplied as they themselves, assuring me again that they would show me what I desired to see.

XV
The Beginnings of Virginia

In April 1606 the Virginia Company charter united the various groups which had been interested for many years in the prospects of American exploitation and settlement. The London syndicate was backed primarily by the London merchants—it was their wealth and endurance which kept the enterprise alive during the long period of experiment which marked the inception of settlement. One important objective was to try to grow in North America products hitherto obtained from Spain since the ordinary trade, revived after peace had been made in 1604, was proving unprofitable on account of Spanish harassment. Another was to attempt to grow some of the products of the Spanish empire in America from which English traders were still excluded. The shortage of timber in England for iron-smelting, glassmaking and such industrial activities could, it was thought, be made good by exploiting American timber. Jamestown was a Company colony; all the men in it were employees and dependents, subject to laws imposed by the Company until well after 1612. They suffered from Company pressures to produce before they could fully acclimatize themselves, just as they were helped by Company supplies when they were in difficulties. They spent much time looking for profitable mines and a watershed which might open a way to the Pacific. Almost all their agricultural and industrial activities were partial failures: their trade with the Indians provided little more than a contribution to their food supplies.

Not until well after 1612 did tobacco provide an economic reason for the continuance of settlement; nor did settlers until some years later have any stake in Virginia's land or any means of collective self-expression. Virginia received, unlike Florida, no direct subvention from the state: it was not a military garrison. Yet the continuance of the colony, in face of Spanish threats, became a matter of prestige, and King James found means of stimulating the Company to greater efforts. The loss of settlers by disease was heavy both before and after 1612. Several times, total abandonment of the colony was avoided only by the chance arrival of reinforcements or supplies. Tenacity amongst the leadership and rank and file alike, together with determination to succeed on the part of the Company, kept the Jamestown settlers going. By 1612 they hoped they had come to stay.

C. M. Andrews, The Colonial Period of American History, I (1934), contains an admirable account of the Virginia settlement. Alexander Brown, The Genesis of the United States (2 vols., 1890, reprinted 1964), is an essential book of reference. Philip M. Barbour, The Three Worlds of John Smith (1964), is a good life of Virginia's most important explorer. John Smith's Works, edited by E. Arber (2 vols., 1907), and Philip M. Barbour's The Jamestown Voyages, 1606–1609 (2 vols., 1969) (with edited versions of the documents to 1609), with William Strachey, The History of Travell into Virginia Britania, ed. Louis B. Wright and V. Freund (1953), make up the major documentation of the Company, 1606–12.

73. George Percy Reports
on the First Landing and the Selection
of the Site of Jamestown,
1607

TOLD TO select a site well inland, up a navigable river, Captain Christopher Newport took the Susan Constant and her two consorts across the lower part of Chesapeake Bay and up the James River in the early days of May 1607. The choice of Jamestown Island as a site for the first settlement was partly due to its combination of isolation from and accessibility to the mainland, but largely because there was deep water nearby, the ships being able to tie up to trees on shore (this choice of a riverbank into which the current was cutting involved the later erosion of the whole site). Purchas printed selections from Percy's "A discourse of the Plantation of the southern colony in Virginia" in his Hakluytus Posthumus, or Purchas his pilgrimes, IV, 1685–1690; an edited text is in Barbour's The Jamestown Voyages; a modernized text, George Percy, Observations Gathered out of "A Discourse of the Plantation of the Southern Colony in Virginia by the English, 1606," was edited by D. B. Quinn (1967).

The six and twentieth day of Aprill, about foure a clocke in the morning, wee descried the Land of Virginia: the same day wee entred into the Bay of Chesupioc directly, without any let or hinderance; there wee landed and discovered a little way, but wee could find nothing worth the speaking of, but faire meddowes and goodly tall Trees, with such Fresh-waters running through the woods, as I was almost ravished at the first sight thereof. . . .

The eighteenth [correctly the 28th] we lanched our Shallop, the Captaine [Christopher Newport] and some Gentlemen went in her, and discovered up the Bay. . . . Wee rowed over to a point of Land, where wee found a channell, and sounded six, eight, ten, or twelve fathom: which put us in good comfort. Therefore wee named that point of Land, Cape Comfort.

The nine and twentieth day we set up a Crosse at Chesupioc Bay, and named that place Cape Henry. Thirtieth day, we came with our ships to Cape Comfort. . . .

When we came over to the other side, there was a many of other Savages which directed us to their Towne, where we were entertained by them very kindly. . . .

The fourth day of May, we came to the King or Werowance of Paspihe: where they entertained us with much welcome. . . .

The eight day of May we discovered up the River. We landed in the Countrey of Apamatica, at our landing, there came many stout and able Savages to resist us with their Bowes and Arrowes, in a most warlike manner, with the swords at their backes beset with sharpe stones, and pieces of yron able to cleave a man in sunder. Amongst the rest, one of the chiefest standing before them crosse-legged, with his Arrow readie in his Bow in one hand, and taking a Pipe of Tobacco in the other, with a bold uttering of his speech, demanded of us our being there, willing us to bee gone. Wee made signes of peace, which they perceived in the end, and let us land in quietnesse.

The twelfth day we went backe to our ships, and discovered a point of Land, called Archers Hope, which was sufficient with a little labour to defend our selves against any Enemy. The soile was good and fruitfull, with excellent good Timber. . . .

The thirteenth day, we came to our seating place in Paspihas Countrey, some eight miles from the point of Land, which I made mention before: where our shippes doe lie so neere the shoare that they are moored to the Trees in six fathom water.

The fourteenth day we landed all our men which were set to worke about the fortification, and others some to watch and ward as it was convenient. . . .

This River which wee have discovered is one of the famousest Rivers that ever was found by any Christian, it ebbes and flowes a hundred and threescore miles where ships of great burthen may harbour in safetie.

74. Powhatan Is Made
an English Subject,
1608

IN THE months between May 1607 and the return of Newport with supplies in January 1608, there had been a good deal of hardship suffered by the colonists. Many had died of disease or malnutrition. There had been dissensions amongst the leadership. Captain John Smith had begun to establish himself as the explorer of the colony, pushing out to find the upper reaches of the Chickahominy River, getting captured and brought prisoner to Powhatan in December and being released in time to greet Newport's arrival, which was shortly followed by the accidental burning down of the greater part of the first settlement at Jamestown. Newport had orders to reconcile Powhatan, the despotic head of the Powhatan confederacy, to the colony. Extract A shows how he did so. When he came out again in September 1608, he had orders to enroll Powhatan (Extract B), as an honorary Englishman, decking him out as a sub-king of King James. Captain John Smith relates (in extracts from A map of Virginia. With a description of the countrey [1612], pp. 16–20, 46) these ceremonies of which he thoroughly disapproved, since he felt that the settlers would pay for any concessions to Powhatan's not unnatural claims to remain ruler of his own territories in spite of the English invasion.

A

But Captaine Newport got in, and arived at James towne [January 8, 1608], not long after the redemption of Captaine Smith. . . . Now the arrivall of this first supply, so overjoyed us, that we could not devise too much to please the mariners. We gave them liberty to truck or trade at their pleasures. But in a short time, it followed that could not be had for a pound of copper, which before was sold for an ounce. Thus ambition, and sufferance cut the throat of our trade, but confirmed their opinion of Newports greatnes, (wherewith Smith had possessed Powhatan) especially by the great presents Newport often sent him, before he could prepare the Pinas to go and visit him, so that this Salvage also desired to see him. A great bruit there was to set him forwarde: when he went he was accompanied, with captaine Smith & Maister Scrivener a very wise understanding gentleman newly arrived & admitted of the Councell, & 30. or 40. chosen men for that guarde. Arriving at Werowocomo, Newports conceipt of this great Salvage, bred many doubts and suspitions of treacheries; which Smith, to make appeare was needlesse, with 20. men well appointed, undertooke to encounter (with that number) the worst that could happen. . . . These being kindly received a shore, with 2. or 300. Salvages were conducted to their towne; Powhatan strained himselfe to the uttermost of his greatnes to entertain us, with great shouts of Joy, orations of protestations, and the most plenty of victual hee could provide to feast us. Sitting upon his bed of mats, his pillow of leather imbroydred (after their rude manner) with pearle & white beades, his attire a faire Robe of skins as large as an Irish mantle, at his head and feet a handsome young woman; on each side his house sate 20. of his concubines, their heads and shoulders painted red, with a great chaine of white beads about their necks, before those, sate his chiefest men in like order in his arbor-like house. With many pretty discourses to renue their olde acquaintaunce; the great kinge and our captaine spent the time till the ebbe left our Barge a ground, then renuing their feasts and mirth we quartred that night with Powhatan: the next day Newport came a shore, and received as much content as those people could give him, a boy named Thomas Savage was then given unto Powhatan who Newport called his son, for whom Powhatan gave him Namontacke his trusty servant, and one of a shrewd subtill capacity, 3. or 4. daies were spent in feasting, dancing, and trading, wherein Powhatan carried himselfe so prowdly, yet discreetly (in his Salvage manner) as made us all admire his natural gifts considering his education, as scorning to trade as his subjects did, he bespake Newport in this manner.

Captain Newport it is not agreeable with my greatnes in this pedling manner to trade for trifles, and I esteeme you a great werowans, Therefore lay me down all your commodities togither, what I like I will take, and in recompence give you that I thinke fitting their value. Captaine Smith being our interpreter, regarding Newport as his father, knowing best the disposition of Powhatan told us his intent was but to cheat us; yet captaine Newport thought to out brave this Salvage in ostentation of greatnes, & so to bewitch him with his bounty, as to have what he listed, but so it chanced Powhatan having his desire, valued his corne at such a rate, as I thinke it better cheape in Spaine, for we had not 4. bushels for that we expected 20. hogsheads. This bred some unkindnes betweene our two captaines, Newport seeking to please the humor of the unsatiable Salvage; Smith to cause the Salvage to please him, but smothering his distast (to avoide the Salvages suspition) glaunced in the eies of Powhatan many Trifles who fixed his humour upon a few blew beads; A long time he importunatly desired them, but Smith seemed so much the more to affect them, so that ere we departed, for a pound or two of blew beads he brought over my king for 2 or 300 bushels of corne, yet parted good friends. The like entertainement we found of Opechanchynough, king of Pamaunke whom also he in like manner fitted, (at the like rates) with blew beads so we returned to the fort [March 9, 1608].

B.

Captaine Newport sent his presents by water which is neare 100 miles, with 50 of the best shot, himselfe went by land which is but 12 miles, where he met with our 3 barges to transport him over. All things being fit for the day of his coronation, the presents were brought, his bason, ewer, bed and furniture set up, his scarlet cloake and apparel (with much adoe) put on him (being persuaded by Namontacke they would doe him no hurt.) But a fowle trouble there was to make hime kneele, to receave his crowne, he neither knowing the majestie, nor meaning of a Crowne, nor bending of the knee indured so many persuasions, examples, and instructions, as tired them all. At last by leaning hard on his shoulders, he a little stooped, and Newport put the Crowne on his head. When by the warning of a pistol, the boates were prepared with such a volly of shot, that the king start[ed] up in a horrible fear, till he see all was well, then remembering himselfe, to congratulate their kindnesse, he gave his old shoes and his mantle to Captain Newoprt.

75. Captain John Smith
Explores the Head of Chesapeake Bay,
1608

IN JUNE 1608 *Captain John Smith had set out to explore Chesapeake Bay north of the York River. His greatest hopes had been raised by the Potomac River as a possible channel into the interior (the James having ceased to be of value for this purpose above the Fall Line at modern Richmond); but the river failed him, turning beyond the site of modern Washington into a shallow, rapid-ridden stream. He was unable to complete his exploration on the first occasion and the extracts given below (from A map of Virginia. With a description of the countrey, pp. 37–40), record his completion of his survey at the northern end of the Bay. His interest in exploring continuing channels into the country is seen by his penetration of the Susquehanna River in order to meet Iroquois tribesmen from whom he learned that he had reached an Amerindian group which was in contact with the French. In the same year Samuel de Champlain learned that by way of Lake Champlain he could eventually make contact with "Florida," or, more accurately, Virginia. The year 1608 thus sees overlapping spheres of commerce and interest already developing between the European intruders. The Spaniards in Florida also were able to get vague reports of English activities on Chesapeake Bay, reaching them through intertribal contacts in the Southeast.*

What happened the second voyage to discover the Bay.

The 20. of July Captaine Smith set forward to finish the discovery with 12. men. . . .

The winde beeing contrary, caused our stay 2 or 3 daies at Kecoughtan the werowans feasting us with much mirth, his people were perswaded we went purposely to be revenged of the Massawomeckes, in the evening we firing 2. or 3. rackets [rockets], so terrified the poore Salvages, they supposed nothing impossible wee attempted, and desired to assist us. The first night we anchored at Stingeray Ile, the next day crossed Patawomecks river, and hasted for the river Bolus, wee went not much farther, before wee might perceive the Bay to devide in 2. heads, and arriving there we founde it devided in 4, all of which we searched so far as we could saile them; 2. of them wee found uninhabited, but in crossing the bay to the other, wee incountered 7. or 8. Canowes-full of Massa-womecks; we seeing them prepare to assault us, left our oares, & made way with our saile to incounter them, yet were we but five (with our captaine) could stand; for within 2. daies after wee left Kecoughtan, the rest (being all of the last supply) were sicke almost to death, (untill they were seasoned to the country) having shut them under our tarpawling, we put their hats upon stickes by the barge side, to make us seeme many, and so we thinke the Indians supposed those hats to be men, for they fled withall pos-sible speed to the shoare, and there stayed, staring at the sailing of our barge, till we anchored right against them. Long it was ere we could drawe them to come unto us, at last they sent 2 of their company unarmed in a Canowe, the rest all followed to second them, if need required; These 2 being but each presented with a bell, brought aborde all their fellowes, presenting the captain with venison, beares flesh, fish, bowes, arrows, clubs, targets, and beare-skins; wee understood them nothing at all but by signes, whereby they signified unto us they had been at warres with the Tockwoghs the which they confirmed by shewing their green wounds; but the night parting us, we imagined they appointed the next morning to meete, but after that we never saw them.

Entring the River of Tockwogh [Sassafras River] the Salvages all armed in a fleete of Boates round invironed us; it chanced one of them could speake the language of Powhatan, who perswaded the rest to a friendly parly: but when they see us furnished with the Massawomeckes weapons, and we faining the invention of Ke-coughtan to have taken them perforce; they conducted us to their pallizadoed towne, mantelled with the barkes of trees, with Scaffolds like mounts, brested about with Barks very formally, their men, women, and children, with dances, songs, fruits, fish, furres, & what they had kindly entertained us, spreading mats for us to sit on, stretching their best abilities to expresse their loves.

Many hatchets, knives, and peeces of yron, & brasse, we see, which they reported to have from the Sasquesahanockes a mighty people, and mortall enimies with the Massawomeckes; The Sasquesahanocks, inhabit upon the chiefe spring of these 4. two daies journey higher then our Barge could passe for rocks. Yet we prevailed with the interpreter to take with him an other interpreter to perswade the Sasquesahanocks to come to visit us, for their language are different: 3. or 4. daies we expected their return then 60. of these giantlike-people came downe, with presents of venison, Tobacco pipes, Baskets, Targets, Bowes and Arrows, 5 of their Werowances came boldly abord us, to crosse the bay for Tockwogh, leaving their men and Canowes, the winde being so violent that they durst not passe.

Our order was, dayly, to have prayer, with a psalm, at which solemnitie the poore Salvages much wondered: our prayers being done, they were long busied with consultation till they had contrived their businesse; then they began in most passionate manner to hold up their hands to the sunne with a most fearefull song, then imbracing the Captaine, they began to adore him in like manner, though he rebuked them, yet they proceeded til their song was finished, which don, with a most strange furious action, and a hellish voice began an oration of their loves; that ended, with a great painted beares skin they covered our Captaine, then one ready with a chaine of white beads (waighing at least 6 or 7 pound) hung it about his necke, the others had 18 mantles made of divers sorts of skinnes sowed together, all these with many other toyes, they laid at his feet, stroking their ceremonious handes about his necke for his creation to be their governour, promising their aids, victuals, or what they had to bee his, if he would stay with them to defend and revenge them of the Massawomecks; But wee left them at Tockwogh, they much sorrowing for our departure, yet wee promised the next yeare againe to visit them; many descriptions and discourses they made us of Atquanahucke, Massawomecke, and other people, signifying they inhabit the river of Cannida, and from the French to have their hatchets and such like tooles by trade, these knowe no more of the territories of Powhatan then his name, and he as little of them.

Thus having sought all the inlets and rivers worth noting, we returned to discover the river of Pawtuxunt, these people we found very tractable, and more civill then any, wee promised them, as also

the Patawomecks, the next yeare to revenge them of the Massa-womecks. Our purposes were crossed in the discoverie of the river of Toppahannock [Rappahannock], for wee had much wrangling with that peevish nation; but at last, they became as tractable as the rest. It is an excellent, pleasant, well inhabited, fertill, and a goodly navigable river, toward the head thereof; it pleased God to take one of our sicke (called Maister Fetherstone), where in Fetherstons bay we buried him in the night, with a volly of shot; the rest (notwithstanding their ill diet, and bad lodging, crowded in so small a barge in so many dangers, never resting but alwaies tossed to and againe) al well recovered their healthes; then we discovered the river of Payankatank, and set saile for James Towne; but in crossing the bay in a faire calme. such a suddaine gust surprised us in the night with thunder and raine, as wee were halfe imployed in freeing out water, never thinking to escape drowning yet running before the winde, at last we made land by the flashes of fire from heaven, by which light only we kept from the splitting shore, until it pleased God in that black darknes to preserve us by that light to find Point comfort, and arived safe at James Towne, the 7 of September, 1608. where wee found Master Skrivener and diverse others well recovered, many dead, some sicke. The late President prisoner for muteny, by the honest diligence of Master Skrivener the harvest gathered, but the stores, provision, much spoiled with raine.

76. Jamestown in
1610

JAMESTOWN WAS REBUILT in 1608 after its burning, and was enlarged when an access of settlers reached it in 1609. Many of those on the great expedition of 1609 were shipwrecked on the Bermudas and made their way to Jamestown, in vessels of their own construction, only in 1610. The arrivals of 1609 and the refugees of 1610 together found the colony impossible to run and were about to abandon it to the Indians when Lord De La Warr arrived as governor with plentiful supplies in June and reestablished them and his reinforcements in Jamestown. William Strachey, who had been in Bermuda, was made secretary of the colony, and when things had got under way he wrote to a lady in England (thought to be Lady Sara Smith, wife of the treasurer of the Company, Sir Thomas Smith) an account of his adventures, "A true reportory of the wracke, and redemption of Sir Thomas Gates Knight; upon, and from the Ilands of the Bermudas: his coming to Virginia, and the estate of that Colonie then, and after under the government of the Lord La Warre," published in Purchas, Hakluytus Posthumus, or Purchas his pilgrimes, IV, 1735–1756. It records a vivid description of a Jamestown that was (on July 15, 1610) finally emerging as an English town in North America. A modernized text was edited by Louis B. Wright, in A Voyage to Virginia in 1609 (1964). A good life of Strachey is S. G. Culliford, William Strachey (1966).

Here (worthy Lady) let mee have a little your pardon, for having now a better heart, then when I first landed, I will briefely describe unto you, the situation and forme of our Fort. When Captain Newport in his first Voyage, did not like to inhabit upon so open a roade, as Cape Henry, nor Point Comfort he plied it up to the River, still looking out for the most apt and securest place, as well for his Company to sit downe in, as which might give the least cause of offence, or distast in his judgement, to the Inhabitants. At length, after much and weary search (with their Barge coasting still before, as Virgill writeth Aeneas did, arriving in the region of Italy called Latium, upon the bankes of the River Tyber) in the Country of a Werowance called Wowinchapuncke (a ditionary [one under dominion] to Powhatan) within this faire River of Paspiheigh, which wee have called the Kings River, a Country least inhabited by the Indian, as they all the way observed, and threescore miles & better up the fresh Channell, from Cape Henry they had sight of an extended plaine & spot of earth, which thrust out into the depth, & middest of the channell, making a kinde of Chersonesus or Peninsula, for it was fastened onely to the Land with a slender necke, no broader then a man may well quaite a tile shard, & no inhabitants by seven or six miles neere it. The Trumpets sounding, the Admirall strooke saile, and before the same, the rest of the Fleete came to an ancor, and here (as the best yet offered unto their view, supposed so much the more convenient, by how much with their small Company, they were like inough the better to assure it) to loose no further time, the Colony disimbarked, and every man brought his particular store and furniture, together with the generall provision ashoare: for the safety of which, as likewise for their owne security, ease, and better accommodating, a certaine Canton and quantity of that little halfe Iland of ground, was measured, which they began to fortifie, and thereon in the name of God, to raise a Fortresse, with the ablest and speediest meanes they could: which Fort, growing since to more perfection, is now at this present in this manner.

A low levell of ground about halfe an Acre, or (so much as Queene Dido might buy of King Hyarbas, which she compassed about with the thongs cut out of one Bull hide, and therein built her Castle of Byzra) on the North side of the River, is cast almost into the forme of a Triangle, and so Pallizadoed. The South side next the River (howbeit extended in a line, or Curtaine six score foote more in length, then the other two, by reason the advantage of the ground doth so require) containes one hundred and forty yards: the West and East sides a hundred onely. At every Angle or corner, where the lines meete, a Bulwarke or Watchtower is raised, and in each Bulwarke a peece of Ordnance or two well mounted. To every side, a proportioned distance from the Pallisado, is a setled streete of houses, that runs along, so as each line of the Angle hath his streete. In the middest is a market place, a Store house, and a Corps du guard, as likewise a pretty Chappell, though (at this time when wee came in) as ruined and unfrequented: but the Lord Governour, and Captaine Generall, hath given order for the repairing of it, and at this instant, many hands are about it. It is in length threescore foote, in breadth twenty foure, and shall have a Chancell in it of Cedar, and a Communion Table of the Blake Walnut, and all the Pewes of Cedar, with faire broad windowes, to shut and open, as the weather shall occasion, of the same wood, a Pulpet of the same, with a Font hewen hollow, like a Canoa, with two Bels at the West end. It is so cast, as it be very light within, and the Lord Governour and Captaine Generall doth cause it to be kept passing sweete, and trimmed up with divers flowers, with a Sexton belonging to it, and in it every Sonday wee have sermons twice a day, and every Thursday a Sermon, having true preachers, which take their weekely turnes, and every morning at the ringing of a Bell, about ten of the clocke, each man addresseth himselfe to prayers, and so at foure of the clocke before Supper. Every Sunday,

when the Lord Governour, and Captaine Generall goeth to
Church, hee is accompanied with all the Counsailers, Captaines,
other Officers, and all the Gentlemen, and with a guard of Hol-
berdiers in his Lordships Livery, faire red cloakes to the number of
fifty, both on each side, and behinde him: and being in the
Church, his Lordship hath his seate in the Quier, in a greene
Velvet Chaire, with a Cloath, with a Velvet Cushion spread on a
Table before him, on which he kneeleth, and on each side sit the
Counsell, Captaines, and Officers, each in their place, and when he
returneth home againe, he is waited on to his house in the same
manner.

And thus inclosed, as I said, round with a Pallizado of Planckes
and strong Posts, foure foote deepe in the ground, of yong Oakes,
Walnuts, &c. The Fort is called in honour of his Majesties name,
James Towne; the principall Gate from the Towne, through the
Pallizado, opens to the River, as at each Bulwarke there is a Gate
likewise to goe forth, and at every Gate a Demi-Culverin, and so in
the Market Place. The houses first raised, were all burnt by a
casualty of fire, the beginning of the second yeare of their seate,
and in the second Voyage of Captain Newport, which since have
bin better rebuilded, though as yet in no great uniformity, either
for the fashion, or beauty of the streete. A delicate wrought fine
kinde of Mat the Indians make, with which (as they can be
trucked for, or snatched up) our people do dresse their chambers,
and inward roomes, which make their houses so much the more
handsome. The houses have wide and large Country Chimnies in
the which is to be supposed (in much plenty of wood) what fires
are maintained; and they have found the way to cover their houses:
now (as the Indians) with barkes of Trees, as durable, and as good
proofe against stormes, and winter weather, as the best Tyle de-
fending likewise the piercing Sunbeames of Summer, and keeping
the inner lodgings coole enough, which before in sultry weather
would be like Stoves, whilest they were, as at first, pargetted and
plaistered with Bitumen or tough Clay: and thus armed for the
injury of changing times, and seasons of the yeare, we hold our
selves well apaid, though wanting Arras Hangings, Tapistry, and
guilded Venetian Cordovan, or more spruse household garniture,
and wanton City ornaments, remembring the old Epigraph:

We dwell not here to build us Bowers,
And Hals for pleasure and good cheere:
But Hals we build for us and ours,
To dwell in them whilst we live here.

True it is, I may not excuse this our Fort, or James Towne,
as yet seated in some what an unwholesome and sickly ayre,
by reason it is in a marish ground, low, flat to the River, and
hath no fresh water Springs serving the Towne, but what wee drew
from a Well sixe or seven fathom deepe, fed by the brackish River
owzing into it, from whence I verily beleeve, the chiefe causes have
proceeded of many diseases and sicknesses which have happened to
our people, who are indccdc strangely afflicted with Fluxes and
Agues; and every particular season (by the relation of the old
inhabitants) hath his particular infirmity too, all of which (if it
had bin our fortunes, to have seated upon some hill, accommodated with fresh Springs and cleere ayre, as doe the Natives of
the Country) we might have, I beleeve, well escaped: and some
experience we have to perswade our selves that it may be so, for of
foure hundred and odde men, which were seated at the Fals, the
last yeere when the Fleete came in with fresh and yong able spirits,
under the government of Captain Francis West, and of one hundred to the Seawards (on the South side of our River) in the
Country of the Nansamundes, under the charge of Captaine John
Martin, there did not so much as one man miscarry, and but very
few or none fall sicke, whereas at James Towne, the same time, and
the same moneths, one hundred sickned, & halfe the number died:
howbeit, as we condemne not Kent in England, for a small Towne
called Plumsted, continually assaulting the dwellers there (especially new commers) with Agues and Fevers; no more let us lay
scandall, and imputation upon the Country of Virginia, because
the little Quarter wherein we are set downe (unadvisedly so
chosed) appeares to be unwholesome, and subject to many ill
ayres, which accompany the like marish places.

Bibliography

Books Mentioned in the Text and a Few General Works

Acts of the Privy Council, 1597. London, 1897.

Adam of Bremen. *History of the Archbishops of Hamburg-Bremen.* Translated by Francis T. Tschan. New York, 1959.

Ailly, Pierre d'. *Ymago Mundi.* Edited by Edmond Buron. 3 vols. Paris, 1930.

Alguns Documentos da Torre de Tombo. Lisbon, 1891.

Anderson, R., and R. C. Anderson. *The Sailing Ship.* New York, 1963.

Andrews, Charles M. *The Colonial Period of American History.* Volume I. New Haven, Conn., 1934.

Andrews, Kenneth R. *Elizabethan Privateering.* Cambridge, 1965.

Aristotle. *Works.* Edited by W. D. Ross. Volume II. Oxford, 1930.

Arnade, C. W. *Florida on Trial, 1593–1602.* Coral Gables, Fla., 1959.

Asher, George M., ed. *Henry Hudson the Navigator.* Hakluyt Society, London, 1860.

Babcock, W. H. *Legendary Islands in the Atlantic.* New York, 1922.

Barbour, Philip L., ed., *The Jamestown Voyages, 1606–1609.* 2 vols. Hakluyt Society, Cambridge, 1969.

———. *The Three Worlds of John Smith.* New York, 1964.

Barrientos, Bartolomé. *The Life of Pedro Menéndez de Avilés.* Edited by Anthony Kerrigan, Gainesville, Fla., 1965.

Berrill, N. J. *The Living Tide.* New York, 1951.

Best, George. *A true discourse of the late voyages of discoverie, for the finding of a passage to Cathaya, by the Northwest, under the conduct of Martin Frobisher.* London, 1578.

Biggar, H. P. "An English Expedition to America," *Mélanges offert à M. Charles Bémont* (Paris, 1913), 254–261.

———. "Jean Ribaut's 'Discoverye of Terra Florida'," *English Historical Review*, XXX (1917), 253–270.

———. *The Precursors of Jacques Cartier, 1496–1534.* Canadian Archives Publications. Ottawa, 1911.

Bigges, Walter [etc.]. *A summarie and true discourse of Sir Frances Drakes West Indian voyage.* London, 1589.

Bishop, Morris. *Champlain*. New York, 1948.

———. *The Odyssey of Cabeza de Vaca*. New York, 1933.

Bolton, Charles K. *The Real Founders of New England*. Boston, 1929.

Bolton, Herbert E. *Coronado, Knight of Pueblos and Plains*. New York and Albuquerque, N.M., 1949.

———. *The Spanish Borderlands*. New Haven, Conn., 1921.

Bourne, Edward G., ed. *Narratives of the Career of Hernando de Soto*. 2 vols. New York, 1904.

Brebner, J. B. *The Explorers of North America, 1492–1806*. London, 1933.

Brereton, John. *A briefe and true relation of the discoverie of the north part of Virginia*. London, 1602.

Bridenbaugh, Carl. *Vexed and Troubled Englishmen, 1590–1642*. New York, 1968.

Brown, Alexander. *The Genesis of the United States*. 2 vols. New York, 1890. Reprinted in 1964.

Bry, Theodor de. *America*. part i, 1590; part ii, 1591. Frankfurt am Main.

Burrage, Henry S. *The Beginnings of Colonial Maine*. Portland, Me., 1914.

———, ed. *Early English and French Voyages, 1534–1608*. New York, 1906.

Calendar of State Papers, Milan. Edited by A. B. Hinds. Volume I. London, 1912.

Cambridge History of the British Empire, The. Volume I. 1929; Volume VI, 1950. Cambridge.

Carpenter, Nathaniel. *Geography delineated*. London, 1634.

Cartier, Jacques. *Brief recit . . . de la navigation faict es ysles du Canada, Hochelage & Saguenay*. Paris, 1545.

———. *A short and briefe narration of the two navigations . . . to Newe France*. Translated by John Florio. London, 1580. Facsimile in D. B. Quinn, *Richard Hakluyt, Editor* (1967).

———. *The Voyages*. Edited by H. P. Biggar. Canadian Archives Publications. Ottawa, 1924.

Carus-Wilson, Eleanora M. *The Overseas Trade of Bristol in the Later Middle Ages*. Bristol Record Society. Bristol, 1937.

Casas, Bartolomé de las. *Obras Escogidas*. Edited by Juan Perez de Tudela. 5 vols. Madrid, 1957–58.

Cell, Gillian T. *The English in Newfoundland, 1580–1660*. Toronto, 1970.

Champlain, Samuel. *Les Sauvages*. Paris, 1603.

———. *Les Voyages*. Paris, 1613.

———. Les Voyages de Nouvelle France occidentale dicte Canada. Paris, 1632.

———. Works. Edited by H. P. Biggar. Champlain Society. Toronto. 7 vols. 1922–36.

———. Voyages. Edited by Edmund F. Slafter. Prince Society, Boston. 3 vols. 1878–82.

———. The Voyages and Explorations of Samuel de Champlain. Edited by E. G. Bourne. 2 vols. New York, 1906.

———. Voyages de Samuel Champlain. Edited by Hubert Deschamps. Paris, 1951.

———. Voyages of Samuel de Champlain. Edited by W. L. Grant. New York, 1907.

Chapin, Henry, and F. G. Walton Smith. The Ocean River. New York, 1952.

Childs, St. Julian R. Malaria and Colonization in the Carolina Low Countries, 1528–1596. Baltimore, 1940.

Collinson, Richard, ed. The Three Voyages of Martin Frobisher. Hakluyt Society. London, 1867.

Colón, Fernando. The Life of the Admiral Christopher Columbus. Translated by Benjamin Keen. New Brunswick, N. J., 1959.

Connor, Jeanette T. Colonial Records of Spanish Florida, 1577–1580. 2 vols. De Land, Fla., 1925–30.

Craven, Wesley F. The Southern Colonies in the Seventeenth Century. Baton Rouge, La., 1949.

Crinò, Sebastiano. Come fuscoperta l'America. Milan, 1943.

Crone, Gerald H. Maps and Their Makers. London, 1953.

Culliford, Samuel G. William Strachey. Charlottesville, Va., 1966.

Cumming, William P. "The Parreus Map (1562) of French Florida," Imago Mundi, XVII (1963), 27–40.

Cummings, W. P., Skelton, R. A., and Quinn, D. B. The Discovery of North America. London, 1971.

———. The Southeast in Early Maps. Princeton, N.J., 1958.

Diaz del Castillo, Bernal. The True History of the Conquest of New Spain. 5 vols. Hakluyt Society. London, 1908–16.

Davis, John. The worldes hydrographical discription. London, 1595.

———. The Voyages and Works. Edited by A. H. Markham. Hakluyt Society. London, 1878.

Day, A. G. Coronado's Quest. Berkeley and Los Angeles, Calif., 1940.

Dodge, Ernest S. Northwest by Sea. New York, 1961.

Elvas, Gentleman of. True Relation of the Hardships suffered by Governor Fernando de Soto . . . during the Discovery of the

Province of Florida. Edited by J. A. Robertson. 2 vols. De Land, Fla., 1933.

——. *Virginia richly valued*. London, 1609.

Fernandez de Navarrete, M. *Obras*. 3 vols. Madrid, 1964.

Fernández de Oviedo, Gonzalo. *Historia General y Natural de las Indias*. 5 vols. Madrid, 1959.

Galvão, Antonio. *The discoveries of the world*. Translated by Richard Hakluyt.

——. *The Discoveries of the World*. Edited by C. R. D. Bethune. Hakluyt Society. London, 1862.

Ganong, W. F. *Crucial Maps in the Early Cartography and Place Nomenclature of the Atlantic Coast of Canada*. Ottawa, 1964.

García, Genero. *Dos Antiquos Relaciones de la Florida*. Mexico, 1902.

Geiger, Maynard. *The Franciscan Conquest of Florida, 1573–1618*. Washington, D.C., 1938.

Gibson, Charles. *Spain in America*. New York, 1966.

Gilbert, Sir Humphrey. *A discourse of a discoverie for a new passage to Cataia*. London, 1576.

Gookin, Warner F., and Philip M. Barbour. *Bartholomew Gosnold*. Hamden, Conn., 1963.

Hakluyt, Richard. *Divers voyages touching the discoverie of America*. London, 1582. Facsimile in D. B. Quinn, *Richard Hakluyt, Editor*. London, 1967.

——. *The principall navigations*. London, 1589.

——. *The principal navigations*. 3 vols. London, 1598–1600.

——. *The Principal Navigations*. 12 vols. Glasgow, 1903–1904.

——. *The Principall Navigations, 1589*. Edited by D. B. Quinn and R. A. Skelton. 2 vols. Hakluyt Society. Cambridge, 1965.

Hallenbeck, Cleve. *Journey and Route of Cabeza de Vaca*. Glendale, N.Y., 1940.

Hammond, George P., and Agapito Rey. *Don Juan de Oñate Colonizer of New Mexico, 1595–1628*. 2 vols. Albuquerque, N.M., 1955.

——. *Narratives of the Coronado Expeditions, 1540–1542*. Albuquerque, N.M., 1940.

——. *The Rediscovery of New Mexico, 1580–1594*. Albuquerque, N.M., 1966.

Harrisse, Henry. *La découverte et évolution cartographique de Terre Neuve*. Paris, 1900.

——. *The Discovery of North America*. London, 1892.

Hay, John, and Peter Farb. *The Atlantic Shore*. New York, 1966.

Hennig, Richard. *Terrae Incognitae*. 2nd ed., 4 vols. Leiden, 1944–56.

Hermannson, Halldór. *The Vinland Sagas*. Ithaca, N.Y., 1944.

Hodge, Frederick W., and T. H. Lewis. *Spanish Explorers in the Southern United States, 1528–1543*. New York, 1907.

Hoffman, Bernard A. *Cabot to Cartier*. Toronto, 1961.

Horgan, Paul. *Conquistadors in North American History*. New York, 1963.

Howe, Henry F. *Prologue to New England*. New York, 1943.

Ingstad, Helge. *Land Under the Pole Star*. London, 1966.

———. "The Norse Discovery of Newfoundland," *The Book of Newfoundland*. Edited by Joseph R. Smallwood. Volume III. St. John's, Newfoundland, 1967, pp. 218–224.

———. *Western Way to Vinland*. New York, 1969.

Innis, Harold A. *The Cod Fisheries*. New Haven, Conn., 1940.

Jameson, J. F. *Narratives of New Netherland, 1609–1664*. New York, 1909.

Jones, Gwyn. *The Norse Atlantic Saga*. London, 1965.

———. *The Vikings*. London, 1968.

Juet, Robert. *Juet's Journal*. Edited by Ronart M. Lunny. Newark, N.J., 1959.

Julien, Charles André. *Les Voyages de Découverte et les Premiers Établissements*. Paris, 1946.

Kimble, George H. T. *Geography in the Middle Ages*. London, 1938.

Laet, Jan de. *Niewe Wereldt*. Leiden, 1625.

Langdon, G. D. *Pilgrim Colony*. New Haven, Conn., 1966.

Laudonnière, René de. *L'Historie notable de la Floride*. Paris, 1586.

———. *A notable historie containing foure voyages . . . into Florida*. London, 1587.

———. *A Notable Historie*. Facsimile with introduction by Thomas R. Adams. Farnham, Surrey, 1964.

Lescarbot, Marc. *Histoire de la Nouvelle France*. Paris, 1609.

———. *Nova Francia*. Translated by Pierre Erondelle. London, 1609.

———. *Nova Francia*. Edited by H. P. Biggar. London, 1928.

———. *Works*. Edited by W. L. Grant. 3 vols. Champlain Society. Toronto, 1907–14.

Levermore, Charles H. *Forerunners and Competitors of the Pilgrims and Puritans*. 2 vols. Brooklyn, N.Y., 1912.

Lewis, Clifford M., and Albert J. Loomie. *The Spanish Jesuit Mission in Virginia, 1570–1572*. Chapel Hill, N.C., 1953.

López de Gómara, Francisco. *Historia General de las Indias*. 2 vols. Madrid, 1932.

Lowery, Woodbury. *The Spanish Settlements Within the Present Limits of the United States, 1513–1574*. 2 vols. New York, 1901–11.

Lussagnet, Susanne. *Les Français en Amérique pendant la deuxième moitié du XVIᵉ Siècle. Les Français en Floride*. Paris, 1958.

Markham, Clements R. *A Life of John Davis*. London, 1891.

Marsh, T. N. "An Unpublished Hakluyt Manuscript," *New England Quarterly*, XXV (1962), 247–252.

Martire, d'Anghiera Pietro. *De Orbe Novo Decades*. Alcalá, 1516.

———. *De Orbe Novo Decades*. Alcalá, 1530.

McCann, Franklin T. *English Discovery of America to 1585*. New York, 1952.

Morandière, M. de la. *Histoire de la Pêche de Morue française à Terre Neuve*. 3 vols. Paris, 1961–66.

Morison, Samuel E. *Christopher Columbus, Admiral of the Ocean Sea*. 2 vols. Boston, 1942.

———. *Christopher Columbus, Mariner*. London, 1956.

———. *Journals and Other Documents on the Life and Voyages of Christopher Columbus*. New York, 1963.

———. *Portuguese Voyages to America in the Fifteenth Century*. Cambridge, Mass., 1940.

Morison, S. E. *The European Discovery of America. The Northern Voyages*. New York, 1971.

Murga Sans, Vicente. *Juan Ponce de León*. San Juan, Puerto Rico, 1959.

Murphy, Henry C. *Henry Hudson in Holland*. Edited by Wouter Nijhoff. The Hague, 1909.

Nansen, Fridtjof. *In Northern Mists*. 2 vols. London, 1911.

Neatby, Leslie H. *In Quest of the North-West Passage*. Toronto, 1958.

Newton, A. P., ed. *The Great Age of Discovery*. London, 1932.

Notestein, Wallace. *The English People on the Eve of Colonization*. New York, 1954.

O'Daniel, V. F. *The Dominicans in Early Florida*. New York, 1930.

Oleson, Tryggvi J. *Early Voyages and Northern Approaches, 1000–1632*. Toronto, 1963.

Oré, Luis Gerónimo de. *Relacion de los Martires que a avido en las Provincias de la Florida*. [Madrid, 1617?].

———. *The Martyrs of Florida, 1513–1616*. Edited by Maynard Geiger. New York, 1936.

Parker, John, ed. *Merchants and Scholars*. Minneapolis Minn., 1965.

Parry, John H. *The Age of Reconnaissance*. London, 1963.

———. *The European Reconnaissance*. New York, 1968.

Penrose, Boies. *Travel and Discovery in the Renaissance*. Cambridge, Mass, 1955.

Percy, George. *Observations Gathered out of "A Discourse of the*

*Plantation of the Southern Colony in Virginia by the English,
1606.*" Edited by D. B. Quinn. Charlottesville, Va. 1967.

Perez Embid, F. *Los Discobrimientos en el Atlántico.* Seville, 1948.

Preston, Richard A. *Gorges of Plymouth Fort.* Toronto, 1953.

Priestley, Herbert I. *The Coming of the White Man, 1492–1848.*
London, 1929.

———. *The Luna Papers, 1559–1561.* 2 vols. De Land, Fla., 1938.

———. *Tristán de Luna.* Glendale, Calif., 1936.

Purchas, Samuel. *Hakluytus Posthumus, or Purchas His Pilgrimes.* 4 vols.
London, 1625.

———. *Hakluytus Posthumus, or Purchas His Pilgrimes.* 20 vols. Glasgow, 1905–06.

Quinn, David B. "The Argument for the English Discovery of America
Between 1480 and 1494," *Geographical Journal,* CXXVII (1961),
277–285.

Quinn, D. B. "Thomas Hariot and the Virginia Voyages of 1602," *William and Mary Quarterly* XXVII (1970), 268–81.

———. " 'Virginia' Indians in the Thames in 1603," *Terrae Incognitae,*
II (1970), 7–14.

Quinn, D. B., and Cheshire, N. C. *The New Foundland of Stephan
Parmenius.* Toronto, 1971.

———. "Edward IV and Exploration," *The Mariner's Mirror,* XXI
(1935), 281–284.

———. "Edward Hayes, Liverpool Colonial Pioneer," *Transactions of
the Historic Society of Lancashire and Cheshire,* CXI (1959),
26–43.

———. "The English and the St. Lawrence, 1580–1602," in Parker, ed.,
Merchants and Scholars, pp. 119–143.

———. "The First Pilgrims," *William and Mary Quarterly,* XXIII
(1966), 359–390.

———. "John Day and Columbus," *Geographical Journal,* CXXXIV
(1967), 203–209.

———. "Martin Pring at Provincetown, 1603?," *New England
Quarterly,* XL (1967), 79–91.

———. *Raleigh and the British Empire.* Revised edition. New York,
1962.

———. *Richard Hakluyt, Editor* (with a facsimile of R. Hakluyt, *Divers
Voyages* [1582], and of J. Cartier, *A Short and Briefe Narration*
[1580]). 2 vols. Amsterdam, 1967.

———, ed. *The Roanoke Voyages, 1584–1590.* 2 vols. Hakluyt Society.
Cambridge, 1955.

————. "The Voyage of Étienne Bellenger to the Maritimes, 1583," *Canadian Historical Review*, XLIII (1962), 328–243.

————, ed. *The Voyages and Colonising Enterprises of Sir Humphrey Gilbert*. 2 vols. Hakluyt Society. London, 1940.

————, and P. G. Foote. "The Vinland Map," *Saga-Book* XVII (1966), 63–89.

————, and P. H. Hulton. *The American Drawings of John White*. 2 vols. London and Chapel Hill, N.C., 1964.

Ramusio, Giovanni Battista. *Navigationi et Viaggi*. 3 vols. Venice, 1550–59.

Ravenstein, Edward G. *Martin Behaim*. London, 1908.

Ribault, Jean. *The whole and true discoverye of Terra Florida*. London, 1563.

————. *The Whole and True Discoverye of Terra Florida*. Edited by Jeanette T. Connor. De Land, Fla., 1927.

Rosier, James. *A true relation of the most prosperous voyage made this present yeere 1605 by Captain George Waymouth, in the discovery of the land of Virginia*. London, 1605.

Ross, Mary. "French Intrusions . . . 1577–1580," *Georgia Historical Quarterly*, VII (1923), 256–269.

Rowse, A. L. *The Elizabethans and America*. London, 1959.

————. *The Expansion of Elizabethan England*. London, 1955.

Ruddock, Alwyn A. "John Day of Bristol," *Geographical Journal*, CXXXIII (1966), 222–233.

Santa Cruz, Alonzo de. *Islario General de Todas las Islas del Mundo*. Edited by Antonio Blasquez. Madrid, 1922.

Skelton, Raleigh A. "English knowledge of the Portuguese Discoveries in the 15th Century," *Congresso International de História dos Discobrimentos, Actas*, II (Lisbon, 1961), 365–374.

————. *Explorers' Maps*. London, 1958.

————, T. E. Marston, and G. D. Painter. *The Vinland Map*. New Haven, Conn., 1965.

Smallwood, Joseph R., ed., *The Book of Newfoundland*. Volume III. St. John's, Newfoundland, 1967.

Smith, John. *A map of Virginia. With a description of the countrey*. Oxford, 1612.

————. *Newes from Virginia*. London, 1608.

Smith, Thomas Buckingham, ed., *Relation of Alvar Nuñez Cabeça de Vaca*. New York, 1871.

Solis de Merás, Gonzalo. *Pedro Menéndez de Avilés*. Edited by Jeanette T. Connor. De Land, Fla., 1923.

Stefansson, Viljalmur, ed. *The Three Voyages of Martin Frobisher.* 2 vols. London, 1938.
————. *Northwest to Fortune.* New York, 1958.
Stevenson, E. L. *The Geography of Claudius Ptolemy.* New York, 1932.
Stokes, I. N. Phelps. *The Iconography of Manhattan Island.* Volume IV. New York, 1922.
Storm, Gustav. *Islandske Annaler indtil 1578.* Christiana, (Oslo), 1888.
Strachey, William. *The History of Travell into Virginia Britania.* Edited by Louis B. Wright and Virginia Freund. Hakluyt Society. London, 1953.
————. *A Voyage to Virginia in 1609.* Edited by Louis B. Wright. Charlottesville, Va., 1964.
Swanton, John R. *The Indians of the Southeastern United States.* Smithsonian Institution, Bureau of American Ethnology, *Bulletin* 137. Washington, D.C., 1946.
Taylor, Eva G. R., ed. *The Original Writings and Correspondence of the Two Richard Hakluyts.* 2 vols. Hakluyt Society. London, 1935.
————. *The Haven-Finding Art.* London, 1956.
————. "The Voyage of Master Hore, 1536," *Geographical Journal,* LXXVII (1933), 469–470.
Teixiera da Mota, A. *Portuguese Navigations in the North Atlantic in the Fifteenth and Sixteenth Centuries.* St. John's, Newfoundland, 1965.
Terrell, John U. *Journey Into Darkness.* New York, 1962.
Thayer, Henry O. *The Sagadahoc Colony.* Portland, Me., 1892.
Thomas, A. H., and I. D. Thornley, eds. *The Great Chronicle of London.* London, 1939.
Trudel, Marcel. *Histoire de la Nouvelle France, 1524–1627.* 2 vols. Montreal, 1963–66.
Tyler, Lyon G. ed., *Narratives of Early Virginia, 1606–1625.* New York, 1907.
United States de Soto Expedition Commission. *Final Report.* Washington, D.C., 1939.
Vásquez de Espinosa, Antonio. *The Compendium and Description of the West Indies.* Translated by C. U. Clark. Smithsonian Institution, *Smithsonian Miscellaneous Collections.* Volume 108. Washington, D.C., 1942.
Vergil, Polydore. *The Anglia Historia of Polydore Vergil.* Edited by Denys Hay. Royal Historical Society. London, 1950.
Verrazzano, Giovanni da. "Giovanni da Verrazzano and His Discoveries in North America 1524," edited by Alessandro Bacchiani

and Edward H. Hall. *American Scenic and Historic Preservation Society, Fifteenth Annual Report*. Albany, N.Y., 1910, pp. 135–226.

Vignaud, Henri. *Toscanelli and Columbus*. London, 1902.

Vigneras, Louis André. "New Light on the 1497 Cabot Voyage," *Hispanic-American Historical Review*, XXXVI (1956), 503–509.

Vigneras, L. A. "The Cartographer Diogo Ribero," *Imago Mundi*, XVI (1962), 76–83.

———. "The Voyage of Esteban Gómez from Florida to the Baccalaos," *Terrae Incognitae*, II (1970), 25–28.

———. "The Cape Breton Landfall: 1494 or 1497," *Canadian Historical Review*, XXXVIII (1957), 219–228.

———. "El Viaje de Estaban Gómez a Norte America," *Revista de Indias*, XVII (1957), 189–207.

———. "État présent des etudes sur Jean Cabot," *Congresso Internacional de História dos Descobrimentos, Actas*, III (1961), 660–668.

———. "A Spanish discovery of North Carolina in 1566," *North Carolina Historical Review*, XLVI (1969), 398–415.

Washburn, Wilcomb E. *Proceedings of the Vinland Map Conference*. Chicago, 1971.

Waters, David W. *The Art of Navigation in England*. London, 1958.

Williamson, Janes A. *The Age of Drake*. London, 1938.

———. *The Cabot Voyages and Bristol Discovery under Henry VII*. Hakluyt Society. Cambridge, 1962.

———. *The Voyages of the Cabots*. London, 1929.

Winship, G. P. "The Coronado Expedition, 1540–1542," *Smithsonian Institution, Bureau of American Ethnology, Fourteenth Report*, pp. 329–637. Washington, D.C., 1896.

———. ed. *Sailors, Narratives of Voyages along the New England Coast, 1524–1624*. Boston, 1905.

Worcestre, William. *Itineraries*. Edited by John H. Harvey. Oxford, 1969.

Wright, Irene A. *Further English Voyages to Spanish America, 1583–1594*. Hakluyt Society. London, 1951.

———. *Spanish Documents Concerning English Voyages to the Carribbean, 1527–1568*. Hakluyt Society. London, 1929.

Wright, Louis B. *Religion and Empire*. Princeton, N.J., 1943.

———, and Elaine W. Fowler. *English Colonization of North America*. New York, 1969.

Wroth, Lawrence C. *The Voyages of Giovanni da Verrazzano 1524–1528*. New Haven, Conn., 1970.

haRpeR ⚜ ᴄoRchbooᴋs

American Studies: General

HENRY ADAMS Degradation of the Democratic Dogma. ‡ *Introduction by Charles Hirschfeld.* TB/1450

LOUIS D. BRANDEIS: Other People's Money, *and How the Bankers Use It. Ed. with Intro, by Richard M. Abrams* TB/3081

HENRY STEELE COMMAGER, Ed.: The Struggle for Racial Equality TB/1300

CARL N. DEGLER: Out of Our Past: *The Forces that Shaped Modern America* CN/2

CARL N. DEGLER, Ed.: Pivotal Interpretations of American History
Vol. I TB/1240; Vol. II TB/1241

A. S. EISENSTADT, Ed.: The Craft of American History: *Selected Essays*
Vol. I TB/1255; Vol. II TB/1256

LAWRENCE H. FUCHS, Ed.: American Ethnic Politics TB/1368

MARCUS LEE HANSEN: The Atlantic Migration: 1607-1860. *Edited by Arthur M. Schlesinger. Introduction by Oscar Handlin* TB/1052

MARCUS LEE HANSEN: The Immigrant in American History. *Edited with a Foreword by Arthur M. Schlesinger* TB/1120

ROBERT L. HEILBRONER: The Limits of American Capitalism TB/1305

JOHN HIGHAM, Ed.: The Reconstruction of American History TB/1068

ROBERT H. JACKSON: The Supreme Court in the American System of Government TB/1106

JOHN F. KENNEDY: A Nation of Immigrants. *Illus. Revised and Enlarged. Introduction by Robert F. Kennedy* TB/1118

LEONARD W. LEVY, Ed.: American Constitutional Law: *Historical Essays* TB/1285

LEONARD W. LEVY, Ed.: Judicial Review and the Supreme Court TB/1296

LEONARD W. LEVY: The Law of the Commonwealth and Chief Justice Shaw: *The Evolution of American Law, 1830-1860* TB/1309

GORDON K. LEWIS: Puerto Rico: *Freedom and Power in the Caribbean. Abridged edition* TB/1371

GUNNAR MYRDAL: An American Dilemma: *The Negro Problem and Modern Democracy. Introduction by the Author.*
Vol. I TB/1443; Vol. II TB/1444

GILBERT OSOFSKY, Ed.: The Burden of Race: *A Documentary History of Negro-White Relations in America* TB/1405

ARNOLD ROSE: The Negro in America: *The Condensed Version of Gunnar Myrdal's* An American Dilemma. *Second Edition* TB/3048

JOHN E. SMITH: Themes in American Philosophy: *Purpose, Experience and Community* TB/1466

WILLIAM R. TAYLOR: Cavalier and Yankee: *The Old South and American National Character* TB/1474

American Studies: Colonial

BERNARD BAILYN: The New England Merchants in the Seventeenth Century TB/1149

ROBERT E. BROWN: Middle-Class Democracy and Revolution in Massachusetts, 1691–1780. *New Introduction by Author* TB/1413

JOSEPH CHARLES: The Origins of the American Party System TB/1049

WESLEY FRANK CRAVEN: The Colonies in Transition: 1660-1712† TB/3084

CHARLES GIBSON: Spain in America † TB/3077

CHARLES GIBSON, Ed.: The Spanish Tradition in America + HR/1351

LAWRENCE HENRY GIPSON: The Coming of the Revolution: 1763-1775. † *Illus.* TB/3007

JACK P. GREENE, Ed.: Great Britain and the American Colonies: 1606-1763. + *Introduction by the Author* HR/1477

AUBREY C. LAND, Ed.: Bases of the Plantation Society + HR/1429

PERRY MILLER: Errand Into the Wilderness TB/1139

PERRY MILLER & T. H. JOHNSON, Ed.: The Puritans: *A Sourcebook of Their Writings*
Vol. I TB/1093; Vol. II TB/1094

EDMUND S. MORGAN: The Puritan Family: *Religion and Domestic Relations in Seventeenth Century New England* TB/1227

WALLACE NOTESTEIN: The English People on the Eve of Colonization: 1603-1630. † *Illus.* TB/3006

LOUIS B. WRIGHT: The Cultural Life of the American Colonies: 1607-1763. † *Illus.* TB/3005

YVES F. ZOLTVANY, Ed.: The French Tradition in America + HR/1425

American Studies: The Revolution to 1860

JOHN R. ALDEN: The American Revolution: 1775-1783. † *Illus.* TB/3011

---

† The New American Nation Series, edited by Henry Steele Commager and Richard B. Morris.
‡ American Perspectives series, edited by Bernard Wishy and William E. Leuchtenburg.
a History of Europe series, edited by J. H. Plumb.
§ The Library of Religion and Culture, edited by Benjamin Nelson.
‖ Researches in the Social, Cultural, and Behavioral Sciences, edited by Benjamin Nelson.
᷂ Harper Modern Science Series, edited by James A. Newman.
° Not for sale in Canada.
+ Documentary History of the United States series, edited by Richard B. Morris.
# Documentary History of Western Civilization series, edited by Eugene C. Black and Leonard W. Levy.
Λ The Economic History of the United States series, edited by Henry David et al.
¶ European Perspectives series, edited by Eugene C. Black.
** Contemporary Essays series, edited by Leonard W. Levy.
* The Stratum Series, edited by John Hale.

RAY A. BILLINGTON: The Far Western Frontier: 1830-1860. † *Illus.* TB/3012
STUART BRUCHEY: The Roots of American Economic Growth, 1607-1861: *An Essay in Social Causation. New Introduction by the Author.* TB/1350
WHITNEY R. CROSS: The Burned-Over District: *The Social and Intellectual History of Enthusiastic Religion in Western New York, 1800-1850* TB/1242
NOBLE E. CUNNINGHAM, JR., Ed.: The Early Republic, 1789-1828 + HR/1394
GEORGE DANGERFIELD: The Awakening of American Nationalism, 1815-1828. † *Illus.* TB/3061
CLEMENT EATON: The Freedom-of-Thought Struggle in the Old South. *Revised and Enlarged. Illus.* TB/1150
CLEMENT EATON: The Growth of Southern Civilization, 1790-1860. † *Illus.* TB/3040
ROBERT H. FERRELL, Ed.: Foundations of American Diplomacy, 1775-1872 + HR/1393
LOUIS FILLER: The Crusade against Slavery: 1830-1860. † *Illus.* TB/3029
DAVID H. FISCHER: The Revolution of American Conservatism: *The Federalist Party in the Era of Jeffersonian Democracy* TB/1449
WILLIM W. FREEHLING: Prelude to Civil War: *The Nullification Controversy in South Carolina, 1816-1836* TB/1359
PAUL W. GATES: The Farmer's Age: *Agriculture, 1815-1860* △ TB/1398
THOMAS JEFFERSON: Notes on the State of Virginia. ‡ *Edited by Thomas P. Abernethy* TB/3052
FORREST MCDONALD, Ed.: Confederation and Constitution, 1781-1789 + HR/1396
BERNARD MAYO: Myths and Men: *Patrick Henry, George Washington, Thomas Jefferson* TB/1108
JOHN C. MILLER: Alexander Hamilton and the Growth of the New Nation TB/3057
JOHN C. MILLER: The Federalist Era: 1789-1801. † *Illus.* TB/3027
RICHARD B. MORRIS, Ed.: Alexander Hamilton and the Founding of the Nation. *New Introduction by the Editor* TB/1448
RICHARD B. MORRIS: The American Revolution Reconsidered TB/1363
CURTIS P. NETTELS: The Emergence of a National Economy, 1775-1815 △ TB/1438
DOUGLASS C. NORTH & ROBERT PAUL THOMAS, Eds.: *The Growth of the American Economy to 1860* + HR/1352
R. B. NYE: The Cultural Life of the New Nation: 1776-1830. † *Illus.* TB/3026
GILBERT OSOFSKY, Ed.: Puttin' On Ole Massa: *The Slave Narratives of Henry Bibb, William Wells Brown, and Solomon Northup* ‡ TB/1432
JAMES PARTON: The Presidency of Andrew Jackson. *From Volume III of the* Life of Andrew Jackson. *Ed. with Intro. by Robert V. Remini* TB/3080
FRANCIS S. PHILBRICK: The Rise of the West, 1754-1830. † *Illus.* TB/3067
MARSHALL SMELSER: The Democratic Republic, 1801-1815 + TB/1406
JACK M. SOSIN, Ed.: The Opening of the West + HR/1424
GEORGE ROGERS TAYLOR: The Transportation Revolution, 1815-1860 △ TB/1347
A. F. TYLER: Freedom's Ferment: *Phases of American Social History from the Revolution to the Outbreak of the Civil War. Illus.* TB/1074
GLYNDON G. VAN DEUSEN: The Jacksonian Era: 1828-1848. † *Illus.* TB/3028

LOUIS B. WRIGHT: Culture on the Moving Frontier TB/1053

American Studies: The Civil War to 1900

W. R. BROCK: An American Crisis: *Congress and Reconstruction, 1865-67* ° TB/1283
T. C. COCHRAN & WILLIAM MILLER: The Age of Enterprise: *A Social History of Industrial America* TB/1054
W. A. DUNNING: Reconstruction, Political and Economic: 1865-1877 TB/1073
HAROLD U. FAULKNER: Politics, Reform and Expansion: 1890-1900. † *Illus.* TB/3020
GEORGE M. FREDRICKSON: The Inner Civil War: *Northern Intellectuals and the Crisis of the Union* TB/1358
JOHN A. GARRATY: The New Commonwealth, 1877-1890 + TB/1410
JOHN A. GARRATY, Ed.: The Transformation of American Society, 1870-1890 + HR/1395
HELEN HUNT JACKSON: A Century of Dishonor: *The Early Crusade for Indian Reform.* † *Edited by Andrew F. Rolle* TB/3063
WILLIAM G. MCLOUGHLIN, Ed.: The American Evangelicals, 1800-1900: An Anthology ‡ TB/1382
ARNOLD M. PAUL: Conservative Crisis and the Rule of Law: *Attitudes of Bar and Bench, 1887-1895. New Introduction by Author* TB/1415
JAMES S. PIKE: The Prostrate State: *South Carolina under Negro Government.* ‡ *Intro. by Robert F. Durden* TB/3085
WHITELAW REID: After the War: *A Tour of the Southern States, 1865-1866.* ‡ *Edited by C. Vann Woodward* TB/3066
FRED A. SHANNON: The Farmer's Last Frontier: *Agriculture, 1860-1897* TB/1348
VERNON LANE WHARTON: The Negro in Mississippi, 1865-1890 TB/1178

American Studies: The Twentieth Century

RICHARD M. ABRAMS, Ed.: The Issues of the Populist and Progressive Eras, 1892-1912 + HR/1428
RAY STANNARD BAKER: Following the Color Line: *American Negro Citizenship in Progressive Era.* ‡ *Edited by Dewey W. Grantham, Jr. Illus.* TB/3053
RANDOLPH S. BOURNE: War and the Intellectuals: *Collected Essays, 1915-1919.* ‡ *Edited by Carl Resek* TB/3043
A. RUSSELL BUCHANAN: The United States and World War II. † *Illus.*
    Vol. I TB/3044; Vol. II TB/3045
THOMAS C. COCHRAN: The American Business System: *A Historical Perspective, 1900-1955* TB/1080
FOSTER RHEA DULLES: America's Rise to World Power: 1898-1954. † *Illus.* TB/3021
JEAN-BAPTISTE DUROSELLE: From Wilson to Roosevelt: *Foreign Policy of the United States, 1913-1945. Trans. by Nancy Lyman Roelker* TB/1370
HAROLD U. FAULKNER: The Decline of Laissez Faire, 1897-1917 TB/1397
JOHN D. HICKS: Republican Ascendancy: 1921-1933. † *Illus.* TB/3041
WILLIAM E. LEUCHTENBURG: Franklin D. Roosevelt and the New Deal: 1932-1940. † *Illus.* TB/3025
WILLIAM E. LEUCHTENBURG, Ed.: The New Deal: *A Documentary History* + HR/1354
ARTHUR S. LINK: Woodrow Wilson and the Progressive Era: 1910-1917. † *Illus.* TB/3023

2

BROADUS MITCHELL: Depression Decade: *From New Era through New Deal, 1929-1941* ∧ TB/1439

GEORGE E. MOWRY: The Era of Theodore Roosevelt and the Birth of Modern America: 1900-1912. † *Illus.* TB/3022

WILLIAM PRESTON, JR.: Aliens and Dissenters: *Federal Suppression of Radicals, 1903-1933* TB/1287

WALTER RAUSCHENBUSCH: Christianity and the Social Crisis. ‡ *Edited by Robert D. Cross* TB/3059

GEORGE SOULE: Prosperity Decade: *From War to Depression, 1917-1929* ∧ TB/1349

GEORGE B. TINDALL, Ed.: A Populist Reader: *Selections from the Works of American Populist Leaders* TB/3069

TWELVE SOUTHERNERS: I'll Take My Stand: *The South and the Agrarian Tradition. Intro. by Louis D. Rubin, Jr.; Biographical Essays by Virginia Rock* TB/1072

Art, Art History, Aesthetics

CREIGHTON GILBERT, Ed.: Renaissance Art ** *Illus.* TB/1465

EMILE MÂLE: The Gothic Image: *Religious Art in France of the Thirteenth Century.* § *190 illus.* TB/344

MILLARD MEISS: Painting in Florence and Siena After the Black Death: *The Arts, Religion and Society in the Mid-Fourteenth Century. 169 illus.* TB/1148

ERWIN PANOFSKY: Renaissance and Renascences in Western Art. *Illus.* TB/1447

ERWIN PANOFSKY: Studies in Iconology: *Humanistic Themes in the Art of the Renaissance. 180 illus.* TB/1077

OTTO VON SIMSON: The Gothic Cathedral: *Origins of Gothic Architecture and the Medieval Concept of Order. 58 illus.* TB/2018

HEINRICH ZIMMER: Myths and Symbols in Indian Art and Civilization. *70 illus.* TB/2005

Asian Studies

WOLFGANG FRANKE: China and the West: *The Cultural Encounter, 13th to 20th Centuries. Trans. by R. A. Wilson* TB/1326

L. CARRINGTON GOODRICH: A Short History of the Chinese People. *Illus.* TB/3015

DAN N. JACOBS, Ed.: The New Communist Manifesto and Related Documents. TB/1078

DAN N. JACOBS & HANS H. BAERWALD, Eds.: Chinese Communism: *Selected Documents* TB/3031

BENJAMIN I. SCHWARTZ: Chinese Communism and the Rise of Mao TB/1308

BENJAMIN I. SCHWARTZ: In Search of Wealth and Power: *Yen Fu and the West* TB/1422

Economics & Economic History

C. E. BLACK: The Dynamics of Modernization: *A Study in Comparative History* TB/1321

STUART BRUCHEY: The Roots of American Economic Growth, 1607-1861: *An Essay in Social Causation. New Introduction by the Author.* TB/1350

GILBERT BURCK & EDITORS OF *Fortune:* The Computer Age: *And its Potential for Management* TB/1179

SHEPARD B. CLOUGH, THOMAS MOODIE & CAROL MOODIE, Eds.: Economic History of Europe: *Twentieth Century #* HR/1388

THOMAS C. COCHRAN: The American Business System: *A Historical Perspective, 1900-1955* TB/1080

ROBERT A. DAHL & CHARLES E. LINDBLOM: Politics, Economics, and Welfare: *Planning and Politico-Economic Systems Resolved into Basic Social Processes* TB/3037

PETER F. DRUCKER: The New Society: *The Anatomy of Industrial Order* TB/1082

HAROLD U. FAULKNER: The Decline of Laissez Faire, 1897-1917 ∧ TB/1397

PAUL W. GATES: The Farmer's Age: *Agriculture, 1815-1860* ∆ TB/1398

WILLIAM GREENLEAF, Ed.: American Economic Development Since 1860 + HR/1353

ROBERT L. HEILBRONER: The Future as History: *The Historic Currents of Our Time and the Direction in Which They Are Taking America* TB/1386

ROBERT L. HEILBRONER: The Great Ascent: *The Struggle for Economic Development in Our Time* TB/3030

DAVID S. LANDES: Bankers and Pashas: *International Finance and Economic Imperialism in Egypt. New Preface by the Author* TB/1412

ROBERT LATOUCHE: The Birth of Western Economy: *Economic Aspects of the Dark Ages* TB/1290

W. ARTHUR LEWIS: The Principles of Economic Planning. *New Introduction by the Author°* TB/1436

WILLIAM MILLER, Ed.: Men in Business: *Essays on the Historical Role of the Entrepreneur* TB/1081

GUNNAR MYRDAL: An International Economy. *New Introduction by the Author* TB/1445

HERBERT A. SIMON: The Shape of Automation: *For Men and Management* TB/1245

RICHARD S. WECKSTEIN, Ed.: Expansion of World Trade and the Growth of National Economies ** TB/1373

Historiography and History of Ideas

J. BRONOWSKI & BRUCE MAZLISH: The Western Intellectual Tradition: *From Leonardo to Hegel* TB/3001

WILHELM DILTHEY: Pattern and Meaning in History: *Thoughts on History and Society.° Edited with an Intro. by H. P. Rickman* TB/1075

J. H. HEXTER: More's Utopia: *The Biography of an Idea. Epilogue by the Author* TB/1195

H. STUART HUGHES: History as Art and as Science: *Twin Vistas on the Past* TB/1207

ARTHUR O. LOVEJOY: The Great Chain of Being: *A Study of the History of an Idea* TB/1009

RICHARD H. POPKIN: The History of Scepticism from Erasmus to Descartes. *Revised Edition* TB/1391

MASSIMO SALVADORI, Ed.: Modern Socialism # TB/1374

BRUNO SNELL: The Discovery of the Mind: *The Greek Origins of European Thought* TB/1018

W. WARREN WAGER, ed.: European Intellectual History Since Darwin and Marx TB/1297

History: General

HANS KOHN: The Age of Nationalism: *The First Era of Global History* TB/1380

BERNARD LEWIS: The Arabs in History TB/1029

BERNARD LEWIS: The Middle East and the West ° TB/1274

History: Ancient

A. ANDREWS: The Greek Tyrants TB/1103

ERNST LUDWIG EHRLICH: A Concise History of Israel: *From the Earliest Times to the Destruction of the Temple in A.D. 70* ° TB/128
THEODOR H. GASTER: Thespis: *Ritual Myth and Drama in the Ancient Near East* TB/1281
MICHAEL GRANT: Ancient History ° TB/1190
A. H. M. JONES, Ed.: A History of Rome through the Fifth Century # *Vol. I: The Republic* HR/1364
Vol. II The Empire: HR/1460
NAPHTALI LEWIS & MEYER REINHOLD, Eds.: Roman Civilization *Vol. I: The Republic* TB/1231
Vol. II: The Empire TB/1232

History: Medieval

MARSHALL W. BALDWIN, Ed.: Christianity Through the 13th Century # HR/1468
MARC BLOCH: Land and Work in Medieval Europe. *Translated by J. E. Anderson* TB/1452
HELEN CAM: England Before Elizabeth TB/1026
NORMAN COHN: The Pursuit of the Millennium: *Revolutionary Messianism in Medieval and Reformation Europe* TB/1037
G. G. COULTON: Medieval Village, Manor, and Monastery HR/1022
HEINRICH FICHTENAU: The Carolingian Empire: *The Age of Charlemagne. Translated with an Introduction by Peter Munz* TB/1142
GALBERT OF BRUGES: The Murder of Charles the Good: *A Contemporary Record of Revolutionary Change in 12th Century Flanders. Translated with an Introduction by James Bruce Ross* TB/1311
F. L. GANSHOF: Feudalism TB/1058
F. L. GANSHOF: The Middle Ages: *A History of International Relations. Translated by Rémy Hall* TB/1411
DENYS HAY: The Medieval Centuries ° TB/1192
DAVID HERLIHY, Ed.: Medieval Culture and Society # HR/1340
J. M. HUSSEY: The Byzantine World TB/1057
ROBERT LATOUCHE: The Birth of Western Economy: *Economic Aspects of the Dark Ages* ° TB/1290
HENRY CHARLES LEA: The Inquisition of the Middle Ages. || *Introduction by Walter Ullmann* TB/1456
FERDINAND LOT: The End of the Ancient World and the Beginnings of the Middle Ages. *Introduction by Glanville Downey* TB/1044
H. R. LOYN: The Norman Conquest TB/1457
ACHILLE LUCHAIRE: Social France at the time of Philip Augustus. *Intro. by John W. Baldwin* TB/1314
GUIBERT DE NOGENT: Self and Society in Medieval France: *The Memoirs of Guibert de Nogent.* || Edited by John F. Benton TB/1471
MARSILIUS OF PADUA: The Defender of Peace. *The Defensor Pacis. Translated with an Introduction by Alan Gewirth* TB/1310
CHARLES PETET-DUTAILLIS: The Feudal Monarchy in France and England: *From the Tenth to the Thirteenth Century* ° TB/1165
STEVEN RUNCIMAN: A History of the Crusades Vol. I: *The First Crusade and the Foundation of the Kingdom of Jerusalem. Illus.* TB/1143
Vol. II: *The Kingdom of Jerusalem and the Frankish East 1100-1187. Illus.* TB/1243
Vol. III: *The Kingdom of Acre and the Later Crusades. Illus.* TB/1298
J. M. WALLACE-HADRILL: The Barbarian West: *The Early Middle Ages, A.D. 400-1000* TB/1061

History: Renaissance & Reformation

JACOB BURCKHARDT: The Civilization of the Renaissance in Italy. *Introduction by Benjamin Nelson and Charles Trinkaus. Illus.* Vol. I TB/40; Vol. II TB/41
JOHN CALVIN & JACOPO SADOLETO: A Reformation Debate. *Edited by John C. Olin* TB/1239
FEDERICO CHABOD: Machiavelli and the Renaissance TB/1193
J. H. ELLIOTT: Europe Divided, 1559-1598 *a* ° TB/1414
G. R. ELTON: Reformation Europe, 1517-1559 ° *a* TB/1270
DESIDERIUS ERASMUS: Christian Humanism and the Reformation: *Selected Writings. Edited and Translated by John C. Olin* TB/1166
DESIDERIUS ERASMUS: Erasmus and His Age: *Selected Letters. Edited with an Introduction by Hans J. Hillerbrand. Translated by Marcus A. Haworth* TB/1461
WALLACE K. FERGUSON et al.: Facets of the Renaissance TB/1098
WALLACE K. FERGUSON et al.: The Renaissance: *Six Essays. Illus.* TB/1084
FRANCESCO GUICCIARDINI: History of Florence. *Translated with an Introduction and Notes by Mario Domandi* TB/1470
WERNER L. GUNDERSHEIMER, Ed.: French Humanism, 1470-1600. * *Illus.* TB/1473
MARIE BOAS HALL, Ed.: Nature and Nature's Laws: *Documents of the Scientific Revolution* # HR/1420
HANS J. HILLERBRAND, Ed., The Protestant Reformation # TB/1342
JOHAN HUIZINGA: Erasmus and the Age of Reformation. *Illus.* TB/19
JOEL HURSTFIELD: The Elizabethan Nation TB/1312
JOEL HURSTFIELD, Ed.: The Reformation Crisis TB/1267
PAUL OSKAR KRISTELLER: Renaissance Thought: *The Classic, Scholastic, and Humanist Strains* TB/1048
PAUL OSKAR KRISTELLER: Renaissance Thought II: *Papers on Humanism and the Arts* TB/1163
PAUL O. KRISTELLER & PHILIP P. WIENER, Eds.: Renaissance Essays TB/1392
DAVID LITTLE: Religion, Order and Law: *A Study in Pre-Revolutionary England.* § *Preface by R. Bellah* TB/1418
NICCOLO MACHIAVELLI: History of Florence and of the Affairs of Italy: *From the Earliest Times to the Death of Lorenzo the Magnificent. Introduction by Felix Gilbert* TB/1027
ALFRED VON MARTIN: Sociology of the Renaissance. ° *Introduction by W. K. Ferguson* TB/1099
GARRETT MATTINGLY et al.: Renaissance Profiles. *Edited by J. H. Plumb* TB/1162
J. H. PARRY: The Establishment of the European Hegemony: 1415-1715: *Trade and Exploration in the Age of the Renaissance* TB/1045
J. H. PARRY, Ed.: The European Reconnaissance: *Selected Documents* # HR/1345
J. H. PLUMB: The Italian Renaissance: *A Concise Survey of Its History and Culture* TB/1161
A. F. POLLARD: Henry VIII. *Introductioh by A. G. Dickens.* ° TB/1249
RICHARD H. POPKIN: The History of Scepticism from Erasmus to Descartes TB/1391
PAOLO ROSSI: Philosophy, Technology, and the Arts, in the Early Modern Era 1400-1700. || *Edited by Benjamin Nelson. Translated by Salvator Attanasio* TB/1458

4

R. H. TAWNEY: The Agrarian Problem in the Sixteenth Century. *Intro. by Lawrence Stone* TB/1315

H. R. TREVOR-ROPER: The European Witch-craze of the Sixteenth and Seventeenth Centuries and Other Essays ° TB/1416

VESPASIANO: Rennaissance Princes, Popes, and XVth Century: *The Vespasiano Memoirs. Introduction by Myron P. Gilmore. Illus.* TB/1111

History: Modern European

RENE ALBRECHT-CARRIE, Ed.: The Concert of Europe # HR/1341

MAX BELOFF: The Age of Absolutism, 1660-1815 TB/1062

OTTO VON BISMARCK: Reflections and Reminiscences. *Ed. with Intro. by Theodore S. Hamerow* ¶ TB/1357

EUGENE C. BLACK, Ed.: British Politics in the Nineteenth Century # HR/1427

D. W. BROGAN: The Development of Modern France ° Vol. I: *From the Fall of the Empire to the Dreyfus Affair* TB/1184 Vol. II: *The Shadow of War, World War I, Between the Two Wars* TB/1185

ALAN BULLOCK: Hitler, A Study in Tyranny. ° *Revised Edition. Iuus.* TB/1123

GORDON A. CRAIG: From Bismarck to Adenauer: *Aspects of German Statecraft. Revised Edition* TB/1171

LESTER G. CROCKER, Ed.: The Age of Enlightenment # HR/1423

JACQUES DROZ: Europe between Revolutions, 1815-1848. ° *a Trans. by Robert Baldick* TB/1346

JOHANN GOTTLIEB FICHTE: Addresses to the German Nation. *Ed. with Intro. by George A. Kelly* ¶ TB/1366

ROBERT & ELBORG FORSTER, Eds.: European Society in the Eighteenth Century # HR/1404

C. C. GILLISPIE: Genesis and Geology: *The Decades before Darwin* § TB/51

ALBERT GOODWIN: The French Revolution TB/1064

JOHN B. HALSTED, Ed.: Romanticism # HR/1387

STANLEY HOFFMANN et al.: In Search of France: *The Economy, Society and Political System In the Twentieth Century* TB/1219

H. STUART HUGHES: The Obstructed Path: *French Social Thought in the Years of Desperation* TB/1451

JOHAN HUIZINGA: Dutch Civilisation in the 17th Century and Other Essays TB/1453

WALTER LAQUEUR & GEORGE L. MOSSE, Eds.: Education and Social Structure in the 20th Century. ° *Volume 6 of the* Journal of Contemporary History TB/1339

WALTER LAQUEUR & GEORGE L. MOSSE,` Ed.: International Fascism, 1920-1945. ° *Volume 1 of the* Journal of Contemporary History TB/1276

WALTER LAQUEUR & GEORGE L. MOSSE, Eds.: Literature and Politics in the 20th Century. ° *Volume 5 of the* Journal of Contemporary History. TB/1328

WALTER LAQUEUR & GEORGE L. MOSSE, Eds.: The New History: *Trends in Historical Research and Writing Since World War II.* ° *Volume 4 of the* Journal of Contemporary History TB/1327

WALTER LAQUEUR & GEORGE L. MOSSE, Eds.: 1914: *The Coming of the First World War.* ° *Volume3 of the* Journal of Contemporary History TB/1306

JOHN MCMANNERS: European History, 1789-1914: *Men, Machines and Freedom* TB/1419

PAUL MANTOUX: The Industrial Revolution in the Eighteenth Century: *An Outline of the Beginnings of the Modern Factory System in England* TB/1079

KINGSLEY MARTIN: French Liberal Thought in the Eighteenth Century: *A Study of Political Ideas from Bayle to Condorcet* TB/1114

NAPOLEON III: Napoleonic Ideas: *Des Idées Napoléoniennes, par le Prince Napoléon-Louis Bonaparte. Ed. by Brison D. Gooch* ¶ TB/1336

FRANZ NEUMANN: Behemoth: *The Structure and Practice of National Socialism, 1933-1944* TB/1289

DAVID OGG: Europe of the Ancien Régime, 1715-1783 ° α TB/1271

GEORGE RUDE: Revolutionary Europe, 1783-1815 ° α TB/1272

MASSIMO SALVADORI, Ed.: Modern Socialism # TB/1374

DENIS MACK SMITH, Ed.: The Making of Italy, 1796-1870 # HR/1356

ALBERT SOREL: Europe Under the Old Regime, *Translated by Francis H. Herrick* TB/1121

ROLAND N. STROMBERG, Ed.: Realsim, Naturalism, and Symbolism: *Modes of Thought and Expression in Europe, 1848-1914* # HR/1355

A. J. P. TAYLOR: From Napoleon to Lenin: *Historical Essays* ° TB/1268

A. J. P. TAYLOR: The Habsburg Monarchy, 1809-1918: *A History of the Austrian Empire and Austria-Hungary* ° TB/1187

J. M. THOMPSON: European History, 1494-1789 TB/1431

DAVID THOMSON, Ed.: France: Empire and Republic, 1850-1940 # HR/1387

H. R. TREVOR-ROPER: Historical Essays TB/1269

W. WARREN WAGAR, Ed.: Science, Faith, and MAN: *European Thought Since 1914* # HR/1362

MACK WALKER, Ed.: Metternich's Europe, 1813-1848 # HR/1361

ELIZABETH WISKEMANN: Europe of the Dictators, 1919-1945 ° α TB/1273

JOHN B. WOLF: France: 1814-1919: *The Rise of a Liberal-Democratic Society* TB/3019

Literature & Literary Criticism

JACQUES BARZUN: The House of Intellect TB/1051

W. J. BATE: From Classic to Romantic: *Premises of Taste in Eighteenth Century England* TB/1036

VAN WYCK BROOKS: Van Wyck Brooks: The Early Years: *A Selection from his Works, 1908-1921 Ed. with Intro. by Claire Sprague* TB/3082

RICHMOND LATTIMORE, Translator: The Odyssey of Homer TB/1389

ROBERT PREYER, Ed.: Victorian Literature ** TB/1302

BASIL WILEY: Nineteenth Century Studies: *Coleridge to Matthew Arnold* ° TB/1261

RAYMOND WILLIAMS: Culture and Society, 1780-1950 ° TB/1252

Philosophy

HENRI BERGSON: Time and Free Will: *An Essay on the Immediate Data of Consciousness* ° TB/1021

LUDWIG BINSWANGER: Being-in-the-World: *Selected Papers. Trans. with Intro. by Jacob Needleman* TB/1365

H. J. BLACKHAM: Six Existentialist Thinkers: *Kierkegaard, Nietzsche, Jaspers, Marcel, Heidegger, Sartre* ° TB/1002

J. M. BOCHENSKI: The Methods of Contemporary Thought. *Trans. by Peter Caws* TB/1377
CRANE BRINTON: Nietzsche. *Preface, Bibliography, and Epilogue by the Author* TB/1197
ERNST CASSIRER: Rousseau, Kant and Goethe. *Intro. by Peter Gay* TB/1092
FREDERICK COPLESTON, S. J.: Medieval Philosophy TB/376
F. M. CORNFORD: From Religion to Philosophy: *A Study in the Origins of Western Speculation* § TB/20
WILFRID DESAN: The Tragic Finale: *An Essay on the Philosophy of Jean-Paul Sartre* TB/1030
MARVIN FARBER: The Aims of Phenomenology: *The Motives, Methods, and Impact of Husserl's Thought* TB/1291
PAUL FRIEDLANDER: Plato: *An Introduction* TB/2017
MICHAEL GELVEN: A Commentary on Heidegger's "Being and Time" TB/1464
J. GLENN GRAY: Hegel and Greek Thought TB/1409
W. K. C. GUTHRIE: The Greek Philosophers: *From Thales to Aristotle* ° TB/1008
G. W. F. HEGEL: On Art, Religion Philosophy: *Introductory Lectures to the Realm of Absolute Spirit.* ‖ *Edited with an Introduction by J. Glenn Gray* TB/1463
G. W. F. HEGEL: Phenomenology of Mind. ° ‖ *Introduction by George Lichtheim* TB/1303
MARTIN HEIDEGGER: Discourse on Thinking. *Translated with a Preface by John M. Anderson and E. Hans Freund. Introduction by John M. Anderson* TB/1459
F. H. HEINEMANN: Existentialism and the Modern Predicament TB/28
WERER HEISENBERG: Physics and Philosophy: *The Revolution in Modern Science. Intro. by F. S. C. Nortrop* TB/549
EDMUND HUSSERL: Phenomenology and the Crisis of Philosophy. § *Translated with an Introduction by Quentin Lauer* TB/1170
IMMANUEL KANT: Groundwork of the Metaphysic of Morals. *Translated and Analyzed by H. J. Paton* TB/1159
IMMANUEL KANT: Lectures on Ethics. § *Introduction by Lewis White Beck* TB/105
QUENTIN LAUER: Phenomenology: *Its Genesis and Prospect. Preface by Aron Gurwitsch* TB/1169
GEORGE A. MORGAN: What Nietzsche Means TB/1198
H. J. PATON: The Categorical Imperative: *A Study in Kant's Moral Philosophy* TB/1325
MICHAEL POLANYI: Personal Knowledge: *Towards a Post-Critical Philosophy* TB/1158
KARL R. POPPER: Conjectures and Refutations: *The Growth of Scientific Knowledge* TB/1376
WILLARD VAN ORMAN QUINE: Elementary Logic *Revised Edition* TB/577
MORTON WHITE: Foundations of Historical Knowledge TB/1440
WILHELM WINDELBAND: A History of Philosophy *Vol. I: Greek, Roman, Medieval* TB/38
Vol. II: Renaissance, Enlightenment, Modern TB/39
LUDWIG WITTGENSTEIN: The Blue and Brown Books ° TB/1211
LUDWIG WITTGENSTEIN: Notebooks, 1914-1916 TB/1441

Political Science & Government

C. E. BLACK: The Dynamics of Modernization: *A Study in Comparative History* TB/1321
KENNETH E. BOULDING: Conflict and Defense: *A General Theory of Action* TB/3024

DENIS W. BROGAN: Politics in America. *New Introduction by the Author* TB/1469
ROBERT CONQUEST: Power and Policy in the USSR: *The Study of Soviet Dynastics* ° TB/1307
ROBERT A. DAHL & CHARLES E. LINDBLOM: Politics, Economics, and Welfare: *Planning and Politico-Economic Systems Resolved into Basic Social Processes* TB/1277
HANS KOHN: Political Ideologies of the 20th Century TB/1277
ROY C. MACRIDIS, Ed.: Political Parties: *Contemporary Trends and Ideas* ** TB/1322
ROBERT GREEN MC CLOSKEY: American Conservatism in the Age of Enterprise, 1865-1910 TB/1137
BARRINGTON MOORE, JR.:Political Power and Social Theory: *Seven Studies* ‖ TB/1221
BARRINGTON MOORE, JR.: Soviet Politics—The Dilemma of Power: *The Role of Ideas in Social Change* ‖ TB/1222
BARRINGTON MOORE, JR.: Terror and Progress—USSR: *Some Sources of Change and Stability in the Soviet Dictatorship* TB/1266
JOHN B. MORRALL: Political Thought in Medieval Times TB/1076
KARL R. POPPER: The Open Society and Its Enemies *Vol. I: The Spell of Plato* TB/1101
Vol. II: The High Tide of Prophecy: Hegel, Marx, and the Aftermath TB/1102
HENRI DE SAINT-SIMON: Social Organization, The Science of Man, and Other Writings. ‖ *Edited and Translated with an Introduction by Felix Markham* TB/1152
JOSEPH A. SCHUMPETER: Capitalism, Socialism and Democracy TB/3008

Psychology

LUDWIG BINSWANGER: Being-in-the-world: *Selected papers.* ‖ *Trans. with Intro. by Jacob Needleman* TB/1365
HADLEY CANTRIL: The Invasion from Mars: *A Study in the Psychology of Panic* ‖ TB/1282
MIRCEA ELIADE: Cosmos and History: *The Myth of the Eternal Return* § TB/2050
MIRCEA ELIADE: Myth and Reality TB/1369
MIRCEA ELIADE: Myths, Dreams and Mysteries: *The Encounter Between Contemporary Faiths and Archaic Realities* § TB/1320
MIRCEA ELIADE: Rites and Symbols of Initiation: *The Mysteries of Birth and Rebirth* § TB/1236
HERBERT FINGARETTE: The Self in Transformation: *Psychoanalysis, Philosophy and the Life of the Spirit* ‖ TB/1177
SIGMUND FREUD: On Creativity and the Unconscious: *Papers on the Psychology of Art, Literature, Love, Religion.* § *Intro. by Benjamin Nelson* TB/45
J. GLENN GRAY: The Warriors: *Reflections on Men in Battle. Introduction by Hannah Arendt* TB/1294
WILLIAM JAMES: Psychology: *The Briefer Course. Edited with an Intro. by Gordon Allport* TB/1034
MUZAFER SHERIF: The Psychology of Social Norms. *Introduction by Gardner Murphy* TB/3072
HELLMUT WILHELM: Change: *Eight Lectures on the I Ching* TB/2019

Religion: Ancient and Classical, Biblical and Judaic Traditions

C. K. BARRETT, Ed.: The New Testament Background: *Selected Documents* TB/86

MARTIN BUBER: Eclipse of God: *Studies in the Relation Between Religion and Philosophy* TB/12
MARTIN BUBER: Hasidism and Modern Man. *Edited and Translated by Maurice Friedman* TB/839
MARTIN BUBER: The Knowledge of Man. *Edited with an Introduction by Maurice Friedman. Translated by Maurice Friedman and Ronald Gregor Smith* TB/135
MARTIN BUBER: Moses. *The Revelation and the Covenant* TB/837
MARTIN BUBER: The Origin and Meaning of Hasidism. *Edited and Translated by Maurice Friedman* TB/835
MARTIN BUBER: The Prophetic Faith TB/73
MARTIN BUBER: Two Types of Faith: *Interpenetration of Judaism and Christianity* ° TB/75
MALCOLM L. DIAMOND: Martin Buber: *Jewish Existentialist* TB/840
M. S. ENSLIN: Christian Beginnings TB/5
M. S. ENSLIN: The Literature of the Christian Movement TB/6
HENRI FRANKFORT: Ancient Egyptian Religion: *An Interpretation* TB/77
MAURICE S. FRIEDMAN: Martin Buber: *The Life of Dialogue* TB/64
ABRAHAM HESCHEL: The Earth Is the Lord's & The Sabbath. *Two Essays* TB/828
ABRAHAM HESCHEL: God in Search of Man: *A Philosophy of Judaism* TB/807
ABRAHAM HESCHEL: Man Is not Alone: *A Philosophy of Religion* TB/838
ABRAHAM HESCHEL: The Prophets: *An Introduction* TB/1421
T. J. MEEK: Hebrew Origins TB/69
JAMES MUILENBURG: The Way of Israel: *Biblical Faith and Ethics* TB/133
H. H. ROWLEY: The Growth of the Old Testament TB/107
D. WINTON THOMAS, Ed.: Documents from Old Testament Times TB/85

Religion: Early Christianity Through Reformation

ANSELM OF CANTERBURY: Truth, Freedom, and Evil: *Three Philosophical Dialogues. Edited and Translated by Jasper Hopkins and Herbert Richardson* TB/317
MARSHALL W. BALDWIN, Ed.: Christianity through the 13th Century # HR/1468
ADOLF DEISSMAN: Paul: *A Study in Social and Religious History* TB/15
EDGAR J. GOODSPEED: A Life of Jesus TB/1
ROBERT M. GRANT: Gnosticism and Early Christianity TB/136
WILLIAM HALLER: The Rise of Puritanism TB/22
ARTHUR DARBY NOCK: St. Paul ° TB/104
GORDON RUPP: Luther's Progress to the Diet of Worms ° TB/120

Religion: The Protestant Tradition

KARL BARTH: Church Dogmatics: *A Selection. Intro. by H. Gollwitzer. Ed. by G. W. Bromiley* TB/95
KARL BARTH: Dogmatics in Outline TB/56
KARL BARTH: The Word of God and the Word of Man TB/13
WHITNEY R. CROSS: The Burned-Over District: *The Social and Intellectual History of Enthusiastic Religion in Western New York, 1800-1850* TB/1242
WILLIAM R. HUTCHISON, Ed.: American Protestant Thought: *The Liberal Era* ‡ TB/1385

SOREN KIERKEGAARD: The Journals of Kierkegaard. ° *Edited with an Intro. by Alexander Dru* TB/52
SOREN KIERKEGAARD: The Point of View for My Work as an Author: *A Report to History.* § *Preface by Benjamin Nelson* TB/88
SOREN KIERKEGAARD: The Present Age. § *Translated and edited by Alexander Dru. Introduction by Walter Kaufmann* TB/94
SOREN KIERKEGAARD: Purity of Heart. *Trans. by Douglas Steere* TB/4
SOREN KIERKEGAARD: Repetition: *An Essay in Experimental Psychology* § TB/117
SOREN KIERKEGAARD: Works of Love: *Some Christian Reflections in the Form of Discourses* TB/122
WOLFHART PANNENBERG, et al.: History and Hermeneutic. *Volume 4 of* Journal for Theology and the Church, *edited by Robert W. Funk and Gerhard Ebeling* TB/254
F. SCHLEIERMACHER: The Christian Faith. *Introduction by Richard R. Niebuhr.* Vol. I TB/108; Vol. II TB/109
F. SCHLEIERMACHER: On Religion: *Speeches to Its Cultured Despisers. Intro. by Rudolf Otto* TB/36
PAUL TILLICH: Dynamics of Faith TB/42
PAUL TILLICH: Morality and Beyond TB/142

Religion: The Roman & Eastern Christian Traditions

A. ROBERT CAPONIGRI, Ed.: Modern Catholic Thinkers II: *The Church and the Political Order* TB/307
G. P. FEDOTOV: The Russian Religious Mind: *Kievan Christianity, the tenth to the thirteenth Centuries* TB/370
GABRIEL MARCEL: Being and Having: *An Existential Diary. Introduction by James Collins* TB/310
GABRIEL MARCEL: Homo Viator: *Introduction to a Metaphysic of Hope* TB/397

Religion: Oriental Religions

TOR ANDRAE: Mohammed: *The Man and His Faith* § TB/62
EDWARD CONZE: Buddhism: *Its Essence and Development.* ° *Foreword by Arthur Waley* TB/58
EDWARD CONZE: Buddhist Meditation TB/1442
EDWARD CONZE et al, Editors: Buddhist Texts through the Ages TB/113
ANANDA COOMARASWAMY: Buddha and the Gospel of Buddhism TB/119
H. G. CREEL: Confucius and the Chinese Way TB/63
FRANKLIN EDGERTON, Trans. & Ed.: The Bhagavad Gita TB/115
SWAMI NIKHILANANDA, Trans. & Ed.: The Upanishads TB/114

Religion: Philosophy, Culture, and Society

NICOLAS BERDYAEV: The Destiny of Man TB/61
RUDOLF BULTMANN: History and Eschatology: *The Presence of Eternity* ° TB/91
RUDOLF BULTMANN AND FIVE CRITICS: Kerygma and Myth: *A Theological Debate* TB/80
RUDOLF BULTMANN and KARL KUNDSIN: Form search. *Trans. by F. C. Grant* TB/96
LUDWIG FEUERBACH: The Essence of Christianity. § *Introduction by Karl Barth. Foreword by H. Richard Niebuhr* TB/11
KYLE HASELDEN: The Racial Problem in Christian Perspective TB/116

MARTIN HEIDEGGER: Discourse on Thinking. *Translated with a Preface by John M. Anderson and E. Hans Freund. Introduction by John M. Anderson* TB/1459
IMMANUEL KANT: Religion Within the Limits of Reason Alone. § *Introduction by Theodore M. Greene and John Silber* TB/FG
H. RICHARD NIEBUHR: Christ and Culture TB/3
H. RICHARD NIEBUHR: The Kingdom of God in America TB/49
JOHN H. RANDALL, JR.: The Meaning of Religion for Man. *Revised with New Intro. by the Author* TB/1379

Science and Mathematics

W. E. LE GROS CLARK: The Antecedents of Man: *An Introduction to the Evolution of the Primates.* ° *Illus.* TB/559
ROBERT E. COKER: Streams, Lakes, Ponds. *Illus.* TB/586
ROBERT E. COKER: This Great and Wide Sea: *An Introduction to Oceanography and Marine Biology. Illus.* TB/551
F. K. HARE: The Restless Atmosphere TB/560
WILLARD VAN ORMAN QUINE: Mathematical Logic TB/558

Science: Philosophy

J. M. BOCHENSKI: The Methods of Contemporary Thought. *Tr. by Peter Caws* TB/1377
J. BRONOWSKI: Science and Human Values. *Revised and Enlarged. Illus.* TB/505
WERNER HEISENBERG: Physics and Philosophy: *The Revolution in Modern Science. Introduction by F. S. C. Northrop* TB/549
KARL R. POPPER: Conjectures and Refutations: *The Growth of Scientific Knowledge* TB/1376
KARL R. POPPER: The Logic of Scientific Discovery TB/576

Sociology and Anthropology

REINHARD BENDIX: Work and Authority in Industry: *Ideologies of Management in the Course of Industrialization* TB/3035
BERNARD BERELSON, Ed., The Behavioral Sciences Today TB/1127
KENNETH B. CLARK: Dark Ghetto: *Dilemmas of Social Power. Foreword by Gunnar Myrdal* TB/1317
KENNETH CLARK & JEANNETTE HOPKINS: A Relevant War Against Poverty: *A Study of Community Action Programs and Observable Social Change* TB/1480
LEWIS COSER, Ed.: Political Sociology TB/1293
ROSE L. COSER, Ed.: Life Cycle and Achievement in America ** TB/1434
ALLISON DAVIS & JOHN DOLLARD: Children of Bondage: *The Personality Development of Negro Youth in the Urban South* || TB/3049
ST. CLAIR DRAKE & HORACE R. CAYTON: Black Metropolis: *A Study of Negro Life in a Northern City. Introduction by Everett C. Hughes. Tables, maps, charts, and graphs* Vol. I TB/1086; Vol. II TB/1087

PETER F. DRUCKER: The New Society: *The Anatomy of Industrial Order* TB/1082
LEON FESTINGER, HENRY W. RIECKEN, STANLEY SCHACHTER: When Prophecy Fails: *A Social and Psychological Study of a Modern Group that Predicted the Destruction of the World* || TB/1132
CHARLES Y. GLOCK & RODNEY STARK: Christian Beliefs and Anti-Semitism. *Introduction by the Authors* TB/1454
L. S. B. LEAKEY: Adam's Ancestors: *The Evolution of Man and His Culture. Illus.* TB/1019
KURT LEWIN: Field Theory in Social Science: *Selected Theoretical Papers.* || *Edited by Dorwin Cartwright* TB/1135
RITCHIE P. LOWRY: Who's Running This Town? *Community Leadership and Social Change* TB/1383
R. M. MACIVER: Social Causation TB/1153
GARY T. MARX: Protest and Prejudice: *A Study of Belief in the Black Community* TB/1435
ROBERT K. MERTON, LEONARD BROOM, LEONARD S. COTTRELL, JR., Editors: Sociology Today: *Problems and Prospects* || Vol. I TB/1173; Vol. II TB/1174
GILBERT OSOFSKY, Ed.: The Burden of Race: *A Documentary History of Negro-White Relations in America* TB/1405
GILBERT OSOFSKY: Harlem: The Making of a Ghetto: *Negro New York 1890-1930* TB/1381
TALCOTT PARSONS & EDWARD A. SHILS, Editors: Toward a General Theory of Action: *Theoretical Foundations for the Social Sciences* TB/1083
PHILIP RIEFF: The Triumph of the Therapeutic: *Uses of Faith After Freud* TB/1360
JOHN H. ROHRER & MUNRO S. EDMONSON, Eds.: The Eighth Generation Grows Up: *Cultures and Personalities of New Orleans Negroes* || TB/3050
ARNOLD ROSE: The Negro in America: *The Condensed Version of Gunnar Myrdal's An American Dilemma. Second Edition* TB/3048
GEORGE ROSEN: Madness in Society: *Chapters in the Historical Sociology of Mental Illness.* || *Preface by Benjamin Nelson* TB/1337
PHILIP SELZNICK: TVA and the Grass Roots: *A Study in the Sociology of Formal Organization* TB/1230
PITIRIM A. SOROKIN: Contemporary Sociological Theories: *Through the First Quarter of the Twentieth Century* TB/3046
MAURICE R. STEIN: The Eclipse of Community: *An Interpretation of American Studies* TB/1128
FERDINAND TONNIES: Community and Society: *Gemeinschaft und Gesellschaft. Translated and Edited by Charles P. Loomis* TB/1116
SAMUEL E. WALLACE: Skid Row as a Way of Life TB/1367
W. LLOYD WARNER and Associates: Democracy in Jonesville: *A Study in Quality and Inequality* || TB/1129
W. LLOYD WARNER: Social Class in America: *The Evaluation of Status* TB/1013
FLORIAN ZNANIECKI: The Social Role of the Man of Knowledge. *Introduction by Lewis A. Coser* TB/1372

71 72 73 74   12 11 10 9 8 7 6 5 4 3 2 1